THE PSYCHOLOGY OF ENTERTAINMENT MEDIA

Blurring the Lines Between Entertainment and Persuasion

Advertising and Consumer Psychology
A Series sponsored by the Society for Consumer Psychology

Aaker/Biel: *Brand Equity & Advertising: Advertising's Role in Building Strong Brands* (1993)

Clark/Brock/Stewart: *Attention, Attitude, and Affect in Response Advertising* (1994)

Englis: *Global and Multi-National Advertising* (1994)

Goldberg/Fishbein/Middlestadt: *Social Marketing: Theoretical and Practical Perspectives* (1997)

Kahle/Chiagouris: *Values, Lifestyles, and Psychographics* (1997)

Kahle/Riley: *Sports Marketing and the Psychology of Marketing Communications* (2003)

Mitchell: *Advertising Exposure, Memory, and Choice* (1993)

Schumann/Thorson: *Advertising and the World Wide Web* (1999)

Scott/Batra: *Persuasive Imagery: A Consumer Response Perspective* (2003)

Shrum: *The Psychology of Entertainment Media: Blurring the Lines Between Entertainment and Persuasion* (2004)

Thorson/Moore: *Integrated Communication: Synergy of Persuasive Voices (1996)*

Wells: *Measuring Advertising Effectiveness* (1997)

Williams/Lee/Haugtvedt: *Diversity in Advertising: Broadening the Scope of Research Directions* (2004)

THE PSYCHOLOGY OF ENTERTAINMENT MEDIA

Blurring the Lines Between Entertainment and Persuasion

Edited by

L. J. Shrum
University of Texas–San Antonio

LAWRENCE ERLBAUM ASSOCIATES, PUBLISHERS

2004   Mahwah, New Jersey   London

Lawrence Erlbaum Associates, Inc., Publishers
10 Industrial Avenue
Mahwah, NJ 07430

Cover design by Sean Sciarrone

Library of Congress Cataloging-in-Publication Data

The psychology of entertainment media: blurring the lines between
entertainment and persuasion/L. J. Shrum, editor.
  p.   cm.
Includes bibliographical references and index.
ISBN 0-8058-4641-7 (h : alk paper)
1. Subliminal advertising.   2. Advertising—Psychological aspects.
3. Mass media—Psychological aspects.   4. Persuasion (Psychology)
5. Manipulative behavior.   I. Shrum, L. J.

HF5827.9.P78   2003
659.1′01′9—dc21   2003040800

Printed in the United States of America
10 9 8 7 6 5 4 3 2 1

Contents

About the Authors   ix

Preface   xv

1 What's So Special About Entertainment Media and Why Do We
Need a Psychology for It?: An Introduction to the Psychology
of Entertainment Media   1
L. J. Shrum

**PART I: EMBEDDING PROMOTIONS WITHIN PROGRAMS:
SUBLIMINAL EMBEDS AND PRODUCT PLACEMENTS**

2 Beyond Gizmo Subliminality   13
Matthew Hugh Erdelyi and Diane M. Zizak

3 Product Placement: The Nature of the Practice and Potential
Avenues of Inquiry   45
John A. McCarty

4 Product Placements: How to Measure Their Impact   63
Sharmistha Law and Kathryn A. Braun-LaTour

5 Mental Models for Brand Placement   79
*Moonhee Yang, Beverly Roskos-Ewoldsen, and David R.
Roskos-Ewoldsen*

6 Embedding Brands Within Media Content: The Impact of
Message, Media, and Consumer Characteristics on Placement
Efficacy   99
Namita Bhatnagar, Lerzan Aksoy, and Selin A. Malkoc

7 The "Delicious Paradox": Preconscious Processing of Product
Placements by Children   117
Susan Auty and Charlie Lewis

PART II: THE PROGRAMS BETWEEN THE ADS:
THE PERSUASIVE POWER OF ENTERTAINMENT FICTION
AND NARRATIVE

 8   Pictures, Words, and Media Influence: The Interactive
        Effects of Verbal and Nonverbal Information on Memory
        and Judgments   137
        Robert S. Wyer, Jr. and Rashmi Adaval

 9   The Power of Fiction: Determinants and Boundaries   161
        Melanie C. Green, Jennifer Garst, and Timothy C. Brock

 10 A Process Model of Consumer Cultivation:
        The Role of Television Is a Function of the
        Type of Judgment   177
        L. J. Shrum, James E. Burroughs, and Aric Rindfleisch

 11 Paths From Television Violence to Aggression: Reinterpreting
        the Evidence   193
        George Comstock

 12 Between the Ads: Effects of Nonadvertising TV Messages on
        Consumption Behavior   213
        Maria Kniazeva

 13 Media Factors That Contribute to a Restriction of Exposure to
        Diversity   233
        David W. Schumann

PART III: INDIVIDUAL DIFFERENCES IN MEDIA USAGE
AND THEIR ROLE AS MEDIATORS AND MODERATORS OF
MEDIA EFFECTS

 14 The Need for Entertainment Scale   255
        Timothy C. Brock and Stephen D. Livingston

 15 People and "Their" Television Shows: An Overview of
        Television Connectedness   275
        Cristel A. Russell, Andrew T. Norman, and Susan E. Heckler

 16 The Interplay Among Attachment Orientation, Idealized Media
        Images of Women, and Body Dissatisfaction: A Social
        Psychological Analysis   291
        Dara N. Greenwood and Paula R. Pietromonaco

17 Marketing Through Sports Entertainment: A Functional
Approach   **309**
Scott Jones, Colleen Bee, Rick Burton, and Lynn R. Kahle

18 Sensation Seeking and the Consumption of Televised Sports   **323**
Stephen R. McDaniel

Author Index   **337**

Subject Index   **351**

About the Authors

Rashmi Adaval is Assistant Professor of Marketing at the Hong Kong University of Science and Technology. She is the author of several book chapters and journal articles and is the recipient of the 2002 Robert Ferber Award for the best dissertation-related article published in the *Journal of Consumer Research*. Her research interests include the role of affect in information processing, the impact of narrative-related information on judgments and decisions, and automaticity.

Lerzan Aksoy is Assistant Professor of Marketing at Koc University in Istanbul, Turkey. She completed her undergraduate degree from Hacettepe University in Ankara, Turkey, received a Fulbright scholarship to pursue an MBA at George Mason University, and in 2001 received her PhD in Marketing from the Kenan-Flagler Business School, University of North Carolina at Chapel Hill. Her research interests include the impact of personalization in the online environment on consumer decision quality, cross-cultural research, efficacy of non-traditional media, and marketing public policy implications. Her teaching interests at the undergraduate and graduate levels include marketing management, consumer behavior, and customer relationship management.

Susan Auty is a lecturer in Marketing at Lancaster University Management School in Lancaster, England. Her recent research has been concerned with the role of brand imagery in consumer choice.

Colleen Bee is a PhD student in the Charles H. Lundquist College of Business at the University of Oregon.

Namita Bhatnagar is currently Assistant Professor of Marketing at the Asper School of Business, University of Manitoba, Canada. She is completing her PhD in Marketing from the Kenan-Flagler Business School, University of North Carolina at Chapel Hill. Her research interests lie in the areas of categorization, cross-channel management of services, and non-traditional forms of marketing through entertainment media.

Kathryn A. Braun-LaTour, PhD, is President of Marketing Memories™ in Auburn, Alabama.

Timothy C. Brock is Professor of Psychology at Ohio State University and past-president of the Society for Consumer Psychology. He has co-edited *Psychological Foundations of Attitudes* (1968), *Cognitive Response in Persuasion* (1981), *Attention, Affect, and Attitude in Response to Advertising* (1994), *Persuasion: Psychological Insights and Perspectives* (1994), and *Narrative Impact: Social and Cognitive Foundations* (2002).

James E. Burroughs is Assistant Professor of Commerce, McIntire School of Commerce, University of Virginia. He received his PhD in Business (Marketing) from the University of Wisconsin-Madison. His research is in the area of consumer behavior and is specifically focused on issues such as materialism, symbolic consumption, and consumer culture.

Rick Burton is the Executive Director of the Warsaw Sports Marketing Center in the University of Oregon's Lundquist College of Business (LCB). He is a senior instructor of sports marketing in the LCB's marketing department and when not teaching, consults for national and international sports leagues and organizations. He is the host of the TV show "The Business of Sport" on ASCN.

George Comstock (PhD, Stanford University) is S.I. Newhouse Professor at the School of Public Communications, Syracuse University. He was science adviser to the Surgeon General's Scientific Advisory Committee on Television and Social Behavior that issued the 1972 federal report, *Television and Growing Up: The Impact of Televised Violence,* and in 1991–93 was chairman of the Department of Journalism and Communication, Chinese University, Hong Kong. His interests include the art and science of research synthesis, the influence of media in the socialization of children, and the dynamics of public opinion. His recent publications include *Television: What's On, Who's Watching, and What It Means* (co-authored with Erica Scharrer) and *Television and the American Child* (with Haejung Paik).

Matthew Hugh Erdelyi (AB, College of Wooster; PhD, Yale University) is currently Professor of Psychology and Stern Professor of Humor at Brooklyn College, CUNY. He has numerous publications on subliminal processes and defense mechanisms, and has published two books, *Psychoanalysis: Freud's Cognitive Psychology* and *The Recovery of Unconscious Memories: Hypermnesia and Reminiscence.*

Jennifer Garst is Assistant Professor of Communication at University of Maryland, College Park. She received training in social psychology with a PhD from Michigan State University and a postdoctoral fellowship at Ohio State University. Her research delves into the processes by which media messages and rhetorical styles subtly influence recipients' beliefs and attitudes.

Melanie C. Green is Assistant Professor of Psychology at the University of Pennsylvania. She received her PhD in social psychology from Ohio State University. Her research areas include the effects of narratives (including fictional stories) on individuals' beliefs and attitudes, and individual influences on the formation of social capital. She recently co-edited *Narrative Impact: Social and Cognitive Foundations* (2002; with Jeffrey Strange and Timothy Brock).

Dara N. Greenwood is a doctoral student in Social Psychology at the University of Massachusetts at Amherst. Her research interests include gender, sexist humor, media perceptions and influence, close relationships, and body image issues.

Susan E. Heckler is Professor of Marketing in the College of Business at the University of St. Thomas in St. Paul, MN. Dr. Heckler holds a PhD degree in Business Administration from the University of Minnesota. Her research interests center on issues concerning marketing communication with specific focus on the role of aesthetic elements in advertisements and individual differences related to elaboration and persuasion. Dr. Heckler's work appears in a number of marketing and advertising scientific journals as well as other editions of ACP publications.

Scott Jones is a PhD student in the Charles H. Lundquist College of Business at the University of Oregon.

Lynn R. Kahle is the James Warsaw Professor of Marketing at the University of Oregon. Topics of his research include social adaptation, values, and sports marketing. His articles have appeared in such outlets as the *Journal of Consumer Psychology, Journal of Consumer Research, Journal of Marketing, Sport Marketing Quarterly, Public Opinion Quarterly, Journal of Personality and Social Psychology,* and *Child Development.* His books include *Social Values and Social Change, Marketing Management,* and *Values, Lifestyles, and Psychographics.* He previously edited the journal *Sport Marketing Quarterly.* He has served as president of the Society for Consumer Psychology, president of the City of Eugene Human Rights program, and chair of the Department of Marketing at the University of Oregon.

Maria Kniazeva is a PhD student and visiting instructor at the McDonough School of Business at Georgetown University. Ethnic Russian, Maria Kniazeva was born in Estonia. She has a Masters in Journalism from Leningrad (now St. Petersburg) State University in Russia and has worked as a professional journalist in Estonia. Before starting her doctoral program, she spent two years at the Graduate School of Management, University of California at Irvine, as an MBA student, Edmund Muskie fellow, and as a recipient of the American Association of University Women international fellowship. Her research interests include

consumer perception of biotechnology and the impact of mass media on attitude formation. She is also the author of the book *America Through The Eyes of a Russian Woman* published in English with a grant received from the United States Information Agency and administered by the International Research & Exchanges Board. Maria Kniazeva can be contacted at: kniazevm@uci.edu

Sharmistha Law, PhD, is Assistant Professor in the Division of Management at the University of Toronto, Ontario, Canada.

Charlie Lewis is Professor of Family and Developmental Psychology at Lancaster University in Lancaster, England. His two main research interests involve the study of parent-child relationships, particularly the role of the father in the contemporary family, and young children's social-cognitive development, especially the development of mental state understanding.

Stephen D. Livingston is a Canadian Social Sciences and Humanities Research Council (SSHRC) doctoral fellow at Ohio State University, currently pursuing graduate studies in social psychology. His research interests include attitude formation and change, stereotyping, and motivated cognition.

Selin A. Malkoc is currently a doctoral student at the University of North Carolina at Chapel Hill. She has undertaken masters-level work at the University of Texas at Dallas and holds an undergraduate degree in business administration from Bilkent University, Turkey.

John A. McCarty currently teaches in the School of Business at The College of New Jersey in Ewing, New Jersey. Prior to taking this position, he taught at the University of Illinois at Urbana-Champaign; American University in Washington, D. C.; and George Mason University in Fairfax, Virginia. He holds a PhD in social psychology from the University of Illinois at Urbana-Champaign.

Stephen R. McDaniel is an associate professor in kinesiology at the University of Maryland. He received a PhD in communication from Florida State University. His research is focused on consumer psychology in the realm of sport marketing and media. His work has appeared in *Advances in Consumer Research, Imagination, Cognition and Personality, Journal of Services Marketing, Psychology & Marketing, Personality and Individual Differences, and Social Behavior and Personality.*

Andrew T. Norman is Assistant Professor of Marketing at Drake University. His research interests center on incongruency and categorization effects, attitude formation, and cognitive processing in various types of marketing communications.

He has also investigated the consumption of television programming as it relates to marketing promotions. Dr. Norman is an active member of the *Association for Consumer Research*, the *American Marketing Association*, and the *Society for Consumer Psychology*.

Paula R. Pietromonaco, PhD, is Associate Professor of Psychology at the University of Massachusetts at Amherst. Her research interests include close relationships, emotion, and social cognition.

Aric Rindfleisch is Assistant Professor of Marketing at the University of Wisconsin-Madison, where he earned his doctorate in 1998. Prior to rejoining UW-Madison, he spent five years as a faculty member at the University of Arizona. He is currently teaching a course on product management. Aric's research, which focuses on understanding interfirm cooperation and consumption values, has been published in the *Journal of Marketing,* the *Journal of Marketing Research,* the *Journal of Consumer Research,* the *Journal of Public Policy & Marketing, Marketing Letters,* and *Business Horizons.*

Beverly Roskos-Ewoldsen (PhD, Indiana University) is Associate Professor of Psychology at the University of Alabama. Dr. Roskos-Ewoldsen's research interests include mental models and the media, spatial cognition, mental imagery, and the cognitive foundations of creativity. She has published her research in journals such as the *Journal of Experimental Psychology: Learning, Memory, and Cognition, Journal of Environmental Psychology, Journal of Mental Imagery,* and *Journal of Clinical and Social Psychology.*

David R. Roskos-Ewoldsen (PhD, Indiana University) is the Reese Phifer Professor of Communication Studies and Professor of Psychology at the University of Alabama. He is founding co-editor of the journal *Media Psychology.* Dr. Roskos-Ewoldsen's research focuses on mental models and the media, and attitudes and persuasion. He has published his research in journals such as *Human Communication Research, Communication Yearbook, Journal of Personality and Social Psychology, Journal of Experimental Social Psychology,* and *Journal of Experimental Psychology: Applied.*

Cristel A. Russell is Assistant Professor of Marketing at San Diego State University. Her research focuses on the increasingly blurred lines between entertainment and marketing. Her work investigating the effectiveness of product placements in audiovisual media appears in the *Journal of Consumer Research* and she is currently working on several follow-up projects related to the product placement industry and consumers' responses to product placements. She also introduced the concept of television connectedness as an important factor

in explaining how television programs affect viewers' perceptions of consumption images in the media.

David W. Schumann holds the William J. Taylor Professorship in Business at the University of Tennessee. His research interests focus on issues related to attitude formation, persuasion, and belief structures in response to marketing communication. He is an APA Fellow in the divisions of consumer psychology and media psychology (Divisions 23 and 46), and is a past president of the Society for Consumer Psychology.

L. J. Shrum (PhD, University of Illinois) is Associate Professor of Marketing at the University of Texas-San Antonio. His research investigates the psychological processes underlying media effects, and particularly the role of media information in the construction of values, attitudes, and beliefs. His work has appeared in such journals as *Journal of Consumer Research, Human Communication Research, Journal of Advertising,* and *Public Opinion Quarterly.*

Robert S. Wyer, Jr., a professor emeritus of Psychology at the University of Illinois at Urbana-Champaign, is currently Visiting Professor of Marketing at Hong Kong University of Science and Technology. He is the author of four books on social information processing (the most recent being *Comprehension and Judgment in Daily Life: The Impact of Situation Models, Narratives and Implicit Theories*). He has been the coeditor of the *Handbook of Social Cognition,* and editor of the *Advances in Social Cognition* series. He was a past editor of the *Journal of Experimental Social Psychology,* and is currently editor of the *Journal of Consumer Psychology.* He is a recipient of the Alexandr von Humboldt Research Prize for Distinguished Scientists and the Thomas M. Ostrom Award for distinguished contributions to social cognition.

Moonhee Yang (MA, Korea University) is a doctoral student in the College of Communication and Information Science at the University of Alabama. Her research interests include mental models of persuasive messages, contextual effect in advertising, and entertainment theory.

Diane M. Zizak (BA Hunter College) has recently completed her PhD in Experimental Psychology at the Brooklyn College campus of The Graduate School at CUNY. Her areas of research include implicit processes and the mere exposure effect.

Preface

One of the bedrock principles of a free-market system of commerce is the notion of a free flow of information to afford a level playing field for all decision makers. Within this framework operates what I will call, for lack of a more creative term, a variation of informed consent: Audience members consent to be persuaded as long as they are informed of the persuasion attempt. At least that's the way it's supposed to work for advertising: a paid, nonpersonal persuasive communication *from an identified source* (Sandage, Fryburger, & Rotzoll, 1983). In fact, that's often one of the reasons given for why advertising may not be all that effective (after all, people know they are being persuaded by a biased source and can appropriately source-discount). And it is likely the flip side of that reason as to why the notion of subliminal advertising is so feared and reviled by consumers—the notion that they could be persuaded without their knowledge and thus without their defense.

That is precisely what this book is about: how the lines between entertainment and persuasion have become increasingly blurred and how these blurred lines might either facilitate or inhibit changes in attitudes, beliefs and perceptions. The chapters that comprise this volume grew out of the 21st Annual Advertising and Consumer Psychology Conference, held at the Omni Berkshire Place in New York City, May 16–18, 2002, which was organized around the blurred lines theme. The best papers from this conference were invited for this volume. In addition, several additional chapters were invited from some of the best-known scholars in psychology, marketing, and communications who are doing work in this area. Taken together, this contributed volume represents a multidisciplinary investigation of an age-old process (persuasion) in a relatively new guise (e.g., product placements, brand films and television programs, sponsorships). Its intent is to explore how persuasion works in these contexts (and, indeed, to expand the notion of what constitutes persuasion), hopefully resulting in a more knowledgeable field and a more knowledgeable consumer.

ACKNOWLEDGMENTS

Because this volume is closely associated with the annual Advertising and Consumer Psychology Conference, it is difficult to separate the contributions to the conference from the contribution to the book. I would like to acknowledge the

support of SCP members, particularly Curt Haugtvedt (for answering count-less operational questions), Marian Friestad, the president of SCP at the time of the conference (for her support of the conference proposal), and Susan Heckler (for her suggestion of media entertainment as a conference topic). I would also like to thank Larry Compeau for his help with all of the conference arrangements and logistics.

This is the first time I have edited a volume of this sort, so it is unclear to me why I was spared the miseries of editing that I have heard so much about. I can truly say that this was an enjoyable, as well as enlightening, experience. I cannot thank the authors enough for their willingness to operate on extremely tight deadlines in an effort to get this volume out in a timely manner. I want to thank the authors who were participants in the conference for helping make both a success. And I especially want to thank the authors of the invited chapters (Bob Wyer, Rashmi Adaval, David Roskos-Ewoldsen, Beverly Roskos-Ewoldsen, and Moonhee Yang) for operating on an even tighter deadline than most.

Finally, with respect to editing and publishing, I would like to thank Linda Bathgate of Lawrence Erlbaum Associates for her guidance and suggestions and Lawrence Erlbaum Associates for their continued support of the Advertising and Consumer Psychology series. I also would like to extend a huge thanks to Julie Colin, my graduate assistant at UTSA, for her enormous help with constructing the indices for this volume. And, last but not least, I would like to thank Tina Lowrey for the countless hours she spent reading everything I wrote and explaining, albeit in a nice way, what I had done wrong.

L. J. Shrum
November 29, 2002

REFERENCE

Sandage, C. H., Fryburger, V., & Rotzoll, K. (1983). *Advertising theory and practice* (11th ed.). Homewood, IL: Richard Irwin.

CHAPTER ONE

What's So Special About Entertainment Media and Why Do We Need a Psychology for It?: An Introduction to the Psychology of Entertainment Media

L. J. Shrum

University of Texas–San Antonio

The title poses a reasonable question. Is there anything unique about entertainment media that warrants a different way of thinking about people's way of thinking? More to the point of the book, is there anything unique about entertainment media that might impact the extent to which the information it conveys has a persuasive effect? Certainly, if current theories of persuasion can just as easily (and accurately) account for effects that occur within entertainment media (e.g., TV programs, films) as they can for effects that occur between entertainment media (e.g., advertisements), Occam's razor would lop off the unneeded new theory devoted to entertainment media.

So what is the answer? To quote Ed Grimley, "It's difficult to say."[1] On the one hand, as Marcia Johnson points out in her forward to *Narrative Impact* (Green, Strange, & Brock, 2002), there are quite a lot of theoretical constructs that can account for certain effects of entertainment media (e.g., situation models, accessibility, source monitoring; Johnson, 2002). On the other hand, as Brock, Strange, and Green (2002) also note in that same volume, current dual processing theories of persuasion, which primarily address rhetorical persuasion, have trouble accounting for certain narrative persuasion effects. In fact, chapters in this book (cf. Chapters 8, 9) make the point that people typically process entertainment (narrative) and promotional (rhetorical) information differently. Consequently, it seems plausible, if not

---

[1]Ed Grimley was a character played by Martin Short on NBC's *Saturday Night Live.*

likely, that the ways in which entertainment and promotion have an effect on audiences are correspondingly different.

Nevertheless, this book is not equipped to answer the question of whether we need a psychology of entertainment media. Rather, it is intended to continue the scientific conversation about the nature of entertainment media and how they may impact the thoughts, feelings, perceptions, and behaviors of their audiences. Ideally, continued conversations on this matter would eventually lead to an answer.

This book is not the first to address the unique aspects of entertainment media. At least two other books come to mind. The first is Zillmann and Vorderer's (2000) *Media Entertainment: The Psychology of Its Appeal*, and the second is the afore-mentioned *Narrative Impact* (Green et al., 2002). Although each of these books has some overlap with this volume, there are important distinctions. The Zillmann and Vorderer book looks principally at what draws us to entertainment media and what it is about entertainment that holds our attention, scares us, and makes us happy. As such, it is primarily concerned with the gratifications that media entertainment provides. The Green et al. book addresses the impact of narratives, or the stories we encounter via books, plays, television, and so forth. As such, it is in the end concerned with issues of narrative effects. Each of these books nicely complements the present volume. The key distinction between those books and the present one is the focus of this book on the blurring between promotion and entertainment. Specifically, what this volume attempts to understand is how entertainment or narrative is information processed and whether this processing is fundamentally different from the processing of promotional or rhetorical information. If so, what are the consequences of these differences in processing on the persuasive impact of both the entertainment aspect and the promotional aspect?

ROADMAP FOR THE CHAPTERS

The chapters that comprise this book are divided into three broad areas. These areas are the potential effects of embedding promotions within entertainment media content, the persuasive power of the entertainment media content itself, and individual differences in the interplay between media usage and media effects.

Part I: Embedding Promotions Within Programs: Subliminal Embeds and Product Placements

Part I is predominantly focused on what is arguably the epitome of what at least I think of as blurred lines: product placement in entertainment media. Product placement generally refers to the deliberate inclusion of brands in stories, usually in television programs and films (but see Chapter 6 for an example of placements in prose). However, this section starts off with a chapter by Matthew Erdelyi and Diane Zizak on subliminal perception and persuasion (Chapter 2). Although embedding subliminal stimuli in ads is not a direct example of blurring the lines (both

the subliminal and surpraliminal stimuli are persuasive attempts), it is a perfect starting point for discussing the psychological processes that may underlie product placement effects. Erdelyi and Zizak provide a comprehensive review of the current status of subliminal processes in experimental psychology, discuss a number of laboratory studies that pertain to these processes, and then illustrate how common real-world phenomena such as jokes, art, and ads can be integrated within this framework. They provide a relatively new take (at least to consumer psychology) on what is considered subliminal and argue that contemporary experimental psychology has focused almost exclusively on degrading stimuli (to make them subliminal) through the use of gizmos—technological devices such as tachistoscopes—at the expense of what Erdelyi and Zizak term *psychological techniques* for degrading the stimulus. In doing so, they extend previous work on the surprisingly close association between cognitive theories of information processing and Freudian concepts such as repression, suppression, reconstruction, and defense, just to name a few (Erdelyi, 1985, 1996).

The remainder of Part I (Chapters 3–7) is devoted to issues regarding product placement. These five chapters are for the most part ordered from the more general to the more specific. In Chapter 3, John McCarty reviews the current state of product placements in film and television. He provides a general overview of the construct, discusses a number of prominent examples of the practice (some likely to be familiar to readers, some not), and reviews academic research on product placement. He then builds on that analysis to delineate some promising areas of inquiry that might help to spur future research on the topic. These areas include issues of salience, involvement, and product characteristics.

In Chapter 4, Sharmistha Law and Kathryn Braun-LaTour address one of the most perplexing issues in product placement research: how to measure the impact of placements. As Law and Braun-LaTour note (and as echoed in Chapters 3, 5, and 7), research on the effects of product placement has been decidedly mixed, even though industry touts numerous success stories, albeit mostly anecdotally. One reason they suggest for the mixed findings from previous research is an overreliance on recall and recognition as the key dependent measures. The authors note that the use of these measures imply (or at least should imply) a process that is for the most part conscious. However, drawing on recent research on learning without awareness, Law and Braun-LaTour suggest that making a distinction between explicit (conscious) and implicit (unconscious) memory (Graf & Schacter, 1985) might be a useful approach to studying product placement effects. They offer a theoretical framework based on this distinction and discuss some of the findings of their own research to bolster their arguments.

In Chapter 5, Moonhee Yang, Beverly Roskos-Ewoldsen, and David Roskos-Ewoldsen also address issues of product placement and memory. However, they take a slightly different approach from Law and Braun-LaTour in that they focus as much, if not more, on earlier stages in information processing, in particular the comprehension stage. They argue that understanding what happens at the time

of viewing is essential to being able to accurately predict product placement effects. Building on the general notion of mental or situation models (Wyer, 2003; Wyer & Radvansky, 1999), they specifically use a landscape model framework (van den Broek, Risden, Fletcher, & Thurlow, 1996) to make predictions regarding the conditions under which product placement effects might be expected. They then present data from an experiment that tested some key assumptions of that model. They conclude by discussing the implications of these findings for product placement effects.

Namita Bhatnagar, Lernan Aksoy, and Selin Malkoc provide their take on product placement issues in Chapter 6. In particular, they focus on contextual factors, such as the fit between the program and the placed brand, the strength of the placement (i.e., number of brand mentions, foreground vs. background), consumer characteristics (e.g., awareness of placement, involvement), and characteristics of the medium (e.g., trustworthiness). They also provide something missing from all of the other chapters: an example of product placement in a novel. They discuss the reactions to such placements from readers (mostly negative) and draw implications regarding process from the differences in the contextual issues between novels and TV programs or film.

Finally, Susan Auty and Charlie Lewis (Chapter 7) conclude Part I by addressing a relatively underresearched product placement effect: the effects of placements on children. Auty and Lewis begin by briefly reporting the results of an experiment they conducted and then using those results to theorize on issues of explicit and implicit memory, mere exposure effects, and the relation of these constructs to choice behavior. Their approach differs slightly from the other product placement chapters, however, in that it focuses almost exclusively on effects on children. This is an important addition to the literature because most product placement research has been conducted with adults. Although the processes underlying product placement effects are not likely to differ as a function of age, the effects may differ because of cognitive development. Indeed, as Auty and Lewis note, the blurred lines between entertainment and promotion/persuasion may be even more blurry for children, who may lack sufficient sophistication to discern whether a plot scene involves product placement, assuming they even know what product placement is. Auty and Lewis's results suggest that product placements can indeed directly influence choice behavior in children, even in the absence of effects on memory. Moreover, issues of memory differ as a function of age.

Part II: The Programs Between the Ads: The Persuasive Power of Entertainment Fiction and Narrative

Part II steps away from attempts to persuade via promotion to persuasion effects of the media entertainment content itself. The first two chapters of Part II focus on general issues involving the interplay between visual and verbal information and the persuasive power of fiction, both part and parcel of what television and film entertainment provide. In Chapter 8, Bob Wyer and Rashmi Adaval address

how verbal and nonverbal (visual) information may interact in their influence on memory and judgment. They make a persuasive argument that visual images can have a substantial effect on how people process subsequent information they receive. This of course is the case when the visual information is relevant to the subsequent judgments, but the authors also argue that this effect holds even when the visual information has little to do with the subsequent information or judgments. They bolster their arguments by reinterpreting some of their prior work, as well as discussing new data, and discussing the implications of these findings for how entertainment media may affect the attitudes and behaviors of audience members.

In Chapter 9, Melanie Green, Jennifer Garst, and Tim Brock address the power of fiction in general, including nonvisual (e.g., novels) as well as visual narratives. They begin by identifying some of the fundamental differences between fiction and nonfiction, particularly in terms of how they are processed, and relate these differences in processing to issues of memory and judgment. They suggest that, contrary to conventional wisdom, research is accumulating suggesting that fiction may actually be more persuasive than nonfiction. They then go on to detail aspects of fiction that may contribute to this superior persuasiveness as well as boundary conditions for this effect.

The next three chapters shift the focus to the effects of television consumption on values, attitudes, and behaviors. In Chapter 10, L. J. Shrum, Jim Burroughs, and Aric Rindfleisch discuss theory and research on the cultivation effect (Gerbner & Gross, 1976). The cultivation effect pertains to the positive relation between television consumption and the holding of beliefs and behaviors congruent with the television message. Shrum et al. specifically focus on the processes that may underlie this relation. They detail a model of how television information influences judgments of set size and probability and then draw on recently collected data to extend this model to the development of judgments such as personal values (in this case, materialism). They suggest that the way in which television information influences judgments is a function of the types of judgments that are made and how they are constructed and that television influences the different judgments in quite different ways.

In Chapter 11, George Comstock looks at a specific type of television effect, the controversial relation between violent television viewing and aggression. Comstock, however, does a number of things that are different from previous discussions on this topic. First, he discusses a number of meta-analyses, including his own work, that clearly show a positive correlation between exposure to violent television or movies and aggression or antisocial behavior. However, as he notes, the real issue is interpreting that positive correlation: Does it reflect a causal effect of television or some other causal mechanism? Comstock suggests that the case for television viewing being the causal factor is quite strong. He points to meta-analyses of experiments that show a very consistent (and very robust) effect on aggressive behavior. Even though certain individual studies may be critiqued for such things as construct validity and generalizability, the consistency of the pattern argues that television is the causal factor, particularly when coupled with

the equally consistent (though less robust in terms of effect size) survey (correlational) findings. Finally, Comstock makes one additional contribution. He suggests that, based on a reexamination of the data, dispositions such as attitudes, norms, and values are not a necessary link between exposure to television violence and aggression. Although the link has been found in a number of studies, it is also the case that direct relations between exposure to television violence and aggression have been observed. He then discusses the implications of this reformulation for the processes underlying media effects on aggressive behavior.

Although the effects of media violence on viewers is probably the best known media effect, there are in fact other effects of viewing television content. As Maria Kniazeva notes in Chapter 12, television programs convey a significant amount of information about consumption behavior. This information can serve as specific cues about what is considered normative, desirable, to be avoided, and so forth. The information may be relatively brand specific or it could be relevant to a general product category. Moreover, Kniazeva argues that, with respect to television effects, the academic literature (at least in marketing) has tended to focus almost entirely on the effects of advertisements, ignoring for the most part the effects of the programs between the ads. In her chapter, Kniazeva outlines the extant literature on non-advertising media effects and discusses the psychological processes that occur at various stages of processing (i.e., encoding, interpretation, retrieval). In doing so, she adds to the growing body of work on the processes underlying media effects.

The previous few chapters have focused on the effects of viewing particular content. In Chapter 13, David Schumann looks at the ironic flipside of not viewing or, at least, not viewing particular types of programs. Schumann explores the ramifications of market segmentation, particularly in regard to how it restricts exposure to diversity. Building on earlier work by Joseph Turow (1997), he develops a complex model of restricting exposure to diversity and, in doing so, provides a blueprint for an extended program of research into what until now has been a relatively ignored topic. He particularly notes that in targeting a consumer segment by pointing out the shared consumption activities of that segment, there is also an underlying inference that the group is different from other segments. Indeed, it is often in the marketer's interest to reinforce not only affiliation or aspiration groups and their favored brands and practices but also avoidance groups and what not to have and do (Lowrey, Englis, Shavitt, & Solomon, 2001). Schumann's model explores the antecedents and consequences of this practice.

Part III: Individual Differences in Media Usage and Their Role as Mediators and Moderators of Media Effects

Several of the previous chapters in Part II mention in some way that particular media effects are likely to vary as a function of at least some type of individual characteristic. The chapters that comprise Part III of this volume focus specifically on several of these individual differences. In Chapter 14, Tim Brock and Stephen

Livingston assert that one of these individual differences is the need for entertainment. They suggest that some people simply crave entertainment more than others. If so, then it seems possible that need for entertainment may moderate the effects of consuming such entertainment by determining how media are processed. As a first step in testing this proposition, Brock and Livingston present data on the development of their Need for Entertainment scale, detailing their efforts to develop and validate the scale items.

Cristel Russell, Andy Norman, and Susan Heckler take a similar approach in Chapter 15. However, rather than looking at individual relations with entertainment in general, Russell et al. explore the extent to which viewers may become connected with particular programs or characters. Specifically, they explore the extent to which individuals differ in such connectedness. They discuss their program of research that includes the development of a connectedness scale and the articulation of the antecedents and consequences of connectedness. They further assert that connectedness may serve as a mediator or moderator of television program effects.

In Chapter 16, Dara Greenwood and Paula Pietromonaco tackle the question of whether frequent viewing of idealized images of women in the media results in greater body dissatisfaction on the part of viewers, especially women. This is a particularly troubling issue because of the relation between body dissatisfaction and the development of eating disorders, such as bulimia. Greenwood and Pietromonaco follow a path very similar to that of Russell et al. Specifically, they suggest that some types of women may be more influenced by media images than others and thus may be more likely to develop eating disorders. They suggest that women's relational styles may moderate the extent to which the media images have an effect on those women. They discuss data from their research program that suggests an interaction among attachment styles, media perceptions, and body image concerns. They also discuss the ambiguous lines between fantasy and reality that are the subject of this volume and suggest that these blurred lines may indeed lead young women to manifest their attachment needs through body image concerns.

The last two chapters of Part III address a specific type of media entertainment, sports entertainment. In Chapter 17, Scott Jones, Colleen Bee, Rick Burton, and Lynn Kahle discuss the factors that make sports entertainment a unique medium for marketing communications. They look at the relationships that fans develop with sports teams and the consequences that may result from these relationships, including compliance, identification, and internalization. They then discuss some strategic implications of these relationships that might be of interest to marketers.

In Chapter 18, Steve McDaniel concludes the individual differences focus by looking at the relation between sensation seeking and the consumption of TV sports. McDaniel reviews research that has looked at the relation between sensation seeking and television viewing in general and then goes on to focus specifically

on recent research on televised sports. He details some of his own work that shows that sensation seeking is indeed related to such things as viewing violent combative sports (indeed, for both women and men).

ENTERTAINMENT MEDIA *IS* SPECIAL

As noted earlier, this book is not equipped to answer at least the second part of the question posed in the title of this chapter, namely, whether we need a separate psychology of entertainment media. However, this book does address the first part: What is so special about entertainment media? All of the chapters in this book provide a perspective on the nature of entertainment media and how it often blends with overt persuasion attempts, such as promotions. And virtually all in some manner speak to the issue of how entertainment media is processed, with the conclusion that media consumers do in fact tend to process entertainment (narrative) and promotional (rhetorical) information differently. This, if nothing else, is what makes entertainment media so special. And it is the premise of at least some of the chapters that this is also what makes it potentially so powerful. It should come as no surprise, then, that marketers would be interested in becoming part of that special processing rather than separate from it.

Perhaps that is fine. This book does not take a position as to whether the blurring of the lines between entertainment and promotion is necessarily good or bad. But in the interest of the free flow of information mentioned in the preface, it is hoped that the chapters in this book can at least contribute to more informed consumers who might then decide whether to provide their consent to be persuaded.

REFERENCES

Brock, T. C., Strange, J. J., & Green, M. C. (2002). Power beyond reckoning: An introduction to narrative impact. In M. C. Green, J. J. Strange, & T. C. Brock (Eds.), *Narrative impact: Social and cognitive foundations* (pp. 1–15). Mahwah, NJ: Lawrence Erlbaum Associates.

Erdelyi, M. H. (1985). *Psychoanalysis: Freud's cognitive psychology*. New York: W. H. Freeman.

Erdelyi, M. H. (1996). *The recovery of unconscious memories: Hypermnesia and reminiscence.* Chicago: University of Chicago Press.

Gerbner, G., & Gross, L. (1976). Living with television: The violence profile. *Journal of Communication, 26,* 182–190.

Graf, P., & Schacter, D. L. (1985). Implicit and explicit memory for new associations in normal and amnesic subjects. *Journal of Experimental Psychology: Learning, Memory, and Cognition, 11,* 501–518.

Green, M. C., Strange, J. J., & Brock, T. C. (Eds.). (2002). *Narrative impact: Social and cognitive foundations.* Mahwah, NJ: Lawrence Erlbaum Associates.

Johnson, M. K. (2002). Foreword. In M. C. Green, J. J. Strange, & T. C. Brock (Eds.), *Narrative impact: Social and cognitive foundations* (pp. ix–xii). Mahwah, NJ: Lawrence Erlbaum Associates.

Lowrey, T. M., Englis, B. G., Shavitt, S., & Solomon, M. R. (2001). Response latency verification of consumption constellations: Implications for advertising strategy. *Journal of Advertising, 30*(1), 29–39.

Turow, J. (1997). *Breaking up America: Advertisers and the new world media.* Chicago: University of Chicago Press.

van den Broek, P., Risden, K., Fletcher, C., & Thurlow, R. (1996). A "landscape" view of reading: Fluctuating patterns of activation and the construction of a stable memory representation. In B. K. Brittion & A. C. Graesser (Eds.), *Models of understanding text* (pp. 165–187). Mahwah, NJ: Lawrence Erlbaum Associates.

Wyer, R. S. (2003). *Social comprehension and judgment: The role of situation models, narratives, and implicit theories.* Mahwah, NJ: Lawrence Erlbaum Associates.

Wyer, R. S., Jr., & Radvansky, G. A. (1999). The comprehension and validation of information. *Psychological Review, 106*, 89–118.

Zillmann, D., & Vorderer, P. (Eds.). (2000). *Media entertainment: The psychology of its appeal.* Mahwah, NJ: Lawrence Erlbaum Associates.

I. EMBEDDING PROMOTIONS WITHIN PROGRAMS: SUBLIMINAL EMBEDS AND PRODUCT PLACEMENTS

CHAPTER TWO

Beyond Gizmo Subliminality

Matthew Hugh Erdelyi
Diane M. Zizak
Brooklyn College and the Graduate School, CUNY

For most of its history, laboratory psychology has probed subliminal perception with gizmos—physical devices such as tachistoscopes—for degrading stimuli to liminal levels. The results have been grudging and often controversial. The real psychological action, it is suggested in this chapter, is found in psychological techniques for degrading the stimulus, among them, *Ebbinghausian subliminality* (in which forgetting degrades the stimulus), *Pavlovian subliminality* (in which the information is induced associatively), and *Freudian subliminality* (in which latent contents are transformed into mitigated manifest contents by dreamwork techniques, such as censorship, displacement, condensation, symbolism, and plastic-word representation). Even when gizmos are used to produce subliminal effects, unacknowledged psychological subliminality is likely to play a role in the effects. In this chapter, we first review the status of subliminal processes in experimental psychology, examine some examples from laboratory studies, and then define and illustrate some of the psychological techniques ubiquitously found in the real world (e.g., in jokes, art, ads) for degrading or subliminalizing stimuli.

GIZMO SUBLIMINALITY

If one reads the methods section of any mainstream experimental article on subliminal perception, one is bound to be treated to an assortment of details about the gizmos—the physical devices and techniques—employed for rendering the

stimulus subliminal. The tachistoscope used might be described along with the exposure durations (e.g., 10 ms, 1 ms). The type of masking—pattern masking, energy masking, metacontrast—will be detailed (if masking is used), with specification of the SOA (stimulus onset asynchrony). One is likely also to learn about the luminances involved, the visual angles, the distance of the subject from the display, and so on.

This tradition of degrading the input with physical devices goes back a century. For example, Otto Pötzl (1917), who did one of the first modern subliminal studies, used a camera shutter for getting stimulus exposures down to 0.01 s (10 ms) and succeeded in reproducing certain peculiar effects that he had observed with neurological patients who had sustained damage to the visual cortex (e.g., the emergence and recovery—in distorted form—of undetected central stimuli in subsequent peripheral percepts and, even, in the content of dreams of the same night). In the 1950s, two-channel and three-channel tachistoscopes became modal, though homespun devices were also occasionally deployed (e.g., carbon paper—multiple carbon copies of some text were made, and the carbon copy that was sufficiently blurred to be judged below the limen of consciousness designated the subliminal stimulus).

Today, of course, we have computers and the accent falls on pixels, refresh times, rise and fall characteristics of the light source, the SOAs employed, and so on. It all strikes one as highly scientific, with gizmos having the aura of science about them. But are gizmos necessary, or even relevant? In this article, we advance the view that gizmos, which started out as useful adjuncts to research as helpful laboratory tools, have usurped the leading role in research on subliminal processes and have distorted and even undermined some of the powerful effects involved. The classic phenomena of unconscious mentation that were introduced into psychology by Freud, Janet, Jung, and even von Helmholtz (of unconscious inference fame), among others, were never about stimulus flashes or otherwise degraded physical stimuli but entailed, instead, psychological processes that were inaccessible to consciousness or which had been rendered unconscious by psychological techniques. It is these psychological techniques for degrading consciousness—which we refer to as *psychological subliminality* in contraposition to gizmo subliminality—that we seek to define and underscore in this chapter.

Pötzl-Fisher Effects

Before we move beyond gizmo subliminality, however, let us examine one striking example of effects produced with a gizmo—a tachistoscope in this case—by the laboratory-minded psychoanalyst Charles Fisher, who translated Pötzl's earlier monograph into English and sought to replicate Pötzl's findings and extend them from dreams to other soft indicators, such as daydreams, fantasy, free-associations, and doodles (Fisher, 1954, 1956, 1988).

FIG. 2.1   Fisher's 1956 stimulus: Two Siamese cats and a parakeet. From "Dreams, Images, and Perception: A Study of Unconscious-Preconscious Relationships," by C. Fisher, 1956, *Journal of the American Psychoanalytic Association, 4*, p. 24. Copyright 1956 "By permission of Leo Goldberger, Ph.D., Editor-in-chief of *Psychoanalysis & Contemporary Thought*." Reprinted with permission.

In a 1956 study, Fisher flashed the stimulus shown in Fig. 2.1 (a parakeet perched between two Siamese cats) for 10 ms. Although none of the subjects reported seeing a bird, there was much evidence of the bird having been registered below full awareness. One subject, for example, reported seeing "two white and black animals which resembled dogs or pigs" (Fisher, 1956, p. 22), which she proceeded to render in a drawing (see Fig. 2.2). Despite the absence of any verbal report about a bird, the drawing does seem to reflect the influence of the bird. The same subject produced drawings of word associations to stimuli provided by the experimenter. To the stimulus word *DOG*, the subject produced the association *HOUSE*, along with the more detailed image of a watchdog standing in front of a house. Her attempt to render this associated image is reproduced in Fig. 2.3. This time the subject herself noted the bird, expressing confusion over its emergence: "She wanted to know what was wrong, could not understand why she continued to draw a bird, stating that she knew very well how to draw a dog and had done so many times (Fisher, 1956, pp. 25–26). If advertisers could get this type of compulsive behavior without awareness of its cause, it would be quite a feat indeed.

FIG. 2.2 Subject's drawing of "two white and black animals which resemble dogs or pigs." From "Dreams, Images, and Perception: A Study of Unconscious-Preconscious Relationships," by C. Fisher, 1956, *Journal of the American Psychoanalytic Association, 4*, p. 23. Copyright 1956 "By permission of Leo Goldberger, Ph.D., Editor-in-chief of *Psychoanalysis & Contemporary Thought*." Reprinted with permission.

FIG. 2.3 Watchdog standing in front of a house. From "Dreams, Images, and Perception: A Study of Unconscious-Preconscious Relationships," by C. Fisher, 1956, *Journal of the American Psychoanalytic Association, 4*, p. 25. Copyright 1956 "By permission of Leo Goldberger, Ph.D., Editor-in-chief of *Psychoanalysis & Contemporary Thought*." Reprinted with permission.

Another subject, who also failed to report seeing a bird in the stimulus flash, responded with the word *FEATHER* to the stimulus word *PILLOW* and produced the drawing reproduced in the top drawing of Fig. 2.4. A bird (or possibly two birds) can be seen in the drawing, along with the outline (to the right) of a cat with its mouth by the head of the top bird. The same subject, when presented the stimulus word *SICK*, responded with the word association *PATIENT* and drew the picture of a sick child in bed (Fig. 2.4, middle drawing). The shape of birds emerges in the folds of the blanket covering the child. This same subject was reexposed to the original stimulus, this time for 0.1 s (100 ms), but still failed to report seeing a bird in the stimulus. Yet her drawing of a cat lapping up some spilled milk (Fig. 2.4, bottom drawing) again shows the "compulsive emergence" (Fisher, 1956, p. 22) of birds. Even at a full 1-s exposure, this subject failed to report seeing the bird.

The Current Status of Subliminal Effects in Experimental Psychology

Fisher's demonstrations were decidedly on the informal side, and a generation ago experimental psychologists would have reacted to these data with a torrent of methodological criticisms. At that time, the smart money was aligned against the reality of subliminal effects. In more recent years, however, there has been a veritable sea change in the mainstream, and these types of effects, in a variety of guises, are readily accepted and produced in the laboratory (e.g., Bargh & Chartrand,1999; Bornstein & Pittman, 1992; Erdelyi, 1970, 1996). The change in the Zeitgeist from extreme skepticism to everyday acceptance has not yet been fully harmonized in the scientific literature. This may be seen in a special issue of *Psychology and Marketing* (Moore,1988), devoted to subliminal advertising, in which the contributing experts simultaneously question the effectiveness of (gizmo) subliminal advertising while underscoring the reality of subliminal perception effects in the laboratory.

In recent times, the focus in the experimental psychology of subliminal processes has been shifting from the methodological to the conceptual. A wide band of subliminal effects, including those of the Pötzl-Fisher variety, can be reliably produced with rigorous methodology. But what do we mean by "subliminal" in these cases? For example, if the subject fails to report a stimulus (e.g., bird), does this mean that the subject has no awareness of the stimulus? Is awareness an either-or state? Is there, in other words, a true threshold or limen such that a stimulus intensity below this limen fails to produce awareness but at or above this limen yields awareness? Almost all contemporary experimental psychologists would now espouse the position that there is no true limen except as a statistical abstraction. As the stimulus is gradually intensified, the probability of its perception increases gradually (in an ogival fashion). There is no step-function cleaving perception into two distinct states, detect and nondetect. Thus, if we hew to the classic threshold or limen concept, we must adopt a statistical conception (e.g., the threshold/limen is the stimulus value at which the probability of detection reaches,

say, 50%). By this (unavoidable) statistical conception, subliminal perception becomes real by definition because 50% of the stimuli at or below the limen are detected. In effect, then, we are left with a more-or-less conception of awareness: The limen defines a region of relative obscuration of awareness.

Modern psychophysicists have by and large opted for cutting the Gordian knot and have outrightly abandoned the concept of the limen (what happens to subliminal if there is no limen?) and have shifted to variations of signal detection theory (e.g., Macmillan & Creelman, 1991; Swets, 1964; Swets, Tanner, & Birdsall, 1961), in which perceptual sensitivity is evaluated by means of the receiver operating characteristic (ROC) curve, which plots hit rates (the probability of the subject saying "yes" when the stimulus is presented) as a function of false-alarm rates (the probability of saying "yes" when nothing, or a nonstimulus distractor, is presented). A metric, d', or some homologue, is used to measure sensitivity, with $d' = 0$ defining a complete absence of sensitity to the stimulus. A low value of sensitivity (e.g., $d' = 1$) can be arbitrarily defined as the limen (Holender, 1986; Macmillan, 1986), which would again cinch the reality of subliminal perception by definition because any $d' > 0$ means greater than null sensitivity. Although Fisher's work preceded the wide-scale application of signal detection theory to subliminal perception, it is a safe bet that his gizmo-induced subliminality (the subject failing to report "bird") did not reflect zero sensitivity ($d' = 0$) to the unreported stimulus item but only a low level of sensitivity (see Erdelyi, 1970, 1996).

PSYCHOLOGICAL SUBLIMINALITY

Note that the terms of the argument have shifted from gizmos to perception. We now are concerned with the subject's performance—50% detection, $d' = 1$—rather than with the particulars of the physical device for calibrating the limen. Subliminality is defined not by the gizmo settings but by how the subject performs; it is a response-defined subliminality not a gizmo-defined subliminality. Because there are many psychological ways of degrading performance, it should be clear that we are not wedded to gizmo techniques of degradation. Indeed, for reasons to be noted later, gizmos may not always be the sensible conduit to subliminality and may, actually, derail some of the most vital subliminal phenomena.

←——

FIG. 2.4 (*facing page*)   Top drawing: pillow with feathers spilling out at the right end. Middle drawing: patient in bed. Bottom drawing: subject's drawing of the stimulus represented at 0.1 s (cat lapping up spilled milk). From "Dreams, Images, and Perception: A Study of Unconscious-Preconscious Relationships," by C. Fisher, 1956, *Journal of the American Psychoanalytic Association, 4*, pp. 22, 29, 30. Copyright 1956 "By permission of Leo Goldberger, Ph.D., Editor-in-chief of *Psychoanalysis & Contemporary Thought*." Reprinted with permission.

We have no preset number of psychological techniques of degradation. There are many. Rather than strive for exhaustiveness, we focus instead on three well-known techniques—or classes of techniques—which can be applied to the willful manipulation of levels of consciousness.

Ebbinghausian Subliminality

Although the designation is new, Ebbinghausian subliminality goes back to the beginning of experimental psychology. Ebbinghaus (1885), who served as his own subject, showed that just-learned materials that are ignored by the subject are rapidly forgotten over time. A plot of Ebbinghaus's data (Fig. 2.5) yields the widely known Ebbinghaus curve of forgetting. Because, as we have shown, there is no unique unarbitrary criterion for subliminality, a region of sufficient obscuration will do, which forgetting can produce. Hence, we have subliminality due to forgetting.

But why designate the forgotten subliminal? Maybe the forgotten material is not subliminal but gone, as is implied by the usual rendering of the Ebbinghaus (1885) outcome as "memory decays with time." There is a straightforward answer: The

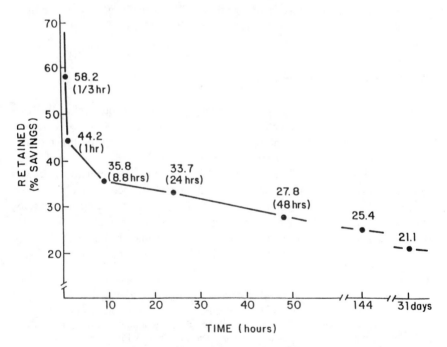

FIG. 2.5   The Ebbinghaus curve of forgetting. From *The Recovery of Unconscious Memories: Hypermnesia & Reminiscence* (p. 2), by M. H. Erdelyi, 1996, Chicago: The University of Chicago Press. © 1996 The University of Chicago Press. Reprinted with permission.

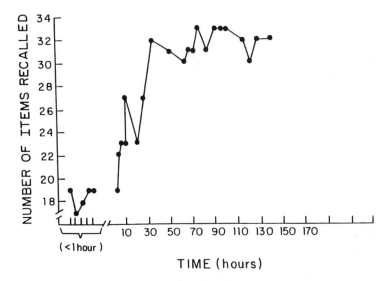

FIG. 2.6 Erdelyi and Kleinbard's (1978) retention function: Picture recall increases with time (hypermnesia). From "Has Ebbinghaus Decayed With Time? The Growth of Recall (Hypermnesia) Over Days," by M. H. Erdelyi and J. Kleinbard, 1978, *Journal of Experimental Psychology: Human Learning and Memory, 4*, p. 278. Copyright 1978 by The American Psychological Association. Reprinted with permission.

forgotten, or at least some of it, may not be gone but may have merely gone underground, below the "threshold of consciousness," as Johann Herbart (1824–1825) suggested decades before Ebbinghaus (see Boring, 1950; Sand, 1988). Fig. 2.6 presents another memory function, introduced in the experimental literature by Erdelyi and Kleinbard (1978). When, instead of avoiding the memories, as had Ebbinghaus, the subject actively thinks of them and seeks to retrieve more of the material, conscious accessibility progressively increases (*hypermnesia*) rather than decreases (*amnesia*).

An important difference between the Ebbinghaus (1885) and the Erdelyi and Kleinbard (1978) studies, other than the ignoring versus thinking of the materials, is the type of stimulus used: nonsense syllables in the case of Ebbinghaus and pictures in the case of Erdelyi and Kleinbard. The stimulus turns out to be a critical factor, as suggested by Fig. 2.7 (also from Erdelyi & Kleinbard, 1978): When recall is repeatedly tested for a list of pictures, memory goes up with time (hypermnesia); the same multiple testing for words, however, fails to produce a reliable increment over time. In a review of the literature, David Payne (1987) found that virtually all multitrial recall studies with pictures produced hypermnesia, but less than 50% of them did so with lists of words. Experimental psychology, unfortunately, has had a predilection for oversimple stimuli (nonsense syllables, lists of words) and for this reason has lost sight of upward-trending memory, which

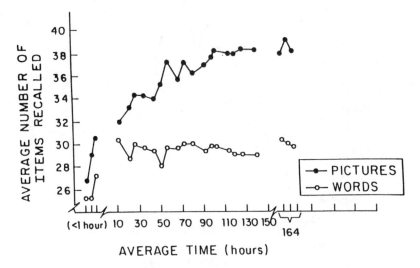

FIG. 2.7   Erdelyi and Kleinbard's (1978) retention functions for pictures and words.
From "Has Ebbinghaus Decayed With Time? The Growth of Recall (Hypermnesia)
Over Days," by M. H. Erdelyi and J. Kleinbard, 1978, *Journal of Experimental
Psychology: Human Learning and Memory, 4*, p. 282. Copyright 1978 by The
American Psychological Association. Reprinted with permission.

had already been experimentally documented by Ballard in 1913 (see Erdelyi,
1996, for an extensive review). The stimulus needs not be, it turns out, pictures.
Poetry, engaging narratives, Socratic stimuli (which subjects themselves generate
from answering riddles) will do. Thus, through retrieval effort or retrieval neglect,
accessibility of memories to awareness can be significantly modulated both upward
and downward.

It should be noted that traditional gizmo subliminality, such as produced by
tachistoscopes, is entwined in these memory effects because testing for perception
necessarily takes place some time after the stimulus (even if only fractions of a
second later), so amnesia and hypermnesia alter the effects of the gizmo. Strictly
speaking, we can never measure subliminal perception because by the time we get
to measuring it, we are already consigned to measuring memory. This conundrum
has been noted before (e.g., Holender, 1986; James, 1890/1950) but tends, perhaps
because it is inconvenient, to be forgotten in mainstream literature.

Pavlovian Subliminality

We now briefly consider the associative induction of meanings, a technique ubiquitous in the advertising world—and the animal lab—but which so far has not been
conceptualized as a subliminal technique in psychology. Ivan Petrovitch Pavlov
(1927) is of course credited with the systematic laboratory study of this type of

conditioning. Pavlovian (classical) conditioning involves, as is universally known in psychology, the association of a *conditioned stimulus* (*CS*) with an *unconditioned stimulus* (*US*), which is defined as any stimulus that at the beginning of the experimental session reliably produces a particular response, designated the *unconditioned response* (*UR*). Thus, the US may be meat powder placed on the tongue of a hungry dog, and the UR is the salivation that ensues. The CS is an initially neutral stimulus, that is, one that does not produce anything like the UR. Thus, the CS could be a tone or bell but not, for example, cheese (because cheese is likely to produce salivation before any conditioning has taken place). The paradigm can be schematized as follows:

$$US_{meat} \longrightarrow UR_{salivation}$$
$$|$$
$$CS_{bell} \longrightarrow -$$

After a number of pairings, classical conditioning may occur; that is, the initially neutral CS now elicits a response (usually) similar to the UR. This learned response to the CS is designated the *conditioned response*, or *CR*. Thus, whereas at the outset the CS was neutral, after conditioning has taken hold, it produces the CR:

$$CS_{bell} \longrightarrow CR_{salivation}$$

Now, in the advertising world this is a standard technique, though meat and bells are not the usual stimuli used. Instead, some exciting stimulus (e.g., a sexy model) is used as the US (which produces something like salivation in the subject) and is paired with the product (e.g., a car):

$$US_{babe/hunk} \longrightarrow UR_{salivation}$$
$$|$$
$$CS_{car} \longrightarrow -$$

After a number of pairings the subject might be expected to respond viscerally to the initially neutral product, for example:

$$CS_{car} \longrightarrow CR_{salivation}$$

The traditional view of classical conditioning was a mechanical one. The CS somehow became a substitute for the US. Modern approaches (e.g., Rescorla, 1988) take a more cognitive tack and suggest (based on much research) that the CS is treated by the subject (dog, rat, or human) informationally, as a predictor of the US. Thus, after conditioning has taken hold, the initially neutral CS becomes predictive of the US. We might say the CS comes to imply the US (CS $\Rightarrow$ US) and then leads to the appropriate preparatory behaviors, the CR.

The human subject may sometimes be aware of the implied message in a Pavlovian ad (this car implies the sexy babe/hunk and the exciting possibilities to follow), but most of the time the veiled communication remains in the background. Indeed, if the message-by-association were too explicit—"get this car and sexy things will happen"—the subject might critically reject the message. As we note later, too much consciousness triggers critical or defensive evaluations of the message and may well lead to its rejection. As long as the implied message ("this car will get you sex with beautiful babes/hunks") is only implied and in the background, the conditioning takes place without conscious criticism overriding the message, and the subject may well wind up behaving the way the advertiser hoped (buying the car because, without being quite conscious why, the car is sexy, and so on).

The technique of *product placement* (aka "embedded advertising") may be thought of as a more veiled version of Pavlovian subliminality. When the juxta-positions occur in what is clearly an advertisement, the subject is more likely to be aware of the implied message and reject it ("What do you take me for? Do you think I am so stupid?"). If, however, the product is associated with the powerful US in the seamless context of a narrative or movie, the classical conditioning is more likely to occur without the subject being aware of the trick and is less likely to reject the message.

It should be noted that Ebbinghausian subliminality will further degrade aware-ness of the associative communication. If interrogated immediately after the US–CS juxtapositions, the subject may report awareness of the contingencies. Sometime later—the advertiser might hope—this weak explicit awareness may wane, leaving, as with the bird-besotted subjects of Fisher, an inexplicable but powerful response tendency ("I know *Consumer Reports* criticized this car, but I really like it; it's sexy, and it makes me feel good. I don't know why, but I want it. I have to have it."). Thus, different techniques for inducing subliminality can overlap and interact.

Freudian Subliminality

We began our discussion of subliminal processes by shifting the accent from the gizmos that produce subliminal perception to the perceptual performance itself. We now take a further step by shifting our emphasis from mere perception—sight—to insight. Instead of raw perception (e.g., "Do you see the point of light?"), our concern becomes the reception of meaning (e.g., "Do you see my point?"). This type of distinction is, perhaps, the most elemental feature of psychoanalysis and is rendered by Freud as the difference between *manifest content* (surface semantic structure; text) and *latent content* (deep, often unconscious semantic structure; subtext). Of course, poets and artists in general have always known this type of distinction. Freud's contribution was to force the obvious—psychological depth—on an inchoate and, later, recalcitrant psychology (e.g., behaviorism).

TABLE 2.1
Dream-Work Techniques (Techniques of Freudian
Subliminality)

I. Censorship
    (a) Omission
    (b) Hints, modification, allusions
    (c) Displacement of accent
II. Condensation
III. (Primitive) Symbolization
IV. Plastic-word representation/dramatization

Interpretation is the way we get from the surface, manifest content of some message to the deeper, latent content. *Insight* is what results—"sight" into the latent content. Interpretation is a difficult problem (Erdelyi, 1985, 1999, 2001), and the insights we achieve are often partial and noisy—liminal or worse. The reverse process, translating (and mistranslating) the latent content into the manifest content is what Freud called, in the context of dream psychology, the dream-work. What is interesting about the process for our purposes is not the dream per se but the techniques involved. In treating jokes, Freud (1905/1960) referred to the equivalent processes as the *joke-work*. In advertising, we might refer to them as the *ad-work* (or "advertising-work"; Williamson, 1987, p. 15).

The dream-work (and its cognates joke-work, ad-work, and so on), is basically a set of techniques for producing a veiled communication—the manifest content. These psychological techniques for veiling or subliminalizing communications are widely used by advertisers, poets, psychotics—really, all of us (albeit often unconsciously). These dream-work techniques, which we generically refer to as the techniques of Freudian subliminality, were extensively discussed by Freud (e.g., 1900/1953, 1905/1960, 1917/1961) and are outlined in Table 2.1.

The first of these dream-work techniques, *censorship*, excludes or degrades troublesome aspects of the latent content in a variety of ways. The bluntest of these is *omission*, which outrightly excludes some feature of the latent content from the manifest content. Censorship, however, often takes subtler forms, semantically degrading aspects of the latent content rather than altogether cutting them out. These softer forms of censorship are referred to by Freud variously as hints, modifications, allusions, and so on. These techniques of Freudian subliminality are widely observed in everyday life—from jokes, art, and psychotic thinking to advertisements.

Let us examine a few examples. Fig. 2.8 reproduces a graffito from the bathroom wall of a Greenwich Village café. The surface (manifest) content does not make much sense. For anyone with a little background knowledge, the latent content expresses (through hints and allusions) a ridiculous proposition along the lines "the cubist Picasso had cubes for testicles." Of course, this latent content is both silly and a tad off-color. Freud (1905) clearly understood that the joke-work was needed to produce comical effects. Without the mitigation of the latent content, the

FIG. 2.8   Graffiti from the bathroom wall of a Greenwich Village café. From *Psychoanalysis: Freud's Cognitive Psychology* (p. 171), by M. H. Erdelyi, 1985, New York: W. H. Freeman. Copyright 1985 by Matthew Erdelyi. Reprinted with permission.

communication strikes one as stupidly childish and even offensive. Psychological subliminality degrades the unacceptable latent content sufficiently so that (many of us) adults can actually enjoy it.

Fig. 2.9 reproduces an ad from a long time ago, brought to one of us by a student who was a stewardess (and took umbrage at the ad, along with many of her colleagues). There is nothing explicitly wrong with the manifest content of the "Only Pat has big, beautiful . . . " ad. There is, however, a cumulative string of hints and allusions—from the phallic nose of the plane to "My Time is Your Time" to "Good Things at Night" and, finally, to "I'm Pat. I'm going to fly you like you have never been flown before"—that point to a veiled communication along the lines of "If a man like you flies with us, you are going to have the sexual thrill of your life." To say this too openly, obviously, would be off-putting (and maybe illegal). So, through hints and allusions, the ad (if we are interpreting it correctly) is trying to get away with the unacceptable latent message by psychological degradation to yield a sufficiently obscure (subliminal) expression. *Displacement of accent* is yet another version of subtle censorship. By misplacing emphasis or putting the emphasis in the wrong place (e.g., displacing the U.S. surgeon general's warning on cigarette boxes to off center and rendering it in fine print), the disturbing message is degraded.

The second technique of Freudian subliminality is *condensation*, by which is meant the merging of two or more independent ideas or images, as in the

FIG. 2.9   Ad: "Only Pat has big, beautiful . . ." From *New York Post*, January 20, 1978, p. 7.

FIG. 2.10 Elephant man. From *The Beatles Illustrated Lyrics* (p. 76), by A. Aldridge, 1969, New York: Dell. Copyright 1969 by Alan Aldridge Associates Limited (London). Reprinted with permission.

mythological figures of the Centaur (man-horse) or the sphinx (woman-lion-serpent). Fig. 2.10 reproduces a composite image from Alan Aldridge's *The Beatles Illustrated* (1969), which students almost always find funny and rarely struggle to interpret. They inevitably laugh at it and understand that the elephant trunk naughtily represents or suggests the penis of the idiotically smiling man. The degradation of the latent content is so slight that it would probably not be subliminal enough for an ad.

Another critical aspect of Freudian subliminality is *symbolization*, in which the latent content is not expressed directly but through a substitute, the symbol.

This substitute, even when clearly understood by the observer (as in the case of euphemisms), can escape unwanted negative reactions. Freudian symbols are well known, and it is worth noting that they need not be laboriously memorized. This is because the symbols are primitive: They are analogic, expressing ideas through similarity of appearance or function (e.g., the elephant trunk, the nose of the airplane, flying, and so on). It's not difficult to figure out the referent. *Plastic-word representation* (or *dramatization*) is a related concept. Freud observed that dreams tend not to be expressed in abstract, verbal formats but rather in concrete picture images or enactive representations (behavioral dramatizations).

These few Freudian techniques usually occur in tandem, and it is often difficult to separate one from the other. Thus, it is not altogether clear whether we should designate the Macho Cologne ad (Fig. 2.11) a type of symbolic statement or plastic-word representation. Similarly, the butter-up ad (Fig. 2.12) combines all the Freudian techniques to communicate something that would be offensive to many observers if it were explicit. The same goes for the famous Joe Camel character (Fig. 2.13a). It is not difficult to discern (though few observers do spontaneously) the two latent contents expressed in the manifest face (see Fig. 2.13b): (1) penis with testicles and (2) penis in vagina. Primitive symbolism, condensation, and hints and allusions suggest the latent message ("Smoke this brand, guys, and your big organ will find its mark," or some such). In a gizmo variant on this theme (Fig. 2.14a), one can discern the subtle embed of a man with an erection (facing right) on the camel that is depicted on each pack of this brand (see Fig. 2.14b for a highlighting of the man with the erection). There is probably more in the camel, some hanky-panky to the right of the man with an erection, but we need not belabor the point.

The latent contents in these ads are degraded because of defensive consider-ations. An explicit, supraliminal presentation of the latent contents would yield strong negative reactions among most observers, with an attendant rejection of the product. A recent ad from Absolut Vodka (Fig. 2.15) masterfully gets away with showing much that would be unacceptable in a public ad. The bottle (a phal-lic symbol) is condensed with a plastic-word representation of the vulva (framed curtains, etc.). The stewardess, pushing her "box," tends to prime the message for the observer. An explicit depiction would yield outrage and rejection by most observers. By subliminalizing the latent content with Freudian techniques, the ad gets away with expressing the forbidden.

These Freudian subliminal techniques were put on the psychological map by Freud, but they are certainly not new. Four centuries before, in his famous triptych, *The Garden of Delights*, Hieronymous Bosch makes use of all these sub-liminalizing techniques to convey debauchery, sex, sadism, and perverted acts—in short, ideas that are taboo and for which Hell is the reward—without being too explicit and therefore offensive. Fig. 2.16, which bears some resemblances to the Absolut Vodka ad, is a detail from the right panel (*Hell*) of the triptych and de-picts, in primitive symbols and plastic-word representations, crude and sadistic images of sexual organs and sexual acts. In the upper left corner, two ears and

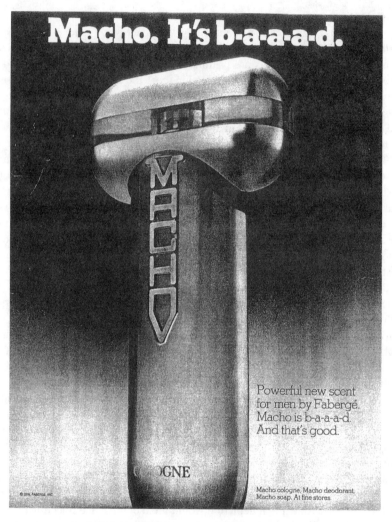

FIG. 2.11 Ad for Macho Cologne (Fabergé, Inc.).

a knife are the manifest content. It is not hard to discern the latent counterpart: testicles with a protruding penis. (The condensation of the knife and penis carries a deeper threatening message, which, incidentally, recurs elsewhere in the painting.) A little to the right is a strange bagpipe instrument. The latent content, if we go by physical resemblance, is the female reproductive system: uterus, fallopian tubes, and the vaginal canal (rendered as a reed instrument, perhaps suggesting a crude invitation, "Let's make music," or some such). The little "nun" immediately below the end of the vaginal canal (musical instrument) is an anatomically accurate rendering of the vulva. This is particularly obvious when we take the nun's skirt off (another crude joke?) and the shafts of light about her head. No student

FIG. 2.12   Ad for Butter Up.

ever spontaneously perceives all these latent contents—though many are moved and vaguely disturbed by the painting—but when they are pointed out, the latent content is readily recognized.

IMPLICATIONS AND CONCLUSIONS

The Contribution of Gizmos, Good and Bad.   Gizmos were introduced into the field as a convenient route to degrading stimuli to subliminal levels. Pötzl, as we saw, succeeded in mimicking with his gizmo (a primitive tachistoscope) the effects

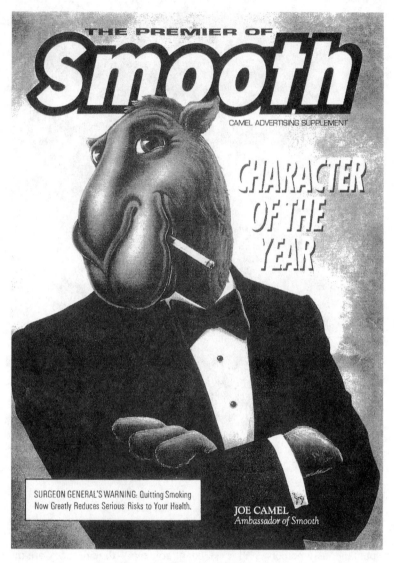

FIG. 2.13a   Joe Camel: ambassador of smooth.

of another "gizmo"—a damaged brain. It is obviously a great convenience to be
able to produce subliminal effects (e.g., emergence and recovery of input in dreams)
with a relatively cheap physical device that can be used with everyday subjects. It is
also of great advantage to be able to manipulate the input systematically in a brief
laboratory session to evaluate the effect of varied levels of stimulus obscuration.

Obviously, there are upsides to using gizmos to produce subliminality. But
there are downsides also. One problem is psychological: Gizmos have the éclat

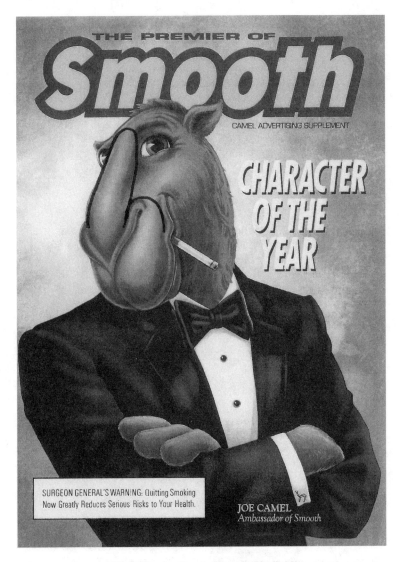

FIG. 2.13b   Joe Camel with embed outlined.

of science, and it is all too easy to get trapped into displacing the accent of research from the substantive issues to the paraphernalia of the instrument. As we
saw, there is probably no actual limen, except as a statistical abstraction to designate the whereabouts of a region of relative obscuration of awareness, and this
limen is not anchored in some gizmo parameter, such as duration, SOA, lumi-
nance, and so on, but is anchored in the subject's performance (e.g., 50% hit rate;
$d' = 1.0$).

FIG. 2.14a   Picture of Camel cigarette pack.

Also, gizmos have their intrinsic limitations. A picture or word can be flashed tachistoscopically, but highly complex materials, as encountered in everyday life (including some advertisements), don't lend themselves to this technique of psychological obscuration. There is a tendency in the experimental literature to gauge subliminal effects by what gizmos are capable of yielding. Thus, Greenwald and his associates (e.g., Draine & Greenwald, 1998; Greenwald, Klinger, &

FIG. 2.14b Picture of Camel cigarette pack with embed outlined.

Schuh, 1995), while pursuing imaginative couplings of gizmos with statistical techniques for assessing effects at chance-level awareness, implicitly assume that the subliminal effects thus demonstrated are coterminous with subliminal effects in general, and they reach the much-cited conclusion that the unconscious is "dumb" or simple (Abrams & Greenwald, 2000; Greenwald, 1992). The amount of information that can be transmitted from a degraded stimulus flash is indeed limited—we

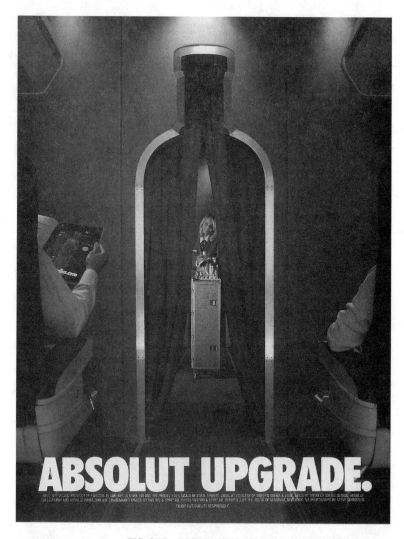

FIG. 2.15   Ad from Absolut Vodka.

would not expect to be able to transmit the contents of the *Encyclopedia Britannica* in a 10-ms flash—but this limit hardly bears on the scope (and genius) of subliminal processes (Erdelyi, 1992, 1999). Thus, perhaps because of the rhetoric of the gizmos, there is a tendency to locate subliminal effects in a contrived experimental paradigm that helps to subliminalize simple, cognitively limited stimulus flashes. It is here where psychological subliminality shifts back the accent to where the vital effects reside—inside the psychological system, which includes memory stores and programs vastly greater in purview and power than that of any paltry encyclopedia.

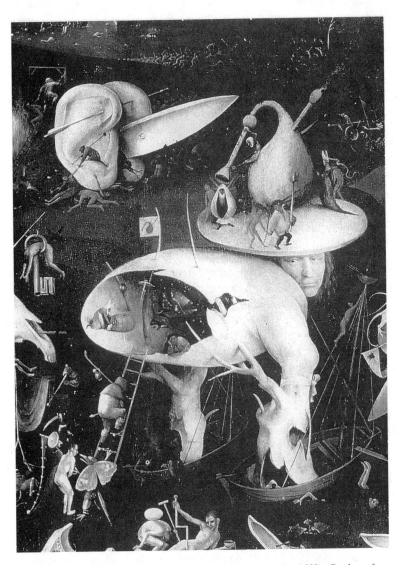

FIG. 2.16 Detail from Hieronymous Bosch's (circa A.D. 1500) *Garden of Earthly Delights*. Copyright by Erich Lessing/Art Resource, NY Bosch Hierorymus (C. 1450–1516). Hell. Right panel from the Garden of Earthly Delights triptych. Copyright Erich Lessing/Art Resource, NY Museo del Prado, Madrid, Spain. Reprinted with permission.

The Interface Between Gizmo and Psychological Subliminality. It is possible to induce subliminality without gizmos but it is not possible to have gizmo subliminality without psychological subliminality. When Pötzl (1917) or Fisher (1954, 1956, 1988) flashed their stimuli and subsequently evaluated soft cognition like fantasy, word-associations, and dreams, they were drawing on the effects not only of the tachistoscope but also of psychological processes that piggybacked on them, such as forgetting. It may be that the tachistoscope functions mainly to speed up psychological degradation of the input. It has been shown with two children (Erdelyi, 1996) that repeated recalls of a story over periods of months can yield the very types of effects (emergence and recovery, displacements, condensations, symbolic representations) as those found by Pötzl and Fisher in dreams and fantasy following tachistoscopic presentation of the stimulus. The tachistoscopic degradation may be thought of as giving the psychological process a head start. Instead of having to wait for days or weeks for forgetting (and other possible psychological processes) to take their toll on the stimulus, a tachistoscopic flash degrades the stimulus immediately and can produce effects in a brief laboratory session.

Why Is Less, More? Do Subliminal Stimuli Produce More Powerful Effects Than Supraliminal Stimuli? There is no general rule that subliminal effects are more powerful than supraliminal ones. It is the case, however, that subliminal communications are sometimes more effective or that they produce different (and more desired) effects than their clearly conscious counterparts. In the various examples of jokes, ads, and art considered previously, we saw that defensive considerations often dictate the mitigation of raw information. Were the communications not toned down by the various techniques of psychological subliminality, untoward emotional reactions might result in the rejection of the communications, which typically involve primitive (sexual, aggressive) impulses about which we are inevitably ambivalent. We tend simultaneously to be attracted to and repelled by such content. Subliminalizing the message allows us to have our cake and eat it too: The taboo can be partaken of without full awareness and, therefore, responsibility.

Such ambivalence is consistent with the realities of the brain. Different subsystems of the brain represent different neurological constituencies. For example, the amygdala may urge aggression on the aggression center of the ventromedial nucleus of the hypothalamus, while the septum, playing the dove, tries to calm down this same center. It is more complicated than this, of course, and other subsystems also play roles in such neural power struggles (e.g., the hippocampus tends to join the hawk factions, while the cerebral cortex can both urge and inhibit aggression). What may be theoretically productive for our consideration is the hypothesis that different levels of stimulus clarity differentially activate different substrates and thus produce different resultant effects.

There is another critical aspect of consciousness that has been noted perennially by psychologists and neuroscientists: Focal consciousness has a general

structuring and inhibitory function of which defense may be only a subset (e.g., Spence & Holland, 1962). If focal consciousness were fully deployed on some sketchy advertising claim, the subject may well reject it on the basis of logic or reality. If, however, consciousness is degraded, it may fail to inhibit more primitive (and credulous) cognitive subsystems. Dan Gilbert (1991) summarizes laboratory evidence showing that when subjects are presented with some communication, the initial (more primitive) response is to believe in the communication. Apparently the cognitive default value is to believe. Only with additional conscious analysis, which might reveal the problems in the communication, will the subject adopt a critical stance and reject the claim, if it is wanting. Thus, it would be to the advantage of the persuader—especially if his or her message is dubious—to degrade this second analytic stage and maximize the role of the credulous earlier stage.

This kind of distinction between a more primitive and a more advanced form of cognition is central to Freudian psychology. The more primitive system, *primary-process thinking*, is suffused with emotions and drives and is characterized by a primitive cognitive style (it is not realistic or logical; it abides contradictions and has no linear time; its language is imagistic and enactive; it fails to make distinctions and displaces and condenses ideas and images). The more advanced cognitive style, *secondary-process thinking*, which is associated with consciousness, is the opposite: It is realistic, logical, discriminating, and inhibiting, and its language is more abstract (e.g., verbal). Dreams and psychotic thinking—and to a lesser extent art, jokes, and ads—illustrate what happens when secondary-process thinking is weakened and thus fails to inhibit the more primitive effusions of primary-process thinking. Art, poetry, and ads are *compromise formations* that favor our more primitive side. Subliminalization achieves this effect by degrading conscious (secondary-process) functioning and thus tilting the psychological balance toward our primitive side. Emotions and ideas may thus be experienced that might otherwise be inhibited by full-throttled consciousness.

An important experimental literature on the mere-exposure effect might illustrate this idea. Zajonc (e.g., 1968, 2001) has documented over the past few decades the pervasiveness of a simple repetition effect: When some neutral (often meaningless) stimulus is repeatedly exposed to the subject, there is a tendency for this repeated stimulus to be preferred by the subject and to be judged more emotionally pleasing. What would happen if these repeated exposures were subliminal? In a seminal study, Kunst-Wilson and Zajonc (1980) showed that when the stimuli were presented so briefly that the subject could do no better than chance in discriminating them later from stimuli that had never been flashed, the subjects nevertheless preferred the stimuli that had been flashed earlier but which had presumably not been seen. It has been more recently documented that this subliminal mere-exposure effect (or KWZ effect) is significantly stronger, by a factor of 2 to 4, than the supraliminal mere-exposure effect (Bornstein, 1989, 1990, 1992;

Weinberger, 1992; Zajonc, 2001). These data, of course, are relevant to adver-tisers (see, e.g., Aylesworth, Goodstein, & Ajay,1999). There is also some evi-dence that Ebbinghausian subliminality will produce the trick: Up to some point, the mere-exposure effect apparently gets stronger over time (Bornstein, 1989, 1992).

Our general stance is not to argue for the pervasive advantage of subliminal over supraliminal stimuli—just as we would not argue that night is superior to day for all purposes: It depends on what we are working with and what our objective might be. We assume that there are optimal levels of awareness for different purposes. To the extent that we can modulate the level of consciousness, which we apparently can do through numerous venues, we may maximize our desired outcomes by optimizing the level of consciousness, which might be, in many cases, in the region of subliminal obscuration.

From a Concretistic to an Abstract Conception of Subliminal Perception.   In effect, the subtext of this paper was to move our overly concretistic conception of subliminal perception, to which experimental psychology has been prone, to a more abstract level. We first showed that subliminality did not depend on any concrete physical device—a gizmo—because psychological techniques of various kinds (only three of which were included in our coverage) could yield the desired obscuration of consciousness. This breakout from the straightjacket of mere phys-ical techniques of stimulus degradation allowed us to consider highly complex (as opposed to "dumb") types of subliminal processing.

A major additional step, broached in Freudian subliminality, is the idea that perception need not be only a sensory experience of some sort but that it is often, especially with humans, a highly conceptual extraction of meaning. We under-scored this idea by contraposing insight with mere sight. It is quite possible for the subject to perceive all the relevant elements of a situation without correctly perceiving a higher order pattern or gestalt ("connecting the dots"). The defense mechanism of denial exactly corresponds to this high-level degradation of percep-tion: The subject, because of emotional vulnerabilities, does not want to "see" the meaning in a situation; hence, the subject fails to put together the fully perceived elements of the situation or puts the elements together incorrectly. Denial, then, is a defensive failure of insight (Erdelyi, 1985).

The extraction of higher order meanings brings us to the everyday realm of subliminal perception because, in virtually every domain of human intercourse— jokes, art, social interactions, and, of course, advertising—the clarity of the sub-text is continually modulated, often downward, for successful (if not always the clearest) communication. It is perhaps not surprising that advertisers—along with clinicians, artists, politicians, and diplomats—whose priority is real-world com-munication over experimental methodology and control—should have intuitively mastered some of these complex, high-level forms of subliminality.

NOTE

Communications may be directed to Matthew Hugh Erdelyi, at the Department of Psychology, Brooklyn College, CUNY, 2900 Bedford Avenue, Brooklyn, NY 11210-2889, or via e-mail at iyledre@aol.com.

REFERENCES

Abrams, R. L., & Greenwald, A. G. (2000). Parts outweigh the whole (word) in unconscious analysis of meaning. *Psychological Science, 11*, 118–124.

Aldridge, A. (1969). *The Beatles illustrated lyrics.* New York: Dell.

Aylesworth, A., Goodstein, R. C., & Ajay, K. (1999). The effect of archetypal embeds on feelings: An indirect route to affecting attitudes? *Journal of Advertising, 28*, 74–81.

Ballard, P. B. (1913). Oblivescence and reminiscence. *British Journal of Psychology, 1*(Suppl. 2), Preface-82.

Bargh, J. A., & Chartrand, T. L. (1999). The unbearable automaticity of being. *American Psychologist, 54*, 462–479.

Boring, E. G. (1950). *A history of experimental psychology (2nd ed.).* New York: Appleton-Century-Crofts.

Bornstein, R. F. (1989). Exposure and affect: Overview and meta-analysis of research, 1968–1987. *Psychological Bulletin, 106*, 265–289.

Bornstein, R. F. (1990). Critical importance of stimulus unawareness for the production of subliminal psychodynamic activation effects: A meta-analytic review. *Journal of Clinical Psychology, 46*, 201–210.

Bornstein, R. F. (1992). Subliminal mere exposure effects. In R. F. Bornstein & T. S. Pittman (Eds.), *Perception without awareness* (pp. 191–210). New York: Guilford.

Bornstein, R. F., & Pittman, T. S. (Eds.). (1992). *Perception without awareness.* New York: Guilford.

Draine, S. C., & Greenwald, A. G. (1998). Replicable unconscious semantic priming. *Journal of Experimental Psychology: General, 127*, 286–303.

Ebbinghaus, H. (1885). *Memory.* (H. A. Ruger & C. E. Bussenius, Trans.). New York: Dover, 1964.

Erdelyi, M. H. (1970). Recovery of unavailable perceptual input. *Cognitive Psychology, 1*, 99–113.

Erdelyi, M. H. (1985). *Psychoanalysis: Freud's cognitive psychology.* New York: W. H. Freeman.

Erdelyi, M. H. (1992). Psychodynamics and the unconscious. *American Psychologist, 47*, 784–787.

Erdelyi, M. H. (1996). *The recovery of unconscious memories: Hypermnesia and reminiscence.* Chicago: University of Chicago Press.

Erdelyi, M. H. (1999). The unconscious, art, and psychoanalysis. *Psychoanalysis and Contemporary Thought, 22*, 609–626.

Erdelyi, M. H. (2001). Studies in historicism: Archeological digs will not resolve the scientific questions of validity and reliability in free-association and interpretation. *Psychological Inquiry, 12*, 133–135.

Erdelyi, M. H., & Kleinbard, J. (1978). Has Ebbinghaus decayed with time? The growth of recall (hypermnesia) over days. *Journal of Experimental Psychology: Human Learning and Memory, 4*, 275–289.

Fisher, C. (1954). Dreams and perception. *Journal of the American Psychoanalytic Association, 3*, 380–445.

Fisher, C. (1956). Dreams, images, and perception: A study of unconscious-preconscious relationships. *Journal of the American Psychoanalytic Association, 4*, 5–48.

Fisher, C. (1988). Further observations on the Pötzl phenomenon: The effects of subliminal visual stimulation on dreams, images, and hallucinations. *Psychoanalysis and Contemporary Thought, 11*, 3–56.

Freud, S. (1953). The interpretation of dreams. In J. Strachey (Ed. & Trans.), *The standard edition of the complete psychological works of Sigmund Freud* (Vols. 4–5). London: Hogarth Press. (Original work published 1900).

Freud, S. (1960). Jokes and their relation to the unconscious. In J. Strachey (Ed. & Trans.), *The standard edition of the complete psychological works of Sigmund Freud* (Vol. 8). London: Hogarth Press. (Original work published 1905).

Freud, S. (1961). Introductory lectures on psychoanalysis. In J. Strachey (Ed. & Trans.), *The standard edition of the complete psychological works of Sigmund Freud* (Vols. 15–16). London: Hogarth Press. (Original work published 1917).

Gilbert, D. T. (1991). How mental systems believe. *American Psychologist, 46*, 107–119.

Greenwald, A. G. (1992). New Look 3. *American Psychologist, 47*, 766–779.

Greenwald, A., Klinger, M., & Schuh, E. (1995). Activation by marginally perceptible ("subliminal") stimuli: Dissociation of unconscious from conscious cognition. *Journal of Experimental Psychology: General, 124*, 22–42.

Herbart, J. F. (1824–1825). *Psychologie als wissenschaft neu gegründet auf erfahrung, metaphysik und mathematik* [Psychology as Science, newly grounded on experience, metaphysics, and mathematics]. Königsberg, Germany: Unzer.

Holender, D. (1986). Semantic activation without conscious identification in dichotic listening, parafoveal vision, and visual masking: A survey and appraisal. *Behavioral and Brain Sciences, 9*, 1–66.

James, W. (1950). *Principles of psychology*. New York: Dover. (Original work published 1890).

Kunst-Wilson, W. R., & Zajonc, R. B. (1980). Affective discrimination of stimuli that cannot be recognized. *Science, 207*, 557–558.

Macmillan, N. A. (1986). The psychophysics of subliminal perception. *Behavioral and Brain Sciences, 9*, 38–39.

Macmillan, N. A., & Creelman, C. D. (1991). *Detection theory: A user's guide*. Cambridge, UK: Cambridge University Press.

Moore, T. E. (Ed.). (1988). Subliminal influences in marketing. [Special issue]. *Psychology and Marketing, 5*(4).

Pavlov, I. P. (1927). *Conditioned reflexes: An investigation of the physiological activation of the cerebral cortex*. London: Oxford University Press.

Payne, D. G. (1987). Hypermnesia and reminiscence in recall: A historical and empirical review. *Psychological Bulletin, 101*, 5–27.

Pötzl, O. (1960). The relationship between experimentally induced dream images and indirect vision. (J. Wolff, D. Rapaport, & S. Annin, Trans.). *Psychological Issues, Monograph 7*, 41–120. (Original work published 1917).

Rescorla, R. (1988). Pavlovian conditioning: It's not what you think it is. *American Psychologist, 43*, 151–160.

Sand, R. (1988). Early nineteenth century anticipation of Freudian theory. *International Review of Psycho-Analysis, 15*, 465–479.

Spence, D. P., & Holland, B. (1962). The restricting effects of awareness: A paradox and an explanation. *Journal of Abnormal and Social Psychology, 64*, 163–174.

Swets, J. A. (Ed.). (1964). *Signal detection and recognition in human observers*. New York: Wiley.

Swets, J. A., Tanner, W. P., & Birdsall, T. G. (1961). Decision processes for perception. *Psychological Review, 68*, 301–340.

Weinberger, J. (1992). Validating and demystifying subliminal psychodynamic activation. In R. F. Bornstein & T. S. Pittman (Eds.), *Perception without awareness* (pp. 170–188). New York: Guilford.

Williamson, J. (1987). *Decoding advertisements: Ideology and meaning in advertising*. New York: Marion Boyars.

Zajonc, R. B. (1968). Attitudinal effects of mere exposure. *Journal of Personality and Social Psychology, 9* (Suppl. 2), 1–27.

Zajonc, R. B. (2001). Mere exposure: A gateway to the subliminal. *Current Directions in Psychological Science, 10*, 224–228.

CHAPTER THREE

Product Placement: The Nature of the Practice and Potential Avenues of Inquiry

John A. McCarty
The College of New Jersey

As marketers continue to vie for the attention of an increasingly fragmented consumer market, they have turned to a variety of communication channels in their efforts to reach customers. One of the channels they have exploited more frequently in recent years is *product placement*, the placing of branded products in movies and television programs. Product placement has been defined as "a paid product message aimed at influencing movie (or television) audiences via the planned and unobtrusive entry of a branded product into a movie (or television program)" (Balasubramanian, 1994, p. 29). It is this unobtrusive entry of a commercial message in a movie or television show that makes product placement different from most other forms of marketing communications. This embedding of commercial messages in another type of communication is a clear example of the blurring of the lines between commercial communications and entertainment, which has become more prevalent in recent years (Solomon & Englis, 1994). This chapter explores the nature of product placement as a marketing communications tool, contrasting it to other communications and discussing the complex and multidimensional nature of the practice. In this chapter I briefly discuss the academic work that has been done on product placement, consider some of the issues that need to be addressed for the field to proceed with future inquires, and suggest some paths that can be taken to understand product placement more fully.

PRODUCT PLACEMENT: A BRIEF DESCRIPTION OF THE PRACTICE

Generally, a product is placed in a movie or television show in return for payment of money or other promotional consideration by the marketer (Gupta & Gould, 1997).[1] Prices can vary for placement, depending on the nature of the placement in the movie (McCarthy, 1994), and can range from nothing to several million dollars (Fournier & Dolan, 1997). The price of product placement can be a function of the type of product that is featured; some product categories are easier to place in a movie than others (McCarthy, 1994). The prominence of the placement in the movie can also affect the price. For example, a placement where the product name is mentioned might cost more than one in which the product logo is simply visible in the background of a scene.

Product placement in movies has actually been around since the 1940s, although it "essentially remained a casual business, an afterthought to most marketers and a low priority for studios" (McCarthy, 1994, p. 30). Brennan, Dubas, and Babin (1999) have suggested that the original motivation for product placements was on the part of the motion picture studios in their effort to add a greater level of reality to the movies by having real brands in the stories. Over time, however, motion picture producers became aware of the commercial value of these placement opportunities, and the practice has become far more prevalent.

In the past decade or so, product placement has become a very sophisticated business, with product placement agencies reviewing scripts in an effort to find product placement opportunities for their marketer clients (McCarthy, 1994). This intensified interest in product placement was likely generated by well-known successes in the 1980s, most notably Reese's Pieces placement in *E.T. The Extra-Terrestrial*, which increased the candy's sales by 66%, and Rayban's placement in *Risky Business*, which tripled the sales of the sunglasses worn by Tom Cruise in the movie (Fournier & Dolan, 1997). Product placement is very common today and, in many instances, involves an arrangement between the movie and the product that includes joint advertising and promotion. For example, the cellular phone service Sprint and Burger King restaurants were brands placed in the movie *Men in Black II*. Television advertising for Sprint that ran during the movie's opening period featured alien characters from the movie; Burger King introduced a special burger that was tied to the theme of the movie. Today, the practice of product placement is not confined to movies and television shows but is being used in music videos and video games as well (Karrh, 1998).

---

[1] In lieu of financial payment, the arrangement for product placement can be a relatively complicated promotional arrangement between the marketer and the movie studio. In these cases, there is often a promotional effort that may be mutually beneficial. For example, for the introduction of the BMW Z3 roadster in the James Bond movie *GoldenEye*, there was an agreement to jointly promote the film and the roadster. BMW does not pay money for product placement as a matter of policy (Fournier & Dolan, 1997). McCarthy (1994) suggested that a promotional arrangement is often preferred to a payment of money because the movie can often benefit more from such arrangement.

The placement of a product in a movie can be as simple as a product being used in one scene (e.g., when a character uses a particular brand of beer or soft drink), a brand being mentioned by a character in the story, or a logo visible in the background of a frame (e.g., when a brand's logo is visible on a billboard or the side of a truck). At the other extreme, a product placement can be a critical and integral part of the movie. In the movie *You've Got Mail*, AOL Internet service was an essential part of the movie and was intimately connected to the plot throughout the entire movie. Not only was the familiar phrase "you've got mail" heard numerous times in the movie when one of the main characters signed on to the Internet service, but AOL was the service through which the main characters communicated for much of the story. Clearly, a product can be placed in a movie or television show in a variety of ways and at a variety of levels. The multifaceted nature of product placement makes it an interesting, albeit complex, marketing practice to understand and strategically use.

PRODUCT PLACEMENT AS MARKETING COMMUNICATION

Given that a product placement can vary from a casual mention of a brand in a single scene of a movie to a brand being a major presence in the story, supported by joint advertising and promotion of the movie and brand, it is perhaps inappropriate to characterize all product placements as essentially the same thing. They can differ quite a bit, and, most likely, the way and at what level viewers process them can vary as well. Having stated this caveat, product placement can be compared to other forms of marketing communications in a number of ways, in that all product placements as a form of marketing communications share some common aspects with one another, but they are different from other forms of marketing communications.

Balasubramanian (1994) considered product placements as one type of a hybrid message, a combination of advertising and publicity. He stated:

> Hybrid messages include *all paid attempts to influence audiences for commercial benefit using communications that project a non-commercial character; under these circumstances, audiences are likely to be unaware of the commercial influence attempt and/or to process the content of such communications differently than they process commercial messages.* (italics in original; p. 30)

As Balasubramanian noted, product placements are generally paid for, just as with advertising, but placements are not identified as paid persuasion efforts by sponsors, which makes them similar to publicity. Therefore, the sponsor gets the best of both of these traditional forms of communication, advertising and publicity. That is, the sponsor has some limited control over the communication (subject to editorial considerations of the movie or television show), but the communication

is not usually identified explicitly as a persuasion attempt; therefore, the effort to persuade is not made salient to the audience.

In a similar discussion, Nebenzahl and Jaffe (1998) considered product placements in their characterization of different kinds of marketing communications and how placements might differ from other kinds of communications. They argued that different marketing communications can be considered along two dimensions: (1) the extent to which the sponsor of the message is disguised, that the message is a paid advertisement is disguised, or both, and (2) the extent to which the persuasive message is secondary to the main message of the communication. Product placements can be contrasted with traditional advertising (and other marketing communications) along these dimensions. In the case of advertising, the sponsor of the product is not disguised, and that it is a persuasive effort by that sponsor is generally clear to the audience. With respect to the second dimension, the advertising (persuasive) message is the salient part of the communication and not secondary to any other message. In contrast, a good product placement is different from an advertisement on both of these dimensions: The placement of the product in a scene in the movie is not connected with the company as an explicit attempt to persuade, and the brand is presented in the context of a story. Considering the second dimension, the persuasive effort is generally secondary to the main communication of the movie or television show.[2] Although Nebenzahl and Jaffe's main interest related to the ethics of the communications as a function of how communications are presented to the audience in relation to these two dimensions (e.g., they argued that product placement would be less ethical than advertising because placement represents a hidden, disguised persuasion attempt), these dimensions can illuminate the ways viewers might process the messages.

Therefore, the discussions of Balasubramanian (1994) and Nebenzahl and Jaffe (1998) indicate that the noncommercial and somewhat hidden secondary nature of product placements make them inherently different from traditional advertising, and this suggests that viewers may not process them in the same way as they would an advertisement. Friestad and Wright's (1994) discussion of consumers' persuasion knowledge is relevant to considerations of how consumers might process product placements differently from advertising, given the hidden and secondary nature of product placements. Friestad and Wright viewed persuasion knowledge as a set of interrelated beliefs consumers hold that relate to persuasion attempts by marketers. These beliefs focus on the perceived goals and tactics marketers use to persuade consumers, the perceived appropriateness and effectiveness of these tactics, as well the consumers' perceptions of their own ability to cope with marketers' persuasion efforts. Friestad and Wright suggested that when consumers are confronted with a communication and the communication is recognized as an

---

[2] A product placement is, in general, secondary to the main communication. However, in the movie *You've Got Mail*, AOL's online service was central to the theme of the story and, therefore, part of the primary communication.

attempt to persuade, a fundamental change of meaning occurs. When consumers recognize a communication as a persuasion attempt, they process the message differently than they would if no such recognition occurred. They may get distracted from the message, disengage from the communication, and develop assessments of the persuasion effort and the company related to the communication. For example, when consumers view an advertisement featuring a spokesperson they admire, their evaluation of the message, the product, the spokesperson, and the company are different than they would be if the consumers are unaware that the advertisement is a paid persuasive attempt. There is a change of meaning with respect to the message that the spokesperson is presenting. The message is interpreted in the context of this persuasion knowledge generated by the awareness that the advertisement is a persuasive communication. For a product placement in a movie or television show, however, a consumer's persuasion knowledge may not be activated because there is a lack of identification of the placement as a persuasion attempt. Therefore, the hidden and secondary nature of product placements may not activate the processes that typically put a consumer on guard in the case of advertising.

It is suggested, therefore, that the stealth nature of product placement is one attribute that might be important in making it work as a promotional tool. However, although the promotional nature of a product placement is often disguised, this is not always the case. The connection of the product placement and the movie is sometimes made clear to consumers through joint advertising and promotion. For example, the launch of the BMW Z3 roadster in the James Bond movie *GoldenEye* included TV and print advertising, a press launch in Central Park, a Nieman Marcus catalog offer, and publicity on Jay Leno's *Tonight Show*; all of these efforts clearly connected the Z3 to the movie *GoldenEye* (Fournier & Dolan, 1997), thus, making it apparent that there was a tie-in between the product and the movie. In particular, the advertising campaign featured both the car and the movie. There are numerous other examples of a product placement in a movie made public via tie-in advertising. Therefore, although it is typically not made salient to viewers that a placement is a promotional effort at the point in time the viewers see the placement, it is somewhat common that the connection between the product and movie is made in advertising and promotional materials. In fact, some professionals argue that promotional tie-ins are key to the success of a product placement. McCarthy (1994) reported that a product placement executive attributed the accompanying promotion to the success of Reese's Pieces in the movie *E. T.*, stating, "Hershey spent a lot of money at retail to let everyone know what *E. T.* was eating" (p. 32) because the bag and candy may not have been apparent in the frames of the movie.

Thus, at first glance it would seem that there is a contradiction between the assumption that product placements derive their success from the disguised nature of them and that many of the successful product placements are ones in which the consumer is made aware of the commercial nature of the placement via the accompanying advertising and promotion. It should be considered, however, that at the time the consumer is seeing or hearing the product placement, the commercial

nature of it is not emphasized, even if the connection has been made in another promotional activity. The product is placed in the context of a story, and it may be that this context is important for the placement's success.

To consider this apparent contradiction, it is instructive to note that product placements are similar to one kind of advertisement in that they involve the presentation of the brand in the context of a story. Wells (1989) discussed two kinds of advertising formats: lectures and dramas. *Lectures* are advertisements that present outwardly to the audience, similar to what a speaker would do in a lecture hall. The television audience is spoken to and is presented with an argument and evidence. According to Wells, an effective lecture presents facts to be believed and should be credible in the presentation of these facts; it is generally clear that there is a persuasion attempt being made. In contrast, Wells suggested that a *drama* advertisement draws the audience into a story. Drama advertisements are like movies, novels, and other stories in that they can present a lesson about how the world works. An important aspect of drama advertisements is that they work by allowing the audience to make an inference about the advertised brand from the story that is presented in the advertisement; this inference may provide a stronger impression than if the audience had been told the point through a lecture format. Wells indicated that an effective drama advertisement must engage the viewer and must be believable as a story. Part of the effectiveness of drama advertisements is that they draw the viewer into the story in such a way that the viewer forgets that the story is a persuasive attempt. With drama advertising, the normal skepticism that consumers may have with respect to advertisements is reduced when they see the product in the context of a story. This idea is consistent with the work of Deighton, Romer, and McQueen (1989) on the use of drama to persuade. In the case of drama commercials, compared with argument commercials (i.e., lecture advertisements), they found that viewers "are less disposed to argue and believe the appeal to the extent that they accept the commercial's verisimilitude and respond to it emotionally" (p. 341).

A product placement could therefore be considered as the ultimate form of drama advertising. The product is in the context of a story, but rather than being in a 30-s story, the product is in a story that generally lasts more than an hour. Thinking of a product placement in this way may help explain a placement's success, even when viewers are aware of the promotional tie-in between the movie and the product through the promotions and advertising. To the extent that the plot of the movie draws viewers in, similar to a drama advertisement, the viewers will see the brand in the story and will not think about it as a persuasion attempt.

Therefore, in the same way that a good story makes us forget that the main character is an actor we may know from other roles,[3] a good product placement

---

[3]For example, when we see Tom Hanks play Forrest Gump in the movie of the same name, we are not thinking about the person as Tom Hanks but as the slow-witted, well-intentioned man who is the main character of the story. We are drawn in to the story, and it is not salient to us that Hanks is an actor whom we have seen in a variety of other roles and has a personal life about which we know some things.

may be one that fits with the story in such a way as to make us forget that it is there to persuade us. This idea of the fit of a product placement is critical and relates to the notion of seamlessness, to which practitioners in product placement have often referred. Dean Ayers of Entertainment Resources Marketing Association states:

> A word that comes up a lot in our work is seamless. Subtly rendered. A blurring of the lines between advertising and entertainment. That's the way placements have to function to be successful. People prefer to see a can of Pepsi or some other familiar brand rather than one that just says "Soda." But nobody wants to pay to see a commercial. You have to pay just the right amount of attention to the product to get this effect. ("It's a Wrap," 1995, p. 4, cited in Fournier & Dolan, 1997, p. 7)

When product placements do not achieve a level of seamlessness, problems can arise. As stated by Gary Mezzatesta of Unique Product Placements, "When the audience snickers and says, 'I wonder how much they paid for that,' you know it's bad" (McCarthy, 1994, p. 32). Thus, when a product placement sticks out as an obvious commercial plug, it may activate viewers' persuasion knowledge as well as distract them from the drama.

Although product placement is likened to drama advertising, there is an important distinction that should be emphasized. A drama advertisement is designed from beginning to end as an advertisement. The purpose of the story is to sell the product. In the case of a product placement, the product placement is generally secondary to the main story. The story that unfolds is not designed as an advertisement for a particular product. Although not intended to do so, it may well be the case that the story incidentally presents a key selling point for a brand. For example, the AOL online service featured in *You've Got Mail* was presented as a useful and exciting way to keep connected to others online. Reese's Pieces in *E. T.* was presented as a tasty snack, desirable to humans and aliens. Numerous examples come to mind of movies that present the luxurious life and suggest the kinds of brands that those who live the luxurious life would use, thus providing a clear, albeit subtle, selling point for a placed product.

THE MULTIDIMENSIONAL NATURE OF PRODUCT PLACEMENTS

Although all product placements share some common characteristics, they can differ in a number of ways. A brand can be visually present in a scene, or it can be mentioned and not seen. A placement can be brief, or the product can be an integral part of a character or the story. Therefore, it is likely that product placements can operate in very different ways, depending on the nature of the placement. Similar to how advertising can work at different levels (i.e., inform, persuade, remind), product placement can operate at different levels, depending on the extent to which and how the placement is woven into the movie.

Russell (1998) characterized product placements as a three-dimensional frame-work: The first dimension is the extent to which a placement is visual. A placement can be purely visual, such as a product placed in the background of a scene (e.g., a truck with the logo of the placed product on the side). The level of visual placement can also vary as a function of the number times it is seen in the movie or whether it is seen at all. Russell's second dimension is the auditory or verbal nature of the placement. The brand may not be mentioned at all in the dialogue of the story, might be mentioned several times, might be mentioned with emphasis, and so forth. Russell's third dimension is the degree to which the placement is connected with the plot of the movie. At one level, a brand can simply be one that is visible in a scene of a movie and not connected to the main part of the story. In this instance, it may only be a prop. For example, in movies we often see a billboard or a brand name on the side of a truck in the background of the action of the scene. At the other end of this dimension, a product placement can be intimately tied to the plot, as in *You've Got Mail*, or be closely connected to the nature of the character, as the type of car that James Bond drives or the brand of wristwatch he wears.

PSYCHOLOGICAL PROCESSES AND PRODUCT PLACEMENT

The dimensions discussed by Russell (1998) illustrate the complexity of inves-tigating how consumers may process product placements. The multidimensional nature of product placements, and how they can differ on each of these dimensions, suggests that a variety of psychological processes are operating when a viewer sees a brand in the context of a movie or television show.

At the most basic level, when product placements are merely seen or mentioned in a story, the process may be as simple as affective classical conditioning or mere exposure. As Baker (1999) explained, affective classical conditioning is the pairing an unconditioned stimulus (e.g., a beautiful scene) with the conditioned stimulus (e.g., a brand of product) such that the good feelings associated with the scene are transferred to the brand. Although often discussed in the context of advertising, it is easy to see how such a psychological process can be used in product placements. Russell (1998) suggested that products in the background of a scene may often be processed by this nonconscious association between the brand and the movie. The conditioning process simply requires a viewer to make an association between the response to the scene or movie (i.e., the good feelings) and the brand that is placed.

If affective conditioning is indeed the process at work for simple and brief product placements, a potential complication for the placement of a brand arises. When viewers are watching a movie or television show, they typically experience a variety of both positive and negative feelings during the course of the story, including joy, anger, fear, disbelief, hatred, and sadness. It may be difficult to predict which feeling will be associated with the brand. There is the possibility that a negative feeling will be linked to the brand. For example, in a scene of the

movie *The Silence of the Lambs*, crumpled Arby's wrappers and cups were among the debris in the rather shabby house of the serial killer hunted by Jody Foster's character in the story. Focus group respondents reported a negative association between Arby's and the character in the movie, indicating that if they ate at Arby's, they would be reminded of the killer (Fournier & Dolan, 1997).

A second possibility is that the construct of mere exposure may explain simple product placements (Vollmers & Mizerski, 1994). Mere exposure suggests that viewers will develop more favorable feelings toward a brand simply because of their repeated exposure to it (Baker 1999). Janiszewski's (1993) work showed that mere exposure may result in more favorable attitudes toward a brand, even though the viewer does not necessarily recall the exposure to the brand. It would seem that mere exposure may help explain some types of product placements, particularly ones involving brands presented as props in one or more scenes of a movie.

Clearly, many product placements are more involved than a simple mention of the brand in the dialogue or the logo visible in the scene. As Russell (1998) suggested, they may have more plot connection and not simply be a prop used in a scene. Product placements are often intimately tied to the character in the story or to the story line. For example, the brands associated with James Bond are closely tied to the nature of the character. In fact, the brands that James Bond uses help define him as a character; they are part of his essence. Although conditioning or mere exposure may well be a part of why these work, there may be more higher order processing related to placement in these circumstances. A transformational process has been suggested as such a possibility (Russell, 1998). *Transformational advertising*, as discussed by Puto and Wells (1984), is advertising that transforms or changes the experience of using a product such that the product becomes more than it would otherwise be, making it "richer, warmer, more exciting, and/or more enjoyable" (p. 638). Numerous examples of transformational advertising come to mind, including advertising for such products as jewelry, perfume, automobiles, and liquor.

In a similar way, a viewer's experience of using a brand can be transformed because the brand is embedded in a movie. The product is not just seen in its functional sense but becomes the brand that is considered in the context of the story. It is, as Puto and Wells's (1984) discussion would suggest, endowed with the characteristics associated with the movie. A BMW is not just a well-made German automobile but is the car that James Bond drives. AOL is not just a way to connect to the Internet but the way that trendy New Yorkers in *You've Got Mail* do so.

A similar notion is that of lifestyle advertising (Solomon & Englis, 1994). Solomon and Englis argued that lifestyle advertising associates a product with a way of life, perhaps presenting it in the context of glamorous life or the good life. These ads can act as models of living. Similarly, a product placed in a movie can profit from the model of living that the story presents. An admirable character using a particular brand tells the audience that this is the "in" or "cool" brand of a particular product category or the way to the good life.

Therefore, many product placements are more than just a matter of a brand being seen or mentioned in a movie; they benefit from their connection to the plot. It would seem that the issue of plot connection is a very fundamental distinction between types of product placements. That is, whether the placement is connected to the plot or simply a prop would seem to be a basic qualitative difference in types of placements. Connection to the plot makes a placement a different phenomenon and brings to bear a whole set of psychological processes that are likely absent for a prop placement. It is suggested, therefore, that product placement is a complex, multidimensional concept that may operate at different levels and affect viewers through a variety of psychological processes. Before considering where future research should head with respect to product placement, the next section briefly reviews the academic work on product placements.

ACADEMIC STUDIES ON PRODUCT PLACEMENT

As the use of product placement has increased over the past 2 decades, there has been an increasing interest in the practice among academic researchers. Until rather recently, studies on product placement have generally related to three topic areas: the prevalence and nature of product placement in movies, the attitudes and beliefs about the practice of product placement, and the effects of placements in movies and television (DeLorme & Reid, 1999). Very recently, research has emerged that is attempting to understand the complexity of product placement. Rather than presenting an exhaustive review of the academic literature, this section summarizes what is known from research on product placement. For a more in-depth discussion of the prior work on product placement, see DeLorme and Reid (1999) or Karrh (1998).

Studies Investigating the Prevalence of Product Placement

Studies investigating the prevalence of product placement (Troup, 1991, cited in DeLorme & Reid, 1999; Sapolsky & Kinney, 1994) have found that the practice is fairly common in movies; Avery and Ferraro (2000) documented a similar prevalence in prime-time television. Both studies on product placement in movies found that the majority of placements were for low-involvement products. The Sapolsky and Kinney study did find, however, that automobiles, a high-involvement product category, accounted for 18% of all placements.

Studies Investigating Consumers' Attitudes and Perceptions About Product Placement

Several studies have investigated the attitudes and perceptions of viewers regarding the practice of product placement (Gupta & Gould, 1997; Nebenzahl & Secunda, 1993; Ong & Meri, 1994). These studies were efforts at determining whether

moviegoers find the practice objectionable, given the stealth and "deceptive"nature of the product placement, as claimed by some consumer groups. Interestingly, these studies found that, in general, the majority of people in the United States don't object to the practice of product placement. In fact, the results of the Nebenzahl and Secunda study showed that the respondents preferred product placements to traditional advertisements, and the authors of that study suggested that this preference relates to the notion that advertisements are perceived as intrusive and annoying, whereas the unobtrusive nature of product placements makes them more palatable to consumers. The study by Gupta and Gould showed that although people generally perceive product placement to be an acceptable practice, perceptions differ by product class. That is, product placements involving products that are controversial (i.e., tobacco products and alcohol) are perceived as less acceptable than noncontroversial products.

Studies Investigating the Effectiveness of Product Placement

The most active area of academic research on product placement relates to the effects of placement on viewers. The effects have generally been considered in terms of memory (recognition and recall), evaluation of the brands, and purchase intention. A 1994 study by Ong and Meri found that recall of placed brands was weak for many of them. Babin and Carder (1996a) found that product placement was mixed with respect to making brands salient to viewers, and this study found no effect of the viewing of product placements on brand evaluations. In another study, Babin and Carder (1996b) investigated the ability of viewers to recognize brands they saw in a movie they had just viewed and to distinguish these from brands not in the film. Results showed that, in general, respondents were able to differentiate between brands they had viewed and brands they had not viewed. Vollmers and Mizerski (1994) found that recall of brands in movie clips was very high, but there was no apparent effect of the placements on the attitude toward the brands.

These early studies on the effects of product placement yielded mixed results with respect to the recall or recognition of brands placed in films; these studies generally showed weak or nonexistent effects of placement on brand evaluations. The mixed and weak results of these early studies on effectiveness are, in part, because these studies generally failed to recognize the multidimensional nature of product placement. That is, they tended to define product placements as similar, re-gardless of modality (visual or verbal) and level of plot connection. Recently, there have been some investigations that have attempted to consider these complexities of product placement.

Gupta and Lord (1998) conducted a study that evaluated the effectiveness of product placements of different modes (visual, audio) and different levels of promi-nence of the placement; the study also compared product placement with adver-tising. Recall was used as the measure of effectiveness. Subjects were shown a

30-min clip from a movie that contained either a product placement, an advertisement edited into the film in a fashion similar to how an ad would interrupt a movie shown on television, or neither of these (the control condition). The respondents viewed a prominent visual placement, a subtle visual placement, an audio-only placement, a visual-only placement, an audio-visual placement, an advertisement, or, in the control condition, no placement or advertisement. The results showed that prominent placements were remembered better than advertisements, and advertisements were remembered better than subtle product placements. An explicit audio product placement was remembered better than a subtle visual placement.

Brennan, Dubas, and Babin (1999) investigated the relationship of type of placement (prop or more integral to the story) and exposure time with recognition of the placement. Their results showed that placements more central to the story were remembered better. The effect of exposure time was a little less clear. Exposure time did not relate to recognition for background placements, but there was some indication that length of exposure was related to recognition for placements that were more central to the story.

Law and Braun (2000) attempted to understand the impact of product placements as a function of the nature of the measurements (explicit memory and implicit choice), the centrality of the placement to the plot, and the modality of the placement. An interesting finding of their study was that products that were seen, but not heard, were least recalled but had more influence on choice than those only heard or seen and heard. The researchers suggest that this work has implications for the way viewers process product placements in that placements that may not be consciously remembered may nevertheless have influences on viewers' brand choices.

Russell (2002) investigated product placements as a function of the modality (visual and auditory) and the degree of connection between the plot and the placement; the focus of the study was the congruency between modality and plot connection. Russell reasoned that congruent instances would be auditory placements with high plot connection or visual placements with low plot connection. Incongruent situations would be auditory placements with low plot connection or visual placements with high plot connection. Her reasoning with respect to congruency relates to the importance that spoken information typically has for story development, relative to visual information. As predicted by Russell, the results showed that incongruent placements were remembered better than congruent ones; however, attitude toward the brands changed more in instances with congruent placements.

Thus, the recent research by Law and Braun (2000) and Russell (2002) points to the complexity of product placement and how it is measured. The results of these two studies suggest that memory for the placements may be independent of the evaluations of the brands that are placed. These studies are a step toward considering the way people process different kinds of placements.

POTENTIAL AVENUES OF RESEARCH

Recent research on product placement is beginning to move beyond simply documenting the memory or evaluative effects of the phenomenon and considering the underlying psychological processes. Future research should focus on understanding the psychological processes that relate to product placement in relation to variables that will help researchers understand how product placements work. This section considers some potential areas of inquiry.

Salience of Product Placement

As I have noted, the seamlessness of the product placement has been recognized by practitioners as an important element of the practice, suggesting that the less the viewers think of the placement as a plug for the product, the more successful the placement will be. Thus, the issue of salience of the placement is an important area of potential research that may help researchers understand the impact that product placement may have on consumers' evaluation of the product. Salience of placements as a promotional effort can occur in different ways. The seamlessness of a product placement is the degree to which the placement fits in the context of the story or is visually appropriate in a scene of the movie.

Other information can confirm to viewers that a product they see is a placement. For example, warnings displayed either before a movie or at the time a placement appears in a movie have been proposed by some consumer groups (Bennett, Pecotich, & Putrevu 1999), and these would explicitly alert viewers to the paid promotional nature of the appearance of the brand in the movie. Advertising and other promotional efforts can alert viewers that a product is a paid placement. The potential research questions of interest relate to how the salience of a product placement as a paid promotional effort bears on the way viewers process the placement and the outcomes of the placement (i.e., memory, evaluation of the placed product).

Three research themes would relate to this issue of salience. One would be the extent to which the placement fits with the story and the presence or absence of cues at the time of the placement that alert the viewer to a paid placement; in other words, the degree of seamlessness of the product placed in the story. Russell's (2002) work on congruity suggests that the salience of the placement as a paid promotion may increase memory for the product but may have an adverse effect on the evaluation of the product. Friestad and Wright (1994) would argue that information that makes the placement salient as a promotion should activate persuasion knowledge and may affect evaluations of the brand.

A second theme would be the effect of explicit warnings to the existence of product placements. As noted, consumer groups have argued for warnings because they view product placements as an intentional commercial message and that viewers have a right to know this. These warnings should make it salient that a product placement is present. One would expect that such warnings would activate

persuasion knowledge. One study thus far has shown that warnings before a movie actually enhance the memory of product placements (Bennett, Pecotich, & Putrevu, 1999), suggesting the warning acts as a cue for memory. This study showed no effects of the warnings on evaluations of the brands. It is important to investigate not only the outcomes of such warnings but also how consumers process the placements in the context of such cues.

As advertising and promotional tie-ins with placements become more prevalent, it will be worthwhile to understand how consumers process placements in the context of the promotions that occur in conjunction with many placements. As this chapter has pointed out, such advertising and promotion may not affect efficacy of placements to the extent that the placements are well integrated into the story. Clearly, such tests may be difficult to perform because they require the investigation of real placements under a variety of promotional conditions.

Involvement and Context

Research on advertising in the context of television programs has shown that higher involvement with the story reduces the involvement viewers have with the commercial (Park & McClung, 1986). A product placement, however, is part of the movie or television show. This raises the question of the relationship of plot involvement with product placement, both placements that are connected to the plot and those that are prop placements. One might expect that high involvement in the story would enhance the effects of product placements that are intimately tied to the plot of the movie because involvement in the story would relate to involvement with products important to the plot. How involvement would affect prop placements that are not tied to the plot is a little less clear. It may be that high involvement would reduce the effects of placement in these cases. A study by Pham (1992) showed that involvement had a curvilinear relationship with recognition of embedded billboards at a soccer game; those who were very involved or not very involved showed less recognition than those experiencing a moderate level of involvement in the game. Assuming that embedded billboards at a sports event are equivalent to products that are props in movies, a similar pattern might be expected for prop placements.

Placement and Product Characteristics

A potentially useful area of research relates to the characteristics of products for which product placement would provide the most benefit. For example, is product placement more beneficial for a relatively unknown brand where association with the story line or character would build awareness and interest or is it more useful for brands for which consumers have prior information where the placement would reinforce existing beliefs? For example, the sales of Red Stripe Beer, a relatively unknown brand, increased more than 50% in 3 months after it was briefly mentioned in a scene of the movie *The Firm* (Buss, 1998). Would the effect on sales of

a brief placement have been as dramatic if consumers had more knowledge about the brand and were relatively indifferent to it?

Another product characteristic of interest is the extent to which the product is utilitarian or value expressive. Products such as liquor, cars, and jewelry are value expressive in that people often buy them to express themselves through their products. These types of products can be a part of an individual's extended self (Belk, 1988). Other products are utilitarian and typically say little about the person who uses them. This distinction is commonly made in advertising, and the kind of advertising used generally varies with the nature of the product. It would be useful to understand how product placements are processed as a function of the level of plot connection and the level of value expressiveness. For example, a utilitarian product tightly woven to the plot may not be processed in the same way as a value expressive product. A utilitarian product, no matter how important to the story, would not be as much a defining characteristic of the character as would the things that typically define someone, such as their clothes, cars, or jewelry. Alternatively, the level of value expressiveness of the product may not be expected to relate to the efficacy of the placement in instances when the product is simply a prop in a scene. It would be useful to understand more about the kinds of products that benefit from different kinds of product placements.

Long-Term Effects of Product Placement

Product placement can likely have both short- and long-term effects on evaluation of the brand. Given temporal limitations, academic studies have only measured the short-term effects of product placement. That is, academic studies have generally measured recall, recognition, evaluation, choice behavior, or all of these effects combined, shortly after study participants viewed a movie or a movie clip. Similar to advertising, however, product placement can have long-term effects on the brand image and equity. Furthermore, product placements can set other things in motion that can have effects on the brand. For example, a product placement can create a word-of-mouth effect such that the long-term effect of the placement reaches well beyond those who may have actually seen the product in a movie. Long-term effects can be difficult to measure but are likely an important contribution of product placement.

CONCLUSION

Over the past decade, there has been an increase in the use of product placement in movies and television shows as marketers attempt to find new ways to communicate with their customers. Although many marketing practitioners seem to have an intuitive understanding of how product placements work in different contexts, academic researchers have lagged behind in their efforts to systematically investigate

the practice. Far more is known about product placement than was known even a decade ago, but it is only recent work that has acknowledged the complexity of the phenomenon. Recent work has begun the task of investigating the psychological processes that may be important to understanding how placements work in a variety of circumstances. As this chapter suggests, however, there is far more to consider in the future.

REFERENCES

Avery, R. J., & Ferraro, R. (2000). Verisimilitude or advertising? Brand appearances on prime-time television. *The Journal of Consumer Affairs, 34*, 217–244.

Babin, L. A., & Carder, S. T. (1996a). Advertising via the box office: Is product placement effective? *Journal of Promotion Management, 3*(1–2), 31–51.

Babin, L. A., & Carder, S. T. (1996b). Viewers' recognition of brands placed within a film. *International Journal of Advertising, 15*, 140–151.

Baker, W. E. (1999). When can affective conditioning and mere exposure directly influence brand choice? *Journal of Advertising, 28*(4), 31–46.

Balasubramanian, S. K. (1994). Beyond advertising and publicity: Hybrid messages and public policy issues. *Journal of Advertising, 23*(4), 29–46.

Belk, R. W. (1988). Possessions and the extended self. *Journal of Consumer Research, 15*, 139–168.

Bennett, M., Pecotich, A., & Putrevu, S. (1999). The influence of warnings on product placements. In B. Dubois, T. M. Lowrey, L. J. Shrum, & M. Vanhuele (Eds.), *European advances in consumer research* (Vol. 4, pp. 193–200). Provo, UT: Association for Consumer Research.

Brennan, I., Dubas, K. M., & Babin, L. A. (1999). The influence of product-placement type and exposure time on product-placement recognition. *International Journal of Advertising, 18*, 323–337.

Buss, D. D. (1998, December). Making your mark in movies and TV. *Nation's Business, 86*, 28–32.

Deighton, J., Romer, D., & McQueen, J. (1989). Using drama to persuade. *Journal of Consumer Research, 16*, 335–343.

DeLorme, D. E., & Reid, L. N. (1999). Moviegoers' experiences and interpretations of brands in films revisited. *Journal of Advertising, 28*(2), 71–95.

Fournier, S., & Dolan, R. J. (1997). *Launching the BMW Z3 roadster.* Boston: Harvard Business School.

Friestad, M., & Wright, P. (1994). The persuasion knowledge model: How people cope with persuasion attempts. *Journal of Consumer Research, 22*, 62–74.

Gupta, P. B., & Gould, S. J. (1997). Consumers' perceptions of the ethics and acceptability of product placements in movies: Product category and individual differences. *Journal of Current Issues and Research in Advertising, 19*(1), 38–50.

Gupta, P. B., & Lord, K. R. (1998). Product placement in movies: The effect of prominence and mode on audience recall. *Journal of Current Issues and Research in Advertising, 20*(1), 47–59.

It's a wrap (but not plain): From Budweiser to BMW, brand names are popping up more and more on screen. (1995, September 3). *The Los Angeles Times*, p. 4.

Janiszewski, C. (1993). Preattentive mere exposure effects. *Journal of Consumer Research, 20*, 376–392.

Karrh, J. A. (1998). Brand placement: A review. *Journal of Current Issues and Research in Advertising, 20*(2), 31–49.

Law, S., & Braun, K. A. (2000). I'll have what she's having: Gauging the impact of product placements on viewers. *Psychology and Marketing, 17*, 1059–1075.

McCarthy, M. (1994, March 28). Studios place, show and win: Product placement grows up. *Brandweek, 35*, pp. 30, 32.

Nebenzahl, I. D., & Jaffe, E. D. (1998). Ethical dimensions of advertising executions. *Journal of Business Ethics, 17*, 805–815.

Nebenzahl, I. D., & Secunda, E. (1993). Consumers' attitudes toward product placement in movies. *International Journal of Advertising, 12*, 1–11.

Ong, B. S., & Meri, D. (1994). Should product placement in movies be banned? *Journal of Promotion Management, 2*(3–4), 159–175.

Park, C. W., & McClung, G. W. (1986). The effect of TV program involvement on involvement with commercials. In R. J. Lutz (Ed.), *Advances in consumer research* (Vol. 13, pp. 544–548). Provo, UT: Association for Consumer Research.

Pham, M. T. (1992). Effects of involvement, arousal, and pleasure on the recognition of sponsorship stimuli. In J. Sherry & B. Sternthal (Eds.), *Advances in consumer research* (Vol. 19, pp. 85–93). Provo, UT: Association for Consumer Research.

Puto, C. P., & Wells, W. D. (1984). Informational and transformational advertising: The differential effects of time. In T. C. Kinnear (Ed.), *Advances in consumer research* (Vol. 15, pp. 638–343). Provo, UT: Association for Consumer Research.

Russell, C. A. (1998). Towards a framework of product placement: Theoretical propositions. In J. W. Alba & J. W. Hutchinson (Eds.), *Advances in consumer research* (Vol. 25, pp. 357–362). Provo, UT: Association for Consumer Research.

Russell, C. A. (2002). Investigating the effectiveness of product placements in television shows: The role of modality and plot connection congruence on brand memory and attitude. *Journal of Consumer Research, 29*, 306–318.

Sapolsky, B. S., & Kinney, L. (1994). You oughta be in pictures: Product placements in the top-grossing films of 1991. In K. W. King (Ed.), *Proceedings of the 1994 conference of the American Academy of Advertising* (p. 89). Athens, GA: American Academy of Advertising.

Solomon, M. R., & Englis, B. G. (1994). Reality engineering: Blurring the boundaries between commercial signification and popular culture. *Journal of Current Issues and Research in Advertising, 16*(2), 1–17.

Troup, M. L. (1991). *The captive audience: A content analysis of product placements in motion pictures.* Unpublished master's thesis, Florida State University, Tallahassee.

Vollmers, S., & Mizerski, R. (1994). A review and investigation into the effectiveness of product placements in films. In K. W. King (Ed.), *Proceedings of the 1994 conference of the American Academy of Advertising* (pp. 97–102). Athens, GA: American Academy of Advertising.

Wells, W. D. (1989). Lectures and dramas. In P. Cafferata & A. M. Tybout (Eds.), *Cognitive and affective responses to advertising* (pp. 13–20). Lexington, MA: Lexington Books.

CHAPTER FOUR

Product Placements: How to Measure Their Impact

Sharmistha Law
University of Toronto at Scarborough

Kathryn A. Braun-LaTour
Marketing Memories ^TM^

With product placement—the deliberate insertion of branded products into an entertainment program aimed at influencing the audience—becoming increasingly popular, research into its effectiveness is a timely topic. In this chapter, we propose that the explicit-implicit memory model suggested by cognitive psychologists offers a promising framework for this area of research. We begin by describing recent occurrences of product placements and what the research in this area has found. We present some of the limitations of the traditional methods of measuring product placements. We argue that the product placement literature can be greatly enhanced by considering the explicit-implicit memory framework, which provides a conceptual vocabulary to help organize empirical observations. This framework also helps formulate research hypotheses on when and how product placements will affect thought and behavior.

In Spielberg's film *Minority Report* a large part of the film's screen time is devoted to product placements—15 brands appear in the film, and reports indicate that these placements offset more than 25 million dollars of the production costs (Grossberg, 2002). Product placement is not a new phenomenon; it dates back to the 1940s, at the start of the movie industry when the goal was to make scenes appear more realistic. However, it was Spielberg's use of Reese's Pieces in *E. T.* that led to the popularization of the practice in movies. A decade later *Seinfeld's* phenomenally successful use of products, such as Junior Mints, led to the common practice of TV placements. *Survivor*, for instance, prominently

featured products and logos from advertisers, such as Target and Dr. Scholl's. A recent study of U.S. national networks (i.e., ABC, CBS, NBC) revealed that as many as 15 branded products appear in every halfhour of television programming, about 40% of which are placements (Avery & Ferraro, 2000). Product placements are now making their way from the small screen to video games (Bannan, 2002).

Most movie and TV studios now have product placement departments, and product placement is seen as a viable promotional medium by corporate America. With advertisers seeking new ways to stand out, and broadcasters looking for new sources of revenue, product placements have grown in number. Practically, placements appear to be a good deal for manufacturers: They often cost less than traditional advertising, appear in a low clutter environment, appeal to a worldwide audience, get recycled with the program, imply a celebrity endorser, and are in an optimal environment where consumers are captive to the product's placement (no remotes!). Despite these benefits, an issue of concern for marketers is whether placements work. And if so, how. Thus far the research on product placements has been mostly anecdotal and is not always reliable. The *E. T.* placement, for instance, succeeded because of Hershey's publicity department. The actual placement was pretty insignificant—a couple of bags in the dark—and there is no direct evidence that the placement itself influenced behavior. The film industry has had no incentive to employ research in this area. For corporate America, the percentage of advertising budgets dedicated to placements was, until recently, too small to justify any rigorous study. But now as placements become more common, and as marketers steer toward unconventional marketing arenas, the need for research in this area increases. A unifying theory based on strong psychological evidence is needed to guide the practical issues marketers face, such as whether their placement will be visual, auditory, or both. Is it worth more to be central to the plot or can even a subtle, less costly placement be effective? Most important, are placements more or less effective than conventional media?

The answers to these questions depend on the quality of the dependent measures employed, and, unfortunately, although the increased use of product placements suggests their effectiveness, the academic research has, at best, produced mixed results. For instance, there is some support for the notion that product placements facilitate brand memory (Babin & Carder, 1996; Vollmers & Mizerski, 1994). Other investigators, in contrast, have found inconsistent or nonsignificant effects of placement on brand memory (Karrh, 1994). It is important to note that to date the measures most commonly used to assess placement effects have been recall and recognition (see Table 4.1). We contend that research in marketing (and in placement effects in particular) has been held back by the research methods employed. Specifically, we believe that the recall and recognition measures are not capable of detecting the more subtle effects of product placements.

Traditionally, marketing researchers have relied on recall and recognition to assess advertising effectiveness. This measurement bias is a by-product of the

TABLE 4.1

Review of Product Placement Research

Researcher	Stimulus	Measure	Test Instructions Reference Viewing Context	Measure Classification
Babin and Carder (1996)	One of two entire movies (*Rocky III* or *Rocky V*), each containing several placements	Brand recognition	Yes	Explicit
d'Astous and Chartier (1999)	Eighteen movie clips consisting of one placement each	Brand recall ("What products or brands do you recall having seen?")	Yes	Explicit
Gupta and Lord (1998)	Thirty-min excerpt of one of three movies (*Big, Project X, Ferris Bueller*) containing a product placement	Brand recognition	Yes	Explicit
		Brand recall	Yes	Explicit
		Brand recognition	Yes	Explicit
		Recall of placement context	Yes	Explicit
Karrh (1994)	Thirty-three-min excerpt of *Raising Arizona* containing five brand placements (Kellogg's Corn Flakes, Huggies diapers, etc.)	Top of mind awareness	No	Emplicit
		Brand familiarity	Yes	Explicit
		Brand recall	Yes	Explicit
		Brand evaluation	Yes	Explicit
Law and Braun (2000)	One of two 10-min excerpts of a TV program, *Seinfeld,* each containing at least six placements	Brand choice	No	Implicit
		Brand recall	Yes	Explicit
		Brand recognition	Yes	Explicit
		Brand attitude	Yes	Explicit
Russell (2002)	Twenty-seven-min screenplay developed for the experiment	Brand attitude	No	Implicit
		Brand recognition	Yes	Explicit
Vollmers and Mizerski (1994)	Two movie clips, each approximately 3 min in length	Brand recall ("Did you notice any branded products in the scenes just viewed?")	Yes	Explicit
		Brand attitude	Yes	Explicit

dominant theory, which states that learning requires attention, effort, and concentration. In other words, only cues available to consciousness should impact behavior. The conclusion then for placement researchers was that to be effective a placement ought to be consciously recalled. Indeed, this conclusion is reflected in the way the industry tests placement effectiveness and, in turn, impacts what marketers pay for certain placements. As an example, CinemaScore, the primary product placement research technique, incorporates after-viewing recall of placements into a formula consisting of projected box office receipts to output a price for the placement. Using that formula they calculated a $28,130 placement fee for Coca-Cola in the movie *Crocodile Dundee*. However, there is no report as to the reliability of this system (Gupta & Lord, 1998).

One of the most important developments in modern cognitive psychology has been the realization that past experience can affect subsequent performance in a multitude of different ways. In addition to the traditional expressions of memory, such as recall and recognition, people also show effects of prior experience that are unaccompanied by conscious recollection of the past, and these effects may manifest themselves as changes in perception, categorization, response accuracy, reasoning, and even motor behavior. The purpose of this chapter is to review evidence from psychology and marketing literature suggesting that learning can occur without awareness, make the distinction between implicit and explicit memory measures, distinguish the research methods used to tap these very different types of memories, and demonstrate how these methods apply to product placement research. We then outline our future research agenda for this area.

EXPRESSIONS OF LEARNING WITHOUT AWARENESS

Memory had been viewed by scientists as a singular system in which information enters the brain, resides in short-term storage and then moves to a longer-term storage. In 1962, that all changed. Debra Milner and colleagues observed a new type of memory on her patient, HM (Milner, 1966). HM had had an epileptic seizure that led to a radical bilateral temporal lobe lesion, resulting in severe difficulty in learning new factual information and an inability to remember daily happenings (anterograde amnesia). In other words, HM appeared to have no functional episodic memory and, hence, could no longer lay down new memories—for instance, or identify a picture that had been taken of him after the operation, he could not tell you the name of the current president. Yet his performance on other typically unrelated tasks of memory showed that information must somehow be reaching and be getting stored in his brain. For example, as part of HM's learning routine, Milner would ask HM to track a moving object. His performance, just like people with intact memories, became increasingly accurate, even though HM was not aware that he had performed the task before.

Distinction Between Explicit and Implicit Memory: Theoretical Overview

These observations led in the 1980s to a critical classification of memory into two dimensions: consciousness (or awareness) and intent, dimensions captured in the distinction between explicit and implicit memory (Graf & Schacter, 1985; Roediger & McDermott, 1993; Schacter, 1987). Explicit memories are both conscious, in the sense that the person is aware of remembering prior events, and intentional, in the sense that the person in some sense wants, or voluntarily intends, to retrieve them. In contrast, implicit memories are unconscious, in the sense that the person is unaware of retrieving or otherwise being influenced by prior events, and their retrieval is thought to occur involuntarily or without intent (Jacoby, 1984). Explicit memory is typically assessed with recall and recognition tasks that require intentional retrieval of information from a specific prior study episode, whereas implicit memory is assessed with tasks that do not require conscious recollection of specific episodes. An early example of a striking dissociation was HM, who showed severe impairment on a test of item recognition but nevertheless showed normal retention of new information as measured on an implicit tracking task.

A major issue concerns the most appropriate way of characterizing and explaining such variety in expressions of memory, with two general perspectives defining the theoretical landscape. The most popular view is that the various expressions of memory reflect the operation of multiple memory systems. Perhaps the strongest advocate of the multiple memory systems approach has been Daniel Schacter of Harvard University, who recommends adopting a cognitive neuroscience approach in which evidence from brain lesion studies, functional dissociations, neuroimaging studies, and studies of nonhuman primates converge to suggest the existence of distinct memory systems (Schacter, 1992). In his research Schacter found distinct areas of the brain are involved in these two types of memory (see Fig. 4.1): For explicit memory to occur, the frontal lobes must be active, which is an effortful process. Implicit memory, on the other hand, relies more on the older sections of the brain, the subcortical areas, such as the cerebellum and another part of the limbic system, the amygdala, where the fight-flight response emerges. Both implicit and explicit memory involve the limbic system—the brain's emotional center—particularly the hippocampus, which is involved in laying down and retrieving memories. According to the memory systems view, then, memory is the process of activating the representations stored in a particular system. Once activated, the representations are able to influence a person's performance with the nature of that influence being dependent on the kind of information or content residing in the representation. Thus, for the systems approach, memory is explained by reference to structural concepts.

The alternative processing approach (pioneered by Henry Roediger) does not postulate multiple memory systems, nor does it rely on an explanation based on underlying memory representations or storage systems. Rather, it views memory as emerging from the interaction between a person with a prior history of

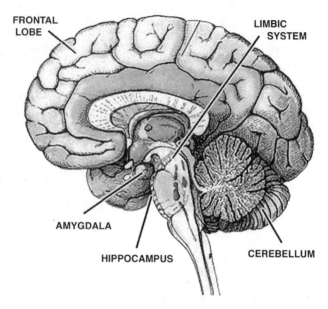

FIG. 4.1   Implicit and explicit memory in the brain.

experiences and the environmental situations (e.g., the memory task demands, processing), which together determine how prior experience gets expressed in subsequent performance.

How to Measure Explicit and Implicit Memory

The debate between systems and process theorists remains alive and contentious. Nevertheless, although these theoretical positions differ from one another in more or less important ways, they are both in agreement that explicit and implicit memory does not respond to experimental manipulations in the same way. To understand the practical distinction between explicit and implicit memory, it is often helpful to consider how their measurement methods differ. Measures of explicit memory are typically quite familiar to marketers. Explicit tests usually take the form of paper-and-pencil surveys in which the consumers might be asked what products they recall seeing in the movie or what types of brands they recognize as having seen in the movie. In contrast, implicit tests are less direct. For the most part, they rely on actual observable behavior. These measures have moved from the observation of different tasks (such as the tracking object in HM's case) to more practical word fragment completion tasks to computerized reaction tests. The distinguishing characteristic of an implicit test is that there is no direct reference to the item being tested.

This distinction between implicit and explicit memory measures is particularly important for marketers because it has been shown that performance on an

implicit memory measure can be uncorrelated or dissociated from performance on an explicit memory test. Indeed, the psychological literature is rampant with examples demonstrating 0 or a negative correlation between implicit and explicit measures (for a review, see Puchinelli, Mast, & Braun, 2001), and these findings have changed the way psychologists believe learning occurs (see Seger, 1994, for a review of implicit learning). This disassociation has been found with "normal" consumers as well, where a person reports no awareness of being influenced, although his or her behavior indicates otherwise (this point is discussed later). Thus far, the usage of these implicit tests in marketing has been limited. The following section presents evidence suggesting why marketers have been reluctant to acknowledge the implicit effects their efforts may be having. We then present research on priming to argue for the use of explicit and implicit measures in gauging the impact of placements on viewers.

CAN THINGS WE ARE UNAWARE OF INFLUENCE US?

Historically, the issue of a marketer influencing behavior without a consumer's awareness of doing so has been likened to brainwashing. Investigations into the possible effects of implicit memory (though not called that at that time) began with a controversial start in 1957 in a New Jersey suburb. James Vicary flashed "drink Coke" and "eat popcorn" slogans at rapid presentations of 1/3,000 s in 5-s intervals during the move *Picnic*. He claimed popcorn sales increased by 58% and Coke sales by 18% during his 2-week run because of those messages. In the post–Korean War paranoid world, this finding touched off a national hysteria. The American Psychological Association was quick to refute Vicary's claim (and there has been question about the validity of his findings because he supplied no verification). They said subliminal advertising was confused, ambiguous, and not as effective as traditional advertising (see Moore, 1980, for a view of how subliminal advertising has been construed by marketers).

Affirmative Evidence From Priming Research

This pronouncement came about a decade too soon. *Priming*, the tendency for a recently presented stimulus to facilitate subsequent judgments or behavior, had not yet been discovered. And research demonstrating the biological foundations for this unique memory system was just being uncovered. In laboratory experiments, the customary way of studying priming (the index of implicit memory) is to expose participants to material (e.g., a list of words, pictures, a passage) in the initial phase. In a later phase, participants are given an ostensibly unrelated task, such as identifying impoverished pictures or fragmented forms of the words. Priming or implicit learning is determined by comparing task performance on items seen earlier (primed) to performance on new (unprimed) items. The typical

finding is that participants will identify the words or pictures better if the items were previously studied, although participants report no knowledge of the prior exposure.

Priming has been found to occur outside the lab setting as well. For instance, consider the "unintentional" plagiarism by ex-Beatle George Harrison. His 1970s hit "My Sweet Lord" sounded much like the 1960s hit "He's So Fine" by the Chiffons, so much so that the Chiffons took him to court. Harrison admitted that he had heard the song before but felt strongly that his song was his own creation. The court concluded that Harrison was guilty of unintentional copying based on what was in Harrison's subconscious memory (Schacter, 1996).

Priming occurs when prior information to which we are exposed influences our behavior without our awareness. Several types of priming effects have been observed in the psychological literature: perceptual, conceptual, and emotional priming. Each is discussed in the following sections.

Perceptual Priming. Perceptual priming occurs when we respond to the modality or surface attributes of the prime rather than its meaning. A branch of this research has been called mere-exposure effects. These researchers find that exposure to objects presented for a very short duration (subliminally) leads to preference for those items, even when they are not aware that they have seen them (Borstein, Leone, & Galley, 1987; Zajonc, 1968). In one study, Bornstein et al. showed individuals pictures of polygons for such a brief duration that they were imperceptible to the individual. The researchers found that when individuals were later shown those polygons interspersed with new ones, the individuals preferred the ones seen previously. Schacter (1996) proposed that the perceptual priming effects are due to the PRS (perceptual representation system), which allows us to identify familiar objects and recognize familiar words, even though PRS does not "know" anything about what the words mean or the objects do. To test his hypothesis, Schacter showed people drawings of objects that were either possible, such as things a person could build out of clay (i.e., things a person is familiar with), or impossible, like an Escher drawing, which could not exist in three dimensions (i.e., things a person is unfamiliar with). Schacter flashed the images on a screen, and each subject had to judge whether the drawing was possible or not. He found a priming effect only with the possible (familiar) objects and theorized that the brain cannot create a unified image of an impossible object, so there is no benefit to receiving such a prime. In general, perceptual priming has been observed to be enhanced to the extent that there is perceptual similarity between study and test stimulus forms. As applied to the product placement arena, then, these findings suggest that to assess perceptual priming effects, the testing measurement needs be as perceptually close as possible to the placement; in other words, visual placements are best tested with a measure showing the product's picture, whereas auditory placements are best tested by having participants hear the product's name, as in a telephone survey.

Conceptual Priming.   Unlike perceptual priming, conceptual priming is based more on semantic memory, in which the meaning of words activates an existing belief and influences behavior. An example is an experiment conducted by John Bargh (Bargh, Chen, & Burrows, 1996), who showed people words either associated with elderly people or words that had no such association. Those exposed to the "old" words walked more slowly down the hall following the experiment than did those who received the neutral words. The words primed the stereotype of elderly people and had an influence on how the subjects behaved. In the area of subliminal advertising, the debate has been whether or not a subliminal implant could invoke a specific behavior, such as buying Coke, or just invoke a more general feeling of being thirsty. The possibility arises that the placement could be doing both: priming the overall desire conceptually, with the perceptual cue triggering a specific choice.

Emotional Priming.   Emotional priming experiments use a prime that has an emotional connotation, such as a picture of a smiling or frowning face. The stimulus is presented very briefly (for approximately 5 ms) and is immediately followed by a masking stimulus, which inhibits further stimulus processing—the mask essentially prevents detection. Following a delay, a neutral target stimulus, such as a drawing, is presented. Robert Zajonc and his colleagues (1968, 1980) found that the liking of the target object is determined by whether the subliminal exposure contained a frown or smile. Thus, even a brief emotional context exposure is likely to affect how the product is perceived.

Evidence of Implicit Memory in Consumer Decision Making

Only recently in the marketing literature has the topic of unconscious memory processes and the role these processes play in influencing consumer decision making been studied. Several researchers have reported priming/implicit memory effects—that is, a change in behavior due to a prior exposure without a deliberate attempt to recollect the prior episode. For example, Law, Hawkins, and Craik (1998) report that fictitious advertising claims appeared more veridical to participants on the second viewing, particularly if they were unable to recognize them as previously studied items. Other implicit effects reported in the consumer behavior literature include the *mere-exposure effect* (the formulation of a positive affect towards a brand as a result of a brief exposure; Janiszewski, 1993), the *false familiarity effect* (mistakenly judging a hypothetical brand to be famous after 24 hours; Holden & Vanhuele, 1999), and *emotional context effects* (where a product presented with favorable music is rated higher than when presented with negative music; Gorn, Goldberg, Chattopadhyay, & Litvack, 1991).

If explicit and implicit measures tap in to different forms of memory, then one would expect stochastic independence between participants' performance on explicit and implicit tests and different experimental manipulations that have a

differential impact on the two. Several marketing researchers have now reported such findings. Janiszewski (1990, 1993) reported positive and reliable effects of exposure on brand evaluations and liking (implicit measures), even when participants failed to recognize having seen the brands (explicit measure), suggesting stochastic independence between the two measures. In the same vein, Shapiro and Krishnan (2001) had participants view print ads of everyday products (e.g., watches, jeans) with fictitious brand names, either under full attention or divided attention conditions (e.g., while listening to a short story). Fifteen minutes or 7 days later, participants either took an explicit recognition test or were required to complete an implicit choice task where no reference was made to the print ads. Performance on the explicit and implicit tests appeared to exhibit stochastic independence: Participants' performance on the recognition test was uncorrelated with their performance on the choice task. Furthermore, although the experimental manipulations (testing delay, attention) were found to significantly impact the explicit measure, they left the implicit measure untouched. These results provide evidence that incidental exposure to advertising or brand names can influence subsequent consumer behavior in a variety of ways, some of which fall outside the consumers' awareness.

PRODUCT PLACEMENTS: IN NEED OF IMPLICIT MEASURES

In a study that is in some ways even more compelling, we demonstrated a double dissociation between explicit and implicit measures, in which performance on explicit and implicit tests responded differentially, and in predictable ways, to experimental manipulations (Law & Braun, 2000). In this study, we examined the effectiveness of product placement by having participants watch one of two excerpts of *Seinfeld* (TV program); containing at least six product placements under the guise of collecting their evaluations of the show. A subset of the placements was central to the plot (e.g., a discussion between Kramer and Elaine's mother about a chocolate éclair), whereas others were more peripheral (such as a box of Tide in a garbage pail). Furthermore, a few of the products were both seen and mentioned, whereas others were either simply seen or only spoken about. Thus, plot centrality and placement modality were the two independent variables in the study. After viewing the *Seinfeld* excerpt, participants completed an implicit choice task and an explicit recognition test. In the implicit choice task, participants were asked to choose a brand from a set of two brand names (where one was a brand present in the *Seinfeld* episode and the other was not present). No reference to the earlier viewing was made. The construction of the explicit recognition test was similar, consisting of previously seen and new brand names, except that in this case participants were instructed to think back to the viewing episode and identify which brands had been present in the video. We expected placement centrality and placement modality would dissociate between explicit and implicit measures of

memory. The results confirmed these expectations: placements that were central to the program were best recalled and recognized though least likely to be chosen. In contrast, placement modality showed an opposite effect on the two measures: seen-only placements showed lower recall and recognition compared with heard-only placements but were chosen most frequently. In other words, the experimental manipulations produced strong double dissociations: Although centrality affected explicit measures and had no impact on the implicit measure, placement modality showed the reverse effect.

One limitation of the Law and Braun (2000) study is that, like other placement research, it relied on existing footage to investigate product placement effects (see Russell, 2002, for an exception). For instance, it was not possible for us to get a *Seinfeld* clip where Pepsi was seen in one version and mentioned in another. And although we can speculate on how the placements should respond based on psychological theory, it has been hard to make definitive conclusions from these data because they are confounded by other uncontrolled factors (such as liking for the actor, strength of the plot, exposure duration). More recently, we replicated and extended these results using more controlled footage (Law, Schimmack, & Braun, 2003). We directed and taped two versions of a 15-min video play where various packaged goods (e.g., cereal, coffee, crackers) were incidentally embedded. Some of the brands were familiar, and others were unfamiliar. Participants were randomly assigned to view one of the two videos, and, either 20 min or a week later, they took either explicit memory tests (recall and recognition) or implicit memory tests (brand choice and preference). Again, the results revealed clear dissociations between the effect of the independent variables brand familiarity and testing delay and the explicit and implicit measures employed. Taken together, these results add to the conclusion that implicit tests of retention measure a form of knowledge (or exposure effects) different from that tapped by standard, explicit tests. More important, these findings confirm that the explicit-implicit distinction is relevant for research on product placement effectiveness.

The question, then, becomes which measure is "right"? As we have argued elsewhere (see Law & Braun, 2000), the answer depends on the goal of the place-ment: Explicit measures are found to be better predictors of behavior when the decision is consequential and deliberate; implicit measures are better predictors when the behavior is spontaneous (Vargas, von Hippel, & Petty, 2001). Thus, if the marketer's intent for a placement is to increase brand awareness and demonstrate brand benefits, as was the case for BMW's placement within *The World Is Not Enough*, explicit measures may be appropriate measures of effectiveness. Simi-larly, for high-involvement buying decisions, such as a sports car, where the status of having a James Bond car is likely to influence the decision, the consumer's abil-ity to consciously remember the placement is key, and explicit measures would likely best predict behavior. But for the majority of buying decisions, in which such explicit awareness is not necessary and may even be discounted, implicit measures that come closer to the consumer's actual behavior are more appropriate. For these

decisions, such as the grabbing of a Coke in the supermarket aisle, consumers' deliberate attempts to search their memory for previously encountered information is highly unlikely (thus, the acknowledgement of a Coke placement within *Seinfeld* is not likely to occur as they hurriedly finish their grocery shopping). As such, implicit measures may be better suited for measuring this type of phenomenon.

There are several ways marketers can gauge the effect a placement has on implicit memory; our consumer buying scenario was an implicit task that came close to the desired behavior, but attitude measures such as those used by Russell (in press) can also indirectly assess placement effects. Response-time software that measures the response latency in product recognition may be another way to get at these more subtle effects on behavior (see Shapiro, MacInnis, Heckler, & Perez, 1999 for an example of another method for studying unconscious perception in marketing).

FACTORS INFLUENCING PRODUCT PLACEMENTS

The company considering buying a product placement has several issues to consider, such as how central the product is to the plot; how the placement appears— visual, auditory, or both; whether it is seen in a positive or negative context; and how to best measure the product category. Based on research into explicit and implicit memory, the following suggestions are made:

- *Product centrality.* Gupta and Lord (1998) found that prominent placements outperform subtle depictions in audience recall. If the manufacturer's goal is conscious recall, centrality to the plot is key. These products are likely to perform well on CinemaScore and other methods employing only explicit memory measures.
- *Modality.* In our study on placements we found it difficult to separate the effects of centrality from modality; typically those products both seen and heard were more central to the plot (Law & Braun, 2000). In general, however, the evidence from the cognitive psychology literature shows that modality tends to have a large effect on perceptual implicit memory tasks (Blaxton, 1989) but little or no effect on explicit memory tasks (Roediger & Blaxton, 1987). In contrast, other research suggests a memory benefit from having both modality presentations: Paivio's (1986) dual processing theory states that two different memory traces will be formed on exposure if a product is both seen and heard. This stronger memory trace is more likely to be expressed on explicit measures of memory. However, if a marketer were faced with a choice between presentation modalities, and the goal was to exert a more subtle influence, visual modality is preferred. We live in a primarily visual world, and our ability to process that type of information is enhanced.

Additionally, because visual information is more available in the environment where consumers makes their choices (such as seeing the cereal box they recently saw on *Seinfeld*), research on perceptual priming effects suggests that this modality match is going to favor a visual placement.

- *Emotional context.* A product placement by definition is embedded within an emotional context of the program. This emotional context will transfer over to the brand. Typically, information from a negative context is better recalled, so a product appearing in a negative way will be remembered better than a favorable presentation. However, in this scenario, there is likely to be a dissociation between the explicit and implicit measures when it comes to behavior, where the affect transfer produces an attitude consistent with the program context. Thus, explicit measures may show enhanced memory for the negative context but implicit measures are more effective in predicting how the emotional context influences actual behavior.

- *Product category.* Across a number of studies, performance on implicit tests, relative to explicit tests, has been shown to be resistant to decay (Gibbons, Neaderhiser, & Walker, 2000; Law et al., 2002; Shapiro & Krishnan, 2001). This suggests that for low-involvement purchases where consumers are expected to make brand choices after a delay (such as choosing between brands of sparkling water at the supermarket), the use of implicit rather than explicit measures will be more appropriate.

CONCLUSION

The general thesis in this chapter—that the measurement of placement effectiveness employ both explicit and implicit tests—has been shaped by the accelerating knowledge of the various expressions of human memory. Cognitive psychologists—and, more recently, marketing researchers—are vigorously experimenting with ways to measure and understand how exposure to a stimulus can affect subsequent judgments, emotions, and behavior, with or without awareness. Whereas product placement researchers have placed emphasis primarily on explicit measures, in which consumers are expected to consciously recall the placement, we argue that it may be productive to entertain and systematically explore the possibility that people can be unaware of the placement and its influence. As such, we propose the use of implicit measures as well—indeed, we suggest that these latter types of tests are often more appropriate in the consumer context.

The current framework and the associated literature suggest a number of directions for future research. First, given that marketers view placements as being a more cost-effective alternative to spending on more traditional media, it is important to investigate whether this is indeed the case. On the one hand, Friestad and Wright (1994) have argued that once people are aware that a persuasion attempt is being made, they indulge in mental counterarguing, message rejection, or

message scrutiny. Consumers exposed to traditional forms of marketing communication (e.g., commercials between programs) are generally aware of the persuasive intent, and this awareness probably counters the persuasive impact of these messages. In the case of product placements, however, awareness is likely to be low for most people, suggesting that the latter may be a more persuasive medium. On the other hand, the advertisements have significantly less control over placements and can seek the viewers' attention more compellingly through traditional commercials. Second, using controlled stimuli, it is important to determine whether placement effects will be discernable once program sponsors are clearly identified. Some consumer advocacy groups (such as the Center for Science in the Public Interest) are concerned about cameo brand appearances in TV programs and believe that mandating the identification of product sponsors is a necessary step toward protecting the public interests. As such, it is relevant to examine whether the presence of sponsor identification helps counter placement effects and under what circumstances such disclosures are most effective. Future research should attempt to see address these questions.

ACKNOWLEDGMENTS

This research was supported by a grant from the Social Sciences and Humanities Research Council of Canada to the first author. Correspondence concerning this chapter should be addressed to Sharmistha Law, Division of Management, University of Toronto at Scarborough, 1265 Military Trail, Scarborough, Ontario, Canada M1C 1A4 (Email: law@rotman.utoronto.ca).

REFERENCES

Avery, R. J., & Ferraro, R. (2000). Verisimilitude or advertising? Brand appearances on prime-time television. *The Journal of Consumer Affairs, 34*(2), 217–244.

Babin, L. A., & Carder, S. T. (1996). Viewers' recognition of brands placed within a film. *International Journal of Advertising, 15*, 140–151.

Bannan, K. J. (2002, March 5). Companies try a new approach and a smaller screen for product placements: Video games. *New York Trmes*, p. C6.

Bargh, J. A., Chen, M., & Burrows, L. (1996). Automaticity of social behavior: Direct effects of trait constructs and stereotype activation on action. *Journal of Personality and Social Psychology, 71*, 230–244.

Bornstein, R. F., Leone, D. R., & Galley, D. J. (1987). The generalizability of subliminal exposure effects: Influence of stimuli perceived without awareness of social behavior. *Journal of Personality and Social Psychology, 53*, 1070–1079.

d'Astous, A., & Chartier, F. (1999). How should we plug our brand? A study of factors affecting consumer evaluations and memory of product placements in movies. In Y. Evrard, W. D. Hoyer & A. Strazzieri (Eds.), *Proceedings of the third international research seminar on marketing communications and consumer behaviour* (pp. 104–117). d'Aix-en-Provence: IAE.

Friestad, M., & Wright, P. (1994). The persuasion knowledge model: How People cope with persuasion attempts. *Journal of Consumer Research, 21,* 1–31.

Gibbons, J. A., Neaderhiser, B. J., & Walker, W. R. (2000). *Forgetting and implicit memory.* Unpublished manuscript, Kansas State University.

Gorn, G. J., Goldberg, M. E., Chattopadhyay, A., & Litvack, D. (1991). Music and information in commercials: Their effects with an elderly sample. *Journal of Advertising Research, 30,* 23–32.

Graf, P., & Schacter, D. L. (1985). Implicit and explicit memory for new associations in normal and amnesic subjects. *Journal of Experimental Psychology: Learning, Memory, and Cognition, 11,* 501–518.

Grossberg, J. (2002, June 21). *Minority Report*'s product placement. *E!Online.* Retrieved August 29, 2002, from http://www.eonline.con/News/Items/0,1,10138, 00.html

Gupta, P. B., & Lord, K. R. (1998). Product placement in movies: The effect of prominence and mode on recall. *Journal of Current Issues and Research in Advertising, 20*(1), 47–59.

Holden, S. J. S., & Vanhuele, M. (1999). Know the name, forget the exposure: Brand familiarity versus memory of exposure context. *Psychology and Marketing, 16*(6), 479–496.

Jacoby, L. L. (1984). Incidental versus intentional retrieval: Remembering and awareness as separate issues. In L. R. Squire & N. Butters (Eds.), *Neuropsychology of memory* (pp. 145–156). New York: Guilford Press.

Janiszewski, C. (1990). The influence of nonattended material on the processing of advertising claims. *Journal of Marketing Research, 27,* 263–278.

Janiszewski, C. (1993). Preattentive mere exposure effects. *Journal of Consumer Research, 20,* 376–392.

Karrh, J. A. (1994). Effects of brand placements in motion pictures. In K. W. King (Ed.), *Proceedings of the 1994 conference of the American Academy of Advertising* (pp. 90–96). Richmond, VA: American Academy of Advertising.

Law, S., & Braun, K. A. (2000). I'll have what she's having: Gauging the impact of product placements on viewers. *Psychology and Marketing, 17*(12), 1059–1075.

Law, S., Hawkins, S. A., & Craik, F. I. M. (1998). Repetition-induced belief in the elderly: Rehabilitating age-related memory deficits. *Journal of Consumer Research, 25,* 95–107.

Law, S., Schimmack, U., & Braun, K. A. (2002). *Study of embedded commerce with explicit and implicit measures of memory.* Unpublished manuscript, University of Toronto, Canada.

Milner, B. (1966). Amnesia following operation on the temporal lobe. In C. W. M. Whitty & O. L. Zangwill (Eds.), *Amnesia* (pp. 109–133). New York: Butterworth.

Moore, T. E. (1980). Subliminal advertising: What you see is what you get. *Journal of Marketing, 26,* 38–47.

Paivio, A. (1986). *Mental representativeness: A dual coding approach.* New York: Oxford University Press.

Puchinelli, N., Mast, F., & Braun, K. A. (2001). *What we know and don't know about what influences behavior: An examination of implicit predictors of behavior.* Unpublished manuscript, Mind of the Market Lab, Harvard Business School, Cambridge, MA.

Roediger, H. L., & Blaxton, T. A. (1987). Effects of varying modality, surface features, and retention interval on priming in word fragment completion. *Memory and Cognition, 15,* 379–388.

Roediger, H. L., & McDermott, K. B. (1993). Implicit memory in normal human subjects. In F. Boller & J. Grafman (Eds.), *Handbook of neuropsychology* (Vol. 8, pp. 63–131). Amsterdam: Elsevier.

Russell, C. A. (2002). Investigating the effectiveness of product placements in television shows: The role of modality and plot connection congruence on brand memory and attitude. *Journal of Consumer Research, 29,* 306–318.

Schacter, D. L. (1987). Implicit memory: History and current status. *Journal of Experimental Psychology: Learning, Memory, and Cognition, 13*(3), 501–518.

Schacter, D. L. (1992). Understanding implicit memory. *American Psychologist, 47*(4), 559–569.

Schacter, D. L. (1996). *Searching for memory.* New York: Basic Books.

Seger, C. A. (1994). Implicit learning. *Psychological Bulletin, 115*(2), 163–196.

Shapiro, S., & Krishnan, H. S. (2001). Memory-based measures for assessing advertising effects: A comparison of explicit and implicit memory effects. *Journal of Advertising, 30*(3), 1–3.

Shapiro, S., MacInnis, D. J., Heckler, S. E., & Perez, A. M. (1999). An experimental method for studying unconscious perception in a marketing context. *Psychology and Marketing, 16*(6), 459–477.

Vargas, P. T., von Hippel, W., & Petty, R. E. (2001). *Using implicit attitude measures to enhance the attitude-behavior relationship.* Unpublished manuscript, Ohio State University.

Vollmers, S., & Mizerski, R. (1994). *A review and investigation into the effectiveness of product placements in films.* In K. W. King (Ed.), *Proceedings of the 1994 conference of the American Academy of Adverstising* (pp. 97–102). Richmond, VA: American Academy of Advertising.

Zajonc, R. B. (1968). Attitudinal effects of mere exposure. *Journal of Personality and Social Psychology Monograph Supplement, 9*, (2, pt 2) 1–27.

Zajonc, R. B. (1980). Feeling and thinking: Preferences need no inferences. *American Psychologist, 35*(2), 151–175.

CHAPTER FIVE

Mental Models for Brand Placement

Moonhee Yang
Beverly Roskos-Ewoldsen
David R. Roskos-Ewoldsen
University of Alabama

The use of brand placement in a movie or television program has been employed by advertisers for more than 50 years as a way of communicating their specific brands to an audience (Babin & Carder, 1996; Sargent et al., 2001). A recent content analysis of 112 hours of prime-time television during the spring of 1997 found that, on average, there were close to 30 brand appearances per hour of prime-time programming (Avery & Ferraro, 2000; Ferraro & Avery, 2000). Apparently, brand placement is perceived as an effective mechanism for reaching audiences.

Unfortunately, it is difficult to ascertain the effectiveness of brand placement because much of the data on brand placement are proprietary. However, many authors cite the effectiveness of Hershey's placement of Reese's Pieces in the movie *E. T.* as the classic example of the potential effectiveness of brand placement (Babin & Carder, 1996; Gupta & Lord, 1998; Karrh, 1998; Ong & Meri, 1994). The consumption of Reese's Pieces increased by 67% within a few months of audience's witnessing a small alien being drawn into a house because a boy left a trail of Reese's Pieces from the alien's hiding place to the boy's house. Despite the resounding success of the Reese's Pieces story, the empirical research on brand placement is less encouraging, suggesting that the practice may not be as effective at increasing sales as some would like to believe (Karrh, 1998; McCarty, this volume).

Of course, increasing sales is not the only goal of brand placement. Brand placement is also used to increase the audience's familiarity with the brand so that

consumers are more likely to remember the brand (d'Astous & Chartier, 2000). The empirical research on this aspect of brand placement has focused on viewers' memory for the brands placed within a movie or television show. This research, which we later discuss, shows a complex relation between brand placement and memory for the brand. No single theory or model has been able to explain this complicated relation.

In this chapter, we present an approach to understanding when brand placements are effective for remembering the brand. We argue that when individuals watch a movie or a television program, their primary focus is on comprehending the story and that an adequate understanding of brand placement requires an understanding of how people comprehend the programming. Based on the research on text comprehension, we know that people construct mental models of a story when attempting to comprehend it (e.g., Wyer & Radvansky, 1999). Thus, in this chapter, we propose a mental models approach to understanding the effects of brand placement on memory for, and attitude toward, the brand. This approach, along with research on the relationship between memory and judgments, provides the foundation for predicting when brand placements will be successful. To preview, we begin this chapter by reviewing the research on brand placement, and then we discuss the mental models approach, including a recent test of the landscape model of text comprehension using video media rather than the usual text media. We conclude by discussing the implications of the mental models approach for understanding when brand placement will be effective.

WHAT ARE THE EFFECTS OF BRAND PLACEMENT?

Why is brand placement used? Because, as already discussed, it is believed to be effective, but, more specifically, brand placement has a number of advantages compared with traditional advertising, such as 15- or 30-s commercials. First, brand placement probably overcomes the problem of zapping (Avery & Ferraro 2000; d'Astous & Chartier, 2000). Though it is easy to run to the kitchen for a beer during a commercial break, a person is less likely to run to the kitchen when Reese's Pieces are being placed on the ground because the viewer presumably wants to watch the movie (Babin & Carder, 1996; d'Astous & Chartier, 2000). Second, brand placements are often associated with well-known actors or actresses, and, as a result, the placement can work as a celebrity endorsement (Avery & Ferraro, 2000). For example, in a study using focus groups, DeLorme and Reid (1999) found that audiences who are young and who admire a particular movie actor or actress are more likely to associate the brand with the actor or actress and to want to buy the product. Likewise, research has shown that when the main actor in a movie uses a product, the viewers' memory for the brand is enhanced, and they also have a slightly more positive evaluation of the product than if the actor had not used the product (d'Astous & Chartier, 2000). Third, brand placement allows

for advertisers to target very specific audiences because the demographics of who attends which kinds of movies are well understood by Hollywood (Nebenzahl & Secunda, 1993). Fourth, brand placement has a longer life than does typical advertisement (Brennan, Dubas, & Babin, 1999; d'Astous & Chartier, 2000). With the release of the 20th anniversary *E. T.*, Hershey's placement of Reese's Pieces may continue to be effective 20 years after the initial placement. Furthermore, to the extent that people purchase the *E. T.* videotape or DVD, the placement's life is extended even further. Fifth, commercials are regulated as a type of commercial speech. However, there is a fair amount of ambiguity concerning brand placements. Is brand placement commercial speech or does it afford the same protections that the movie is provided? These questions have not been decided by the courts, so brand placements currently enjoy more freedom than more traditional commercial speech (Avery & Ferraro, 2000). Sixth, audiences seem to have positive attitudes toward brand placements (Nebenzahl & Secunda, 1993). Indeed, audiences have indicated that brand placements enhance the viewing experience because they make the movie more realistic (Avery & Ferraro, 2000). Finally, audiences probably have less-critical responses to brand placements than they do to standard commercials (Babin & Carder, 1996). When people know that someone is trying to persuade them, they tend to react more critically to a message (Petty & Cacioppo, 1986). However, when brand placement occurs in a show viewers are watching, they probably do not perceive the placement as persuasive in nature and are less likely to respond critically to the placement (Babin & Carder, 1996).

Influence of Brand Placement on Memory and Evaluations

With the aforementioned advantages of brand placement, the increase in sales of a brand after the success of movie or television program would almost seem assured (Sargent et al., 2001). However, brand placement does not always guarantee success, even though the advertisers may invest an enormous amount of money for the expense of placing their product on the specific movie or television program. Moreover, considering the increasing number of brand placements in movies and television programs, there has been little research regarding its effectiveness (Karrh, 1998; Ong & Meri, 1994). Instead, most of the research on brand placement has focused on memory for the placement.

The research on memory for brand placement generally finds that memory is improved for a brand that is placed within a movie compared with the same brand that is not placed within a movie (Karrh, 1998). However, the early research on the effect of brand placement on brand memory was rather mixed (Babin & Carder, 1996; Ong & Meri, 1994). For example, Ong and Meri (1994) found no improvement in memory for some brand placements and remarkably large improvements in memory for other brand placements. In particular, 77% of viewers recalled seeing Coke while watching the movie *Falling Down*, but only 18% recalled seeing Hamm's Beer in the same movie (Ong & Meri, 1994).

These early findings shifted the research question to the factors that moderate the effect of brand placement on brand memory. As a result, more recent research has focused on the nature of the placement and whether it moderates the effectiveness of the brand placement on later memory for the brand. This research has considered whether the placement was creative (background shot) versus on-set (foreground) and also the product's size or position on the screen. The basic finding of this research is that placements that are more visually prominent tend to result in greater memory for the brand than do less-prominent placements (Brennan, Dubas, & Babin, 1999; d'Astous & Chartier, 2000; Gupta & Lord, 1998; Law & Braun, 2000). As we later discuss, this makes sense within a mental models perspective because information that is prominent is more likely to be noticed and encoded into one's mental model of the story. Unfortunately, what has not been explored is the degree to which the brand is integral to the story. We argue that the functions a brand can serve within a story should influence how much a product is encoded into one's mental model of a story.

A recent study shows an additional effect of brand placement on memory for the brand. Specifically, Law and Braun (2000) found that brand placement not only influenced explicit measures of memory, such as recognition and recall tasks, but it also influenced implicit measures of memory. In their study, Law and Braun had participants imagine that they were helping a friend purchase items for the friend's new apartment. Participants were more likely to choose items for the friend's new apartment that had appeared in a recently watched episode of *Seinfeld*, compared with control items that did not appear in the episode. The results suggest that brand placement can prime the brand in memory, which could influence later judgments or behaviors related to that brand (see Roskos-Ewoldsen, Klinger, & Roskos-Ewoldsen, in press, or Roskos-Ewoldsen, Roskos-Ewoldsen, & Carpentier, 2002, for a discussion of media priming).

Another focus of research on brand placement has been on the effectiveness of brand placement on brand evaluations. The results of this line of research are clear. With few exceptions, this research suggests that brand placements have little or no effect on the evaluation of the brand or on purchase intentions (Babin & Carder, 1996; Karrh, 1998; Ong & Meri, 1994). These results are puzzling, given that prominent placements improve memory for the brand. A partial answer for the ineffectiveness of brand placement on attitudes toward the brand may be found in the results of DeLorme and Reid's (1999) focus group study. Their participants indicated that they were more likely to notice brand placements if the brand was one that they already like and use. This finding is consistent with the research showing that people are more likely to attend to those items in their environment toward which they have accessible attitudes (Fazio, Roskos-Ewoldsen, & Powell, 1994; Roskos-Ewoldsen, 1997; Roskos-Ewoldsen & Fazio, 1992). If people already have strong attitudes toward the brand, which indicates that they already have a consolidated attitude stored in memory, their attitude is unlikely to change (Roskos-Ewoldsen, 1997; Roskos-Ewoldsen & Fazio, 1997). Thus, the brand's

placement may serve to reinforce an already existing attitude, but it is not going to result in a more positive evaluation of the brand or stronger intentions to purchase it.

The Ethics of Brand Placement

Within the literature concerning brand and product placement, one of the issues that has received extensive coverage concerns the ethics of certain brands or products within movies and television shows. Specifically, is it ethical to place cigarette brands (prior to the voluntary ban on brand placement by the cigarette industry in 1990) or cigarettes as a product (after the ban in 1990) in movies if the placement may influence adolescents to start smoking?[1] Although the ethical issues are beyond the scope of this chapter, we believe that the research in this area deserves special attention because it claims some of the strongest effects of brand and product placement.

Several content analyses of television and movies suggest that cigarettes appear in movies at a much higher rate than they should, given the prevalence of smoking in the general population (Christenson, Henriksen, & Roberts, 2000; Diener, 1993; Everett, Schnuth, & Tribble, 1998; Hazan, Lipton, & Glantz, 1994; Roberts, Henriksen, & Christenson, 1999; Sargent et al., 2001; Stockwell & Glantz, 1997). In a content analysis of four episodes of 42 of the most popular television shows among adolescents and adults in the fall of 1998, Christenson et al. (2000) found that approximately 22% of all television episodes contained either references to smoking or smoking behavior, though smoking occurred more often in shows aimed at adults than in shows aimed at adolescents. In addition, in a content analysis of 200 movies from 1996 and 1997, Roberts et al. (1999) found that 89% of all movies included references to smoking or smoking behavior, and 17% of the characters who appeared to be under the age of 18 smoked. Clearly, cigarettes and other tobacco products are prevalent in movies and television.

Some researchers have argued that the prevalence of smoking and cigarettes in movies and on television is responsible, at least in part, for adolescents' smoking initiation (Basil, 1997; Chapman & Davis, 1997; Stockwell & Glantz, 1997). Indeed, several studies suggest that the presence of cigarettes might influence whether adolescents start smoking. For example, Distefan, Gilpin, Sargent, and Pierce (1999) found evidence suggesting that adolescents who are susceptible to smoking initiation are also more likely to like movie stars who smoke both on and off the screen. Distefan et al. (1999) interpreted this result as indicating that teenagers become susceptible to smoking initiation because the actors or actresses they like smoked. However, this interpretation should be treated with caution.

---

[1]The tobacco industry voluntarily stopped paying for brand placement in movies in 1990. However, cigarettes continue to be used in movies at approximately the same rate as before the ban for a number of reasons, including the smoking status of the actor or actress, the director's belief that smoking makes the film more realistic or fits with the characters persona, and so forth (Shields, Carol, Balbach, & McGee, 1999).

Given the correlational nature of the study, it is difficult to know whether it is the portrayals of smoking that influence an adolescent to think about smoking, or whether adolescents who are thinking about smoking are more likely to notice and like stars who smoke. In addition, the relationship between being at risk for smoking and liking movie stars who smoke on or off screen is weak ($r < .09$) and not statistically significant.[2] Finally, the measure of being at risk for smoking that Distefan et al. (1999) used overestimates the extent to which adolescents actually become smokers. Pierce, Choi, Gilpin, Farkas, and Merritt (1996), using the same measure of susceptibility to smoking, found that only 13% of adolescents who were susceptible in 1989 were smokers in 1993.[3]

Two experimental studies looking at the effect of smoking in movies have also been cited as indicating that portrayals in movies influence smoking initiation. Hines, Saris, and Throckmorton-Belzer (2000) found that male regular and occasional smokers who watched film clips that included smoking indicated a stronger desire to smoke a cigarette than those who watched a clip that did not include smoking. In addition, when they watched a clip that contained smoking, occasional and regular smokers rated their likelihood of smoking in the future higher than did those who watched a clip that did not contain smoking. However, there was no effect of smoking in the film clip on nonsmokers' ratings of their likelihood of smoking in the future, and female characters who smoked were consistently rated more negatively than when the same characters were portrayed as not smoking.[4]

In the second experimental study, Gibson and Maurer (2000) had participants watch two different clips from the movie *Die Hard*. In one clip, Bruce Willis smokes, and in the second clip he does not smoke. Nonsmokers who were low in need for cognition rated themselves as more likely to become friends with a person who smokes after viewing the clip in which Bruce Willis smoked than did those who watched the clip in which he did not smoke. However, there was no effect of the presence of smoking in the movie clip on general attitudes toward smoking or on willingness to smoke in the future. There were no effects of the clip for nonsmokers who were high in need for cognition.

---

[2]The correlation was calculated using the frequencies that the authors provided in Table 5 (Distefan et al., 1999).

[3]This percentage is extrapolated from Table 2 in Pierce, Choi, Gilpin, Farkas, and Merritt (1996, p. 357).

[4]Hines, Saris, and Throckmorton-Belzer (2000) argued that their results did show that nonsmokers rated themselves as more likely to smoke after watching a clip that contained smoking than when the clip did not contain smoking because there was a significant main effect of experimental condition. However, inspection of the means for nonsmokers (Figure 4, p. 2261) shows that there was no effect of whether the characters in the film clip smoked or did not smoke on nonsmokers' likelihood of smoking in the future. The significant main effect was a result of the interaction between smoking status and experimental condition and does not mean that all participants were affected by the experimental manipulation. Unfortunately, the authors did not conduct post hoc tests to determine which means were significantly different from each other.

One of the main problems with discussions of the ethical aspects of product placement in movies or on television is that scholars tend not to consider the context of product use in a movie or television program. Yet one would think that how smoking is portrayed should influence the effect the depiction of smoking has on the audience. In other words, the context in which the smoking occurs should influence the audience's reaction to the smoking. Although most portrayals of smoking on television and in movies are neutral, there are more negative than positive portrayals. Of television episodes that contained smoking, 23% involved negative statements about smoking, compared with just 13% that involved positive statements. In movies, antagonists are more likely to smoke (38%) than protagonists (22%), and negative statements about smoking occur in 22% of movies, whereas only 7% include positive statements about smoking (Christenson et al., 2000; Roberts et al., 1999). Given this context, it is curious that we assume that smoking portrayals would lead to more smoking, not less.

To summarize, the extant research on the influence of the portrayal of smoking on television or in movies is consistent with the more generic research on brand placements. Both literatures indicate that brand or product placements have no influence on attitudes toward the brand or product. Further, brand placements seem to have no influence on behavior related to the brand product, unless one is already a smoker.

MENTAL MODELS AND THE MEDIA

When people watch television programs or movies, there are many different goals they may have, such as being entertained, informed, or distracted from problems at home or at work. However, a basic goal that all viewers of the media have is to have a coherent understanding of what they are watching. To accomplish this, viewers construct mental representations of the movie as the movie unfolds. This representation includes information about the characters and situations within the movie and prior expectations based on knowledge about the genre of movies or the actors and actresses starring in the movie. This combination of information provides the basis for understanding the movie as it unfolds and for predicting future events in the movie. Unfortunately, little research has focused on how people create a coherent understanding of what they are watching (but see Livingstone, 1987, 1989, 1990). This focus on the understanding—or coherence—of a movie, and on the cognitive representation that undergirds it, is central to the mental models approach. In our opinion, understanding personal discourse, the media, or the world in general requires constructing a coherent mental model to represent the event. To the extent that a person can construct such a model, the person is said to understand the event (Halford, 1993; Wyer & Radvansky, 1999). We argue that understanding the effects of product placements within television and movies requires an understanding of how people create coherent understandings of movies or television shows.

The mental models approach reflects the observation that thinking typically occurs within and about situations (Garnham, 1997). Mental models are the cognitive representations of (a) situations in real, hypothetical, or imaginary worlds, including space and time; (b) entities found in the situation and the states those entities are in; (c) interrelationships between the various entities and the situation, including causality and intentionality; and (d) events that occur in that situation (Garnham, 1997; Johnson-Laird, 1983; Radvansky & Zacks, 1997; Wyer & Radvansky, 1999; Zwaan & Radvansky, 1998). Mental models are distinct from network models of memory, but the entities and events within a mental model are hypothesized to be linked to relevant representations within a semantic network (Radvansky & Zacks, 1997; Wyer & Radvansky, 1999). In other words, mental models are hypothesized to exist alongside, as well as coupled with, the semantic networks that are hypothesized by network models of memory.

van Dijk (1998) argues that mental models involve the merger of semantic memory (knowledge of the world) and episodic memory (memory for our past experiences). However, this argument can be misleading. In particular, it might give the impression that mental models involve only the representation of past situations we have personally experienced (what van Dijk refers to as experience mental models). However, when defining mental models as cognitive representations of situations, the term *situation* is used very broadly. For example, we can have mental models of ownership, which include the interrelationships of owners and the objects that are owned (Radvansky & Zacks, 1997). Likewise, mental models can be used in a reasoning task to represent the possible worlds in which the premises of an argument are true and to manipulate the possible worlds to discover what may occur (Johnson-Laird, 1983).

The mental models approach has been used to understand a number of different phenomena, including reasoning and problem solving (Greeno, 1984; Johnson-Laird, 1983), language processing (Garnham, 1997), children's understanding of the world (Halford, 1993), text comprehension and discourse (Graesser, Singer, & Trabasso, 1994; Morrow, Greenspan, & Bower, 1987; van Dijk & Kintsch, 1983; Zwaan & Radvansky, 1998), children's implicit theories of physics (Gentner & Gentner, 1983), spatial cognition (Radvansky, Spieler, & Zacks, 1993), media priming (Roskos-Ewoldsen et al., 2002), political commercials (Biocca, 1991), and ideology (van Dijk, 1998). We believe that they also can be used to understand the influence of brand placements in movies and on television on people's memory for and attitudes about the brand.

To begin at a broader level, the mental models approach provides a flexible framework for how we understand the media. First, mental models can exist at many levels of abstraction (Johnson-Laird, 1983). If you are a reader of mysteries, you might have a mental model for Agatha Christie novels, more specific mental models for her Poirot and Miss Marple mysteries, and maybe even more specific mental models for specific stories from the Poirot or Miss Marple series. Brand placements should be less likely to be represented in more abstract mental models,

unless the brand is an integral part of the situation. Second, new information can be integrated into existing mental models (Wyer & Radvansky, 1999). A person's mental model of Shrewsbury, the setting for Ellis Peters' Brother Cadfael mysteries, could be updated as more information is provided about Shrewsbury and the abbey where Brother Cadfael lives. Similarly, rumination about the content of a mental model would result in updating the mental model (Zwaan & Radvansky, 1998). For example, if a brand's first placement is subtle (i.e., not integral to the story), it is not likely to be represented in one's mental model. However, a subsequent placement that is more prominent, and integral to the story, is much more likely to be included in the mental model, and the mental model may be updated further to include the initial, more subtle placement. Third, mental models can represent both static situations, such as a mental model of the town of Shrewsbury (a *state-of-affairs model*; Radvansky & Zacks, 1997), and dynamic situations, such as a mental model of a specific mystery that is occurring at the abbey (a *course-of-event model*; Radvansky & Zacks, 1997).

Several lines of research on mental models corroborate their usefulness for understanding how we understand the media. Research has found that the mix of linguistic and pictorial information improves the construction of mental models (Glenberg & Langston, 1992; Wyer & Radvansky, 1999). For this reason, the media should be particularly effective at influencing the construction of mental models. Consistent with this, Gupta and Lord (1998) found that verbal references to a brand did not improve memory over simple visual placements of a brand in a movie. Research has also shown that previously created mental models will influence how new information is interpreted and that they will influence the mental model that is constructed to understand the current event (Radvansky & Zacks, 1997; Wyer & Radvansky, 1999). In terms of television shows, mental models allow us to understand information across scenes of the program and across episodes of a series (Zwaan & Radvansky, 1998). Furthermore, the mental model that one constructs of a show will drive the type of inferences one draws about the show (see Graesser et al., 1994). Finally, as already discussed, mental models can vary in their degree of abstraction, so frequent viewers of a particular genre should have richer abstract mental models appropriate for understanding the nuances of that genre. Indeed, research has found that the mental models people construct are dependent on the genre of the story they are reading (Zwaan, 1994). Thus, genre differences found in media studies may well reflect the types of mental models people construct of the media event.

The mental models approach also provides a framework for understanding the effects of media on our perceptions and behavior. For example, Segrin and Nabi (2002) recently found that people who watch romantic TV programming have more idealistic expectations about marriage than people who do not watch romantic programs. We argue that viewing this genre of TV shows and movies resulted in the creation of mental models that incorporated the idealistic images of marriage in the media. In other words, we argue that our expectations concerning

marriage are a result of our mental models of marriage, which are influenced, at least in part, by the genre of TV that we watch. Wyer and Radvansky (1999) provide another example. They argued that the influence of the media on perceptions of a "mean world" (see Gerbner et al., 1977) may result from one's use of mental models that were constructed from watching violent media when attempting to understand the social world. From our perspective, given the amount of violence on TV, it is likely that heavy viewers of TV construct abstract mental models that incorporate violence. Further, the abstractness of the mental model would increase the likelihood of its use to understand situations beyond the media. More generally, we believe that mental models can be used to explain media effects such as cultivation and the influence of the media on perceptions of reality.

We have used the mental models approach to investigate how a movie is understood (Roskos-Ewoldsen, Roskos-Ewoldsen, Yang, Crawford, & Choi, 2002). When watching a movie, generating a coherent understanding of that movie can be difficult because of limitations in both attentional resources and short-term memory. Indeed, sometimes movies are designed to take advantage of these limitations to create ambiguity. Consider the movie *Falling Down*. In the movie, Michael Douglas plays a defense engineer (Defens) who has been fired from his job. The movie begins with him stuck in a traffic jam near downtown Los Angeles. He abandons his car and proceeds to start walking home. Everyone he encounters, mostly stereotypic characters such as a threatening ghetto gang, a rude convenience store owner, and a White supremacist, all upset him. He reacts with increasing violence. As he walks across L.A., he calls his ex-wife, telling her that he is coming home to see his daughter for her birthday. She is clearly frightened by the phone call, indicating that there is more to the situation. By the end of the movie, viewers are convinced that Defens is insane.

There are three interpretations of the movie, based on the movie cover and comments about the movie on the Internet. One interpretation portrays Defens as an average man who is fighting back against an insane society (hero interpretation). A second interpretation is that the movie is a comedy about a man dealing with exaggerated everyday pressures (comedy interpretation). The third interpretation is that the movie is about a man on the edge of insanity who finally goes over the edge because of the pressures from society (insane interpretation).

The ambiguity in the film is created, at least in part, because the director takes advantage of the viewers' short-term memory limitations. Defens could be interpreted as a caring father because he calls home on his daughter's birthday to tell his wife he's coming home for the party. However, Defens had just trashed a corner grocery store because the owner made him buy a Coke to get change for the phone call, but charged too much for the can of Coke, not leaving enough change for the call. This viewer has two conflicting impressions of Defens. Because of limitations in short-term memory, the viewer may focus on the caring aspect, attributing the ex-wife's behavior to something else. In this case, the mental model would be congruent with the hero interpretation. On the other hand, the viewer may focus

on the ex-wife's frightened appearance. In this case, the mental model would be congruent with the insane interpretation.

In our investigation of people's mental models of this movie (Roskos-Ewoldsen, Roskos-Ewoldsen, Yang et al., 2002), we had 89 participants watch the movie. At the end of the movie, we had them rate the similarities of the main characters. That is, for every pair of characters, participants rated their similarity on an 11-point scale. We converted the similarity ratings to dissimilarity ratings and then submitted the dissimilarity ratings to a multidimensional scaling analysis. The solution is a depiction in a multidimensional space of participants' perceptions of the characters. We viewed this solution as a snapshot of the participants' mental model of the movie. After the similarity ratings, participants rated on an 11-point scale their acceptance of each of the interpretations. Almost everyone thought that Defens was insane. However, about half of the participants thought that he also was a hero, whereas the other half did not. We looked at the multidimensional scaling solution separately for those who thought of Defens a hero and those who did not. Briefly, the people who considered Defens a hero had a different mental model of the movie than those who did not endorse this interpretation. Although this research is preliminary, we believe that it merits further attention.

Landscape Model of Text Comprehension

Within the broader mental models approach, we have been working with the landscape model (van den Broek, Risden, Fletcher, & Thurlow, 1996; van den Broek, Young, Tzeng, & Linderholm, 1999). As with the more general mental models framework, the landscape model is concerned with how people generate a coherent understanding of a story. The landscape model gets its name from the observation that information is being activated at various levels and that the activation dissipates across time. If one were to construct a matrix of the concepts relevant to the movie and the scenes in the movie, one would have a landscape of activations. This landscape forms the basis for the representation of the story's mental model in memory.

We prefer the landscape model to other models because it focuses on coherence by looking at the relationship between the online processing of a story and the memorial representation of that story. Other models have a more limited focus. These other models use methodologies that tap whether participants make one or two inferences during the reading of a text. Rather than explaining a limited number of inferences that are made while reading the text, the landscape model focuses more on the memorial representation that results from reading a text. By looking at participants' memory for the text, the landscape model takes advantage of the well-established finding that greater levels of activation of a particular concept result in greater memory for that concept. Thus, by using the theory's predictions for how active various concepts are in working memory, one can test whether those concepts are indeed more likely to be recalled when participants are asked to recall a story.

The landscape model assumes that there are four general sources of activation of concepts while attending to a story (van den Broek et al., 1996; van den Broek et al., 1999). First, the immediate environment will activate concepts in memory. Specifically, concepts within the current sentence (for a book) or scene (for a movie) will be activated. Second, because activation dissipates across time (Higgins, Bargh, & Lombardi, 1985), concepts from the immediately proceeding sentence of scene should still be activated, albeit at a lower level of activation. Furthermore, concepts from previous scenes are hypothesized to have higher levels of activation if they were the focal point of the previous scene, if they were related to active goals of the protagonists or antagonists in the previous scene, or if they involved events that were antecedents to some subsequent event. Third, concepts from earlier in the story may be reactivated because they are necessary for maintaining the coherence of the story. Fourth, world knowledge necessary for understanding the story will be activated.

Clearly, not all information that is activated in memory is activated at the same level. The landscape model assumes that information that is explicitly mentioned or is visually central to the scene will receive the highest level of activation in memory. For example, when watching the scene in *Falling Down* where Defens trashes a corner grocery store, Defens would be activated at a higher level overall than the can of Coke he ultimately buys because Defens is more central to the story than the can of Coke is. However, within this sequence, Defens holds a can of Coke to his forehead to cool down. In this specific scene, Coke should be as activated as Defens. Concepts with the next-highest level of activation are those that are required to maintain the coherence of the story. During the grocery story scene, the reason that Defens went into the store—because he needed change to make a phone call—should be activated in memory because it makes the scene coherent. At the next level of activation are concepts that enable actions to occur (enablers). The can of Coke is an enabler in the grocery store because the shopkeeper will not give Defens change, forcing him to buy a can of Coke to obtain change. Finally, concepts with the lowest level of activation involve background knowledge that is not tied to making the story coherent but is nonetheless activated because of associative linkages in memory.

For these reasons, the landscape model predicts that the brand Coke is likely to be recalled from the movie *Falling Down*. As a recap, first, Coke is visually salient in several scenes, such as when Defens uses a can of Coke to cool his forehead. Later in the movie, Coke is again prominently featured because Defens is seen drinking the Coke as he walks through what appears to be a park. Further, in the grocery store scene, the can of Coke is an enabler because it allows Defens to attempt to get change to make a phone call. In addition, the excessive cost of the Coke provides a coherent explanation for Defens's trashing of the grocery store. Finally, Coke is seen on billboards and in restaurants throughout the movie. Thus, Coke is activated a number of times, and the levels of activation should be high because of the various functions that Coke serves in the movie. Interestingly, Ong and Meri (1994) found that 77% of the people they interviewed as they exited

the movie *Falling Down* recalled seeing Coke in the movie. This level of recall is substantially higher than for any other product in the movie.

Testing the Landscape Model With Video Stimuli

The landscape model has been tested with text-based stories (van den Broek et al., 1996; van den Broek et al., 1999). It does an excellent job of accounting for participants' memory for a text-based story. Indeed, the landscape model does a better job of predicting participants' memory for text than any existing model of text comprehension (van den Broek & Gustafson, 1999). However, the stories used to test the model were simple short stories. For example, one story about a knight and a dragon is 13 sentences long and includes 26 concepts. We were curious how well the landscape model would do with more complex stories, such as those found in many movies. The addition of video adds a level of complexity to the model because both the text (dialogue) and the visual elements of the story can activate concepts and influence one's mental model of the story.

We tested the landscape model using a short clip (2 m 17 s) from the fifth episode of an animated series called *Cowboy Bebop*, which has 26 episodes. Each episode is about 30 min long. The series recounts the story of three bounty hunters in a futuristic period. This particular clip began with shots of spaceships flying through space. Then it focused on a meeting between two well-dressed crime bosses and their guards, who are striking an agreement to end the conflicts between their two gangs. After the meeting, one of the crime bosses leaves in his spaceship. As he takes off, the ship explodes. Then an assassin enters the apartment of the other crime boss and kills him and his guards.

To test the landscape model, we first had to break down the story into coherent units of meaning (i.e., segments). With a text-based story, the units of meaning typically correspond to sentences. With a movie, breaking the story down into units of meaning is more difficult because the visual scenes (i.e., camera shots) and dialogue interact to create the units of meaning. For example, a single sentence of dialog may correspond to a single camera shot, or it may have several camera shots. Conversely, several sentences of dialog may occur within a single camera shot. In our case, the video clip was divided into 23 segments based on the meaningful change of the story. Four judges familiar with the landscape model agreed on these segments. These same judges identified 89 concepts, including visual and verbal concepts, across the 23 segments of the clip.

The next step was to determine the theoretically derived activation weights for each of the 89 concepts. To accomplish this, we followed the procedures outlined by van den Broek et al. (1996).[5] Two trained judges, who were blind to the

---

[5]The activation weights could also be determined empirically, which would provide a better fit between the predictions of the model and recall data. However, we decided to use van den Broek, Risden, Fletcher, and Thurlow's (1996) procedure to more directly compare our test of the model with their reported test.

experimental hypothesis, coded the level of activation of the 89 concepts, using a 5-point scale, for each segment. A concept was assigned a score of 5 if it was either explicitly mentioned in the dialogue or was a central feature of the visual scene for that idea unit. A concept was assigned a score of 4 if it aided in creating a coherent understanding of the unit of meaning or was causally related to what was occurring. A concept that acted as an enabler was assigned a value of 3. As an example, when the second crime boss is murdered, the sword that is used to cut his throat is an enabler for the murder. During that scene, *sword* was assigned an activation of 3. Finally, a concept that could be inferred from the scene or dialog was assigned a value of 2. For example, the concept *Mafia* might be activated in one of the earlier scenes involving one of the crime bosses cutting his thumb and using it to sign a contract while the other crime boss watched. In addition to these assignments, the landscape model assumes that the activation of a concept will dissipate across subsequent segments if it is not reinstated. Thus, those concepts that were not reactivated in the next idea unit were assigned a value that was half of their value from the previous idea unit. The activation level of these concepts was reduced to 0 during the next idea unit. The intercoder reliability for the two judges was 86% overall. The result of this coding was a theoretically driven 89 (concepts) × 23 (segments) matrix of activation values, which constitutes the landscape of activations for the video clip (Table 5.1).

Next, we compared this theoretically driven activation landscape to an empirically derived activation landscape. To develop the empirically derived landscape, 15 students were recruited from basic communication classes at the University of Alabama. None of the participants had ever watched the animated series *Cowboy Bebop*. The research participants watched the same 23 segments that the two trained judges had watched. After viewing each segment, the participants rated how much the segment made them think of each concept, using an 11-point scale (0 = *not at all* to 10 = *very much*).

To determine the level of agreement between the theoretically and empirically driven activations, we first calculated the reliability among the participants' ratings from the empirically driven activations. For the 15 participants, Cronbach's alpha was calculated across all of the concepts for each of the 23 segments. The reliability of the participants' ratings, averaged across the segments, was .77, which suggests that the participants generally agreed on the degree of activation of the concepts. Given this level of agreement, it was possible to test the validity of the model's predictions concerning the levels of activation. Specifically, we calculated the correlation between the theoretically derived activation from the trained judges and the perceived degree of activation from the participants' ratings (van den Broek et al., 1996). The correlation between theoretical activations and the average activations from the student participants was .66. When evaluating the model's prediction, it is important to remember that the reliability of the participants' ratings (.77) serves as an upper limit on the correlation between the model's predictions and the participants' ratings. At best, the model could account for 59% (77^2) of the variance in the participants' ratings. Thus, the model's accounting for 44% of

TABLE 5.1
Activation of Concepts in the Short Animated Clip From *Cowboy Bebop* (Partial List of Concepts)

	Segments																							*Total*
Concepts	*1*	*2*	*3*	*4*	*5*	*6*	*7*	*8*	*9*	*10*	*11*	*12*	*13*	*14*	*15*	*16*	*17*	*18*	*19*	*20*	*21*	*22*	*23*	*Activation*
Space ship	5	3	5	2.5	0	0	0	0	0	0	0	0	5	4	5	2.5	0	0	0	0	0	0	0	32.0
Fly	5	3	2	1	0	0	0	0	0	0	0	0	5	4	5	2.5	0	0	0	0	0	0	0	27.5
Ring-shaped gates	5	2.5	0	0	0	0	0	0	0	0	0	0	0	0	0	0	0	0	0	0	0	0	0	7.5
Planet Surface	5	5	2.5	1	0	0	0	0	0	0	0	0	0	0	0	0	0	0	0	0	0	0	0	13.5
City	0	5	5	2	1	0	0	0	0	0	0	0	5	3	5	2.5	0	0	0	0	0	0	0	28.5
Plateau	0	5	2.5	0	0	0	0	0	0	0	0	0	0	0	0	0	0	0	0	0	0	0	0	7.5
Planet	5	3	1.5	0	0	0	0	0	0	0	0	0	0	0	0	0	0	0	0	0	0	0	0	9.5
Deck	0	0	5	2.5	0	0	0	0	0	0	0	0	5	2	1	0	0	0	0	0	0	0	0	15.5
Building	0	0	0	5	2.5	0	0	0	0	2	3	2	1	0	0	2	1	0	0	0	0	5	2.5	26.0
Moving Clouds	0	0	0	5	2.5	2	2	2	1	0	0	0	0	0	0	2	1	0	0	0	0	0	0	17.5
Windows	0	0	0	5	2.5	0	0	0	0	0	0	0	0	0	0	0	0	0	0	0	0	0	0	7.5
Blood	0	0	0	0	0	0	0	0	0	0	0	0	0	0	0	2	5	5	2.5	0	5	3	2	24.5
Dripping on floor	0	0	0	0	0	0	0	0	0	0	0	0	0	0	0	0	0	0	0	0	5	3	1.5	9.5
Men standing	0	0	0	0	0	0	0	0	0	0	0	0	0	0	0	0	0	0	0	0	0	5	2.5	7.5
Spike (a character)	0	0	0	0	0	0	0	0	0	0	0	0	0	0	0	0	0	0	0	0	0	5	2.5	7.5
Not do this	0	0	0	0	0	0	0	0	0	0	0	0	0	0	0	0	0	0	0	0	0	5	2.5	7.5
Bird man smiles	0	0	0	0	0	0	0	0	0	0	0	0	0	0	0	0	0	0	0	0	5	5	2.5	12.5
Black feathers	0	0	0	0	0	0	0	0	0	0	0	0	0	0	5	2.5	0	0	0	0	5	2.5	0	15
Cawing	0	0	0	0	0	0	0	0	0	0	0	0	0	0	5	2.5	5	5	2.5	0	5	5	5	35.5

the variance is an encouraging result. So far in our study, the landscape model had done a very good job of predicting the empirically derived activation levels of the various concepts in the story, despite the increase in the complexity of the story and the addition of a visual element.

The final step in testing the model involved the model's hypothesis that the activation of a concept while watching the animated clip contributes to the formation of a stable memorial representation of the story (van den Broek et al., 1996). To test how well the model predicted memory for the story, 14 research participants from the same participant pool watched the same clip from *Cowboy Bebop*. However, the clip was shown in its entirety, rather than in 23 segments. After watching the clip, the participants completed several measures of visual and verbal working memory as a distracter task (10 min in length) and then completed a free recall test. In the free recall test, participants wrote down everything they could remember from the video clip they watched. For each participant, two trained coders decided whether the participant had recalled each of the 89 concepts. From this we derived the number of participants who recalled each concept. This served as our dependent variable. From the theoretically derived activations, we calculated the number of segments (out of 23) in which a concept had been activated. We also calculated the total activation of each concept by adding together its activation levels across all 23 segments. These two variables served as our independent variables. A regression analysis found that the number of segments in which each of the concepts was activated and the total level of activation of each concept (node strength) together accounted for 19% of the variance in participants' recall of the story ($R = .44$).

Based on these results, we are confident that the landscape model can be used to understand how people construct mental representations of movies or television shows. In addition, the model does a moderately good job of predicting those factors that will be recalled from the movie or television show. Clearly, there is more work to be done from this aspect.

IMPLICATIONS OF THE LANDSCAPE MODEL
FOR PRODUCT PLACEMENT

Watching a movie or television show involves, at its most basic level, building a representation of what is occurring in the show. Based on previous research on text comprehension, we have argued elsewhere that comprehension of media shows involves the construction of mental models (Roskos-Ewoldsen, Roskos-Ewoldsen, Yang et al., 2002). However, mental models in general, and the landscape model in particular, seem far removed from the study of the influence of brand and product placements in movies and television. Yet we feel that to understand the influence of brand placements on viewers' memory for the brand, understanding how the viewer comprehends the show is critical. It is through this comprehension process that the mental representation of the movie or television show is created. Further,

the mental representation of the movie or television show is going to determine whether the brand placement is going to be recalled or not.

We think there are three important implications of the research on the landscape model. First, the landscape model clearly specifies the likelihood that a brand placement will be recalled at a later time. The greater the activation of the brand while viewing the movie, the greater the likelihood that the brand will be recalled in the future. Simply presenting the brand a number of times within the movie increases the likelihood that it will receive some level of activation, but the level of activation will be minimal, and, consequently, later recall of the brand will be unlikely. If a brand is tied to the comprehension of the show, it will receive higher levels of activation. A brand will receive a very high level of activation if it is a central focus within a scene. In *E.T.*, Reese's Pieces was the central focus of the scene in which the young Elliott placed the candy on the ground to draw *E. T.* from his hiding place to the house. A brand will also receive higher levels of activation by acting as an enabler—when the brand plays a role in allowing some form of action or movement to occur within the story. Coke was an enabler in the movie *Falling Down*. Finally, a brand will be activated if it aids in comprehending the story. When E. T. is found in Elliott's house, Reese's Pieces should be reactivated because they aid in understanding how E. T. got into the house (by following the trail of candy).

We believe that these examples highlight how the landscape model can explain the extent to which brand placements influence memory for the brand. Although past research has focused on whether the placement was visually prominent or not, we believe that the critical issue is not visual prominence per se but rather the degree to which the placement functions as an aid to comprehending the program. Clearly, the use of any generic candy would have worked to draw E.T. into the house. By placing Reese's Pieces in the scene, Hershey took advantage of the candy's role in comprehending a series of scenes in the movie.

A second implication of the mental models framework for understanding brand placement is that mental models provide a mechanism for understanding how the context of a placement will influence the effects of the placement. Although we are not aware of any experimental tests of the role of context on brand placements, in-tuitively, context should play a role on the impact of the placement. Hypothetically, let us assume that a new form of alcoholic beverage is developed and advertised via a brand placement. We think it is highly unlikely that the company that makes the new beverage would pay for a placement that occurs within a scene where the imbiber of the new alcoholic beverage gets violently ill after a night of heavy drinking. Even if the imbiber of the beverage indicated enjoyment of the beverage, such a placement would probably not result in overly positive attitudes toward the brand among the majority of viewers. The context of the placement has to influence the impact of the placement. The mental models perspective, by focusing on the comprehension process, necessitates consideration of the larger context.

A final implication of our analysis is that brand placement is not likely to influence attitudes toward the brand. The majority of research on brand placement

has not found much of an influence of placements on attitudes or behavior toward the brand. As we argued earlier, to the extent that viewers already have well-developed attitudes toward the product, the placement is not likely to influence their attitudes because viewers rely on their existing attitudes (Roskos-Ewoldsen & Fazio, 1997; Roskos-Ewoldsen, Arpan-Ralstin, & St. Pierre, 2002). We believe that brand placement has significant effects on attitudes or behavior toward the brand only in those situations in which the brand is relatively novel, as was the case with Reese Pieces in the initial showing of *E. T.* If a brand is relatively novel, we believe that the beliefs about the brand that are developed due to the placement influence attitudes toward the brand. Furthermore, as discussed in our example of the new alcoholic beverage, we believe that context and the comprehension process play a significant role in determining what those beliefs about the brand are going to be.

REFERENCES

Avery, R. J., & Ferraro, R. (2000). Verisimilitude or advertising? Brand appearance on prime-time television. *Journal of Consumer Affairs, 34,* 217–244.

Babin, L. A., & Carder, S. T. (1996). Advertising via the box office: Is product placement effective? *Journal of Promotion Management, 3,* 31–51.

Basil, M. D. (1997). The danger of cigarette "special placements" in film and television. *Health Communication, 9,* 190–198.

Biocca, F. (1991). Viewer's mental models of political ads: Toward a theory of semantic processing of television. In F. Biocca (Ed.), *Television and political advertising: Vol. 1. Psychological processes* (pp. 27–91). Hillsdale, NJ: Lawrence Erlbaum Associates.

Brennan, I., Dubas, K. M., & Babin, L. A. (1999). The influence of product-placement type and exposure time on product-placement recognition. *International Journal of Advertising, 18,* 323–337.

Chapman, S., & Davis, R. M. (1997). Smoking in movies: It is a problem. *Tobacco Control, 6,* 269–271.

Christenson, P. G., Henriksen, L., & Roberts, D. F. (2000). *Substance use in popular prime-time television* (Contract No. 282-98-0013). Washington, DC: U. S. Office of National Drug Control Policy.

d'Astous, A., & Chartier, F. (2000). A study of factors affecting consumer evaluations and memory of product placements in movies. *Journal of Current Issues and Research in Advertising, 22,* 31–40.

DeLorme, D. E., & Reid, L. N. (1999). Moviegoers' experiences and interpretation of brand in films revisited. *Journal of Advertising, 28,* 71–95.

Diener, B. J. (1993). The frequency and context of alcohol and tobacco cues in daytime soap opera programs: Fall 1986 and fall 1991. *Journal of Public Policy and Marketing, 12,* 252–257.

Distefan, J. M., Gilpin, E. A., Sargent, J. D., & Pierce, J. P. (1999). Do movie stars encourage adolescents to start smoking? Evidence from California. *Preventive Medicine, 28,* 1–11.

Everett, S. A., Schnuth, R. L., & Tribble, J. L. (1998). Tobacco and alcohol use in top grossing American films. *Journal of Community Health, 23,* 317–324.

Fazio, R. H., Roskos-Ewoldsen, D. R., & Powell, M. C. (1994). Attitudes as determinants of attention and perception. In S. Kitayama & P. M. Niedenthal (Eds.), *The heart's eye: Emotional influences on perception and attention* (pp. 197–216). Orlando, FL: Academic Press.

Ferraro, R., & Avery, R. J. (2000). Brand appearance on prime-time television. *Journal of Current Issues and Research in Advertising, 22,* 1–15.

Garnham, A. (1997). Representing information in mental models. In M. A. Conway (Ed.), *Cognitive models of memory* (pp. 149–172). Cambridge, MA: MIT Press.

Gentner, D., & Gentner, D. R. (1983). Flowing waters or teeming crowds: Mental models of electricity. In D. Gentner & A. L. Stevens (Eds.), *Mental models* (pp. 99–129). Mahwah, NJ: Lawrence Erlbaum Associates.

Gerbner, G., Gross, L., Eleey, M. F., Jackson-Beeck, M., Jeffries-Fox, S., & Signorielli, N. (1977). TV violence profile no. 8: The highlights. *Journal of Communication, 27,* 171–180.

Gibson, B., & Maurer, J. (2000). Cigarette smoking in the movies: The influence of product placement on attitude toward smoking and smokers. *Journal of Applied Social Psychology, 30,* 1457–1473.

Glenberg, A. M., & Langston, W. E. (1992). Comprehension of illustrated text: Pictures help to build mental models. *Journal of Memory and Language, 31,* 129–151.

Graesser, A. C., Singer, M., & Trabasso, T. (1994). Constructing inferences during narrative text comprehension. *Psychological Review, 101,* 371–395.

Greeno, J. G. (1984). Conceptual entities. In D. Gentner & A. L. Stevens (Eds.), *Mental models* (pp. 227–252). Hillsdale, NJ: Lawrence Erlbaum Associates.

Gupta, P. B., & Lord, K. R. (1998). Product placement in movies: The effect of prominence and mode on recall. *Journal of Current Issues and Research in Advertising, 20,* 47–59.

Halford, G. S. (1993). *Children's understanding: The development of mental models.* Hillsdale, NJ: Lawrence Erlbaum Associates.

Hazan, A. R., Lipton, H. L., & Glantz, S. A. (1994). Popular films do not reflect current tobacco use. *American Journal of Public Health, 84,* 998–1000.

Higgins, E. T., Bargh, J. A., & Lombardi, W. (1985). Nature of prime effects on categorization. *Journal of Experimental Psychology: Learning, Memory, and Cognition, 11,* 59–69.

Hines, D., Saris, R. N., & Throckmorton-Belzer, L. (2000). Cigarette smoking in popular films: Does it influence viewers' likelihood to smoke? *Journal of Applied Social Psychology, 30,* 2246–2269.

Johnson-Laird, P. N. (1983). *Mental models.* Cambridge, MA: Harvard University Press.

Karrh, J. A. (1998). Brand placement: A review. *Journal of Current Issues and Research in Advertising, 20,* 31–49.

Law, S., & Braun, K. A. (2000). I'll have what she's having: Gauging the impact of product placements on viewers. *Psychology and Marketing, 17,* 1059–1075.

Livingstone, S. M. (1987). The implicit representation of characters in *Dallas*: A multidimensional scaling approach. *Human Communication Research, 13,* 399–420.

Livingstone, S. M. (1989). Interpretive viewers and structured programs. *Communication Research, 16,* 25–57.

Livingstone, S. M. (1990). Interpreting a television narrative: How different viewers see a story. *Journal of Communication, 40,* 72–84.

Morrow, D. G., Greenspan, S. L., & Bower, G. H. (1987). Accessibility and situation models in narrative comprehension. *Journal of Memory and Language, 26,* 165–187.

Nebenzahl, I. D., & Secunda, E. (1993). Consumers' attitudes toward product placement in movies. *International Journal of Advertising, 12,* 1–11.

Ong, B. S., & Meri, D. (1994). Should product placement in movies be banned? *Journal of Promotion Management, 2,* 159–175.

Petty, R. E., & Cacioppo, J. T. (1986). The elaboration likelihood model of persuasion. In L. Berkowitz (Ed.), *Advances in experimental social psychology* (Vol. 19, pp. 123–205). New York: Academic Press.

Pierce, J. P., Choi, W. S., Gilpin, E. A., Farkas, A. J., & Merritt, R. K. (1996). Validation of susceptibility as a predictor of which adolescents take up smoking in the United States. *Health Psychology, 15,* 355–361.

Radvansky, G. A., Spieler, R. T., & Zacks, R. T. (1993). Mental model organization. *Journal of Experimental Psychology: Learning Memory and Cognition, 19,* 95–114.

Radvansky, G. A., & Zacks, R. T. (1997). The retrieval of situation-specific information. In M. A. Conway (Ed.), *Cognitive models of memory* (pp. 173–213). Cambridge, MA: MIT Press.

Roberts, D. F., Henriksen, L., & Christenson, P. G. (1999). *Substance use in popular movies and music* (Contract No. 277-95-4013). Washington, DC: U. S. Office of National Drug Control Policy.

Roskos-Ewoldsen, B., Roskos-Ewoldsen, D. R., Yang, M., Crawford, Z., & Choi, J. (2002). *Mental models of a movie*. Manuscript in preparation.

Roskos-Ewoldsen, D. R. (1997). Attitude accessibility and persuasion: Review and a transactive model. In B. Burleson's (Ed.), *Communication yearbook 20* (pp. 185–225). Beverly Hills, CA: Sage.

Roskos-Ewoldsen, D. R., Arpan-Ralstin, L. A., & St. Pierre, J. (2002). Attitude accessibility and persuasion: The quick and the strong. In J. P. Dillard & M. Pfau (Eds.), *The persuasion handbook: Developments in theory and practice* (pp. 39–61). Thousand Oaks, CA: Sage.

Roskos-Ewoldsen, D. R., & Fazio, R. H. (1992). On the orienting value of attitudes: Attitude accessibility as a determinant of an objects' attraction of visual attention. *Journal of Personality and Social Psychology, 63*, 198–211.

Roskos-Ewoldsen, D. R., & Fazio, R. H. (1997). The role of belief accessibility in attitude formation. *Southern Communication Journal, 62*, 107–116.

Roskos-Ewoldsen, D. R., Klinger, M. R., & Roskos-Ewoldsen, B. (in press). Media priming. In R. W. Preiss, M. Allen, B. M. Gayle & N. Burrell (Eds.), *Media effects research: Advances through meta-analysis*. Mahwah, NJ: Lawrence Erlbaum.

Roskos-Ewoldsen, D. R., Roskos-Ewoldsen, B., & Carpentier, F. (2002). Media priming: A synthesis. In J. B. Bryant & D. Zillmann (Eds.), *Media effects in theory and research* (2nd ed.). Mahwah, NJ: Lawrence Erlbaum Associates.

Sargent, J. D., Tickle, J. J., Beach, M. L., Dalton, M. A., Ahrens, M. B., & Heatherton, T. F. (2001). Brand appearances in contemporary cinema films and contribution to global marketing of cigarettes. *Lancet, 357*, 29–32.

Segrin, C., & Nabi, R. L. (2002). Does television viewing cultivate unrealistic expectations about marriage? *Journal of Communication, 52*, 247–263.

Shields, D. L. L., Carol, J., Balbach, E. D., & McGee, S. (1999). Hollywood on tobacco: How the entertainment industry understands tobacco portrayal. *Tobacco Control, 8*, 378–386.

Stockwell, T. F., & Glantz, S. A. (1997). Tobacco use is increasing in popular films. *Tobacco Control, 6*, 282–284.

van den Broek, P., & Gustafson, M. (1999). Comprehension and memory for texts: Three generations of reading research. In S. R. Goldman, A. C. Graesser, & P. van den Broek (Eds.), *Narrative comprehension, causality, and coherence: Essays in honor of Tom Trabasso* (pp. 15–34). Mahwah, NJ: Lawrence Erlbaum Associates.

van den Broek, P., Risden, K., Fletcher, C., & Thurlow, R. (1996). A "landscape" view of reading: Fluctuating patterns of activation and the construction of a stable memory representation. In B. K. Brittion & A. C. Graesser (Eds.), *Models of understanding text* (pp. 165–187). Mahwah, NJ: Lawrence Erlbaum Associates.

van den Broek, P., Young, M., Tzeng, Y., & Linderholm, T. (1999). The landscape model of reading: Inferences and the online construction of a memory representation. In H. van Oostendrop & S. R. Goldman (Eds.), *The construction of mental model representations during reading* (pp. 71–98). Mahwah, NJ: Lawrence Erlbaum Associates.

van Dijk, T. A. (1998). *Ideology: A multidisciplinary approach*. London: Sage.

van Dijk, T. A., & Kintsch, W. (1983). *Strategies of discourse comprehension*. New York: Academic Press.

Wyer, R. S., Jr., & Radvansky, G. A. (1999). The comprehension and validation of information. *Psychological Review, 106*, 89–118.

Zwaan, R. A. (1994). Effects of genre expectations on text comprehension. *Journal of Experimental Psychology: Learning, Memory, and Cognition, 20*, 920–933.

Zwaan, R. A., & Radvansky, G. A. (1998). Situation models in language comprehension and memory. *Psychological Bulletin, 123*, 162–185.

CHAPTER SIX

Embedding Brands Within Media Content: The Impact of Message, Media, and Consumer Characteristics on Placement Efficacy

Namita Bhatnagar
University of Manitoba

Lerzan Aksoy
Koc University

Selin A. Malkoc
University of North Carolina at Chapel Hill

The need to rise above the cacophony of marketing messages aimed constantly toward the consuming public has fueled interest in nontraditional ways for companies to get these communications across. The confluence of commercial persuasion and entertainment media, which frequently falls under the category of blurred communications (Solomon & Englis, 1996), is one such solution. Brand sponsors pay for messages that are embedded within featured entertainment, but the sponsors' identity is kept hidden. Tremendous growth in popularity and industry organization over the past 2 decades makes it critical for marketing researchers to gain deeper insights into the phenomenon of embedded brands. This chapter provides a broad commentary on issues we believe warrant further exploration, given the current state of knowledge in the area. The impact of various message, media, and consumer characteristics on the effectiveness of blurred communications is specifically examined.

The most established form of blurred communications is product-related information that gets placed or embedded within the content of visual media. This communication draws on elements from different types of promotional methods, most notably from advertising (i.e., in which the brand sponsor has control over the message content) and publicity (i.e., in which the disseminating medium is also perceived to be the message source). Whereas most attention has been given to placements that occur in movies and television programs, blurred communication is increasingly spanning into other popular media, such as books, magazines, newspapers, and even video games and music.

Product placements have been of growing interest to researchers as well as to practitioners of marketing in recent years (DeLorme & Reid, 1999; Gupta, Gould, & Lord, 1998; Karrh, 1994; Magiera, 1990). Actual efficacy of the practice, however, has not been well tested empirically. Evidence that is available is ambiguous and tends not to extend much beyond brand memory and evaluation. In field settings, the entwined nature of joint promotional campaigns makes it difficult to tease apart the effects of placements from other forms of marketing efforts. Although quantitative measures, such as box office ticket sales, are sometimes used as proxies for the number of impressions created, such estimates are at best approximations of the true impact of placements. A richer notion of the success of a placement must surely incorporate more than mere exposure to placements, memory for placed brands, and attitudes toward them. Some amount of academic conjecture, unaccompanied by empirical validation for the most part, also surrounds the notion of skepticism and trust in placed claims, mainly in the context of consumer deception and implications for public policy (Rothenberg, 1991). The implications of skepticism and trust in placed claims for brand sponsors and not least for participating media add interesting facets to the construct of placement efficacy and warrant further investigation.

Past research has argued for the superiority of blurred communications over more conventional forms of marketing practices on several grounds. Obvious among these are reasons such as the wide reach and longevity of featured entertainment. Consensus additionally appears to have formed for the idea that the hidden commercial intent of placed messages enhances persuasion outcomes (Balasubramanian, 1994). In other words, people do not know that companies pay to place their brands within popular media. Unless consumers realize that marketers are attempting to persuade them, the likelihood of setting up mental barriers, becoming skeptical, and carefully scrutinizing brand claims is low. As a result, some researchers argue that placements are deceptive and need to be regulated, primarily because they may be mistaken for unbiased endorsements by the media vehicles involved. This begs the question whether audiences are unaware of the commercial motives behind product placements. Ample anecdotal evidence about product placements is catalogued in the trade press, and it is increasingly common to encounter brands insinuated within entertainment content. Given this, marketers who still believe in the complete naiveté of audiences may very well be revealing the same about themselves. If consumers are indeed aware of the commercial nature of placements, then serious implications arise for the level of credence that is put in claims made and, importantly, the degree of trust that is placed in the medium.

Broadening the concept of efficacy to include issues such as trust would help marketers understand conditions under which placements can become more or less successful and those under which they can actually be harmful. Messages generated by credible sources are typically more believable, except when biases, where none are expected, get noticed. A backlash against placements at the grassroots level, especially for well-respected and credible media, is not inconceivable. The criticism

surrounding author Fay Weldon's book *The Bulgari Connection* is illustrative of reactions that can be generated against placements that become too obvious, particularly when they occur in media that are thought to be free of commercial biases. For example, in critiquing the book, Kim (2002) makes the following assertion: "A 'commissioned book' represents a violation of one area of society free from the corporate sector's drive to push its 'swooshes'—or its brands. With the heavy hand of corporate marketing entering the popular literature arena, a new wave of cynicism is sure to wash over us." [on-line]

Ruskin (2001) has this to say about *The Bulgari Connection* in an open online letter to book reviewers: "Is it a novel to be reviewed, or is it an advertisement to be commented upon in the business pages? *The Bulgari Connection* is like a Kodak Moment or a Budweiser Whassup! It is an advertisement; and we should call it that and deal with it accordingly."

Excessively placing the Bulgari jewelry brand generated tremendous amounts of cynicism and ill will toward the book itself and exemplifies potential backlashes that disseminating media need to guard against. Conditions where consumers do not place greater faith in messages contained within credible media need further investigation (e.g., when people are highly involved and motivated to process information for themselves). To summarize, we address conditions that are thought to influence the degree of placement efficacy and set forth propositions with broad implications for various constituencies: (1) for marketing practitioners (implications for companies, e.g., success of placements; and for media used, e.g., generation of potential consumer backlash); (2) for marketing theorists (implications for trust in brand claims and trust in the medium given variations in message, media, and consumer characteristics); and (3) for public policy legislators (implications for regulation of placements given the presence of consumer deception).

The rest of the chapter is organized as follows: The next section examines the significance of persuasive communications for companies. We then formally describe the practice of product placements and advantages attributed to them. This is followed by an examination of placement efficacy in terms of memory and attitudes toward brands and claims made, trust in these claims, and trust in the placing medium. Conditions under which placements are more or less effective are then investigated. The effects of message, media, and consumer characteristics on placement efficacy are examined to this end. Finally, broad conclusions based on relationships proposed throughout the chapter are made.

SIGNIFICANCE OF PERSUASIVE COMMUNICATIONS

With profits and long-term survival at stake, companies strive to make consumers aware of, be interested in, try, and ultimately adopt the products and services they have to offer. Given the frenetic pace of the current competitive environment, companies relentlessly bombard consumers with persuasive messages in attempts

to create, reinforce, or alter attitudes and subsequent purchase behaviors. It is therefore in the interest of companies to thoroughly understand whether persuasive attempts with these objectives in mind are effective or not.

One way to understand attitude change and persuasion is by examining the process by which communications are disseminated (Kotler & Armstrong, 2001). On a simplistic level, the communications process may be decomposed into its constituent elements (i.e., the message source, its content, the media that carry the message, the recipients, and the feedback generated thereafter). Characteristics of all elements must be examined to determine the influence each has on overall effectiveness.

Companies can choose any one or more of several media options available to them (e.g., television, radio, magazines, newspapers) for disseminating messages. All media possess unique characteristics. For example, certain associations may be made with print media that cannot be made with visual media. Some readers may choose to believe that newspapers by and large have unbiased content, whereas most movie viewers believe movies are purveyors of entertainment. Or unique characteristics may be associated with specific vehicles within a particular medium. Take, for example, a TV soap opera, such as *Melrose Place*, versus a TV news show, such as *20/20*; a tabloid magazine, such as the *National Inquirer*, versus a news magazine like *U. S. News and World Report*; any mainstream movie, such as the James Bond movies versus a nonmainstream film, such as *In the Bedroom*. In each case, contents of the former are more likely to be characterized as fluff and the latter as substance. Suspicions of commercial motives may be weaker for the latter versus the former. For example, articles appearing in *U. S. News and World Report* are more likely to be associated with editorial independence and unbiased reporting than those appearing in the *National Inquirer*. Consumer reactions to brand inclusions within media content may therefore be contingent on the characteristics of the media vehicle involved.

In decoding embedded messages, recipients make interpretations based on their perceptions about the message source, what the message contains, and the medium that transmits it. Where a sponsor is not noticed, as is believed to be the case with placements, the medium delivering a message is also perceived to be the source. Audience reactions to the message should be captured within the feedback loop so that the source can determine the degree to which its communication objectives are achieved. Various characteristics of these communication elements (e.g., source and media credibility, strength of message, fit of message within content, recipient involvement, and persuasion knowledge) play a role in memory, attitude formation, and persuasion and are further elaborated on in this chapter.

WHAT ARE PRODUCT PLACEMENTS?

Whereas blurred communications span all entertainment media, product placement, the most established form of blurred communications, occurs in movies and is not a new phenomenon. Long before an alien was eating Reese's Pieces in the

1980s movie *E. T.: The Extra-Terrestrial* (Winski, 1982), tobacco companies had actors and actresses smoking cigarettes in movies of the 1920s (Schudson, 1984). In this multimillion dollar industry, once informal arrangements between Hollywood executives and brand sponsors are now organized symbiotic relationships. Brands usually insinuate themselves into media content in return for commercial considerations (Gupta & Gould, 1997), allowing producers to generate revenues and corporations to promote their brands at the same time. More formally, blurred or hybrid messages are a category of communications where brand sponsors pay for a message but are not identified (Balasubramanian, 1994; Sandler & Secunda, 1993; Solomon & Englis, 1996). Of these, product placements refer to instances where commercial motives exist for the inclusion of branded products in movies and T.V. programs (Balasubramanian, 1994). Just as several media are available for message dissemination, brand placements can occur in any media. The term *product placements* is used loosely here to refer to branded inclusion in any medium, not just in movies or T.V. programs, to ease understanding. Some advantages of such nontraditional methods of communication proposed in past literature are briefly touched on later in this chapter. Please refer to McCarty (this volume) for more detailed assessments of the practice.

ADVANTAGES OF PRODUCT PLACEMENTS

Several key advantages of placing products, given positive brand associations and positive positioning, have been proposed in past literature (DeLorme & Reid, 1999; Gould, Gupta, & Grabner-Krauter, 2000). Some advantages deal with cost-effectiveness, width of message reach, longevity of message life, and implied endorsements, and other advantages pit placements against more traditional forms of promotion such as advertising (where there is less integration within naturalistic settings) and publicity (where there is less control over message content). Arguments in favor of product placements are briefly elaborated on here.

First, some have argued that integrating brands within programming provides a potentially cost-effective alternative to advertising (Magiera, 1990). Although difficult to quantify the worth of placements, their cost is a fraction of that for most advertising. Second, entertainment media have wide local, national, and global audiences (Balasubramanian, 1994). Although no standard measurement system has been developed for the industry, Creative Entertainment Services uses ticket sales as a proxy for the number of impressions arising from movie placements. More specifically, box office earnings divided by average ticket price yields a large number of impressions for movie audiences. The number of tickets sold for a moderately successful movie worldwide well exceeds the reach of an average advertisement. Third, these brand impressions continue to accumulate over the extended period of a feature presentation's life. Entertainment vehicles have potentially longer shelf lives (e.g., feature films, television programs, and music have afterlives on home videos, foreign distribution, cable casts, and network broadcasts), and impressions

continue to be formed long after their initial release. Fourth, embedding brands within a context reinforces the impact of the message and creates an appearance of brand endorsement (Balasubramanian, 1994). And, finally, emergence of a payment structure gives sponsor companies greater control over the manner of brand portrayal. Potentially harmful negative brand associations can be avoided in this way.

Balasubramanian (1994) further contends that placements help companies overcome the downsides of both publicity and advertising. Cohen (1988) describes advertisements as messages that are paid for by clearly identified sponsors and publicity as messages that are not paid for and over which the publicized company has no control. On the one hand, sponsors have control over advertised content, and audiences perceive disseminating media as unbiased sources of publicity. On the other hand, advertised messages are biased by nature, and companies have no control over the content of publicity. Placed messages, which are paid for but do not identify the message sponsor, have the potential to overcome consumers' skepticism toward advertisements. In this case, participating media are thought to be the unbiased message sources, and the actual brand sponsors retain control over the message. The effects of product placements have been gauged in various ways in past literature. We elaborate on these and other ways of construing placement efficacy, from the point of view of the brand sponsor as well as the media involved.

MEASURES OF PLACEMENT EFFICACY

It is oftentimes hard to gauge the effect of placements on marketing outcomes, especially given the integrated nature of the promotional mix employed by most firms. Despite gains in popularity, it is unusual for promotional campaigns to consist solely of placements. The integrated marketing plan for the launch of BMW's Z3 roadster (Fournier & Wojnicki, 1999) is a good case study in joint promotions. The portfolio of promotional methods used included a 90-s placement within the James Bond movie *GoldenEye*, television and print advertisements that cross-promoted the car with the movie, public appearances by the actors, plugs on television talk shows, and features within the Neiman Marcus Christmas catalogue. The sensitivity of U.S. auto sales (frequently used as an indicator of public confidence) to the state of the economy further confounds results in this particular product category. The impact of the external environment, along with difficulties in isolating consumer responsiveness to different components of joint promotional campaigns, makes it hard to assess the pure effect of placements in field settings. With rigorous empirical testing arguably in the nascent stage, simulations in laboratory settings (with some consequent control over external influencers) have vast potential for adding to knowledge in the area.

Numerous studies have attempted to examine the effectiveness of placements. Most of these have looked at effects on brand recall, recognition, and attitudes.

Additional investigations must depend on how we understand the efficacy construct and its myriad interpretations. Expanding placement effectiveness to mean more than just good attentional and memory outcomes is key for gaining deeper insights into the manner by which consumers process placed communications. Other candidate indicators can include implications for placed brands (e.g., Do hidden commercial motives allow consumers to have greater faith in placed information?) as well as for media that carry placements (e.g., Do consumers feel betrayed by the medium if the hidden commercial motives are discovered?). These and other measures of placement efficacy are elaborated on in the following sections.

Memory for Placed Information

Most prior empirical studies have looked at brand recognition, recall, and attitudes as measures of placement efficacy. Some researchers find that placements do not lead to significantly altered brand evaluations (Karrh, 1994). Support has, however, been building for the positive impact of placements on aided and unaided brand recall (Babin & Carder, 1996; Baker & Crawford, 1996; Gupta et al., 1998; Ong & Meri, 1994; Steortz, 1987; Vollmers & Mizerski, 1994; Zimmer & DeLorme, 1997). Interpreting these results in the context of psychological theories sheds some light on why memory for placed information may be strong.

Memory research suggests that novel or unexpected information stands out more than information that is expected (Von Restorff, 1933). Consumers expect brand information to be contained within advertisements and other conventional tools of marketing. If an element of surprise or novelty, on the other hand, is associated with encountering product placements, we might expect consumers to remember information that is placed better than information that is advertised.

Indeed, results of multiple studies carried out by the authors (Bhatnagar, Aksoy, & Malkoc, 2002) indicate that people have stronger memories for brands and claims that are placed versus those that are advertised. Of the people who remembered the brands and brand claim, more had difficulties in remembering where exactly placed messages were encountered. This raises the intriguing possibility that the effects of placed messages are more powerful, yet the internalization process is subtler when compared with the effects of advertised messages.

Attitudes Toward Placed Brands

Companies expect consumers to form attitudes toward brands based on the contexts in which they are presented. The seamless manner of brand inclusion within media content makes it easier for people to make paired associations between the context and the placed brand, thereby exploiting tenets of the theory of classical conditioning (Gorn, 1982). Sponsors have some degree of control over the manner in which their brands get portrayed, and it is probably safe to assume that products generally get placed within positive contexts. Sponsors hope these positive feelings engendered via storylines translate into the formation of positive attitudes

toward placed brands. The paid-for nature of placements thus gives companies a modicum of leverage in avoiding adverse brand associations and the subsequent formation of negative brand attitudes (Balasubramanian, 1994).

The extensively researched phenomenon of learning has additional implications for purchase intent toward placed brands. More specifically, within the modeling paradigm, people are thought to learn through formed associations. Bandura (1977) suggests that product demonstrations help people to learn how to use products more quickly. Product placements are similar to actual demonstrations in that they enable consumers to see how and when to use—and who uses—a particular product. Modeling behaviors according to what gets demonstrated can therefore facilitate learning for consumers and increase the adoption likelihood for placed products and services.

Trust in Brand Claims and Trust in Media

The degree of trust consumers are willing to put in brand claims and the trust exhibited toward disseminating media are both excellent indicators of the effects of placements. We focus on the influence of consumers' trust toward brand claims in this section and later further elaborate on the impact of consumers' trust placed in the medium (i.e., media credibility).

A proposed advantage of product placements over other forms of persuasion (e.g., advertisements) is the natural and covert method of message delivery. Placed information is usually embedded within a social context and can be assimilated into the storyline. Key arguments for the effectiveness of these embedded messages center on the hidden commercial intent of placements. Past research (Boush, Friestad, & Rose, 1994; Calfee & Ringold, 1988; Friestad & Wright, 1994) suggests that consumers react with skepticism to cope with noticeable persuasion attempts (e.g., through advertisements and salespeople clearly sponsored by companies). Skepticism toward claims induces closer scrutiny of them and limits consumer deception (Aksoy & Bloom, 1999).

Proponents of the view that placements overcome skepticism and closer examination of product-related claims (Balasubramanian, 1994) base their arguments on the assumption that media productions successfully hide the commercial nature of placements by incorporating brands into the storyline in a natural way. Advertisements are clearly sponsored and delineated from editorial content. It is hard, however, for consumers to determine whether product-related content in movies, T.V. programs, books, newspapers, magazines, and the like is commercially sponsored or not. If the paid nature of product inclusions is not apparent, then unbiased endorsements by the media may be inferred where none exist. Past literature uses these arguments to suggest that consumers' trust in placed claims is higher than their trust in advertised claims. All of this would be true if we were to accept that no conditions exist under which consumers get suspicious of brand placements as marketing attempts and not entertainment.

If the persuasive intent underlying placements becomes apparent, consumers should be just as, if not more, skeptical of placed claims as they are of advertised claims. Consumers who notice paid placements where they are not expected, and feel betrayed, might actually react more negatively than when they notice advertisements (in which the persuasive intent is overt). Conditions that potentially increase or decrease the effectiveness of product placements, for brand sponsors and for media, are discussed at greater length later in this chapter.

CONDITIONS INFLUENCING PLACEMENT EFFICACY

Characteristics of constituent elements of the communication process are expected to impact effectiveness of the process as a whole. In general, media that successfully hide the identity of brand sponsors are perceived as the source of branded messages. Given this, we examine message characteristics (i.e., fit of the placed message with the context, strength of the placement), media or perceived source characteristics (i.e., media credibility), and recipient characteristics (i.e., involvement with placed claims, awareness of persuasive intent), and propose various relationships they have with placement efficacy.

Influence of Message Characteristics on Placement Efficacy

Fit of the Placement With the Context.   The degree of fit or congruence between placed brands and the contexts in which they appear is expected to determine the extent to which attitudes toward contexts transfer onto placed brands. This idea is borrowed from branding literature that claims attitudes are found to successfully transfer between parent brands and brand extensions when perceived fit between the two is high (Aaker & Keller, 1990).

Extending this idea to product placements, good fit of the actors or the context with placed products should engender a transfer of positive attitudes from the former to the latter. Greater fit is also expected to enhance attention to, memory for, and believability of brand portrayals and claims made because the relevance of the message within a given context is high. A good example is the case of the BMW Z3 roadster that was placed within the 17th James Bond movie *GoldenEye*. Both the car and the character can be described as sophisticated and sexy. The roadster, with superior technological features, is the vehicle of choice for the British spy, who is portrayed as technologically savvy. In line with the concept of good fit, attitudes toward one component in our example (the actor) are expected to transfer to the other (the car), given the high level of complementarities between the two on relevant attributes. Placed brands, on the other hand, that do not quite fit into storylines are likely to both be noticed as well as raise suspicions of superfluity and of media motives other than artistic expression. In other words, placements that are out of context are expected to be scrutinized negatively and result in lower

levels of trust in brand claims and in the medium. To reiterate, we propose that placement efficacy (e.g., attitudes toward placed brands, trust in placed claims, trust in the medium) increases with the degree of perceived fit between storylines and placed brands. If this holds true, then marketing practitioners need to identify common and meaningful dimensions of contexts and products along which to fashion successful placements.

Strength of the Placement. An additional message characteristic that we believe has the potential to influence placement efficacy is the strength or the intensity of the placement. This construct is somewhat confounded with the previous notion of fit between contexts and placements in that the greater the fit, the stronger the placement is expected to be. Product placement consultants also negotiate the strength of placements with producers on the basis of several other criteria. The number of brand mentions; visual or verbal inclusion, or both; appearances in the foreground or background; actual usage; and integration with the context are all examples of how placement strength can be manipulated. Stronger placements are typically accompanied by higher price tags. Payment structures are usually contingent on a product's intended use and the anticipated degree of exposure (Magiera, 1990). Costs reportedly ranged from $20,000 for only visual product displays to $40,000 for brand name mentions to $60,000 for depicting actual usage in Walt Disney's movie *Mr. Destiny*. With such costs involved, marketing managers who demand maximum returns on their investments must better understand the relationship between placement strength and persuasive outcomes.

Given the menu of possible placement options, it is important to examine whether the levels of attention and persuasion vary with differing strengths of placements. A nonlinear relationship between placement strength and efficacy is anticipated. More specifically, an inverted, U-shaped relationship between the two is proposed (see Fig. 6.1). Say, for instance, we operationalize placement strength as an increasing function of the number of times the brand name is mentioned.

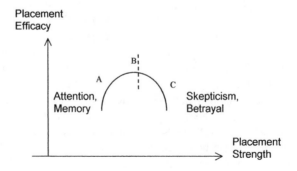

FIG. 6.1   Effect of the strength of product placements on placement efficacy.

The rationale behind the proposed relationship would then be as follows: Initially, measures of placement efficacy, such as brand recall and recognition, are expected to rise with the number of brand mentions (i.e., placement strength) as people are exposed to the brand more extensively. Eventually, however, the incremental gain in efficacy from each additional brand mention is expected to decline (region A). Increasing the number of mentions beyond a certain point (B) might actually make audiences skeptical, and perhaps feel betrayed, leading to a decline in absolute levels of placement efficacy (region C).

Successful product placements are supposed to be subtle and should blend in with the context. When placements become too obvious, consumers are likely to infer manipulative intent and become less susceptible to persuasion attempts. Placements that make consumers think, "I wonder how much this cost (the brand sponsor)?" is no more effective than advertising the brand, and, as argued previously, may even be worse. The controversy surrounding *The Bulgari Connection*, as discussed earlier, is illustrative of consumer reactions against excessive brand placements, especially in types of media that are expected to be sacrosanct and free of marketing motives. The relationship between media characteristics (i.e., media credibility) and consumer characteristics (i.e., involvement with the product category, awareness of persuasive intent) with placement efficacy are discussed next.

Influence of Media and Consumer Characteristics on Placement Efficacy

Consumer Awareness of Persuasive Intent.   The lack of consumer awareness that placements (i.e., payments in exchange for brand inclusion) occur is considered central to the effectiveness of placements. This has implications for trust in brand claims and trust in the medium.

As discussed previously, the degree of skepticism for consumers who are able to discern commercial motives underlying placements may be similar to or greater than the skepticism toward advertised claims. Kelley's (1972) work on attributions has implications for the influence of consumer awareness of persuasive intent on trust in media. It is suggested that message recipients evaluate the motives of message communicators and infer reporting biases (Eagly, Wood, & Chaiken, 1978) in which communicators are seen as insincere in reporting accurate versions of events. Such attributions of communicator insincerity and manipulativeness (Mills & Jellison, 1967) result in lower degrees of persuasiveness. In the case of placements, consumers may infer reporting bias on the part of the medium if commercial motivations underlying brand inclusions become known. Results of our own research indicate that perceptions of motive purity for participating media decline when placed messages are noticed (Bhatnagar et al., 2002).

Further, according to the persuasion knowledge model (Friestad & Wright 1994), individuals develop beliefs about how, why, and when marketers attempt to influence them. Individuals therefore develop persuasion knowledge and devise strategies to cope with this knowledge. Viewers who become skeptical closely

scrutinize messages whenever persuasive attempts are inferred, thereby lowering message effectiveness and persuasion.

Increased exposure to and familiarity with placements also has the potential to influence placement efficacy. Increased familiarity will likely influence the individuals' ability to recognize a placement and manage the persuasion attempt. Friestad and Wright (1994), for example, suggest that persuasion knowledge of marketers' tactics is not static. It changes over time and increases with the number of persuasion attempts. This is the same as saying that consumers become more aware of the persuasive intent underlying placements as the placements become increasingly common. Academic research as well as anecdotal evidence suggests that, at least within the United States, consumers' awareness of commercial content in entertainment media is on the upswing. For example, DeLorme and Reid (1999) found that consumers' immunity to specific types of persuasion attempts rises as the degree of exposure increases. Repeated exposures enable consumers to realize the underlying marketing motive. After 30 in-depth interviews, DeLorme and Reid also concluded that most moviegoers were aware of product placements, and their attitudes and interpretations of brands inclusions varied according to the age group they represented. Some evidence also exists for greater consumer acceptance of product placements as legitimate forms of marketing practice (Nebenzahl & Secunda, 1993). This contention, however, is not always supported, especially in the case of highly credible media, where consumer backlash is possible. The following sections elaborate on the impact of media characteristics, (viz., media credibility) and consumer characteristics (viz., involvement) on believability of claims and trust toward the medium.

Credibility of the Medium.   Believability and persuasiveness of messages are influenced by the identity of the perceived source (Balasubramanian, 1994). In the case of advertisements, persuasive agendas are overt and the identities of brand sponsors obvious. For placements, however, where persuasive agendas are covert, the medium can be mistaken for the message source. Characteristics of the media used are thus important in determining the extent to which placements persuade consumers.

Message sources (the media in this case) that are characterized as highly credible are more likely to be believed (Choo, 1964). Though perceptions of both expertise as well as trustworthiness underlie the source credibility construct (Dholakia, Sternthal, & Leavitt, 1978), we constrain our arguments to the latter dimension (i.e., perceptions of trustworthiness) for the present. Eagly et al. (1978) suggest that people who believe a source to be biased or untrustworthy in some way are more likely to resist persuasion. In addition to resisting persuasion, we believe consumers may also feel betrayed when perceiving biases that contradict their initial expectations of ethical conduct. A backlash, fueled by consumer resentment, is therefore possible in reaction to placements noticed in media reputed to be credible and free of commercially motivated biases. On the other hand, conditions may exist

under which consumers do not use media credibility as a predictor of claim believability. We therefore examine mitigating circumstances, specifically the level of involvement consumers have within a product category, when credibility enjoyed by the medium no longer influences claim believability next.

Consumer Involvement With Placed Claims. An examination of the persuasive communications process is incomplete without an inspection of message targets. To this end, we examine audience involvement with placed claims and its influence on persuasion. Different people have different levels of personal interest for most product categories and for information about them. Messages that are personally relevant and of interest to some may be passed over without much thought or consideration by others. These variations in involvement result in the activation of different cognitive processes (Petty & Cacioppo, 1979). The elaboration likelihood model (ELM) posits that highly involved individuals use the central route to persuasion: They carefully attend to message content and generate cognitive responses to arguments used (Petty, Cacioppo, & Schumann, 1983). In contrast, less-involved individuals tend to use the peripheral route to persuasion: They are not motivated to attend to message content and look to cues for discerning message suitability. Examples of cues used within the present context can include attitudes toward and perceived credibility of specific media vehicles (such as specific movies), perceived endorsers (such as actors who use products within the movie), and perceived message sources (also the specific media vehicles here).

Marketers need to take such cues into consideration, especially in communicating with target audiences consisting of individuals having little or no personal stake in a marketing message, taking the specific instance of audiences using source credibility as a cue for determining whether to trust the message content and its source. According to tenets of the ELM, we would expect trust in messages and consequent persuasion for less-involved consumers to be greater when credible media are used. For target audiences consisting mostly of very involved consumers, however, a focus on attributes related to the accuracy and relevance of claims is likely more persuasive.

Marketers again need to consider the potential danger of a backlash from consumers, especially where highly involved individuals are faced with placements in highly credible media. Because highly involved individuals are more likely to pay attention to a placement in that product category and scrutinize claims closely, they are also more likely to notice the persuasive intent of brand inclusions. This underlying manipulative intent, when detected, has the potential to generate feelings of betrayal and possibly a backlash, particularly for media that are expected to be highly credible. This has important implications not only for marketing managers that need to make decisions about placing products but also for media that consider entering into such agreements with companies. Characteristics of target audiences thus warrant judicious investigation prior to the design and implementation phase of placements.

CONCLUSION

Message sponsors typically pay for blurred messages while keeping their identities hidden. The most common form of blurred messages is product placements, a creative yet covert method of brand insinuation into popular culture. It can be hard to discern where editorial comment ends and commercial persuasion begins within the entertainment-information mix inhabited by placed messages. Measures of placement efficacy and conditions under which this efficacy can be enhanced or mitigated are discussed in the following sections.

Placement Efficacy and Its Measures

We address the question of how placement efficacy is best measured. Companies' motives for using product placements can range from improving brand and claim memory to instilling trust in claims to fostering positive brand attitudes, with a view to enhancing persuasive outcomes. It is therefore critical for practitioners and researchers in the field of marketing to think of placement efficacy in terms of more than just the memory and attitudinal variables that have been explored in past literature. Placement efficacy has traditionally been examined from the perspective of companies desiring to use placements within their promotion mix. The effects (especially adverse consumer reactions) of placements with respect to media perceptions are, however, academically underresearched. A more comprehensive measure of placement effectiveness must also incorporate measures such as trust in brand claims and effect on trust in the medium. Because placements affect perceptions of brands as well the media involved, media managers must ensure that placements—though they are lucrative revenue sources—do not adversely influence trust placed in a medium. In this way, we suggest additional variables for gauging placement success and attempt to broaden the manner in which placement efficacy is construed.

Proposed relationships of various message (fit with context, strength of placement), media (media credibility), and consumer (involvement with placed claims, awareness of persuasive intent) characteristics with placement efficacy that were touched on previously are briefly summarized in the following sections.

Influence of Message Fit and Strength on Placement Efficacy. Message

characteristics such as fit with the context are important. People pay more attention to and internalize claims that have a good fit with the context they are placed in. A nonlinear relationship between placement strength and efficacy is further proposed. Efficacy is expected to be low when placements are extremely weak or extremely strong. When placements are too weak, it is hard for audiences to notice them, and when they are extremely strong, consumers become suspicious that a marketing effort is in progress and become skeptical of the claims. At optimum efficacy level,

a placement should be strong enough to get noticed and internalized but not so strong that it generates negative scrutiny.

Influence of Media Credibility on Placement Efficacy. Media credibility is expected to impact placement efficacy in two ways: Placed messages in highly credible media are more likely be believed, and consumers may generate a backlash against credible media if commercially motivated messages get noticed. Credible media are considered honest in their reporting, and consumers could feel betrayed if underlying commercial motives become apparent.

Influence of Consumer Involvement on Placement Efficacy. Finally, the impact of consumer characteristics (such as the level of involvement) was examined. When a message is personally relevant or important to consumers, the likelihood of scrutiny is higher. At high levels of involvement, consumers are more likely to ignore media characteristics (like credibility) as cues and scrutinize claims closely.

Two additional issues regarding placements warrant further investigation: implications of placements for consumer deception (and hence public policy legislation) and the examination of placements in media beyond movies and television programs.

Government Regulation of Placement Practices

The virtues of product placements have frequently been extolled by past researchers. Chief among these are hidden commercial sponsorship and seamless integration within media content. It is assumed here that audiences are largely unaware of the commercial intent behind brand placements. Consumers who are unaware that they are targets for persuasive messages are less likely to become skeptical and scrutinize claims. Arguments for the advantage of placements over other overt forms of marketing are to a large part based on this assumption. If this holds true, there is an implicit conflict between the need to make a placement effective and the need to protect consumers from being misled. This raises questions about the ethicality of such practices and the government regulation of industry practices. We can turn the argument around and contend that audiences are sophisticated, and conditions do exist where consumers realize that brands are commercially placed within media content. Consumers who are aware and accepting of placements as legitimate forms of marketing efforts engage in critical thinking, thereby obviating the need for government legislation.

Placements in Varied Media

Most previous research has looked at the effects of placements in visual entertainment media like movies and television programs. Different media, however, are associated with different characteristics, and other forms of media are extensively

used in conveying embedded messages as well (e.g., print media). Generalizing wisdom garnered from research in visual media to understand placements in another medium might not be optimal, not least due to potential differences on relevant media characteristics. The additional examination of placements in media like books and magazines have worth, given that companies are increasingly looking to creatively cut through the clutter of traditional communication methods.

In summary, therefore, placing products within entertainment content has varied implications for marketing practitioners (What are the best practices for designing effective placements? What types of media are most desirable?), marketing theory (What are the implications of media credibility, audience involvement, and awareness for trust in claims and trust in the medium?), and for public policymakers (Do placements deceive consumers, thereby warranting regulation?). In closing, we reiterate that much needs to be done within the area of blurred communications and particularly product placements. Fresh insights into best practices for the industry need to emerge as an outcome of further investigations.

REFERENCES

Aaker, D. A., & Keller, K. L. (1990). Consumer evaluations of brand extensions. *Journal of Marketing, 54*, 27–41.
Aksoy, L., & Bloom, P. (1999). *The effects of cultural orientation and trust toward marketers on the level of consumer deception.* Proceedings of the Cross-Cultural Research Conference, Association for Consumer Research, Cancun, Mexico.
Babin, L. A., & Carder, S. T. (1996). Viewers' recognition of brands placed within a film. *International Journal of Advertising, 15*, 140–151.
Baker, M. J., & Crawford, H. A. (1996). Product placements. In E. A. Blair & W. A. Kamakura (Eds.), *Proceedings of the Winter Marketing Educator's Conference* (p. 312). Chicago: American Marketing Association.
Balasubramanian, S. K. (1994). Beyond advertising and publicity: Hybrid messages and public policy issues. *Journal of Advertising, 23*, 29–46.
Bandura, A. (1977). *Social learning theory.* Engelwood Cliffs, NJ: Prentice Hall.
Bhatnagar, N., Aksoy, L., & Malkoc, S. (2002, May). *Efficacy of brand placements versus advertisements: The impact of brand familiarity and media credibility on attitude towards brand claims, trust in brand sponsors and trust in the communication medium.* Paper presented at meeting of the Advertising and Consumer Psychology Conference, New York.
Boush, D. M., Friestad, M., & Rose, G. M. (1994). Adolescent skepticism toward TV advertising and knowledge of advertiser tactics. *Journal of Consumer Research, 21*, 165–175.
Calfee, J. E., & Ringold, D. J. (1988). Consumer skepticism and advertising regulation: What do the polls show? In M. J. Houston (Ed.), *Advances in consumer research* (Vol. 15, pp. 244–248). Provo, UT: Association for Consumer Research.
Choo, T. (1964). Communicator credibility and communication discrepancy as determinants of opinion change. *Journal of Social Psychology, 64*, 1–20.
Cohen, D. (1988). *Advertising.* Glenview, IL: Scott Foresman.
DeLorme, D. E., & Reid, L. N. (1999). Moviegoers' experiences and interpretations of brands in films revisited. *Journal of Advertising, 27*, 71–95.

Dholakia, R. R., Sternthal, B., & Leavitt, C. (1978). The persuasive effect of source credibility: Tests of cognitive reponses. *Journal of Consumer Research, 4,* 252.

Eagly, A. H., Wood, W., & Chaiken, S. (1978). Causal inferences about communicators and their effect on opinion change. *Journal of Personality and Social Psychology, 36,* 424–435.

Fournier, S., & Wojnicki, A. (1999). *Launching the BMW Z3 Roadster.* Cambridge, MA: Harvard Business School Publishing.

Friestad, M., & Wright, P. (1994). The persuasion knowledge model: How people cope with persuasion attempts. *Journal of Consumer Research, 21,* 1–31.

Gorn, G. J. (1982). The effect of music in advertising on choice behavior: A classical conditioning approach. *Journal of Marketing, 46,* 84–101.

Gould, S. J., Gupta, P. B., & Grabner-Krauter, S. (2000). Product placements in movies: A cross-cultural analysis of Austrian, French and American consumers' attitudes toward this emerging international promotional medium. *Journal of Advertising, 29,* 41–59.

Gupta, P. B., & Gould, S. J. (1997). Consumers' perceptions of the ethics and acceptability of product placements in movies: Product category and individual differences. *Journal of Current Issues and Research in Advertising, 19,* 37–50.

Gupta, P. B., Gould, S. J., & Lord, K. R. (1998). Product placement in movies: The effect of prominence and mode on audience recall. *Journal of Current Issues and Research in Advertising, 20,* 47–59.

Karrh, J. A. (1994). Effects of brand placements in motion pictures. In K. W. King (Ed.), *Proceedings of the 1994 conference of the American Academy of Advertising* (pp. 90–96). Athens, GA: American Academy of Advertising.

Kelley, H. H. (1972). Attribution in social interaction. In E. E. Jones, D. E. Kanouse, H. H. Kelley, R. E. Nisbett, S. Valins, & B. Weiner (Eds.), *Attribution: Perceiving the causes of behavior* (pp. 1–26). Morristown, NJ: General Learning Press.

Kim, E. (2002). Buy this space: The evil power of the swoosh. *The Daily Tar Heel.* Retrieved June 30, 2002, from http://www.dailytarheel.com/vnews/display.v/ART/2002/01/22/3c4d727eee4d1?in_archive=1

Kotler, P., & Armstrong, G. (2001). *Principles of marketing.* Upper Saddle River, NJ: Prentice Hall.

Magiera, M. (1990). Disney plugs up new film. *Advertising Age, 63,* 4.

Mills, J., & Jellison, J. M. (1967). Effect on opinion change of how desirable the communication is to the audience the communicator addressed. *Journal of Personality and Social Psychology, 6,* 98–101.

Nebenzahl, I. D., & Secunda, E. (1993). Consumers' attitudes toward product placement in movies. *International Journal of Advertising, 12,* 1–11.

Ong, B. S., & Meri, D. (1994). Should product placement in movies be banned? *Journal of Promotion Management, 2,* 159–175.

Petty, R. E., & Cacioppo J. T. (1979). Issue involvement can increase or decrease persuasion by enhancing message relevant cognitive responses. *Journal of Personality and Social Psychology, 37,* 1915–1926.

Petty, R. E., Cacioppo, J. T., & Schumann, D. (1983). Central and peripheral routes to advertising effectiveness: The moderating role of consumer involvement. *Journal of Consumer Research, 10,* 135–146.

Rothenberg, R. (1991, May 31). Critics seek F.T.C. action on products as movie stars. *New York Times,* p. D1.

Ruskin, G. (2001). *Authors ask editors to treat Fay Weldon's new work as an ad, not a book.* Retrieved June 30, 2002, from http://lists.essential.org/pipermail/commercial-alert/2001/000094. html

Sandler, D. M., & Secunda, E. (1993). Point of view: Blurred boundaries—Where does editorial end and advertising begin? *Journal of Advertising Research, 33,* 73–80.

Schudson, M. (1984). *Advertising, the uneasy persuasion.* New York: Basic Books.

Solomon, M., & Englis, B. G. (1996). Consumption constellations: Implications for integrated communications strategy. In E. Thorson & J. Moore (Eds.), *Integrated communication: Synergy of persuasive voices* (pp. 65–86). Mahwah, NJ: Lawrence Erlbaum Associates.

Steortz, E. M. (1987). *The cost efficiency and communication effects associated with brand exposure within motion pictures.* Unpublished master's thesis, University of West Virginia.

Vollmers, S., & Mizerski, R. (1994). A review and investigation into the effectiveness of product placements in films. In K. W. King (Ed.), *Proceedings of the 1994 conference of the American Academy of Advertising* (pp. 97–102). Athens, GA: American Academy of Advertising.

Von Restorff, H. (1933). Uber die wirkung von bereichsbildungen in spurenfeld. [About the effects of the formation of categories in fields of small entities.]. *Psychologisch Forschung, 18,* 299–342.

Winski, J. M. (1982). Hershey befriends extra-terrestrial. *Advertising Age, 53,* 1.

Zimmer, M. R., & DeLorme D. (1997, July 30–August 2). *The effects of brand placement type and a disclaimer on memory for brand placements in movies.* Paper presented at the meeting of the Association for Education in Journalism and Mass Communication, Chicago.

CHAPTER SEVEN

The "Delicious Paradox": Preconscious Processing of Product Placements by Children

Susan Auty
Charlie Lewis
Lancaster University

> *Here is what is offensive. . . . Movies that strew product placement through scenes (not just S***bucks but P*zza H*t and S*ven-El*ven) hoping we will notice only subliminally.*
>
> (from a review by Andrews in the *Financial Times* of *I Am Sam*, May 9, 2002, p. 16)

In the relatively short space of 50 years, children's lives have been transformed by the easily accessible moving images of television and video, which have blurred the lines between reality and fantasy, between fact and fiction, and between entertainment and commercial communication. Quite a lot of research has been done on the social effects of these media on children (for a review see John, 1999, and for longitudinal evidence about children's behavior after the introduction of TV in St. Helena, see Charlton, Davie, Panting, Abrahams, & Yon, 2001). Yet the research literature presents contradictory evidence about whether these media exert a negative or positive effect on children's understanding of the world (Sheppard, 1994). In turn, apart from studies of smoking initiation, almost no research has been done on how TV- and film-mediated understanding affects children's choice of the branded goods commonly displayed within programming. Product placement, or the appearance of branded goods within entertainment, is not strictly subliminal communication, as suggested in the film review cited at the beginning of this chapter, because products usually have exposure times measured in seconds rather than

117

milliseconds, often with some verbal labeling. However, as Erdelyi and Zizak (this volume) point out, subliminality was initially understood to be an inaccessibility to consciousness, in which case product placement may be considered to be subliminal. Its effects are taken to be tacit or implicit because recollection of the brands may be unreliable or unavailable. If the effect is subliminal—unconscious influence on choice—then there is a need to understand how it works on children, whose cognitive defenses against the possibility of such influence have not been developed.

Studies of adolescent smoking behavior indicate that when an actor is shown smoking in a film, viewers may associate a type of person with the brand that is shown. Adolescents absorb the images of the actors and use them in developing their own attitudes toward smoking and also their own identity as a smoker (Sargent et al., 2001). Product placement, however, extends into a wide range of products aimed at a wide range of ages, including very young children. Indeed, the most often quoted example of successful placement is Reese's Pieces in the film *E. T.* A consideration of how product placement works from a psychological point of view, especially in the developing child, is overdue.

AN EXPERIMENT WITH CHILDREN

In an attempt to see if product placement has any effect on children's behavior, we recently conducted an experiment to see if children notice product placement in movies, and, if they do, if it has any concomitant effect on their choice within the product category (Auty & Lewis, 2002). We showed 105 children (i.e., four classes), 6–7 years old and 11–12 years old, a brief clip from the movie *Home Alone*. Half were shown a scene in which Pepsi Cola is mentioned and spilled on the table; the other half were shown a similar scene with food and milk but no branded products. Having obtained parental permission to offer them a soft drink, we invited the children individually to help themselves to a drink from a choice of Coke or Pepsi before asking them to describe what they saw in the clip. Every participant was interviewed separately in a fixed-format interview with successive prompts to see if those in the treatment group would more easily recall the brand Pepsi by name. Those who were exposed to the branded clip were significantly more likely to choose Pepsi than Coke. This effect on choice was more pronounced for those who had seen the film before, even if they were not, after prompting, able to recall seeing Pepsi. Notably, the 6–7 year olds in the branded group were less able to recall the brand than the older children were but were just as likely to choose Pepsi to drink.

This result raises many psychological and ethical questions about the practice of product placement. Some of the psychological questions follow:

- Why should product placement have this effect?
- Why should conscious memory of the product not be necessary to produce the effect?

- Why does prior exposure appear to strengthen this effect?
- How long does the effect last on each reminder occasion?
- What implications does this effect have for children's exposure to entertainment that includes product placement?

The main ethical issue that stems from these implications is if product placement is found in further studies to have a discernible effect on product choice, are there grounds for banning the practice in films and other forms of entertainment (e.g., cartoons promoting toys) targeted at children?

In this chapter, we suggest preliminary answers to some of these questions based on related literature on the psychology of advertising, development, and information processing. We examine the issues that might warrant greater regulation of product placement in the entertainment industry and pose some research questions designed to examine the effect of product placement on children in detail. An initial model of how product placements may be processed is put forward for further comment and refinement.

PROCESSING PRODUCT PLACEMENT INFORMATION

In the study just described, the surprising dissociation between the children's ability to recall having seen Pepsi and their choice of this brand over its more successful competitor in the market is, of course, the very effect—increased interest, sales— that advertisers strive for. Yet until relatively recently psychological models of memory have been hard-pressed to account for them. However, research within psychology in the past 15 years has suggested a need to separate out consciously controlled processes that involve well-known techniques of recognition and recall (explicit memory) from nonconscious types of memory in which exposure to an item influences later processing of the item or attitudes toward it without the person necessarily being aware of such an influence.

Perhaps the best demonstration of such effects is the research on adults' recall of advertisements in popular magazines, which was conducted by Tim Perfect and his colleagues (e.g., Perfect & Askew, 1994), similar to earlier work by Janiszewski (1988). They divided participants into two groups. One group was told that they were involved in research on ads (deliberate exposure), whereas the second group was asked to look at the articles in a magazine to judge its layout and readability (incidental exposure). Not surprisingly, the deliberate exposure group was able to distinguish between advertisements seen in the magazines from those not previously seen. However, there was a clear effect in both groups on a range of measures of the effectiveness of the ads. Even though they had not recognized whether they had seen an advertisement, the incidental group still rated pictures seen previously as more appealing, distinctive, and eye-catching. Findings reported

more recently by Shapiro, MacInnis, and Heckler (1997) have again confirmed this affective influence of incidental exposure.

These results tie in with a series of experiments on memory for more abstract stimuli. Not only does the exposure to a picture make adults and children more able to recognize decomposed pictures that present only a small amount of information (Parkin & Streete, 1988), but also subliminally presented abstract geometric shapes (e.g., polygons) are not recognized as having been seen before, although they tend to be identified as preferable to new stimuli on affective rating scales (Kunst-Wilson & Zajonc, 1980). So both laboratory data and experiments with advertisements appear to show that mere exposure to stimuli influences our reactions to them without our being aware of these effects. Mere exposure has frequently been used to explain the effect of advertising, particularly of products that arouse little involvement on the part of the consumer. Perfect and Askew (1994) refer to this dissociation between awareness and response as a delicious paradox. Before we attempt to explore the effect of product exposure in children we must consider what this paradox implies for our understanding of memory and the place of implicit processes within it.

EXPLICIT AND IMPLICIT MEMORY

The dissociation of implicit and explicit memory is widely accepted within models of memory, although there are still divisions about whether it represents two memory systems or different thresholds of activation (Whittlesea & Price, 2001). To understand the mere-exposure effect that we found, a dual system is a useful starting point because it separates the effects of exposure and active recall. A typical dual system model is Parkin's (1997) distinction between the explicit (declarative) systems of semantic and episodic memory, which are by definition accessible to recollection, and a group of lower level (procedural) functions that form implicit memory, which do not require recollection but do not necessarily preclude it. In this scheme processes such as everyday motor or learned responses do not demand consciously recalled events. Parkin's differentiation suggests that implicit memory is not a single process so much as a range of related skills that share the delicious paradox of being dissociable from conscious reflection. We feel that such a distinction can be used to understand the conscious/nonconscious differences reported above.

Kihlstrom (1987) in his review of the cognitive unconscious notes that "a great deal of information processing takes place outside of working memory" (p. 1448). An argument that supports the effectiveness of subliminal advertising and "other forms of surreptitious social influence" (among which we might include product placement) concerns the role of a priming stimulus that "can activate procedural knowledge, and thus affect the way that consumers think about products, or perhaps even their actual buying behavior" (p. 1448). Unconscious procedural knowledge

is described both as innate and automatic; it may work in a social domain as well as for more overtly cognitive operations, such as tying a knot:

> Speakers may like one face more than another, while being unable to say exactly why they have that preference. A large number of social judgments and inferences, especially those guiding first impressions, appear to be mediated by such unconscious processes. . . . Thus, people may reach conclusions about events—for example, their emotional valence—and act on these judgments without being able to articulate the reasoning by which they were reached. (p. 1447)

Fluency

If implicit memory is dissociable from other types of recall, how does implicit memory work? This is no easy problem to tackle, particularly because to date there are no brain imaging data to suggest different pathways for explicit and procedural functions. Psychologists since William James (1892) have pointed out that remembering does not simply involve recalling an event. Jacoby (e.g., Jacoby, Kelley, & Dywan, 1989) has long argued that the very reconstructive nature of memory is the key to our understanding of implicit processes: "Subjective experience involves an attribution or unconscious attribution that is as much a function of the present as it is of the past" (p. 392). However, "the tie between representation and subjective experience is actually a loose one" (p. 393). He devised the concept of fluency to explain the workings of implicit memory.

This concept involves attributional processes in which we identify familiarity or pastness in a relatively automatic way—akin to labeling emotions as a consequence of one's physiological arousal. Sanyal (1992) suggested that some consumer choices might be influenced by perceptual fluency, but little research has been carried out that might confirm or refute his theory. Chung and Szymanski (1997) found in their experiments with low-involvement goods that consumers seem to rely on visual perceptions and then make choices because the item seen previously pops out at them as being somehow familiar. This supports Jacoby's view that it is cognition about the cause of arousal that determines the feeling that is experienced, and such reactions are based on influences that are both perceptual (e.g., seeing a bottle of Pepsi for the second time in 4 hours) and conceptual (e.g., having familiarity with and views about soda brands). Familiarity, as Yonelinas (2002) points out in his discussion of Jacoby's model, "is not limited to perceptual fluency, but rather can also reflect conceptual fluency (i.e., enhanced processing of the meaning of the stimuli)" (p. 445).

Divisions and Links in Explicit and Implicit Memory

Much debate surrounds the relationship between declarative (explicit) and procedural (implicit) memory. A brief review of the distinctions made in cognitive psychology should serve to illustrate the complexity of the issues. Theoretical

attempts simply to equate perceptual processing with unconscious memory and conceptual processing with conscious memory were unable to explain experimental findings (see Yonelinas, 2002, for a review of recollection and familiarity). According to Yonelinas, the absence of a neat division between the two may be in part explained by Tulving's (1982) model of declarative memory as comprising both episodic and semantic subsystems, each relying on different areas of the brain. Episodic memory is a record of personal history entailed in recollection, whereas semantic memory is a general knowledge store entailed in the experience of "knowing." Tulving (1982) at first believed that perceptual implicit memory somehow used semantic memory to produce a feeling of familiarity but revised this in later work (Tulving & Schacter, 1990) to distinguish familiarity from perceptual memory. Familiarity was allowed to include the possibility of a link between the episodic and semantic systems. Retrieval in the declarative memory system is still believed to be independent, allowing either episodic or semantic memory to feed in to the sense of familiarity. Perceptual implicit memory, in this view, remains separate, and, as noted previously, Jacoby (Jacoby et al., 1989) argues that familiarity is influenced by conceptual fluency and thus conceptual implicit memory.

Under the familiarity or fluency model, the initial exposure to a stimulus may be such as to elude conscious awareness of the event, but its effect may be evident from a change in task performance that may be attributed only to that event. According to this conception of preconscious perception of product placement, the viewer is exposed to the product and pays attention to it at some sensorimotor level—to use Piaget's term—but below the level of conscious recollection. This perception is sufficient for the item to be more easily processed on a subsequent occasion but without awareness of any prompt. The sense of familiarity aroused by the reminder as a result of the prior exposure (possibly combined with prior knowledge) leads to the ease of processing.

Explaining the Mere-Exposure Effect

Toth (2000) points out that the fluent reprocessing that arises from prior exposure is conceptually similar to the mere-exposure paradigm first put forward by Zajonc (1968). Jacoby's (Jacoby et al., 1989) fluency theory, indeed, seems to us to provide a mechanism for the mere-exposure theory and therefore to provide a coherent explanation for the effect produced by product placement. Preference for such a product becomes "a misinterpretation of the effects of the past as a pleasing quality of the stimulus rather than as a feeling of familiarity" (Jacoby et al., 1989, p. 402). The processing fluency should be even greater if the scene has been seen more than once, as we found in our experiment.

Toth (2000) highlights research concerning the context specificity of unconscious memory that is particularly relevant to product placement (e.g., Hayman & Tulving, 1989). Indeed, Johnstone and Dodd (2000) discovered that when *Spice*

Girls—The Movie was promoted in Pepsi ads, but Pepsi did not appear in the movie, people were unable to make an association between the two in an explicit test of brand salience. This lack of a link may simply be a function of the explicit measures used. However, it fits in with our suggestion that implicit memory—both procedural and conceptual—can be used to explain the effect of product placement where the context remains constant: The reminder of prior exposure leads to familiarity and hence to choice.

HOW PRODUCT PLACEMENT INFLUENCES CHOICE

Our proposed model of how exposure to product placement influences choice (see Fig. 7.1) builds on Parkin's (1997) model of memory and suggests that incidental exposure will take the implicit route to memory, where classical conditioning, perceptual learning, and verbal priming (especially when the product name is spoken while it is shown on screen) may singly or jointly combine with semantic memory. Semantic memory is our conscious understanding of concepts and their relation to one another; it may be linked to episodic memory, which Parkin (1997) compares to

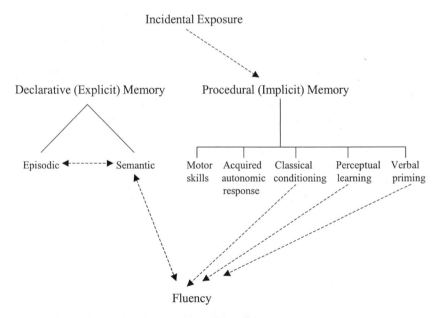

FIG. 7.1 A model based on a dual memory system showing the proposed processing of product placements, where the dotted lines represent responses that may be activated to produce the effect of fluency. Adapted from Figure 5.1 by Parkin, A. (1997). In N. Cowan (Ed.), *Development of Memory in Childhood* (p. 118) © Psychology Press. Reprinted with permission.

a black box flight recorder in that it is the record of events in their specific temporal order. Our double-headed arrows between the two types of declarative memory and between semantic memory and fluency are intended to suggest that earlier memories of pleasurable experience with a product may interact in a nonconscious way with implicit memory in producing the fluency effect, such that when offered a choice from the product category, the person will experience positive affect toward the placed product.

Duration of the Effect

If one accepts that the operation of implicit memory accounts for the observed effect of product placement on choice, the question of most interest then is, how long does this effect last when a reminder stimulus is presented? The literature on the processing of picture identification, which involves participants identifying previously seen pictures from increasingly detailed fragments, suggests that the priming effect of the initial exposure lasts for at least 48 hours and possibly more than a week (Hayes & Hennessy, 1996). Indeed, the length of time that priming effects last is still a matter of debate. Earlier research by Sloman, Hayman, Ohta, Law, and Tulving (1988) found effects lasting months and even up to a year using implicit memory tests.

In light of the findings on context specificity, it is notable, too, that priming effects were found by Hayes and Hennessey (1996) to transfer to new pictures that closely resemble the original items in specific features, as in two different views of a horse. The latter finding suggests that the prime is not being exclusively encoded photographically but also conceptually: "Every time an object is perceived, a single representation which incorporates both perceptual and conceptual features is constructed and it is this representation that mediates priming" (Hayes & Hennessy, 1996, p. 37). Such a theory helps to explain why even the 6–7 year olds seemed to be able to transfer the old image of Pepsi from the movie to the new bottle in making their choice of a drink, although it may have affected their ability to recall the brand. Other studies (e.g., Cermak, Talbot, Chandler, & Wolbarst, 1985) have found that priming effects are greater for words than for nonwords. These findings support the link between semantic memory and implicit memory, as suggested by our proposed model.

IMPLICIT MEMORY IN CHILDREN

The distinction between implicit and explicit memory is especially important for the understanding of children's perceptions of promotional material because implicit memory does not appear to be affected by increasing maturity, whereas explicit measures may fail with children, simply because children are not capable of the retrieval required by the task. Many researchers have found that performance

on a wide range of explicit memory tests improves substantially from early child-hood to adolescence (for a review, see Kail, 1990).

How can we be confident that implicit memory is relatively well attuned in children? The research suggests that even infants show the same fluency effects as adults. For example, Rovee-Collier (1989) conditioned 6-month-old infants to kick in the presence of a hanging mobile toy suspended over their crib. Two weeks later, she found that they kicked when the mobile was presented but not when a slightly modified one was placed on the crib. This and her subsequent work (e.g., Gerhardstein, Adler, & Rovee-Collier, 2000) suggest that implicit skills are present at an early age and continue to be differentiated from slowly developing explicit skills. Such effects are demonstrable in laboratory and applied research with children. Parkin and Streete (1988) found evidence of implicit memory using fragmented picture recognition in children age 3 years, despite their having deficits in explicit memory compared with older children (ages 5 and 7 years). Drummey and Newcombe (1995), moreover, show that perceptual priming occurs in 3-year-old children, even when recognition memory is no more than at chance level. Parkin (1993) suggests that the newborn child may "possess a range of implicit learning abilities that enable the development of crude classifications such as familiar-unfamiliar" (p. 204).

Implicit Learning and Behavior

The experimental data appear to carry over to real-world research. For example, Naito (1990) and Naito and Komatsu (1993) have found implicit learning in young children, leaving open the possibility suggested by Krishnan and Chakravarti (1999) that positive affect toward cigarettes and alcohol may be learned early on from advertising and acted on in later life without conscious links to ad exposure. Of particular interest in the research into implicit memory is again the notion of priming and context specificity. Naito and Komatsu (1993) suggest that reactivation of a primed stimulus is "highly specific to the contextual information of the original training, because the reactivation treatment was made ineffective by a change in the reminder" (p. 237). This leads to the implication that in the case of product placement, the film context is an important part of the reminder, and reactivation would probably not occur if an advertising message were to be substituted for the film clip in an experiment.

Familarity and processing fluency seem to be the keys to explaining our findings described at the outset of this chapter. Brightly colored packages of branded goods may be perceived implicitly in a manner similar to other familiar stimuli, such as faces, which have been found (when priming occurs) to be recognizable very early in life (Ellis, Ellis, & Hosie, 1993). Given that memory performance is a function in part of one's knowledge base (Naito & Komatsu, 1993) and that children have fewer knowledge pegs of products on which to hang their memories, one could theorize that more of their product perceptions in films and TV will be at a preconscious

level and lead to implicit rather than explicit memories. In this view, the exposure acts as a priming for later exposures simply because it makes the branded product accessible to more fluent processing and a greater need to attribute meaning to the increased fluency because the fluency is experienced as positive affect.

Given the relatively slow development of mnemonic skills like rehearsal of the grouping or "chunking" of information and also the lack of an understanding of the processes of memory (Kail, 1990), our thesis is that young children use implicit processing skills to construct a "language" based on the peripheral and unanalyzed information acquired from their viewing for use in an implicit script of everyday behavior. They acquire feelings about the way things are done that contribute to their learned behaviors, such as consumer choices.

Product Placement and Children's Behavioral Scripts

Does this language of behavior serve to enhance children's position in the family, allowing them as they develop to interpret and take part in the family's consumer decisions? Peracchio's (1993) research suggests that 5-year-olds are capable of explicitly learning scripts for consumer behavior from repeated viewings of audiovisual narratives about consumer–product exchanges. Do these scripts benefit from the implicit memories of product placement? In this view, accessible and inaccessible perceptions are interconnected and provide information for each other in a way that becomes, with development, increasingly elaborate and systematic. The implication is that images of the products in placements are perceived but not analyzed until the conceptual system "determines what gets perceptually processed" (Mandler, 1988, p. 132). This view is consistent with the developing child making greater use of implicit memories as these become important, perhaps for social reasons. Drummey and Newcombe (1995) seem to concur with this possibility when they suggest that "developmental changes in the understanding and use of the relations between explicit and implicit memory may account in part for age-related growth in explicit memory" (p. 563).

Then the question arises, does the script get put into action invariably once it has been written, or are children subject to competing scripts depending on the reactivation or repetition priming of stimuli? Such a view would suggest the importance of primacy and recency effects, first detected in the learning of nonsense syllables by Ebbinghaus (1885) and found to be particularly relevant for measuring the impact of television advertising (Krugman, 1965). Some form of activation of the priming stimulus, which needs to be context specific, such as another viewing of the film or at least the relevant scene, seems to be required for choice to be affected by implicit memories. Also important to processing fluency might be existing familiarity with the product. Baker (1999) found that prior familiarity appears to inoculate brands against attempts to influence choice through the use of preconscious methods. This finding suggests that getting written into the script at an early stage is an important consideration for brands, perhaps another manifestation of the primacy effect.

Are Children Especially Susceptible to Product Placement?

It is perhaps not surprising that young children are captivated by pictorial images. Much research has been done on the differences between the information processing of children and adults from television versus print or radio (e.g., Walma van der Molen & van der Voort, 2000). Whereas in adults reading or audio messages are more effectively learned than those from television, in children early studies have indicated more complete and accurate recall of stories from television over print. This result occurs regardless of reading proficiency (Walma van der Molen & van der Voort, 2000).

Work with very young children (ages 4–10) by Roberts and Blades (2000) points to another area of potential difference in how children process information from visual images: their ability to distinguish the source of their information. Differing explanations are provided for the greater confusion of sources for 4-year-olds than for 10-year-olds under conditions of direct questioning but not in free recall. The only generalizable finding from this research is that age and time between events are both significant mediators in accurate recall. Clearly, an apparent confusion between fiction and reality has implications for children's ability to construct a realistic view of product usage from their knowledge acquired from entertaining programming.

The influence of prior knowledge is an important consideration in any examination of the processing of product placement messages in children. From studies of advertising's effect on children, we know that full understanding of the commercial intentions of advertising messages is not usually established until about 8 years of age, and many 10-year-olds still do not grasp the persuasive intentions (Macklin 1987; Oates, Blades, & Gunter, 2001). Certainly young children respond to advertising. Among very young children (3- to 6-year-olds), 81% can describe the product after having seen the logo for Coca-Cola (Dammler & Middelman-Motz, 2002). Moore and Lutz (2000) found that 7-year-olds "used commercials as a means of discovering heretofore unrecognized opportunities and desires" (p. 42), such as compiling a birthday list. Moreover, these children demonstrated unprompted knowledge of line extensions and brand differences, and 10-year-olds showed increasing insight into the relationship between advertising and products.

Advertising Literacy in Children

Advertising literacy is generally believed to become sophisticated only from early adolescence because it is closely related to an ability to understand the psychological dimensions of a narrative as well as the figurative meanings of language (see Moore & Lutz, 2000; Ritson & Elliott, 1995). In many ways it appears as if a sophisticated understanding of advertising will actually militate against effective commercial communications because it will stimulate counterargument (d'Astous & Chartier, 2000). In older children and adults, there is always the

possibility that conscious countercontrol may offset the emotional response to product placements (Ye & van Raaij, 1997).

Moreover, if a conscious link is made, it may have a negative effect on any subsequent choice decision. If higher order analysis accompanies the initial exposure, then any positive affect may be offset by the negative attitudes formed, assuming resistance to overt placements by the audience, who may perceive it as manipulation. Adults may be able to guard against preconscious perceptions simply by noting the appearance of a product as a placement with a commercial origin. Brucks, Armstrong, and Goldberg (1988), however, found that children 8–12 years of age need cues to produce counterarguments and suggest that cues would not be effective for children younger than 8 years. Hence, one could argue that product placement is likely to be most effective in young children, precisely because it is almost always preconscious, allowing affect without (conscious) cognition: a delicious paradox with potentially insidious and powerful effects.

ETHICAL IMPLICATIONS

If children are being exposed to implicitly processed commercial messages almost every time they watch a film or video, and, increasingly, every time they play a video game (Nelson, 2002), there is a need to understand more precisely what kind of influence these messages are having on their choices. That children do not display explicit recall or even any recognition of the placed product does not mean that they are not affected by these messages, especially cumulatively. It may seem fairly benign to have Pepsi Cola mentioned and drunk at a family meal in *Home Alone*, and the alternative of a generic cola without a doubt would detract from the verisimilitude of the scene. Nevertheless, an awareness of the potential power of product placement messages is needed by program makers and regulators if only to protect children from unsuitable messages. For products such as cigarettes and alcohol, the brand of the product is not the important issue—rather it is the invisible scripting that may be going on in children, leaving them with implicit perceptions of smoking and (often excessive) drinking as behavior associated with being grown up. It is notable that smoking initiation among adolescents in the United States resumed its upward trend after a dip from 1980–1984. Over the entire 1980s, expenditure on cigarette advertising decreased, while expenditure on promotion (including promotional allowances, sampling, entertainment and store displays) went up almost threefold in real terms (Centers for Disease Control and Prevention, 1995). Depiction of smoking in films, but not television, followed a similar trend (Pechmann & Shih, 1999). Can it be that the dip in smoking initiation in the early 1980s was associated with Larry Hagman's ban on smoking by characters in the TV series *Dallas*, supported by less-publicized abstentions in other television programs?

SUMMARY AND CONCLUSION: A BLUEPRINT FOR RESEARCH ON CHILDREN AND PRODUCT PLACEMENT

There is a need for much more experimental research into the effect of product placement on children. Several questions have arisen in the course of this exploratory chapter:

- How much exposure is needed for an effect to be produced, both in terms of length of time on the screen and number of repetitions?
- How long do the effects last?
- At what age do children start noticing product placement explicitly?

The research addressed in this chapter suggests that exposure and choice are closely related, despite this association not being accessible to conscious awareness. Memory research also seems to show that fluency effects last more than a week, but we need to explore whether product placement might have such lasting effects.

Questions specifically related to how implicit memory may interact with explicit memory also need to be addressed:

- What is the relationship (if any) between explicit and implicit memory? What determines the direction of the influence?
- To what extent is prior familiarity with the stimulus a factor in the effectiveness of product placement? Is the effect more or less pronounced in the case of novel products?
- Are children more susceptible than adults to the influence of implicit memory?

These are crucial questions both in our understanding of human memory and how market researchers can apply theories of memory to real-world issues, such as product placement. We believe that research on such applied effects and complex theories of memory can exert a mutual influence on one another, as some of the research we have discussed in this chapter suggests (e.g., Perfect & Askew, 1994). We also believe that comparisons between children and adults often help in our understanding of the way memory influences our actions.

Assuming that future experiments confirm the influence of product placement on children's choice, ethical issues are also raised:

- What might be the effect of regulating such placements?
- And, hence, what would be the best form of regulation?

The role of implicit memory in children's development is also worthy of more research. As most data on product placement come out of the laboratory, we

need to examine how this form of marketing communication works in the real world—particularly how it filters into other aspects of behavior, for example, the following:

- How does it influence negotiations between parents and children in the choice of products?
- How does it affect children's peer discussions and, indeed, their role in those discussions about products?

Finally, the theory and data reported in this chapter suggest that the practical issue of how advertising research is currently conducted should also be investigated. The findings of recent research into memory need to be diffused throughout the advertising industry. If the delicious paradox of exposures that influence choice without conscious recollection is confirmed, should agencies continue to measure the effectiveness of ads by eliciting day-after recall? When the influence of their messages might be much more subtle than simple awareness, especially in the case of children, does it make sense to test advertising communications—their creative elements and minimum effective frequencies—using measures of explicit memory?

ACKNOWLEDGMENTS

We wish to thank Diarmaid McDonald and Philip Sheppard for collecting the experimental data on product placement. We are grateful to Steve Dewhurst for his suggested modifications to an earlier version of this chapter.

REFERENCES

Andrews, N. (2002). The true meaning of "offensive." *Financial Times* (May 9), 116.
Auty, S., & Lewis, C. (2002, May). *The effect of product placement on children.* Paper presented at the 21st Annual Advertising and Consumer Psychology Conference, New York.
Baker, W. E. (1999). When can affective conditioning and mere exposure directly influence brand choice? *Journal of Advertising, 28*(4), 31–46.
Brucks, M, Armstrong, G. M., & Goldberg, M. E. (1988). Children's use of cognitive defenses against television advertising: A cognitive response approach. *Journal of Consumer Research, 14*, 471–482.
Centers for Disease Control and Prevention. (1995). Trends in smoking initiation among adolescents and young adults—United States, 1980–1989. *Morbidity and Mortality Weekly Report, 44*(28), 521–525.
Cermak, L. S., Talbot, N., Chandler, K., & Wolbarst, L. R. (1985). The perceptual priming phenomenon in amnesia. *Neuropsychologia, 23*, 615–622.

Charlton, T., Davie, R., Panting, C., Abrahams, M., & Yon, L. (2001). Monitoring children's behaviour in a remote community before and six years after the availability of broadcast TV. *North American Journal of Psychology, 3*, 429–440.

Chung, S. W., & Szymanski, K. (1997). Effects of brand name exposure on brand choices: An implicit memory perspective. In M. Brucks & D. MacInnis (Eds.), *Advances in consumer research* (Vol. 24, pp. 288–294). Provo, UT: Association of Consumer Research.

Dammler, A., & Middelman-Motz, A. V. (2002). "I want the one with Harry Potter on it." *International Journal of Advertising & Marketing to Children, 3*, 3–8.

d'Astous, A., & Chartier, F. (2000). A study of factors affecting consumer evaluations and memory of product placements in movies. *Journal of Current Issues and Research in Advertising, 22*(2), 31–40.

Drummey, A. B., & Newcombe, N. (1995). Remembering versus knowing the past: Children's explicit and implicit memories for pictures. *Journal of Experimental Child Psychology, 59*, 549–565.

Ebbinghaus, H. (1885). *Memory: A contribution to experimental psychology.* Retrieved June 6, 2002, from http://psychclassics.yorku.ca/Ebbinghaus/memory9.htm

Ellis, H. D., Ellis, D. M., & Hosie, J. A. (1993). Priming effects in children's face recognition. *British Journal of Psychology, 84*, 101–110.

Gerhardstein, P., Adler, S. A., Rovee-Collier, C. (2000). A dissociation in infants' memory for stimulus size: Evidence for the early development of multiple memory systems. *Developmental Psychobiology, 36*, 123–136.

Hayes, B. K., & Hennessy, R. (1996). The nature and development of nonverbal implicit memory. *Journal of Experimental Child Psychology, 63*, 22–43.

Hayman, C. A. G., & Tulving, E. (1989). Is priming in fragment completion based on a "traceless" memory system? *Journal of Experimental Psychology: Learning, Memory and Cognition, 14*, 941–956.

Jacoby, L. L., Kelley, C. M., & Dywan, J. (1989). Memory attributions. In H. L. Roediger & F. I. M. Craik (Eds.), *Varieties of memory and consciousness: Essays in honour of Endel Tulving* (pp. 391–422). Hillsdale, NJ: Lawrence Erlbaum Associates.

James, W. (1892). *Principles of psychology.* London: MacMillan.

Janiszewski, C. (1988). Preconscious processing effects: The independence of attitude formation and conscious thought. *Journal of Consumer Research, 15*, 199–209.

John, D. R. (1999). Consumer socialization of children: A retrospective look at twenty-five years of research. *Journal of Consumer Research, 26*, 183–213.

Johnstone, E., & Dodd, C. A. (2000). Placements as mediators of brand salience within a UK cinema audience. *Journal of Marketing Communications, 6*, 141–158.

Kail, R. V. (1990). *The development of memory in children.* New York: W. H. Freeman.

Kihlstrom, J. F. (1987). The cognitive unconscious. *Science, 237*, 1445–1451.

Krishnan, H. S., & Chakravarti, D. (1999). Memory measures for pretesting advertisements: An integrative conceptual framework and a diagnostic template. *Journal of Consumer Psychology, 8*, 1–37.

Krugman, H. E. (1965). The impact of television advertising: Learning without involvement. *Public Opinion Quarterly, 29*, 349–356.

Kunst-Wilson, W. R., & Zajonc, R. B. (1980). Affective discrimination of stimuli that cannot be recognized. *Science, 207*, 557–558.

Macklin, M. C. (1987). Preschoolers' understanding of the informational function of television advertising. *Journal of Consumer Research, 14*, 229–239.

Mandler, J. M. (1988). How to build a baby: On the development of an accessible representational system. *Cognitive Development, 3*, 113–136.

Moore, E. S., & Lutz, R. J. (2000). Children, advertising, and product experiences: A multimethod inquiry. *Journal of Consumer Research, 27*, 31–48.

Naito, M. (1990). Repetition priming in children and adults: Age-related dissociation between implicit and explicit memory. *Journal of Experimental Child Psychology, 50*, 462–484.

Naito, M., & Komatsu, S. (1993). Processes involved in childhood development of implicit memory. In P. Graf & M. E. J. Masson (Eds.), *Implicit memory: New directions in cognition, development, and neuropsychology* (pp. 231–260). Hillsdale, NJ: Lawrence Erlbaum Associates.

Nelson, M. R. (2002). Recall of brand placements in computer/video games. *Journal of Advertising Research, 42*, 80–92.

Oates, C., Blades, M., & Gunter, B. (2001). Children and television advertising: When do they understand persuasive intent? *Journal of Consumer Behaviour, 1*, 238–245.

Parkin, A. J. (1993). Implicit memory across the lifespan. In P. Graf & M. E. J. Masson (Eds.), *Implicit memory: New directions in cognition, development, and neuropsychology* (pp. 191–206). Hillsdale, NJ: Lawrence Erlbaum Associates.

Parkin, A. J. (1997). The development of procedural and declarative memory. In N. Cowan (Ed.), *The development of memory in childhood* (pp.113–137). Hove, UK: Psychology Press.

Parkin, A. J., & Streete, S. (1988). Implicit and explicit memory in young children and adults. *British Journal of Psychology, 79*, 361–369.

Pechmann, C., & Shih, C. F. (1999). Smoking scenes in movies and antismoking advertisements before movies: Effects on youth. *Journal of Marketing, 63*, 1–13.

Peracchio, L. A. (1993). Young children's processing of a televised narrative: Is a picture really worth a thousand words? *Journal of Consumer Research, 20*, 281–293.

Perfect, T. J., & Askew, C. (1994). Print adverts: Not remembered but memorable. *Applied Cognitive Psychology, 8*, 693–703.

Ritson, M., & Elliott, R. (1995). A model of advertising literacy: The praxiology and co-creation of advertising meaning. In M. Bergadaa (Ed.), *Proceedings of the European Marketing Academy Conference, 24*, 1035–1044.

Roberts, K. P., & Blades, M. (2000). Children's memory and source monitoring of real-life and televised events. *Journal of Applied Developmental Psychology, 20*, 575–596.

Rovee-Collier, C. (1989). The joy of kicking: Memories, motives and mobiles. In P. R. Solomon, G. R. Goethals, & B. R. Stephans (Eds.), *Memory: An interdisciplinary approach*. New York: Springer Verlag.

Sanyal, A. (1992). Priming and implicit memory: A review and a synthesis relevant for consumer behavior. In J. Sherry & B. Sternthal (Eds.), *Advances in consumer research* (Vol. 19, pp. 795–805). Provo, UT: Association of Consumer Research.

Sargent, J. D., Tickle, J. J., Beach, M. L., Dalton, M. A., Ahrens, M. B., & Heatherton, T. F. (2001). Brand appearances in contemporary cinema films and contribution to global marketing of cigarettes. *The Lancet, 357*, 29–32.

Shapiro, S., MacInnis, D. J., & Heckler, S. E. (1997). The effects of incidental ad exposure on the formation of consideration sets. *Journal of Consumer Research, 24*, 94–104.

Sheppard, A. (1994). Children's understanding of television programmes: Three exploratory studies. *Current Psychology, 13*(2), 124–137.

Sloman, S. A., Hayman, C. A. G., Ohta, N., Law, J., & Tulving, E. (1988). Forgetting in primed fragment completion. *Journal of Experimental Psychology: Learning, Memory and Cognition, 14*, 223–239.

Toth, J. P. (2000). Nonconscious forms of human memory. In E. Tulving & F. I. M. Craik (Eds.), *The Oxford handbook of memory* (pp. 245–261). Oxford, UK: Oxford University Press.

Tulving, E. (1982). Synergistic ecphory in recall and recognition. *Canadian Journal of Psychology, 36*(2), 130–147.

Tulving, E., & Schacter, D. L. (1990). Priming and human memory systems. *Science, 247*, 301–306.

Walma van der Molen, J. H., & van der Voort, T. H. A. (2000). Children's and adults' recall of television and print news in children's and adult news formats. *Communication Research, 27*, 132–160.

Whittlesea, B. W. A., & Price, J. R. (2001). Implicit/explicit memory versus analytic/nonanalytic processing: Rethinking the mere exposure effect. *Memory and Cognition, 29*, 234–246.

Ye, G., & van Raaij, W. F. (1997). What inhibits the mere-exposure effect: Recollection or familiarity? *Journal of Economic Psychology, 18*, 629–648.

Yonelinas, A. P. (2002). The nature of recollection and familiarity: A review of 30 years of research. *Journal of Memory and Language, 46*, 441–517.

Zajonc, R. B. (1968). Attitudinal effects of mere exposures. *Journal of Personality and Social Psychology, 9*(2, pt. 2), 1–27.

II. THE PROGRAMS BETWEEN THE ADS: THE PERSUASIVE POWER OF ENTERTAINMENT FICTION AND NARRATIVE

Pictures, Words, and Media Influence: The Interactive Effects of Verbal and Nonverbal Information on Memory and Judgments

Robert S. Wyer, Jr.
Rashmi Adaval
Hong Kong University of Science and Technology

Rambo had conquered Asia. In China, a million people raced to see First Blood *within ten days of its Beijing opening, and black marketers were hawking tickets at seven times the official price . . . In Chengdu I heard John Rambo mumble his* First Blood *truisms in sullen machine-gun Mandarin and saw the audience break into tut-tuts of head-shaking admiration as our hero kerpowed seven cops in a single scene . . . "I think he's very beautiful" cooed a twenty-three year old Chinese girl to a foreign reporter. "So vigorous and so graceful. Is he married?"*

Pico Iyer (1988, p. 3)

The darkened hall of the movie theatre lulls us into a zone where we can play out our fantasies. We mentally cheer as the good guys win over the evil ones. We watch with bated breath as apocalyptic events threaten our planet. We get teary eyed when a character beats all odds to find happiness. When we finally step out of the movie theatre into the glare of the lobby, our return to reality may not be completely successful.

The images created by the entertainment media, whether encountered in a darkened movie theatre or in sitcoms, soaps, news reports, and advertising, do appear to blur the lines between reality and what we perceive it to be. These images can have a persisting influence on people's attitudes, beliefs, and behavior in ways that we have only recently begun to uncover. O'Guinn and Shrum (1997) paint a compelling picture of the consequences of excessive television viewing. They

find that heavy viewers of television are more likely than infrequent viewers to overestimate the frequency with which individuals drive luxury cars, have swimming pools in their backyards, or manifest other characteristics of an affluent lifestyle (see Shrum, Burroughs, & Rindfleish, this volume). These effects occur in part because people are typically unmotivated or unable to identify the sources of information they have acquired (Hasher, Goldstein, & Toppin, 1977; Jacoby, Kelley, Brown, & Jasechko, 1989; Johnson, Hashtroudi, & Lindsay, 1993). Thus, they fail to distinguish between their memories for actual events they have read about or personally experienced and their memories of fictional events they have seen on television. Consequently, they often retrieve and use these latter events to estimate the likelihood that the events occur in daily life. In many instances, people are unaware of the biasing influence of the media on their estimates. But even when they are conscious of bias, they do not know how much they should adjust to compensate for it (Petty & Wegener, 1993). Consequently, they can often fail to adjust enough or, at other times, can adjust too much. In the latter case, the biasing factors could have a negative, contrast effect on the judgments they report (for evidence of these overadjustments, see Isbell & Wyer, 1998; Ottati & Isbell, 1996).

However, the impact of the entertainment media on reactions to real-world events may be even more pervasive than Shrum et al.'s (this volume) research suggests. For example, concepts and knowledge that become easily accessible in memory as a result of exposure to movies and television can affect the interpretation of new information and the implications that are drawn from it. To this extent, the concepts can influence the impact of the information on judgments and decisions to which it is relevant.

These effects are discussed in this chapter. We focus in particular on the way in which visual images, stimulated by pictures or video presentations of the sort people encounter in movies or on television, can influence the impact of information that people receive subsequently. We first discuss how concepts activated by visual stimuli can influence reactions to information to which these stimuli are objectively irrelevant. We then consider how people's visual image of a stimulus person can influence the criteria they use to assess the implications of other, verbal information about the person and the effectiveness of applying these criteria. These effects can depend on whether the stimuli that induce these visual images are conveyed at the same time as the written information or are created beforehand. The influences of verbal and visual information on one another are reciprocal, however. In the final section of the chapter, we consider the way in which people's communications about events they have experienced visually (e.g., in a movie) can influence their later memory for these events and, therefore, their beliefs and opinions. The research we discuss, most of which was conducted in our own laboratory, was generally not designed to have a direct bearing on the interface between entertainment and persuasion. However, its implications for this interface should be apparent.

EFFECTS OF MEDIA-CREATED VISUAL IMAGES ON RESPONSES TO ACTUAL PEOPLE AND EVENTS

To reiterate, Shrum et al.'s (this volume) research clearly demonstrates that exposing television viewers to fictional events can influence their perceptions that similar events actually occur in the real world. To this extent, it can influence their beliefs and attitudes about the persons and objects to which the events are relevant. This influence could occur for two reasons.

First, people might come to regard situations that occur frequently on television as normative. This could have both desirable and undesirable consequences. On one hand, exposure to women and African Americans as heads of state, lawyers, or scientists could increase people's perceptions that their occupancy of these roles is commonplace and, therefore, could also increase their acceptance of individuals holding these positions in the real world. On the other hand, individuals might use the situations and events that occur frequently on television as standards of comparison in evaluating their own life circumstances and may be motivated to engage in behavior that attains these standards. Thus, if heavy television viewers overestimate the proportion of people with possessions that exemplify an affluent lifestyle (O'Guinn & Shrum, 1997), they may be more inclined than other individuals to evaluate their own life circumstances unfavorably in relation to this implicit standard of affluence and may try to acquire these possessions or engage in other activities that require them to live beyond their means. These influences of television could underlie the acquisition of materialistic values at a very early age.

Other considerations arise when the situations that occur on television are undesirable. For example, exposure to violence and aggression on television could increase people's perceptions that this behavior is common and, perhaps, inevitable. If this is so, it could decrease their concern about the violence they encounter in the real world. (For a more detailed discussion of the effects of television violence on desensitization to aggression, see Drabman & Thomas, 1975.)

A second possible effect of exposure to violence is quite different. Lerner, Miller, and Holmes (1976; see also Lerner & Simmons, 1966) suggest that people are motivated to believe that the world is just (i.e., that people not only get what they deserve but also deserve what they get). Movies and television shows in which individuals are maimed or killed could activate viewers' concerns about injustice and, therefore, could increase their need to reestablish their belief in a just world when they encounter actual situations. In other words, heavy television users might be more inclined than occasional viewers to believe that perpetrators of violence will be punished. At the same time, they might also be inclined to believe that the victims of violence and aggression are responsible for their victimization and, therefore, that they deserve the fate that has befallen them. (For a summary of evidence that just-world considerations often mediate perceptions of rape, see Wagstaff, 1982). Perhaps ironically, this tendency should be most evident when

the aggression has extremely negative consequences and hence the threat to one's belief in a just world is particularly great.

Media Influences on Reactions to Rape: An Empirical Example

Effects of Exposure to Aggressive Acts and Outcomes

To summarize, exposure to violence in the media could increase tolerance for aggression in the real world for two somewhat opposing reasons. On one hand, it could increase perceptions that aggression is normal and socially sanctioned and that one should not be particularly upset by its occurrence. This is most likely to occur if the aggression is relatively mild. If the aggression is extreme and ostensibly hard to justify, however, it could stimulate the need to believe in a just world, leading individuals to believe that the victims of aggression deserve their fate.

Wyer, Bodenhausen, and Gorman (1985) examined these possible effects in a study of the beliefs that mediate reactions to rape. We were interested in the extent to which activating aggression-related concepts in one context would influence reactions to rape situations that people encounter in an unrelated context. To do so, we asked participants to engage in two apparently different experiments. The first study was ostensibly concerned with the things shown in the media that college students find objectionable. On this pretense, we exposed participants to slides of 12 pictures. Nine of these pictures showed objects and events that participants were unlikely to consider offensive. The other three pictures varied over conditions. In one case, these pictures showed aggressive acts that were relatively common (police subduing a criminal, a boxing match, etc.) and, therefore, were likely to activate concepts that aggression is normal and socially sanctioned. In a second condition, the pictures portrayed severely negative outcomes of aggression that activated the concept that human beings were cruel and inhumane (a lynching episode, a dead soldier with a hole in his head, etc.). (Our assumptions concerning the concepts activated by the pictures were confirmed on the basis of normative data obtained prior to the experiment.) The third, control set portrayed stimuli that might be considered unpleasant but were unrelated to aggression (deformed babies, a smoking advertisement, etc.).

Participants rated each of the 12 pictures in terms of how objectionable it was. Then, they were told that the experiment (which took about 10 min) was over but that, because there was time remaining, we would like them to help another faculty member who was conducting a study in a different room down the hall. When they arrived at this room, however, they found a sign on the door indicating that the experimenter would return shortly and that while they were waiting they should complete a questionnaire that was lying on the table. This questionnaire introduced the "new" study as an investigation of the factors people consider important in judging criminal cases, that different participants were being asked to

consider different types of crimes, and that the one they would personally be asked to consider was rape. (The nature of the crime was handwritten on the instruction page to give the impression that participants were assigned this type of crime by chance.) The questionnaire contained descriptions of four rape cases that varied in terms of whether the alleged rapist was an acquaintance of the victim or a total stranger and whether the victim did or did not try to resist. Participants read each scenario and then reported several reactions. Two questions concerned (1) their belief that the defendant should be convicted and (2) their belief that the defendant actually was convicted. Three others concerned the victim's responsibility for the incident (whether she provoked the rape, whether she could have avoided it, etc.).

We assumed that the pictures to which participants were exposed in the first experiment would activate concepts that they would use to construe the implications of the rape scenarios they encountered in the second experiment. Therefore, if socially sanctioned acts of aggression activate the concept that aggressive behavior is normal, exposure to these acts should decrease beliefs that the defendant should be convicted and, for that matter, that he actually was. This was not the case, however. Participants' beliefs that the defendant was and should be convicted are shown in the first two rows of Table 8.1, averaged over the four scenarios. Exposure to aggressive acts only slightly decreased beliefs that the defendant was convicted relative to control conditions and actually increased beliefs that he should be convicted. Neither of these effects was significant.

Exposure to extremely negative outcomes of aggression also failed to influence beliefs that the defendant should be convicted. However, it increased the belief that the defendant actually *was* convicted. This pattern of results is consistent with the hypothesis that exposure to extremely negative consequences of aggression threatened participants' perception that the world is just. Consequently, it motivated them to reaffirm this perception by believing that the defendant got what he deserved.

If this interpretation is correct, however, it should also be manifested in the participants' belief that the victim deserved what she got, as reflected in judgments

TABLE 8.1

Judgments of the Defendant and Victim As a Function of Concepts Activated by Priming Stimuli

		Primed Concept	
	Control	Aggression Is Normal and Socially Sanctioned	Humans Are Cruel and Inhumane
Belief that defendant should be convicted	8.97	9.62	8.70
Belief that defendant was convicted	3.95	3.47	5.10
Belief that victim was responsible	2.97	3.07	4.20

Note. Judgments are reported along a scale from 0 (*not at all likely*) to 10 (*very likely*). Based on data from Wyer, Bodenhausen, and Gorman (1985).

that she was partly responsible for her fate. This was also the case, as shown in the third row of Table 8.1. Although exposure to socially acceptable acts of aggression had relatively little influence on participants' perceptions of the victim's responsibility, exposure to severely negative outcomes of aggression substantially increased these perceptions. Moreover, this was true regardless of whether the rapist was a stranger or an acquaintance and regardless of whether or not the victim resisted. Thus, activating concepts that the rapist was cruel and inhumane not only increased the belief that the defendant got what he deserved but also increased the belief that the victim deserved what she got.

The implications of these findings for the impact of the media on perceptions of rape must remain speculative. The effects of situationally primed concepts on judgments are often of short duration. However, the effects of frequent exposure to stimuli on concept accessibility are much more enduring (Higgins, 1996; Higgins, Bargh, & Lombardi, 1985). It therefore seems reasonable to assume that frequent exposure to extreme violence could induce a chronic tendency to maintain a belief in a just world that is manifested in a variety of contexts. To this extent, it could have effects similar to those that Wyer et al. (1985) observed.

Other Determinants of Reactions to Rape

Concepts associated with aggression are not the only mediators of reactions to rape. Zillman and Bryant (1982) found that exposing college students to massive doses of pornography over a period of several weeks increased their tolerance for rape, and this effect was reflected in the attitudes that participants reported several months later. Pornography could activate concepts of women as sex objects who enjoy being dominated and as interested in sexual pleasure alone. These concepts could stimulate empathy with the defendant in a rape case and could also influence judgments of the victim's responsibility for the incident.

Additional data obtained by Wyer et al. (1985) bear on this possibility. In two additional conditions, the priming stimuli portrayed women as sex objects. In one case, the stimuli were sexually arousing, consisting of nude centerfolds, one of which showed a woman masturbating. In a second set, however, the pictures included a cartoon, a picture of a stripper, and a branded woman, none of which elicited sexual arousal.

Pictures had no influence on either the belief that the defendant should have been convicted or the belief that he actually was. However, pictures did have an impact on judgments of the victim's responsibility for the rape, the nature of which depended on participants' sex. Specifically, pictures that depicted women as sex objects increased men's perceptions that the victim was responsible for the incident but decreased women's perceptions of her responsibility. In other words, exposing male participants to the stimulus pictures appeared to activate concepts of women as sex objects, as we expected. However, exposing female participants to these stimuli appear to have activated the concept that *men think of women as*

sex objects, inducing reactance and, therefore, decreasing perceptions of the rape victim's responsibility.

The implications of these findings for the impact of the media, like the effects of activating aggression-related concepts, should be treated with caution. Nevertheless, to the extent that frequent activation of concepts increases their chronic accessibility in memory, these findings suggest that frequent portrayals of women as sex objects in the media is likely to polarize existing differences between males and females in their attitudes toward the victims of rape without necessarily influencing their beliefs that the rapist should be punished.

Effects of Image-Activated Stereotypes on Behavior

As we speculated earlier in this section, frequent portrayals of minority group members in responsible social roles could increase perceptions of their suitability for these positions in the real world. This increase may be accompanied by a decrease in stereotype-based beliefs about the attributes of these individuals. As Devine (1989; see also Lepore & Brown, 1997) points out, however, people may have knowledge of the stereotype even if they do not consider it to be valid. Consequently, exposure to members of the stereotyped group can activate trait and behavioral concepts that are associated with the group, and these concepts, once activated, can be applied in other situations to which the stereotype is objectively irrelevant. Moreover, these effects can occur without awareness.

This possibility was demonstrated by Bargh, Chen, and Burrows (1996) in research on the effects of concept activation on overt behavior. In one study (Bargh et al., 1996, Experiment 3), European Americans were subliminally exposed to either Black or White faces while they performed a boring task. After completing the task, participants were told that, due to a computer malfunction, they would have to perform the task again. Participants' nonverbal reactions to this request were unobtrusively observed. Participants manifested more signs of irritation and antagonism if they had been exposed to Black faces than if they had been exposed to White faces. This suggests that exposure to the faces of African Americans, who are stereotyped as being hostile and aggressive (Devine, 1989), activated concepts associated with this behavior, and this disposed participants to behave similarly. Moreover, these effects occurred without awareness of the stimuli that led to the stereotype's activation.

That activating a stereotype influences the behavior of individuals to whom the stereotype does not apply is intriguing. The processes that underlie this effect, however, are not completely clear. One possible explanation is suggested by Prinz's (1990) speculation that to comprehend another's behavior people spontaneously imagine performing the behavior themselves, thereby establishing an association between a representation of others' behavior and a representation of their own. As a result of this association, factors that activate concepts about another's behavior

can increase the disposition to behave similarly under conditions in which the behavior is applicable.

The activation of a stereotype alone is unlikely to stimulate the behaviors that exemplify it, of course. Participants in Bargh et al.'s (1996) study would undoubtedly not have conveyed hostility spontaneously if the situation had not been one that disposed them to feel irritation for other, stereotype-unrelated reasons (i.e., the request to repeat a boring task). In other situations, the same stereotype could activate quite different behaviors. This was demonstrated in an unpublished study by Colcombe and Wyer (2001). In this study, participants who had been exposed to priming conditions identical to those administered by Bargh et al. were asked to perform a mathematics test. In this study, participants performed less well on the test if they had been subliminally exposed to Black faces than if they had been exposed to White ones. African Americans are stereotyped as unmotivated to try hard in academic achievement situations, so activating the stereotype increased participants' own disposition to behave similarly. These results, in combination with Bargh et al.'s (1996) findings, suggest that the particular behavior that is influenced by activating a stereotype depends on situational factors as well as the stereotype itself.

Moreover, the concepts associated with the stereotype may need to be activated without participants' awareness. In other conditions of Colcombe and Wyer's (2001) study, Black and White faces were primed overtly rather than subliminally. In these conditions, participants performed better when they had been exposed to Black faces. Consciousness of the stereotype of African Americans as doing poorly in achievement situations apparently stimulated participants to try harder, so they could distance themselves from the stereotyped group.

These contingencies become particularly important when evaluating the implications of these findings for the effects of the media on behavior. It obviously would be inappropriate to assume that exposing television viewers to members of a stereotyped group increases their likelihood of manifesting stereotype-related behavior in general. This should only occur if situations arise in which the stereotype-activated behavior is applicable. Moreover, if people are conscious of the stereotype at the time a behavioral decision is made, they may try to compensate for its influence and thus might be less inclined to make a stereotype-related decision than they otherwise would.

On the other hand, people do not need to be unaware of the stereotype itself for it to have an impact. They need only be unaware of the potential relatedness between the situation in which the stereotype is activated and the situation in which the behavior occurs. It is therefore conceivable that frequently exposing people to members of a stereotyped group in the media will increase the likelihood of behaving in stereotype-related ways under conditions in which the behavior is relevant. Moreover, this may occur primarily when individuals are not consciously thinking about the group and the behaviors associated with it. To avoid these effects, it may be necessary to change people's perceptions of the stereotype itself. Media exposure to stereotyped group members who behave in stereotype-inconsistent ways might be one way to accomplish this.

EFFECTS OF VISUAL STIMULI ON INFORMATION PROCESSING

To reiterate, visual portrayals of persons and social events can influence people's attitudes and behaviors to which these portrayals are objectively irrelevant. Visual images are even more likely to influence the processing of information about individuals and events to which they directly pertain. The nature of this influence is less obvious than it might appear, however. For example, pictures might seem intuitively likely to provide information about their referents and, therefore, to have a direct impact on judgments of these referents. In fact, however, research in the consumer domain has provided very mixed evidence that pictures of a product have an impact on product evaluations over and above the effects of verbal product descriptions (Costley & Brucks, 1992; Edell & Staelin, 1983; but see Sengupta & Fitzsimons, 2000, for an alternative view).

An understanding of the combined influence of verbal and visual information is complicated by the fact that the two types of information can elicit different types of cognitive activity. Pictures, for example, are likely to be processed holistically or configurally, creating a general impression that is independent of any particular feature (for a theoretical analysis of this possibility, see Wyer & Radvansky, 1999). Verbal information, however, might be processed either holistically or more analytically, depending on the type of information and the format in which it is conveyed. For example, a person's opinions on a set of social issues might be evaluated in terms of their implications for whether the person is socially liberal or conservative. However, the favorableness of each opinion could also be assessed independently and these individual assessments later combined mechanistically to form an overall evaluation (cf. Anderson, 1971; Fishbein & Hunter, 1964). When verbal information can be easily evaluated using either a piecemeal or a holistic processing strategy, the presence of pictures may create a cognitive set to think holistically, therefore influencing the conclusions drawn from it relative to conditions in which the pictures were not conveyed. Other verbal information, however, might be presented in a way that is much easier to process in one way than the other. In this case, the holistic strategy activated by pictures could facilitate or interfere with this processing, depending on its compatibility with that required.

Two quite different sets of studies bear on these possibilities. Although the studies were conducted in the domain of political judgment, they have more general implications.

The Effects of a Politician's Image on Responses to Issue Stands

The media often show political figures in situations that have little objective relevance to an evaluation of their qualifications for public office. Yet these portrayals create an image of these individuals that influences people's general perceptions of their sincerity, integrity, self-confidence, and general personality. These perceptions can be used as a basis for evaluating the individuals independently of their

stands on specific issues. The role of image has been well known in the political arena since the 1960 Kennedy-Nixon debates, which increased Kennedy's popularity despite the fact that Nixon's positions on the issues were more compelling (Englis, 1994).

However, a politician's image not only can have a direct influence on judgments of the candidate but also can affect responses to other, more substantive information. For example, persons who receive information about a politician's stands on social issues might normally assess each individual issue position and evaluate the candidate on the basis of the number of these positions with which they agree. However, if people have formed a global image of the politician, and if this global criterion for judgment is salient, it could induce a tendency to use general criteria to evaluate the implications of other available information as well. Thus, for example, it might stimulate individuals to assess the implications of the person's issue stands for his or her general political ideology and to base their judgments on this ideology independently of their agreement with specific issues.

A study by Wyer et al. (1991) suggests that this may be the case. Nonacademic employees were recruited for a study of the way people make judgments of political candidates on the basis of the sort of information they might receive during an election campaign. On this pretence, they were given two types of information about a member of the U. S. House of Representatives who had recently run for the Senate in a neighboring state. First, participants were shown a videotaped, nonpolitical speech of the candidate's remarks at a bicentennial celebration at which he was asked to present an award to a local dignitary. The speech, delivered by a graduate student in theatre who was an accomplished character actor, was identical in content in all conditions. However, it was delivered in either a forceful, articulate manner that conveyed a favorable image or in a bumbling manner, with inappropriate pauses, fidgeting, and other mannerisms, that conveyed an unfavorable impression.

The second type of information was ostensibly an audiotaped portion of a radio program that had been sponsored by the League of Women Voters. In this program, commentators reviewed the candidate's votes on several recent bills that had come before the House. His votes on six of the bills (e.g., a proposal to increase military spending by 15%, a proposal to allow prayer in public schools) conveyed either a consistently conservative or consistently liberal ideology. (Votes on four other bills had no ideological significance.)

This information was conveyed in three conditions. In *no-delay* conditions, participants listened to the radio program describing the candidate's issue stands immediately after they watched the videotape of his speech. Then, after doing so, they reported their impression of the candidate along a 100-point "feeling thermometer." The procedure in two other conditions was similar, except that a 24-hour delay was introduced either (a) between seeing the videotaped speech and exposure to the candidate's issue positions (*delayed-information* conditions)

or (b) between exposure to the candidate's issue stands and judgments (delayed-judgment conditions).

In all conditions, participants, after evaluating the candidate, reported their personal positions on each of the issues to which the candidate's votes pertained. Finally, they indicated their own party affiliation and ideological orientation. These latter data, in combination with the candidate's issue stands, were used to define two independent variables. First, participants' reported ideology was coded as either similar or dissimilar to the candidate's, as implied by the liberal or conservative orientation of his issue stands. Second, participants were classified as either generally in agreement or generally in disagreement with the candidate's specific issue positions, based on the proportion of ideologically relevant issue stands with which they agreed. (Each participant agreed with at least one liberal and one conservative issue position, regardless of his or her general ideology. Therefore, indices of ideological similarity and agreement level could be obtained for each participant.)

Evaluations of the candidate are shown in Table 8.2 as a function of each informational variable and delay conditions. These evaluations were obviously affected by the favorableness of the candidate's image as conveyed in the videotape. Moreover, the candidate's image had more effect when it was salient at the time of judgment (i.e., under no-delay conditions) than when it was not. The effects of agreement and ideological similarity are of greater interest, however. When the candidate's image was not salient to participants at the time they received

TABLE 8.2
Candidate Evaluations As a Function of Delay Conditions, Image, Agreement
With the Candidate's Issue Stands, and Ideological Similarity

	No-Delay Conditions	Delayed-Information Conditions	Delayed-Judgment Conditions
Candidate's image			
Favorable	51.0	53.8	47.7
Unfavorable	35.6	44.6	42.9
Difference	15.4	9.2	4.8
Participants' agreement with issue stands			
Agree	42.3	64.5	48.1
Disagree	33.2	30.9	40.1
Difference	9.1	33.6	8.0
Ideological similarity to candidate			
Similar	49.6	48.1	57.3
Dissimilar	26.0	47.3	31.0
Difference	23.6	0.8	26.3

Note. Judgments are reported along a 100-point "feeling thermometer" from 0 (*very unfavorable*) to 100 (*very favorable*). Based on data from Wyer et al. (1991).

information about his issue stands (under delayed-information conditions), they based their evaluations of the candidate on their agreement with his issue positions, and the candidate's similarity to them in general ideology had virtually no effect. However, when participants learned about the candidate's issue stands immediately after they had viewed his image-inducing speech, they based their evaluations on the candidate's general ideology, and their agreement with him on specific issues had little influence. This was true under both no-delay and delayed-judgment conditions. Thus, the indirect effect of the candidate's image on the processing of issue information (unlike its direct effects on judgments) was not a function of its salience at the time judgments were reported. Rather, it depended on the salience of the candidate's image at the time the issue stand information was conveyed.

In summary, the salience of the candidate's image at the time his issue stands were learned altered the way in which the implications of these issue stands were construed. That is, when a global image of the candidate was not salient, participants assessed their agreement with his stands on specific issues and based their judgments on this criterion independently of the ideological implications of the candidate's positions. When the candidate's image was salient at the time his issue positions were learned, however, participants applied a global criterion in assessing the implications of his issue positions as well. Consequently, their agreement with the candidate on specific issues had relatively little effect.[1]

It is important to keep in mind that the influence of the candidate's image in this study was only evident when it was particularly salient at the time the issue stand information was presented. As we have noted earlier, however, the accessibility of previously acquired knowledge is likely to be a function of the frequency with which participants have been exposed to it as well as the recency with which they have encountered it, and the effects of frequency are much more enduring (Higgins, 1996; Higgins, Bargh, & Lombardi, 1985). To this extent, Wyer et al.'s (1991) results suggest that the frequent exposure to politicians in the media could produce a general tendency to evaluate them on the basis of their general ideology independently of their specific issue positions. It is interesting to speculate that an incumbent president, who is often shown in newspapers or on television, is more likely to be evaluated on the basis of global ideological criteria, whereas less

---

[1] An alternative interpretation of these results might be that participants experienced overload when the candidate's videotaped speech and his issue stands were conveyed in temporal proximity, and, therefore, they devoted less cognitive effort to an assessment of the candidate's issue positions. If this were the case, however, they would presumably be inclined to use the candidate's image as a heuristic, leading it to have greater effect on judgments than it otherwise would. In fact, the candidate's image had no greater effect under delayed-judgment conditions (when the two types of information were presented together) than under delayed-information conditions. Therefore, this alternative interpretation does not seem viable.

well-known challengers, whose public images are less well established, are more often evaluated on the basis of their stands on specific issues.

Facilitative and Interfering Effects of Visual Images on Verbal Information Processing

The preceding studies suggest that when verbal information can be evaluated easily using either holistic or piecemeal criteria, making salient visual images of the individual may influence the criterion that is applied. Similar considerations suggest that when the information is conducive to only one type of processing, visual images that are salient at the time could either facilitate or interfere with this processing, depending on the type of information involved.

A series of studies by Adaval and her colleagues (Adaval, Isbell, & Wyer, 2003; Adaval & Wyer, 1998) bear on this possibility. Based on earlier research by Pennington and Hastie (1986, 1988, 1992), Adaval and colleagues assumed that when information about a person or object is conveyed in the form of a narrative (i.e., a temporally related sequence of events), people would construct a story about the sequence of events as a whole and would base their judgments on the implications of the story without considering the implications of each individual event in isolation. In contrast, individuals who receive the same information in an unordered list might be more inclined to engage in piecemeal processing of each feature separately and to integrate its implications using a mechanistic computational strategy (cf. Anderson, 1971; Fishbein & Hunter, 1964). If this is so, and if pictures dispose individuals to employ a global processing strategy, they should facilitate the processing of the first type of information, leading the information to have more effect. However, pictures could interfere with processing of the second type of information, leading the information to have less impact.

Studies in both the political domain (Adaval et al., 2003) and consumer decision making (Adaval & Wyer, 1998) suggest that this is true. In two studies by Adaval et al. (2003), participants received information about the events that occurred in the course of a politician's career and were asked to form an impression of him. The information was conveyed in a brochure that began with a brief overview of the politician's career, followed by more specific descriptions of the events that had occurred. In one case, however, the information was conveyed in a narrative. For example, the brochure describing one politician ("Thomas Winters") began:

> Thomas Winters was a well-known political figure between 1950 and 1975. He was a veteran of World War II and served as an executive of General Motors before becoming Governor of Michigan. He then served two years as a U. S. Senator, and ended his career as a special envoy to China.

This paragraph was followed by a series of paragraphs, each describing a different event that occurred during the politician's career and the point at which it occurred,

for example:

> He left General Motors to become Governor of Michigan. There, he showed sensitivity to public interests. Upon assuming office, for example, he went on television to oppose the construction of a nuclear waste processing plant near Detroit that would contaminate the city's water supply.

Other activities included urging the government to halt the bombing in Vietnam, donating his summer home for use by a charitable organization, hosting the Pope during his visit to America, and helping to revise the state budget to provide support for crime prevention.

In contrast, the brochure, under list-format conditions, described the events in the politician's life in bullet form and did not indicate their temporal relatedness. Thus, the brochure pertaining to Winters began:

> Thomas Winters was a well-known political figure between 1950 and 1970. He was:
>
> * A member of the U. S. Senate
> * A World War II veteran
> * A General Motors executive
> * Governor of Michigan
> * Special envoy to China

Although the individual events were conveyed in the same order they were presented in narrative-format conditions, they were also conveyed in bullets that had no temporal implications:

> * Was sensitive to the interests of the public while Governor of Michigan.
> * Went on television to oppose the construction of a nuclear waste processing plant that would contaminate the city's water supply.

In some conditions, the verbal description of each life event was accompanied by a black-and-white photograph of the politician ostensibly engaged in activities related to the event (giving a speech, talking to someone, etc.) or, in some cases, the event itself. (Thus, for example, a statement that the politician had headed a committee to investigate how to decrease violent crime was accompanied by a picture of a policeman at the scene of a killing.) The pictures were taken from books and magazines. (Pictures of Henry Kissinger were used for one of the two politicians, and pictures of Robert McNamara were used for the other. Pretesting indicated that neither politician's face was familiar to the college student population from which participants were drawn.) Participants, after reading the brochures, reported their impressions of each politician along a scale from −5 (*very unfavorable*) to +5 (*very favorable*) and then recalled the events they had read about.

Evaluations of the politicians are shown in Table 8.3 as a function of information presentation format and the presence or absence of pictures. As these data show, participants in no-picture conditions evaluated politicians less favorably

TABLE 8.3
Impressions of Politicians and Number of Events Recalled As a
Function of Format, the Presence of Pictures, and Presentation Order

	Narrative Format	List Format
Impressions of politician		
Pictures	3.98	3.63
No pictures	3.58	3.95
Number of items recalled		
Pictures	5.79	4.92
No pictures	5.04	4.98

Note. Judgments are reported along a scale from –5 (*very unfavorable*) to 5 (*very favorable*). Based on data from Adaval et al., 2003, Experiment 1.

when the information about them was conveyed in a narrative than when it was listed. However, introducing pictures increased evaluations in the former condition and decreased it in the latter. As a result, evaluations of the politicians when pictures were presented were more favorable when the information was conveyed in a narrative than when it was listed. Although these differences were small in magnitude, the interaction of format and pictures was reliable ($p < .05$). As shown in the bottom half of Table 8.3, the number of events that participants recalled in each condition showed a similar pattern. This is consistent with the assumption that differences in processing difficulty mediated the effects we observed.

The information-processing strategies that underlie these effects may be activated and applied spontaneously, with little conscious awareness. This was suggested in a second study in which participants were explicitly told the strategy they should use. That is, participants in piecemeal-instruction conditions were told to "imagine the specific events that occurred in each politician's life," and to "use these individual events as a basis for your impression." In contrast, participants under holistic-instruction conditions were told to "imagine each politician's life as a whole and to use this as a basis for your impression." Participants' self-reports of the strategy they employed confirmed the assumption that they attempted to comply with these instructions. Nevertheless, participants' candidate evaluations showed a pattern very similar to that observed in the first study. These data are summarized in Table 8.4. That is, pictures increased judgments based on information that was conveyed in a narrative and decreased the extremity of judgments based on information that was conveyed in a list, and these effects did not depend significantly on the criteria participants were told to use.

The interfering effects of pictures when verbal information was conveyed in a list may be limited to conditions in which the pictures accompany this information. If an image of a person or event is constructed before verbal information about it is received, as in the study by Wyer et al. (1991), this interference might not be apparent. This possibility was examined in an additional study by Adaval et al. (2003). The design of this experiment was similar to that of the earlier ones. In

TABLE 8.4

Impressions of Politicians As a Function of Format, Task
Demands, the Presence of Pictures, and Presentation Order

	Narrative Format	List Format
Holistic instructions		
Pictures	3.94	3.61
No pictures	3.46	4.03
Piecemeal instructions		
Pictures	3.76	3.12
No pictures	4.00	4.02
Mean		
Pictures	3.85	3.37
No pictures	3.73	4.03

Note. Judgments are reported along a scale from –5 (*very unfavorable*) to 5 (*very favorable*). Based on data from Adaval et al., 2003, Experiment 2.

this case, however, pictures of the politicians were presented at the beginning of the brochure, before the written descriptions of the candidate's life events were conveyed, rather than in the context of these events. Under these conditions, pictures tended to increase evaluations of the politicians regardless of the format in which the information was conveyed. Interestingly, this increase was particularly pronounced among individuals who typically were not disposed to form visual images spontaneously on the basis of verbal information. Participants who typically formed visual images apparently formed these images on their own without the aid of pictures, so the addition of these pictures had little effect.

These results suggest that stimulating people to form visual images of a person or object at one point in time can sometimes increase the influence of verbal information they receive later. In this regard, Nisbett and Ross (1980) have argued that concrete, imageable information about an object often has greater impact on judgments than abstract ("pallid") consensus information that objectively is more reliable. Moreover, this impact can often increase as time goes on (cf. Reyes, Thompson, & Bower, 1980). The results of the present study expand on this possibility. That is, pictures of a person or object at one point in time may increase the ability to imagine the events described by subsequent information about their referent, thereby concretizing these events and leading the events to have more impact than they otherwise would.

Implications for Images Conveyed in the Media

In the research described in this section, the visual information we presented concerned the same people to whom the verbal information pertained. However, it was not particularly relevant to an understanding of this information. Nevertheless, it had an impact on the way the verbal information was processed and the inferences that were drawn from on it. Thus, a political candidate's videotaped

speech that had no implications for his political orientation influenced the way in which descriptions of his issue stands were processed and the conclusions drawn from them. Pictures of a politician that were peripheral to the verbal descriptions of events in his life likewise influenced the inferences that recipients made about the politician on the basis of these events.

Communications about people in the media usually consist of both visual and verbal material, presented either simultaneously or at different times. The results we obtained suggest that even though the verbal descriptions of an individual might provide an accurate characterization of him or her, nonverbal components of media communications (presented either simultaneously or separately) can affect the impact of these descriptions. In other words, although the visual characterizations of a person and his or her activities might be intended solely to stimulate interest and provide enjoyment, it could actually influence the conclusions people draw from the verbal information about the person and the extent to which they are persuaded by it.

COMMUNICATING ABOUT MEDIA CONTENT: THE EFFECTS OF VERBAL CODINGS OF VISUAL INFORMATION ON MEMORY

Our discussion thus far has implications for the way in which visual stimuli of the sort people encounter in the media can influence the interpretation of verbal information to which it is often remotely relevant. However, the influence of visual and verbal information on one another can be reciprocal. In some instances, verbal descriptions of observations that people communicate to others, perhaps for the purpose of being entertaining, can later influence their memory for the events that were observed and, therefore, can potentially influence the impact of these events on judgments they make at a later point in time.

These possibilities are suggested indirectly by evidence that once people have made an initial judgment of a person or object, they often retrieve and use this judgment as a basis for later ones without consulting the information on which the first judgment was based (Carlston, 1980; Higgins & Lurie, 1983: Lingle & Ostrom, 1979; Sherman, Ahlm, Berman, & Lynn, 1978). More directly relevant is a study by Higgins and Rholes (1978). They showed that when people describe a person to someone who either likes or dislikes this person, they tend to tailor their communication to the values of the intended recipient. Once they have done so, however, they base their own liking for the person on the implications of the message they wrote, rather than on the original information they received about the person. Participants in the course of preparing their communication apparently formed a new representation of the person they were describing, and this representation was later retrieved from memory and used to attain goals to which it was relevant independently of the implications of the information on which it was based.

This possibility has potentially important implications for the issues of concern in this chapter. When people watch a movie or television show, they are likely to construct a mental representation of it that is coded in a modality similar to that in which it was presented (i.e., both visually and acoustically; see Wyer & Radvansky, 1999). Later, however, they may be called on to describe the events they saw to another. Alternatively, they may communicate their impressions of one or more of the characters. In doing so, they presumably encode their initial observations in terms of more abstract concepts that are relevant to the communication they are generating. If they are later asked to make judgments of the people or events conveyed in the original movie, they might retrieve and use this verbally coded representation in the course of communicating about it, without considering the original, nonverbally coded material. To this extent, their judgments may be less accurate than they would be if this more abstract representation had not been used.

Two studies by Adaval and Wyer (2003) examined these effects. Participants watched the initial 12-min segment of Albee's *Who's Afraid of Virginia Woolf*. The segment portrays an animated conversation between a man and woman after coming home from a late-night party. Some participants were told before watching the movie that they would later be asked to describe what went on, whereas others were told they would be asked to report their impressions of the protagonists. In two other conditions, participants were told at the outset to watch the movie as they would if they were seeing it in a theatre and were not informed of the task they were asked to perform until afterward. After watching the movie, participants in all four conditions were asked to spend 5 min either writing down what went on or describing their impressions, depending on the objective they had been assigned. Participants in a fifth, control condition did not receive specific objectives either before or after watching the movie and spent 5 min after watching the movie describing a typical day at school. After completing the writing task, all participants were then administered a recognition memory task in which they were asked to identify both things the protagonists said during the interaction or things they had done.

We expected that participants who watched the movie would form a detailed mental representation of it that (like the movie itself) was coded both visually and acoustically. However, when they later conveyed their impressions of the protagonists, or described the sequence of events that occurred, they presumably formed a semantically coded representation that was relevant to their communication objective. However, the features of this latter representation were likely to be coded more abstractly than features of the representation they had formed while watching the movie. Consequently, if participants use the representation as a basis for their recognition responses, they are likely to be less accurate than they would be if this abstract verbal representation had not been formed.

The content of the abstract representation that participants form, however, should depend on their communication objective. If participants are describing the sequence of events that occurred, both things the protagonists said and things they did are relevant. Consequently, protagonists' statements and their nonverbal

behaviors should both be depicted in the abstract representation they formed when they were asked to describe this sequence. We therefore expected that participants who had formed this representation would use it to verify both protagonists' statements and their behaviors, so their accuracy in identifying both types of items would be diminished relative to conditions in which they had not performed this task.

In contrast, suppose participants are describing their impressions of the protagonists. In the particular movie segment that participants observed, protagonists' statements were quite relevant to an understanding of their personality but their nonverbal behaviors were generally uninformative. Therefore, the representation that participants construct in the course of describing their impressions should convey the implications of things the protagonists said but not the things they did. If this is so, these participants should be likely to consider this representation to be a sufficient basis for verifying protagonists' statements but might resort to the less-accessible representation they had formed while watching the movie to verify nonverbal behaviors. Consequently, their accuracy in recognizing statements should be adversely affected, but their accuracy in recognizing nonverbal behaviors should not.

Results were largely consistent with these conjectures. The two studies differed primarily in the nature of the recognition task that the participants performed. In one experiment, recognition items were verbal descriptions of the things protagonists said and did along with an equivalent number of items that were not conveyed in the movie. In the second study, recognition items consisted of acoustic recordings of protagonists' actual utterances and visual frames extracted from the movie. The results of both studies are summarized in Table 8.5, which shows

TABLE 8.5
Effects of Communication Objectives and the Point At Which These
Objectives Were Induced on Recognition of Protagonists' Statements
and Nonverbal Behaviors

	Experiment 1		Experiment 2	
	Statements	Behaviors	Statements	Behaviors
Event-description objectives				
Induced before watching movie	−.189[a]	−.360	−.070	−.046
Induced after watching movie	−.065	−.297	−.044	−.095
Impression-description objectives				
Induced before watching movie	.130	.000	.045	.046
Induced after watching movie	−.108	.021	−.022	.046

Note. Based on Adaval and Wyer (2003).
[a]Recognition accuracy in Experiment 1 was based on a measure that controls for guessing (Hilgard, 1951). This measure could not be applied reliably in Experiment 2 because there were too few distracters. Consequently, accuracy in this study was inferred from the proportion of items that participants identified correctly. In each case, cell entries refer to differences between the accuracy obtained under each task-objective condition and accuracy observed in comprehension-only conditions.

the difference in recognition accuracy at each combination of task objectives and the time these objectives were induced and the accuracy under control conditions. Asking participants to communicate the sequence of events that occurred decreased their recognition accuracy relative to control conditions, and this was true regardless of when these objectives were induced. In contrast, asking participants to describe their impressions of the protagonists after watching the movie only decreased their accuracy of identifying things the protagonists said and did not appreciably influence their recognition of nonverbal behaviors. Moreover, the effects of impression-formation objectives were evident only when task objectives were induced after participants had watched the movie.[2]

More generally, these studies show not only that conclusions drawn from verbal information can be influenced by visual stimuli but also that memory for visually coded information can be influenced by verbal communications. In the studies we conducted, the events described in the visual material were fictitious. However, it is reasonable to suppose that similar effects could occur when people communicate about actual events they see on television. To this extent, not only may exposure to information in the entertainment media influence the impact of other information, but also communications about media content, perhaps for the purpose of being entertaining, can influence memory for the original events and, therefore, beliefs and attitudes to which the events are relevant.

CONCLUDING REMARKS

Much of the information conveyed in the media is intended to entertain or to stimulate interest. This is particularly true of information that is conveyed in pictures or video vignettes. The research reviewed in this chapter suggests that this information can have an impact on how people think about verbal information they receive in either the same context or in different contexts and, therefore, the conclusions they draw from it. To this extent, it can have an impact on the attitudes

---

[2]The effects of inducing task objectives before participants watched the movie require further consideration. Participants are likely to include all of the statements and behaviors that they consider to be of sufficient interest to communicate to others in the representation they formed spontaneously in the course of comprehending what went on. Thus, the content of the representation that participants formed when they had an event-description objective was likely to be similar in content regardless of whether they were informed of this objective before or after they saw the movie, so the goal-specific representation they formed was also likely to be similar in the two cases. As this reasoning implies, describing the sequence of events that occurred decreased recognition accuracy, regardless of when participants were informed they would have to generate this description. In contrast, participants who expect to communicate their impressions of the participants may include things in the representation they form while watching the movie that are relevant to their impressions but would not be depicted in the representation they would form when they are only trying to comprehend what is going on. The implications of these additional features may then be included in the communication they generate later, and their recognition may benefit, as results suggest.

and beliefs that are formed from this information in ways in which recipients are often unaware and that the communicator may not always intend. As we acknowledged at the outset, the research we have reported was not designed with the explicit intention of examining the impact of the media on attitudes, values, and behavior. Moreover, the effects we discussed were largely induced by situation-specific factors, the effects of which are likely to dissipate over time. As we have noted, however, frequent exposure to stimuli is likely to increase their chronic accessibility and, therefore, to have an influence that persists over time and situations. Enduring effects of the sort we have described nevertheless remain to be established. The work we have summarized suggests directions in which future research might take.

ACKNOWLEDGMENTS

The research reported in this chapter was supported by grants MH 5-2616 from the National Institute of Mental Health and HKUST 6053/01H from the Research Grants Council of the Hong Kong Special Administrative Region, China.

REFERENCES

Adaval, R., Isbell, L. M., & Wyer, R. S. (2003). *Political information processing: The impact of pictures and information presentation format on impressions of politicians*. Unpublished manuscript, Hong Kong University of Science and Technology.

Adaval, R., & Wyer, R. S. (1998). The role of narratives in consumer information processing. *Journal of Consumer Psychology, 7*, 207–245.

Adaval, R., & Wyer, R. S. (2003). *Memory for social interactions: Effects of post-information processing objectives on the recognition of protagonists' statements and nonverbal behaviors.* Unpublished manuscript, Hong Kong University of Science and Technology.

Anderson, N. H. (1971). Integration theory and attitude change. *Psychological Review, 78*, 171–206.

Bargh, J. A., Chen, M., & Burrows, L. (1996). Automaticity of social behavior: Direct effects of trait construct and stereotype activation on action. *Journal of Personality and Social Psychology, 71*, 230–244.

Carlston, D. E. (1980). Events, inferences and impression formation. In R. Hastie, T. Ostrom, E. Ebbesen, R. Wyer, D. Hamilton, & D. Carlston (Eds.), *Person memory: The cognitive basis of social perception* (pp. 89–120). Hillsdale, NJ: Lawrence Erlbaum Associates.

Colcombe, S. J., & Wyer, R. S. (2001). *The effects of image-based priming on lexical access, conceptual activation, and behavior.* Unpublished manuscript, University of Illinois at Urbana-Champaign.

Costley, C. L., & Brucks, M. (1992). Selective recall and information use in consumer preferences. *Journal of Consumer Research, 18*, 464–474.

Devine, P. G. (1989). Stereotypes and prejudice: Their automatic and controlled components. *Journal of Personality and Social Psychology, 56*, 5–18.

Drabman, R. S., & Thomas, M. A. (1975). Does TV violence breed indifference? *Journal of Communication, 25*, 86–89.

Edell, J. A., & Staelin, R. (1983). The information processing of pictures in print advertisements. *Journal of Consumer Research, 10*, 45–61.

Englis, B. G. (1994). The role of affect in political advertising: Voter emotional responses to the nonverbal behavior of politicians. In E. M. Clark et al. (Eds.), *Attention, attitude and affect in response to advertising* (pp. 223–247). Hillsdale, NJ: Lawrence Erlbaum Associates.

Fishbein, M., & Hunter, R. (1964). Summation versus balance in attitude organization and change. *Journal of Abnormal and Social Psychology, 69*, 505–510.

Hasher, L., Goldstein, D., & Toppin, T. (1977). Frequency and the conference of referential validity. *Journal of Verbal Learning and Verbal Behavior, 16*, 107–122.

Higgins, E. T. (1996). Knowledge activation: Accessibility, applicability and salience. In E. T. Higgins & A. W. Kruglanski (Eds.), *Social cognition: Handbook of basic principles* (pp. 133–168). New York: Guilford.

Higgins, E. T., Bargh, J. A., & Lombardi, W. (1985). The nature of priming effects on categorization. *Journal of Experimental Psychology: Learning, Memory, and Cognition, 11*, 59–69.

Higgins, E. T., & Lurie, L. (1983). Context, categorization and recall: The "change of standard" effect. *Cognitive Psychology, 15*, 525–547.

Higgins, E. T., & Rholes, W. S. (1978). "Saying is believing": Effects of message modification on memory and liking for the person described. *Journal of Experimental Social Psychology, 14*, 363–378.

Hilgard, E. R. (1951). Methods and procedure in the study of learning. In S. S. Stevens (Ed.), *Handbook of experimental psychology*. New York: Wiley.

Isbell, L. M., & Wyer, R. S. (1998). Correcting for mood-induced bias in impression formation: The roles of chronic and situation-induced motivation. *Personality and Social Psychology Bulletin, 25*, 237–249.

Iyer, P. (1988). *Video night in Kathmandu*. London: Bloomsbury.

Jacoby, L. L., Kelley, C., Brown, J., & Jasechko, J. (1989). Becoming famous overnight: On the ability to avoid unconscious influences of the past. *Journal of Personality and Social Psychology, 56*, 326–338.

Johnson, M. K., Hashtroudi, S., & Lindsay, D. S. (1993). Source monitoring. *Psychological Bulletin, 14*, 3–28.

Lepore, L., & Brown, R. (1997). Category and stereotype activation: Is prejudice inevitable? *Journal of Personality and Social Psychology, 72*, 275–287.

Lerner, M. J., Miller, D. T., & Holmes, J. G. (1976). Deserving and the emergence of forms of justice. In L. Berkowitz (Ed.), *Advances in experimental social psychology* (Vol. 9, pp. 133–162). New York: Academic Press.

Lerner, M. J., & Simmons, C. H. (1966). Observer's reactions to the "innocent victim": Compassion or rejection? *Journal of Personality and Social Psychology, 4*, 203–210.

Lingle, J. H., & Ostrom, T. M. (1979). Retrieval selectivity in memory-based impression judgments. *Journal of Personality and Social Psychology, 37*, 180–194.

Nisbett, R. E., & Ross, L. (1980). *Human inference: Strategies and shortcomings of social judgment*. Englewood Cliffs, NJ: Prentice-Hall.

O'Guinn, T. C., & Shrum, L. J. (1997). The role of television in the construction of consumer reality. *Journal of Consumer Research, 23*, 278–294.

Ottati, V. C., & Isbell, L. M. (1996). Effects of mood during exposure to target information and subsequently reported judgments: An on-line model of misattribution and correction. *Journal of Personality and Social Psychology, 71*, 39–53.

Pennington, N., & Hastie, R. (1986). Evidence evaluation in complex decision making. *Journal of Personality and Social Psychology, 51*, 242–258.

Pennington, N., & Hastie, R. (1988). Explanation-based decision making: Effects of memory structure on judgment. *Journal of Experimental Psychology: Learning, Memory and Cognition, 14*, 521–533.

Pennington, N., & Hastie, R. (1992). Explaining the evidence: Tests of the story model for juror decision making. *Journal of Personality and Social Psychology, 62*, 189–206.

Petty, R. E., & Wegener, D. T. (1993). Flexible correction processes in judgment: Correcting for context-induced contrast. *Journal of Experimental Social Psychology, 29*, 137–165.

Prinz, W. (1990). A common coding approach to perception and action. In O. Neumann & W. Prinz (Eds.), *Relationships between perception and action* (pp. 167–201). Berlin: Springer-Verlag.

Reyes, R. M., Thompson, W. C., & Bower, G. H. (1980). Judgment biases resulting from differing availabilities of arguments. *Journal of Personality and Social Psychology, 39*, 2–12.

Sengupta, J., & Fitzsimons, G. (2000). Disruption vs. reinforcement: The effects of analyzing reasons for brand preferences. *Journal of Marketing Research, 37*, 318–330.

Sherman, S. J., Ahlm, K., Berman, L., & Lynn, S. (1978). Contrast effects and the relationship to subsequent behavior. *Journal of Experimental Social Psychology, 14*, 340–350.

Wagstaff, G. F. (1982). Attitudes toward rape: The "just world" strikes again? *Bulletin of the British Psychological Society, 35*, 277–279.

Wyer, R. S., Bodenhausen, G. V., & Gorman, T. F. (1985). Cognitive mediators of reactions to rape. *Journal of Personality and Social Psychology, 48*, 324–378.

Wyer, R. S., Budesheim, T. L., Shavitt, S., Riggle, E. J., Melton, R. J., & Kuklinsky, J. H. (1991). Image, issues and ideology: The processing of information about political candidates. *Journal of Personality and Social Psychology, 61*, 533–545.

Wyer, R. S., & Radvansky, G. A. (1999). The comprehension and validation of social information. *Psychological Review, 106*, 89–118.

Zillmann, D., & Bryant, J. (1982). Pornography, sexual callousness, and the trivialization of rape. *Journal of Communication, 32*, 10–21.

CHAPTER NINE

The Power of Fiction: Determinants and Boundaries

Melanie C. Green
University of Pennsylvania

Jennifer Garst
University of Maryland, College Park

Timothy C. Brock
Ohio State University

Entertainment media often present fictional portrayals of events, and individuals regularly alter their real-world beliefs in response to fictional communications (e.g., Green & Brock, 2000; Strange & Leung, 1999). Whereas marketing practitioners have seized on the selling potential inherent in entertainment media (e.g., with product placements in sitcoms and movies), psychologists are only beginning to understand the nature and mechanisms of fictional influence. In this chapter, we focus on entertainment programs themselves, rather than advertisements or persuasive messages per se. We offer an overview of research on the persuasive power of fictional communications and provide a conceptual framework for studying the effects of fiction and narrative. Evidence suggests that two mechanisms, low elaborative scrutiny and high experienced transportation, may underlie the influence of fictional communications. Furthermore, promising areas of research are outlined that begin to elucidate the boundary conditions under which fiction can have an influence and the factors that determine the staying power of that influence.

Nonfiction, with its pretension of veridicality, and fiction, with its patina of verisimilitude but no necessary pretension to accuracy, are popularly understood as distinct realms. However, research in a variety of domains shows that the fact-fiction distinction is overstated: Individuals may blur the boundaries between the real and the imaginary, as evidenced by the developmental study of children's mental theories of reality (Flavell, 1999), suggestibility of both children and adults

to false suppositions (Bruck & Ceci, 1999; Loftus, 1992), confusion between actual perceptions and thoughts in studies of reality monitoring (Johnson, 1998), and "making of fact" in news media, the courts, and novels (Bruner, 1998). The extent to which individuals integrate products of imagination into their real-world belief structures is of critical importance, yet this topic has received little attention in the persuasion domain.

Despite people's immersion in narratives in their everyday lives, the study of narratives in persuasion contexts has been relatively neglected by psychological science. An authoritative reference in the field of persuasion and attitude change contains more than 60 pages of references but has no mention of the impact of narratives and fiction on attitude or belief change (Eagly & Chaiken, 1993). Research in persuasion has been skewed toward the investigation of rhetoric, or primarily fact-based advocacy messages, such as advertisements, speeches, and editorials, that contain arguments specifically designed to sway a reader to a particular position. The rare exceptions to this trend have suggested that narrative is a powerful form of communication (e.g., Adaval & Wyer, 1998; Deighton, Romer, & McQueen, 1989; Wyer, Adaval, & Colcombe, 2002). Outside of the persuasion arena, the power of a narrative format has been demonstrated by studies in several domains, ranging from jury decision making (Pennington & Hastie, 1988) to likelihood estimates (Gregory, Cialdini, & Carpenter, 1982). In the current conceptual review, we are interested in narratives because they are the primary vehicles for fiction. Although it is certainly possible to find instances of nonnarrative fiction, fiction is often isomorphic with narrative.

Together and separately, narratives and fiction have been underexplored by science, despite their prevalence in the lives of individuals and their importance for understanding domains such as consumer behavior. We review the evidence for the power of fiction and present a theoretical framework for investigating the effects of fiction. Our proposed framework suggests that elaborative scrutiny and the experience of being transported into a narrative world can affect how much influence is exerted by fictional communications.

FICTION MATTERS: BROADER IMPACT OF FICTIONAL COMMUNICATION

Understanding the conditions under which fiction can have an influence—and the staying power of that influence—is important for individuals interested in the intersection of entertainment media and consumer psychology for at least three broad reasons: the potential use of fiction to intentionally persuade, the prevention of persuasion via fiction when information is inaccurate or misleading, and the illumination of ways in which individuals negotiate the boundaries between imagination and reality. Theory-driven understanding of individuals' responses to fiction helps to achieve all of these goals.

First, authors, educators, and media practitioners sometimes want individuals to gain information from works with fictional components. For instance, *Sesame Street* creates fictional situations but teaches children real information about numbers and letters. Entertainment-education programs have been useful in conveying family-planning information and other prosocial messages in developing nations (Slater, 2002). The first author is part of a research team developing a computer game (Heart Sense) to reduce prehospitalization delay for heart attack victims; the computer game conveys serious health information using the setting of a fictional village with fictional characters. Understanding the ways in which individuals might extract valuable real-world information from within a fictional setting is an important factor in determining or increasing the effectiveness of these entertainment media.

The second reason why fiction matters is the reverse of the first: Individuals may be persuaded when they should not be, such as when false information about a medical condition or treatment is presented in a fictional entertainment program. It may be dangerous or harmful if individuals come to believe false information as a result of persuasion via fiction. Similarly, it may be detrimental to a company if their product is presented in a misleading light. A related danger, as noted by Strange (2002), is that "a particular peril of stories is that they are equally good at communicating prototypical and atypical cases, and rarely announce how representative they are" (p. 279).

This perilous aspect of fiction's power has gained the most attention in society at large; efforts to suppress fictional forms of expression are widespread (Strange, Green, & Brock, 2000). Interestingly, censors—including parents and school boards who attempt to ban books such as the *Harry Potter* series from classrooms and libraries—often assume that fiction can have harmful effects on attitudes and beliefs but do not have empirical support for this assumption (DelFattore, 2002).

A final reason for exploring fiction is to come to a deeper understanding of how individuals approach issues of reality and of truth. Understanding the range of circumstances under which individuals will accept information that may not be accurate is relevant beyond the persuasion domain. Creators of entertainment media will want to be cognizant of how likely their audience will be to accept information embedded in their fictional-based programs. Designers of virtual reality simulations may draw on understanding of the psychology of fiction and narrative engagement to enhance the reality of their simulations.

THE POWER OF FICTION: PERCEPTION AND REALITY

Cultural Default: Nonfiction and Fiction As Separate Realms?

Despite these important reasons to focus on how individuals interpret fictional communications, our cultural default may be to assume that nonfiction and fiction should be understood as distinct realms, with information gained from fiction

treated as at least potentially less reliable. Bookstores and libraries are divided into fiction and nonfiction sections. Journalists lose their jobs and professional reputations if they are caught fabricating parts of stories. Most entertainment products are clearly distinguished as fiction, such as a sitcom, or nonfiction, such as a news report, although the line between the two is becoming increasingly blurred (Bruner, 1998). It seems reasonable to think that we should learn more about the world from a newscast, which at least attempts to be an accurate reflection of real events, rather than from a television drama, which may engage in inordinate amounts of artistic license.

However, evidence *against* nonfiction's superior persuasiveness has been increasing in studies of narratives (e.g., Green & Brock, 2000; Murphy, 1998; Slater, 1990). For example, Strange and Leung (1999) showed that narratives labeled as news (nonfiction) or as fiction had equivalent influence on readers' perceptions of a social problem. Green and Brock (2000) showed that both specific and general beliefs were affected by exposure to a narrative, regardless of whether the narrative was labeled as nonfiction or fiction. On a larger scale, the cultivation literature suggests that repeated exposure to fictional television programs can create a view of the world as dangerous (e.g., Gerbner & Gross, 1976; Shrum, Wyer, & O'Guinn, 1998).

Automatic Acceptance

Additional psychological evidence suggests that individuals do not always separate information into tidy categories, accepting one and rejecting the other. For example, following Spinozan philosophy, Gilbert (1991) proposed that the default response to information is to initially believe every assertion encountered. His experiments (in a nonnarrative context) indicated that individuals may later discount information that is known to have come from a false source, but immediate assent is a relatively automatic process in response to information comprehension. Correction for inaccurate information may generally occur without difficulty, but if a person is prevented from engaging in correction processes, the belief may persevere (Gilbert, Krull, & Malone, 1990; Gilbert, Tafarodi, & Malone, 1993). Similarly, Gerrig (1993) claimed that individuals do not automatically create a separate mental category for fictional information, as compared with factual communication.

In a related vein, Reeves and Nass (1996) suggested that "the automatic response is to accept what seems to be real as in fact real" (p. 8). Prentice and colleagues (Prentice, Gerrig, & Bailis, 1997) found that people accepted false assertions, such as "chocolate helps you lose weight" and "mental illness is contagious," if those assertions were embedded in fictional narratives (Wheeler, Green, & Brock, 1999). The findings that people are susceptible to assertions embedded in a narrative may be extended, for example, to product endorsements contained within entertainment programs. If people either do not want to or are not able to separate out fictional information from nonfictional information, they may be affected by it.

WHAT IS FICTION? RECOGNITION AND TRUTH STATUS

Recognition of Fictional Context

In some instances, individuals may be persuaded by fiction because they do not know, do not believe, or do not remember that the information is fictional. (See Strange, 2002, for a full discussion of these modes of context failure and Johnson, 1998, for a discussion of reality monitoring.) For example, a reader may miss a disclaimer that a story is a work of fiction or may not accept an author's claim that resemblance to real persons and places is coincidental. Furthermore, there are forms of media where nonfiction and fiction are becoming blurred, such as docudramas or narratives based on a true story. Although these context failures and mixed formats are interesting in their own right, they are beyond the scope of the current review. Our conceptual analysis addresses cases where individuals are fully aware that they are reading a fictional work.

Fiction Versus Falsehood

Even when a work is clearly identified as fiction, investigations of fictional impact are made more complex by the nature of fiction as a category. Fiction is most often defined as an imaginative work that is not necessarily true. Some authors of fiction might engage in extensive research so that, even if the characters in their stories never actually lived, the places and historical events surrounding them match reality. (A recent book, *Novel History* [Carnes, 2001], brings together historians and novelists to discuss exactly this issue.) Accepting information from a fictional source may not constitute an error in judgment if the focal information is reliable. However, some authors may not be constrained by actual history and may make up people and places with abandon. In practice, there is a huge continuum in the accuracy of presented information, ranging from minor changes in details that serve to increase entertainment value to playing very loose with facts (e.g., Carnes, 2001). For example, Oliver Stone's film *JFK* was widely criticized for ignoring the historical record, whereas the television drama *E.R.* has been praised for the accuracy of its medical information. Without consulting external references, a reader often has no solid basis for determining what information translates to the real world and what should remain in the realm of fantasy.

FICTION AS A CUE TO PROCESSING STYLE

We propose that either fiction or narrative may serve as a cue to a reader to engage in a less-critical, more immersive form of mental engagement. The idea that stories are treated differently from scientific or logical argument, and may be held to different truth standards than rhetorical messages, is not new (see, e.g., Bruner,

1986). Prentice and Gerrig (1999) suggested that fiction tends to be processed nonsystematically and that fiction has its greatest influence when readers respond experientially rather than rationally. From a cognitive perspective, Zwaan (1994) found that *genre expectations*—being told a passage was a news story versus an excerpt from a novel—affected the types of mental representations formed by readers. Readers who believed they were reading a literary work had longer reading times and a better representation of surface information, such as the exact words used by the author, whereas those who thought they were reading a news story had better recall of situational information, indicating a deeper level of representation. However, the effects of these different processing styles have not been systematically explored in the domain of attitude change.

We further propose that this less-critical processing of fiction may take an unengaged or engaged form. In the unengaged form of fictional processing, an individual may simply refrain from critical or evaluative processing (see Prentice & Gerrig, 1999). The person may be focused on relaxation, may feel that the material is not particularly important, or may simply wish to be distracted or passively entertained (see Brock & Livingston, this volume). Thus, he or she may be passively influenced by the communication. The engaged form of fictional processing is what Green and Brock (2000) have termed *transportation into a narrative world*, as described in the next section.

Unengaged Form of Fictional Processing: Low Elaborative Scrutiny

There is some empirical evidence (Garst, Green, & Brock, 2000) suggesting that fiction/nonfiction labeling may affect how individuals process information. Within the framework of a dual-process model of persuasion (elaboration likelihood model; Petty & Cacioppo, 1986; Petty & Wegener, 1998), Garst et al. (2000) exposed participants to a rhetorical persuasive message (a speech) about a university policy requiring essay examinations for seniors. Approximately half of the participants read a speech containing arguments that an independent pretest sample had rated as relatively strong and convincing (e.g., "studying for essay exams fosters better quality learning"). The other half read a speech containing arguments pretested to be weaker and less compelling (e.g., "teachers take longer to grade essay exams"). Pilot testing confirmed that both strong and weak messages could be credibly presented as fact or fiction.

Participants in the fact condition read a transcript, formatted in two columns and credited to TV (channel) 8 News. The following introduction was used: "The speech you will be assessing was . . . recently given by John Nelson . . . on a live television broadcast . . . the speaker . . . is a real person and the speech transcript is factual." Participants in the fiction condition read a script, formatted in a single column and credited to the American Television Writers' Guild. The following

introduction was used:

> The speech you will be assessing was created as part of a fictional television drama. The actor giving the speech plays the part of John Nelson . . . on a made-for-television drama . . . The character . . . is not real nor is the speech real. In fact, the television writers totally made up the speech in order to further develop the plot line of the drama.

Participants' need for cognition (Cacioppo, Petty, & Kao, 1984), their dispositional tendency to enjoy and engage in effortful thought, was also measured.

Results revealed that both high and low need-for-cognition participants scrutinized the message labeled as fact (i.e., participants' attitudes and thoughts were responsive to whether they read strong or weak arguments), but only participants who were high in need for cognition scrutinized the fictional message. It appears that, under some circumstances, individuals are less likely to ponder information reported to be fiction than they are fact. An important implication of these results is that imagination-based assertions may have a substantial effect on attitudes because people are accepting information labeled as fiction without careful scrutiny. Of course, this fiction-labeled information could easily include commercial appeals.

Interestingly, in the Garst et al. (2000) research, both fact- and fiction-labeled messages changed attitudes, and, indeed, fiction was as effective as fact in persuading students to support the new exam policy. Fact and fiction differences manifested themselves in how much readers scrutinized the information, not by how persuasive the information was. That is, fact and fiction did not differ in their overall effects on attitude change.

The parity of influence by messages labeled as fact and fiction could not be attributed to an unsuccessful instantiation of the fact/fiction label or to insufficient power to detect the effect. Recipients had good recall of the fact/fiction label of the messages they read. Furthermore, because messages labeled as fiction were persuasive even when the position being advocated (mandatory essay exams) was both pertinent to the college student participants, and contrary to their initial attitudes, the power of fictional framing does not appear to be limited to topics or advocacies that are irrelevant or agreeable.

Engaged Form of Fictional Processing: Transportation Into Narrative Worlds

Recent research by Green and Brock (2000) focused on the phenomenological experience of being absorbed in a story—a process called transportation into a narrative world—as a mechanism of narrative impact (see also Gerrig, 1993). Most people have had the sensation of being "lost in a book" (Nell, 1988), swept up into the world of a story so completely that they forget the world around them.

Instead of being aware of their physical surroundings, transported readers see the action of the story unfolding before them. They react emotionally to events that are simply words on a page. Transportation resembles flow, or optimal experience (Csikszentmihalyi, 1990).

A transported individual is cognitively and emotionally involved in the story and may experience vivid mental images tied to the story's plot. Green and Brock (2000) developed and validated a scale to measure the extent of transportation experienced by readers and conducted a series of studies demonstrating that highly transported individuals showed more story-consistent beliefs on both story-specific and general attitudinal measures than did individuals who were less transported. Transportation was also associated with increased positivity toward sympathetic characters and a reduction in negative thoughts in response to the story.

Although most of the studies of transportation to date use written materials, the experience of transportation is not limited to the reading of written material. Narrative worlds are broadly defined with respect to modality; the term *reader* may be construed to include listeners, viewers, or any recipient of narrative information. Thus, transportation theory (Green & Brock, 2000, 2002) is broadly applicable to most entertainment media: books, television, radio, and computer-based stories.

How does the phenomenological experience of being "lost in a book" translate into belief change?

First, transportation may aid in suspension of disbelief and reduction of counterarguing about the issues raised in the story. If individuals are putting aside real-world facts, they may not use these facts to contradict implications of the narrative. The mental correction literature suggests that individuals need both motivation and ability to correct beliefs based on untrue, inaccurate, or incomplete information (e.g., Gilbert, 1991; Gilbert et al., 1993). The reduction of negative cognitive responding resulting from transportation could be due to ability factors—the person's mental resources are so engaged in experiencing the story that they are not able to disbelieve story conclusions. Transportation's reduction of counterarguing could also be based on motivation—if people are being swept along by an exciting tale, interrupting it to counterargue story points would destroy the pleasure of the experience. Even after finishing a narrative, individuals may not be motivated to go back and evaluate the implications of the story, especially if they do not believe the story has had any effect on them (e.g., Perloff, 1999). This reduction of counterarguing may also allow product-related information contained in an entertainment context to influence viewers. Transported individuals may be less likely to critically evaluate the products and product claims found within the narrative world.

The traditional means of assessing acceptance of a rhetorical passage is through the use of cognitive responses (Petty, Ostrom, & Brock, 1981). After reading a persuasive message or story, participants list all thoughts, positive or negative, about the message. In our studies (Green & Brock, 2000), however, thought listings did not seem to provide a sensitive measure of unfavorable responses individuals

had while reading the narratives. To address this concern, we created a new measure of story acceptance/rejection called Pinocchio Circling. Once participants had finished reading the narrative, they were instructed to go back over the story and circle any "false notes," or parts of the story that did not ring true to them. False notes were described as something in the story that contradicts a fact or does not make sense. The instructions explained that sometimes authors leave clues when they are being untruthful, just as Pinocchio's nose grew after he told a lie. For narrative communication, identification of false notes may be roughly analogous to counterarguing for rhetorical communication.

We hypothesized that participants who were more transported into the story would be less likely to find false notes in the story; they would be less critical of the story. If highly transported participants showed less false noting, this finding would be supportive of the idea that transportation is correlated with reduced critical thinking and counterarguing. In our studies, there were no right or wrong answers for this task. Pinocchio Circling was intended to be simply a measure of participants' own acceptance or rejection of parts of the story.

Results using this measure supported our theorizing; for example, in a study using a story about a little girl murdered by a psychiatric patient (adapted from Nuland, 1994), highly transported participants circled significantly fewer false notes than their less-transported counterparts. Pinocchio Circling may prove to be a meaningful and sensitive measure of cognitive processing of narrative texts.

Another means by which transportation may affect beliefs is by making narrative events seem more like personal experience. Research has shown that direct experience with attitude objects can result in strong and enduring attitudes (Fazio & Zanna, 1981). If a reader or viewer feels as if he or she has been part of narrative events, the lessons implied by those events may seem more powerful. Work on source monitoring suggests that imagined events may be misremembered as real to the extent that the memories have qualities similar to real memories—for example, concreteness and vivid detail (Johnson, Hashtroudi, & Lindsay, 1993). Narratives, particularly ones into which readers have become transported, are likely to meet those criteria.

Recent advances in virtual reality technology provide a fertile avenue for increased exploration of the transportation mechanism. Individuals transported into imaginary worlds where they can interact with their environments on a physical and sensory level may show even greater belief change. Of course, researchers are still attempting to perfect techniques that allow an increased sense of presence in virtual worlds (Biocca, 2002).

Finally, one effect of transportation is to create strong feelings toward characters in a narrative. Because the narrative world becomes real to a transported individual, sympathetic characters may come to seem like friends, fellow travelers on an adventure. By the same token, readers may develop a passionate hatred of story villains. This attachment to characters may play a critical role in narrative-based belief change and thus may serve as another route by which transportation leads

to belief change. Source credibility is usually an external "given" in persuasive communications (see Eagly & Chaiken, 1993; Hass, 1981); however, for narrative communications, attachment to a protagonist may be an important determinant of the persuasiveness of a story. If a viewer likes or identifies with a particular character, statements made by the character or implications of events experienced by that character may carry special weight. This attachment may extend to objects or consumer products used by (or praised by) protagonists; viewers may form more positive attitudes toward the products through this association.

RESPONDING TO FICTION: JUDGMENT CRITERIA

Even though individuals may not critically evaluate every assertion in a fictional work (due to either the unengaged or engaged form of fictional processing, or both), readers nonetheless have standards by which to judge a fictional work. Fictional information must be compelling in some way for readers to accept the information.

Plausibility Criterion

Oatley (1999) claimed that fiction "may be twice as true as fact" (p. 101). This statement is based on the idea of fictional narratives as mental simulations, where one definition of truth is coherence within a complex structure. Oatley also noted that personal insight is another type of truth that may emerge from a story, even one that does not reflect empirical reality. His ideas appear to capture naive theories of fiction; readers confronted with a work of fiction may be less concerned with its objective truth status (whether the events described actually occurred) and more concerned with whether the work meets some plausibility criterion (realistic characters, settings, or sensible ideas). It is expected that people's appraisal of a narrative as realistic (or not) will have an impact on the narrative's influence (see Busselle & Greenberg, 2000, for a recent review of judgments about television realism). Instead of assuming that introducing materials as nonfictional or fictional would make all readers think the narratives are real or less real, the audience's perception of the perceived plausibility of the stimulus should be taken into account.

BOUNDARY CONDITIONS ON EFFECTS OF FICTION

As noted previously, an increasing body of evidence suggests that fictional information is often integrated into real-world belief structures. We suggest that both factors internal and external to the narrative or message, as well as factors that arise from an interaction between internal and external forces, may help determine whether fictional information is accepted or rejected. Internal factors may include the type

of information given within the text, such as context details versus context-free assertions (see later discussion) or the ease with which information is compared with real-world facts. External factors may include information about the message, prior beliefs of the reader, explicit information about the validity of assertions contained in the narrative, or circumstances that might motivate readers to be especially critical in their approach to the material. Factors such as familiarity with the narrative content arise from an interaction of factors external to the text (prior knowledge of the reader) and internal to the text (content). We review a subset of these factors.

Context Details Versus Context-Free Assertions

In their discussion of narrative fiction, Gerrig and Prentice (1991) distinguish between context details and context-free assertions. Context details are setting elements that are particular to the fictional world and that tend not to be integrated into real-world belief structures. For example, changing the name of the president of the United States in a fictional work is unlikely to affect real-world political beliefs.

On the other hand, context-free assertions are more general claims that are not bound to particular settings. For example, Gerrig and Prentice's (1991) experimental narrative included the (false) statements that "chocolate helps you lose weight" and "mental illness is contagious." This type of information could theoretically apply to the real world as well as to the story world and thus would be more likely to have an impact on real-world beliefs. Gerrig and Prentice found significantly slower reaction times when identifying context-free assertions presented in the story but no such interference effect for context details. The reaction time data indicated that the false context-free assertions from the story were interfering with the verification of real-world facts, suggesting that fictional information had been incorporated into long-term memory. Thus, Gerrig and Prentice concluded that fictional context-free assertions, but not fictional context details, tend to be integrated into real-world knowledge.

Work by Green and Brock (2000) suggests that context-free information need not necessarily take the form of an assertion in the story for it to influence beliefs. For example, a story that implies that the world is an unjust place can affect just-world beliefs (Rubin & Peplau, 1975), even if the author or characters do not specifically assert that life is not fair. Lessons drawn from the events in a narrative or the experiences of the characters can have the same effects as context-free assertions. The boundary conditions for the power of context-free narrative implication, as well as narrative assertion, remain relatively unexplored.

Relevance

In the persuasion literature, enhanced personal relevance is a classic manipulation to encourage increased scrutiny of persuasive messages (Petty & Cacioppo, 1979, 1990). The elaboration likelihood perspective (e.g., Petty & Cacioppo, 1986) states

that individuals might be most likely to take source information into account—accepting nonfictional information but rejecting fictional information—under conditions of high personal relevance. However, studies by Garst et al. (2000) using persuasive speeches containing strong and weak arguments advocating changes in exam formats found no differences in the persuasive power of factual/fictional source labeling, even under high personal relevance. The effects of personal or self-relevance on the acceptance of fiction remain to be tested with narrative materials.

Familiarity

Slater (1990) found that ostensibly nonfictional written messages tended to influence readers' beliefs about category group members' characteristics to a greater extent than ostensibly fictional ones. However, this trend only occurred when the social category was relatively familiar (e.g., Contra guerrillas and English gentleman farmers). When the category was unfamiliar (e.g., Eritrean guerrillas and Dutch gentleman farmers in Java), the impact of the fictional message was equal to or greater than that of the nonfictional message.

Similarly, Prentice et al. (1997) found that fictional persuasion only occurred when the story was set at a distant campus rather than at the participants' own university. In the Prentice et al. study, weakly supported claims were embedded in the narrative. The authors claimed that familiar settings evoked cognitive scrutiny that would lead to the rejection of these tenuous propositions. However, Wheeler et al. (1999) failed to replicate the home-away difference in fictional persuasion. Instead, these investigators found persuasion via fiction in both home-school and away-school conditions. The status of familiarity of settings, groups, and topics as a boundary condition on fictional influence remains uncertain.

The boundary conditions we have discussed here—context-free assertions versus context details, personal relevance, and familiarity—are a subset of possible boundary conditions on fiction's influence. Given the accumulating evidence for the broad scope of fiction's power, extending our knowledge of possible limits on fictional influence would be useful for both researchers and persuasion practitioners.

STRENGTH OF ATTITUDE AND BELIEF CHANGE VIA NARRATIVES AND FICTION

The boundary conditions described previously suggest when fiction might be more or less likely to affect beliefs. Another key question is the nature of the beliefs or attitudes that are created through fiction. Not all attitudes are created equal; some types of attitude change may be transient, whereas others are more long lasting. Green and Brock (2000) suggested that narrative-based belief change may be relatively persistent over time and resistant to counterpersuasion. They base this claim

on findings that narratives are a preferred mental structure for storing and retrieving information (e.g., Schank & Abelson, 1995) and on the idea that narratives are able to effectively bring together both cognitive and affective contributions to attitude change. Attitudes and beliefs that have both cognitive and emotional foundations have been shown to be more persistent (Rosselli, Skelly, & Mackie, 1995). Finally, narratives may have the additional benefit of creating mental images, which can re-evoke story themes and messages when recalled (see Green & Brock, 2002). These qualities of narrative-based attitudes may also increase other aspects of attitude strength.

The prediction about the effects of fiction labeling, per se, is less clear. One possibility is that attitudes changed by a communication labeled as fictional will be equally as strong as those changed by a message labeled as nonfiction. Research to date has shown that in the majority of cases, individuals do not discount fictional information at the time of reading. It may be that the parity between nonfiction and fiction extends to attitude strength as well. An alternative hypothesis is that differences between nonfiction and fiction may not emerge as differences on evaluations or attitudes but, rather, may show up in attitude strength measures. Individuals may be less certain of or confident in their beliefs if those beliefs were formed by reading a message (narrative or nonnarrative) labeled as fiction. Additionally, if fiction promotes less careful scrutiny of the presented information, the attitude that will result will be weaker and less able to withstand subsequent counterpropaganda (see Petty, Haugtvedt, & Smith, 1995, for a review).

CONCLUSION

Although the relative strength of attitudes changed by fiction and narrative remains an open question, it is clear that individuals regularly alter their real-world beliefs and attitudes in response to fictional communications (Garst et al., 2000; Green & Brock, 2000; Prentice et al., 1997; Slater, 1990; Strange & Leung, 1999; Wheeler et al., 1999). Despite the prevalence of fiction in everyday life, there has been relatively little empirical investigation of how individuals may be influenced by products of imagination. Similarly, individuals often shift their beliefs in response to stories or narratives, yet persuasion researchers have paid much more attention to traditional persuasive messages, such as editorials or advertisements.

In their recent review of the use of dual-process models (elaboration likelihood model, Petty & Cacioppo, 1986; heuristic-systematic model, Chaiken, Liberman, & Eagly, 1989) to explore distinctions between fictional and nonfictional communication, Prentice and Gerrig (1999) wrote they "have been hesitant to embrace either of these [dual-process] models, however, because neither of them seems to capture the phenomenological experience of reading (or hearing or viewing) a work of fiction" (p. 543). Our theoretical framework attempts to capture that experience. We reviewed evidence that low elaborative

scrutiny (unengaged form of fictional processing) and high experienced transportation (engaged form of fictional processing) can affect fictional communications' power to change beliefs and attitudes. Furthermore, we outlined promising areas of research that begin to elucidate the boundary conditions under which fiction can have an influence and the factors that determine the staying power of that influence.

Our analysis confirms what censors have suspected for centuries—that fiction can be a powerful tool for shaping attitudes and opinions. Stories are especially influential when we become drawn into them—when our cognitive resources, our emotions, and our mental imagery faculties are engaged. It is important that we begin to explore the full range of implications of the pervasive influence of fictional work (Green, Strange, & Brock, 2002).

REFERENCES

Adaval, R., & Wyer, R. S., Jr. (1998). The role of narratives in consumer information processing. *Journal of Consumer Psychology, 7*, 207–245.

Biocca, F. (2002). The evolution of interactive media: Toward "being there" in nonlinear narrative worlds. In M. C. Green, J. J. Strange, & T. C. Brock (Eds.), *Narrative impact: Social and cognitive foundations* (pp. 97–130). Mahwah, NJ: Lawrence Erlbaum Associates.

Bruck, M., & Ceci, S. J. (1999). The suggestibility of children's memory. *Annual Review of Psychology, 50*, 387–418.

Bruner, J. S. (1986). *Actual minds, possible worlds.* Cambridge, MA: Harvard University Press.

Bruner, J. (1998). What is a narrative fact? *The Annals of the American Academy of Political and Social Science, 560*, 17–27.

Busselle, R. W., & Greenberg, B. S. (2000). The nature of television realism judgments: A reevaluation of their conceptualization and measurement. *Mass Communication and Society, 3*, 249–268.

Cacioppo, J. T., Petty, R. E., & Kao, C. F. (1984). The efficient assessment of need for cognition. *Journal of Personality Assessment, 48*, 306–307.

Carnes, M. C. (2001). *Novel history: Historians and novelists confront America's past (and each other).* New York: Simon & Schuster.

Chaiken, S., Liberman, A., Eagly, A. H. (1989). Heuristic and systematic information processing within and beyond the persuasion context. In J. S. Uleman & J. A. Bargh (Eds.), *Unintended thought* (pp. 212–252). New York: Guilford.

Csikszentmihalyi, M. (1990). *Flow: The psychology of optimal experience.* New York: Harper & Row.

Deighton, J., Romer, D., & McQueen, J. (1989). Using drama to persuade. *Journal of Consumer Research, 16*, 335–343.

DelFattore, J. (2002). Controversial narratives in the schools: Content, values, and conflicting viewpoints. In M. C. Green, J. J. Strange, & T. C. Brock (Eds.), *Narrative impact: Social and cognitive foundations* (pp. 131–155). Mahwah, NJ: Lawrence Erlbaum Associates.

Eagly, A. H., & Chaiken, S. (1993). *The psychology of attitudes.* New York: Academic Press.

Fazio, R. H., & Zanna, M. P. (1981). Direct experience and attitude-behavior consistency. In L. Berkowitz (Ed.), *Advances in experimental social psychology* (Vol. 14, pp. 161–202). New York: Academic Press.

Flavell, J. H. (1999). Cognitive development: Children's knowledge about the mind. *Annual Review of Psychology, 50*, 21–45.

Garst, J., Green, M. C., & Brock, T. C. (2000, June). *Parity of truth and tale in persuasion: Equivalence of outcomes despite differences in underlying processes.* Paper presented at the annual convention of the International Communication Association, Acapulco, Mexico.

Gerbner, G., & Gross, L. (1976). Living with television: The violence profile. *Journal of Communication, 26,* 172–199.

Gerrig, R. J. (1993). *Experiencing narrative worlds: On the psychological activities of reading.* New Haven, CT: Yale University Press.

Gerrig, R. J., & Prentice, D. A. (1991). The representation of fictional information. *Psychological Science, 2,* 336–340.

Gilbert, D. T. (1991). How mental systems believe. *American Psychologist, 46,* 107–119.

Gilbert, D. T., Krull, D. S., & Malone, P. S. (1990). Unbelieving the unbelievable: Some problems in the rejection of false information. *Journal of Personality and Social Psychology, 59,* 601–613.

Gilbert, D. T., Tafarodi, R. W., & Malone, P. S. (1993). You can't not believe everything you read. *Journal of Personality and Social Psychology, 65,* 221–233.

Green, M. C., & Brock, T. C. (2000). The role of transportation in the persuasiveness of public narratives. *Journal of Personality and Social Psychology, 79,* 401–421.

Green, M. C., & Brock, T. C. (2002). In the mind's eye: Transportation-imagery model of narrative persuasion. In M. C. Green, J. J. Strange, & T. C. Brock (Eds.), *Narrative impact: Social and cognitive foundations* (pp. 315–341). Mahwah, NJ: Lawrence Erlbaum Associates.

Green, M. C., Strange, J. J., & Brock, T. C. (Eds.). (2002). *Narrative impact: Social and cognitive foundations.* Mahwah, NJ: Lawrence Erlbaum Associates.

Gregory, W. L., Cialdini, R. B., & Carpenter, K. M. (1982). Self-relevant scenarios as mediators of likelihood estimates and compliance: Does imagining make it so? *Journal of Personality and Social Psychology, 43,* 89–99.

Hass, R. G. (1981). Effects of source characteristics on cognitive responses and persuasion. In R. E. Petty, T. M. Ostrom, & T. C. Brock (Eds.), *Cognitive responses in persuasion* (pp. 141–172). Hillsdale, NJ: Lawrence Erlbaum Associates.

Johnson, M. K. (1998). Individual and cultural reality monitoring. *The Annals of the American Academy of Political and Social Science, 560,* 179–193.

Johnson, M. K., Hashtroudi, S., & Lindsay, D. S. (1993). Source monitoring. *Psychological Bulletin, 114,* 3–28.

Loftus, E. F. (1992). When a lie becomes memory's truth: Memory distortion after exposure to misinformation. *Current Directions in Psychological Science, 1,* 121–123.

Murphy, S. T. (1998). The impact of factual versus fictional media portrayals on cultural stereotypes. *The Annals of the American Academy of Political and Social Science, 560,* 165–178.

Nell, V. (1988). *Lost in a book: The psychology of reading for pleasure.* New Haven, CT: Yale University Press.

Nuland, S. (1994). Murder and serenity. In *How we die* (pp. 118–139). New York: Knopf.

Oatley, K. (1999). Why fiction may be twice as true as fact: Fiction as cognitive and emotional simulation. *Review of General Psychology, 3,* 101–117.

Pennington, N., & Hastie, R. (1988). Explanation-based decision making: Effects of memory structure on judgement. *Journal of Experimental Psychology: Learning, Memory, and Cognition, 14,* 521–533.

Perloff, R. M. (1999). The third-person effect: A critical review and synthesis. *Media Psychology, 1,* 353–378.

Petty, R. E., & Cacioppo, J. T. (1979). Issue involvement can increase or decrease persuasion by enhancing message-relevant cognitive responses. *Journal of Personality and Social Psychology, 37,* 1915–1926.

Petty, R. E., & Cacioppo, J. T. (1986). The elaboration likelihood model of persuasion. In L. Berkowitz (Ed.), *Advances in experimental social psychology* (Vol. 19, pp. 123–205). Orlando, FL: Academic Press.

Petty, R. E., & Cacioppo, J. T. (1990). Involvement and persuasion: Tradition versus integration. *Psychological Bulletin, 107,* 367–374.

Petty, R. E., Haugtvedt, C. P., & Smith, S. M. (1995). Elaboration as a determinant of attitude strength: Creating attitudes that are persistent, resistant, and predictive of behavior. In R. E. Petty & J. A. Krosnick (Eds.), *Attitude strength: Antecedents and consequences* (pp. 93–130). Mahwah, NJ: Lawrence Erlbaum Associates.

Petty, R. E., Ostrom, T., & Brock, T. C. (1981). *Cognitive responses in persuasion.* Hillsdale, NJ: Lawrence Erlbaum Associates.

Petty, R. E., & Wegener, D. T. (1998). Attitude change: Multiple roles for persuasion variables. In D. T. Gilbert, S. T. Fiske, & G. Lindzey (Eds.), *The handbook of social psychology* (4th ed., Vol. 1, pp. 323–390). Boston: McGraw-Hill.

Prentice, D. A., & Gerrig, R. J. (1999). Exploring the boundary between fiction and reality. In S. Chaiken & Y. Trope (Eds.), *Dual-process theories in social psychology* (pp. 529–546). New York: Guilford.

Prentice, D. A., Gerrig, R. J., & Bailis, D. S. (1997). What readers bring to the processing of fictional texts. *Psychonomic Bulletin & Review, 5,* 416–420.

Reeves, B., & Nass, C. (1996). *The media equation: How people treat computers, television, and new media like real people and places.* New York: Cambridge University Press.

Rosselli, F., Skelly, J. J., & Mackie, D. M. (1995). Processing rational and emotional messages: The cognitive and affective mediation of persuasion. *Journal of Experimental Social Psychology, 31,* 163–190.

Rubin, Z., & Peplau, L. A. (1975). Who believes in a just world? *Journal of Social Issues, 31*(3), 65–89.

Schank, R. C., & Abelson, R. P. (1995). Knowledge and memory: The real story. In R. S. Wyer, Jr. (Ed.), *Advances in social cognition* (Vol. 8, pp. 1–85). Hillsdale, NJ: Lawrence Erlbaum Associates.

Shrum, L. J., Wyer, R. S., Jr., & O'Guinn, T. C. (1998). The effects of television consumption on social perceptions: The use of priming procedures to investigate psychological processes. *Journal of Consumer Research, 24,* 447–458.

Slater, M. D. (1990). Processing social information in messages: Social group familiarity, fiction versus nonfiction, and subsequent beliefs. *Communication Research, 17,* 327–343.

Slater, M. D. (2002). Entertainment education and the persuasive impact of narratives. In M. C. Green, J. J. Strange, & T. C. Brock (Eds.), *Narrative impact: Social and cognitive foundations* (pp. 157–181). Mahwah, NJ: Lawrence Erlbaum Associates.

Strange, J. J. (2002). How fictional tales wag real-world beliefs: Models and mechanisms of narrative influence. In M. C. Green, J. J. Strange, & T. C. Brock (Eds.), *Narrative impact: Social and cognitive foundations* (pp. 263–286). Mahwah, NJ: Lawrence Erlbaum Associates.

Strange, J. J., Green, M. C., & Brock, T. C. (2000). Censorship and the regulation of expression. In E. F. Borgatta & R. J. V. Montgomery (Eds.), *Encyclopedia of sociology* (rev. ed. pp. 267–281). New York: MacMillan.

Strange, J. J., & Leung, C. C. (1999). How anecdotal accounts in news and in fiction can influence judgments of a social problem's urgency, causes, and cures. *Personality and Social Psychology Bulletin, 25,* 436–449.

Wheeler, S. C., Green, M. C., & Brock, T. C. (1999). Fictional narratives change beliefs: Replications of Prentice, Gerrig, and Bailis (1997) with mixed corroboration. *Psychonomic Bulletin & Review, 6,* 136–141.

Wyer, R. S., Adaval, R., & Colcombe, S. J. (2002). Narrative-based representations of social knowledge: Their construction and use in comprehension, memory, and judgment. In M. P. Zanna (Ed.), *Advances in experimental social psychology* (Vol. 34, pp. 131–197). New York: Academic Press.

Zwaan, R. A. (1994). Effect of genre expectations on text comprehension. *Journal of Experimental Psychology: Learning, Memory, and Cognition, 20,* 920–933.

CHAPTER TEN

A Process Model of Consumer Cultivation: The Role of Television Is a Function of the Type of Judgment

L. J. Shrum
University of Texas–San Antonio

James E. Burroughs
University of Virginia

Aric Rindfleisch
University of Wisconsin–Madison

Bring up the issue of media effects in any group and it is likely to unleash a torrent of opinions. Virtually everyone has their own theory. This is true regardless of whether the group is composed of academics, business folks, or members of the PTA. Moreover, people tend to hold their theories with pretty high confidence and are often willing to vociferously defend their positions. But why is this so? Perhaps one reason is experience. Everyone, regardless of their profession or hobby, has extensive experience with both the independent and dependent variables. That is, (virtually) everyone watches television (most watch it a lot), listens to the radio, or reads magazines and newspapers. Likewise, everyone makes countless judgments on a daily basis: developing beliefs, forming or reinforcing attitudes, updating personal values, constructing perceptions. A second reason may be that consistent empirical evidence of media effects has been remarkably difficult to pin down. Although the body of evidence is mounting to support the notion that the media have a moderate if not a strong effect on individual judgments (e.g., see Comstock, this volume), there seems to be just enough confounding or conflicting data to call these findings into question and keep alive the debate as to whether the media's influence is that substantial at all.

We would like to suggest a third reason as to why there seems to be little consensus on whether media effects are either prevalent or strong, a reason that may directly relate to the previous two: a lack of understanding of the processes that underlie media effects. With respect to lay opinions about the existence and strength

of media effects, the link between media exposure and individual judgments may not be clear because the processes that are involved in these relations are not clear. Most people are unaware of the underlying causes of their thoughts, feelings, and behaviors, much of which occurs relatively unconsciously (Bargh, 1997; Erdelyi & Zizak, this volume). Despite this, most people cling to the notion that their decisions are willful and for the most part conscious. Consequently, the lack of awareness of the effects of a potential input, such as media consumption, on people's judgments may contribute to their disbelief in the efficacy of media effects.

The lack of understanding of the processes underlying media effects has also hampered academic research. This is especially true for research on the effects of television viewing, particularly for research that has attempted to test cultivation theory (Gerbner & Gross, 1976; for reviews, see Gerbner, Gross, Morgan, Signorielli, & Shanahan, 2002; Shanahan & Morgan, 1999). Just as everyday conversations regarding media effects can be intense, so can academic debates on the same issue. Indeed, these debates on media effects in general and cultivation effects in particular have spawned almost a cottage industry of replies and re-joinders in the premier academic journals (for a review, see Shanahan & Morgan, 1999). For almost every effect reported (or so it seems), an alternative explanation or a reanalysis of the data has been forthcoming. But as we have argued elsewhere (Burroughs, Shrum, & Rindfleisch, 2002; Shrum, 1995, 2002), an understanding of the processes that underlie media effects has the potential to reconcile conflicting findings and interpretations. That is, a process focus would suggest that conditions may exist that either facilitate or inhibit particular media effects, and the presence or absence of these conditions across studies may contribute to these inconsistent findings.

In this chapter, we focus on a particular media effect (the cultivation effect) and attempt to articulate a process model that can account for a variety of effects within the cultivation paradigm. In keeping with the theme of the book, we look at some of the unintended persuasion effects that may occur through the consumption of entertainment media, such as television. In the course of developing a model to explain these effects, we look specifically at the role of television programming in the shaping of product perceptions and the desire for these products, suggesting that television at the least has an influence on primary (product category) demand if not selective (brand) demand.

A PROCESS MODEL OF CULTIVATION EFFECTS

Cultivation Theory

Cultivation theory is a broad theory that relates media content with particular outcomes. The theory has two components. The first is that the content of television programs—whether they be "fiction," such as soap operas, or "fact," such as

news—presents a systematic distortion of reality.[1] That is, the world as it is portrayed on television differs in important and sometimes dramatic ways from how the real world is constituted. For example, the world of television tends to be more affluent (O'Guinn & Shrum, 1997), more violent (Gerbner, Gross, Morgan, & Signorielli, 1980), more maritally unfaithful (Lichter, Lichter, & Rothman, 1994), and more populated with doctors, lawyers, and police officers (DeFleur, 1964; Head, 1954; Lichter et al., 1994; Smythe, 1954) than the real world. The second component is that frequent exposure to these distorted images results in their internalization: The more people watch television, the more they develop values, attitudes, beliefs, and perceptions that are consistent with the world as it is portrayed on television. The internalization of the television message may result in the learning of television "facts": TV viewing has been shown to be positively correlated with estimates of the number of doctors, lawyers, and police officers in the real world (Shrum, 1996, 2001), the prevalence of violence (Gerbner et al., 1980; Shrum, Wyer, & O'Guinn, 1998), and the prevalence of ownership of expensive products (O'Guinn & Shrum, 1997; Shrum, 2001). In addition, internalization can take the form of learning the "lessons" of television: Heavy television viewing has been shown to be associated with greater anxiety and fearfulness (Bryant, Carveth, & Brown, 1981), greater faith in doctors (Volgy & Schwarz, 1980), greater pessimism about marriage (Shrum, 1999b), and greater interpersonal mistrust (Gerbner et al., 1980; Shrum, 1999b).

Research on aspects of the cultivation effect has been a contentious area. Although studies supporting cultivation theory are not in short supply, there have been a number of critiques of cultivation, including critiques of theory, method, analysis, and interpretation (cf. Hirsch, 1980; Hughes, 1980; Newcomb, 1978). These critiques, though having some validity, have been dealt with at length elsewhere (Gerbner, Gross, Morgan, & Signorielli, 1994; Morgan & Shanahan, 1996; Shanahan & Morgan, 1999; Van den Bulck, 2003). Suffice it to say that the critiques revolve around trade-offs in the measurement of the independent variable, television viewing, and consequent issues of causal direction. Gerbner and colleagues (Gerbner et al., 2002) take the position that measurement of television viewing best captures their concept of cultivation. More specifically, it better approximates

---

[1] We put *fact* and *fiction* in quotes to signify that, like the topic of the book, the lines between what is fact and fiction is quite blurry. On the one hand, soap operas are clearly fictional in the technical sense, but they also hold some grain of truth, or at least ring true to some degree. On the other hand, news programs presumably present factual information, yet content analyses consistently show that news presentations can be significantly distorted, for example emphasizing dramatic crimes such as murder and other violence and tending to show African Americans and Latinos as criminals more often than base rates would suggest is representative (Dixon & Linz, 2000). In the middle is reality TV, which shows heavily edited but nevertheless actual footage of such things as crime and police response. But just as with the editing process for news, selective editing tends to portray certain races or classes of people (e.g., Black and Hispanic characters) as criminal suspects more often than as police officers, whereas the opposite is true for white characters (Oliver, 1994).

a pattern of viewing over years because television, in their view, tends to be a fairly habitual process, and thus measurement of viewing provides more validity than does a brief exposure to a particular stimulus (e.g., a program segment, an entire program, or even a series of programs) under experimental conditions. Others point out that the resulting correlational data leave causality ambiguous. Indeed, most of the critiques of cultivation revolve around third-variable or reverse causality explanations (Hirsch, 1980; Hughes, 1980; Zillmann, 1980). Experiments have been used to address these causal issues (for a review, see Ogles, 1987). However, experiments can be criticized because they may provide only a short exposure to particular television or film content, which may not fully capture the long-term nature of cultivation.

Two important (and somewhat interrelated) reasons for the contentious debate regarding the reliability and validity of the cultivation effect are that the effects have been, for the most part, small ones, and the effects have not always consistently obtained. Moreover, when they have obtained, implementation of certain statistical controls (e.g., demographics, activities outside the home, population size) has been shown to reduce the cultivation effect to nonsignificance in some instances (cf. Hirsch, 1980; Hughes, 1980). Indeed, meta-analyses of studies investigating the cultivation effect find an overall correlation coefficient of about .09, and this relation tends to vary slightly, but not significantly, across various demographic and situational variables (Morgan & Shanahan, 1996). The issues of small effect size and lack of reliability make cultivation effects particularly vulnerable to claims that the noted effects are spurious. That is, some other unmeasured variable may easily account for the entire relation between television viewing and judgments when the effects sizes are small.

The issue of small effect sizes has been addressed through a variety of arguments. First, small effect sizes, if real, are not trivial. As Gerbner et al. (2002) note, there are many instances in which a very small shift on some variable (e.g., global warming, voting behavior) has important consequences. Variables such as violence and aggression likely fall into this category as well (Bushman & Anderson, 2001). Second, and more pertinent to the focus of this chapter, small main effects may simply be masking larger effects within certain groups. This notion formed the basis of Gerbner et al.'s (1980) refinements to cultivation theory that introduced the concepts of mainstreaming and resonance, which postulated that direct experience variables may moderate the cultivation effect (see also Shrum & Bischak, 2001). This notion also forms the basis of our focus on psychological processes: Variables that affect the judgment processes may also moderate the cultivation effect.

Psychological Processes and Cultivation

The debate over measurement and causality long predates the issues raised within the context of cultivation theory, and it seems unlikely that it will be resolved anytime soon. We tend to agree with both sides—measurement of television viewing

best captures the effects of viewing over time, but the resulting correlational data are always open to alternative explanations. However, as we have argued elsewhere (Shrum, 1995, 1999c, 2002), there may be a method to retain the traditional practice of measuring television viewing yet bolster the confidence one has that the data can speak to the issue of causality. This method involves the development of a psychological process model of cultivation effects. The logic is that if a process model of cultivation effects could be developed and validated—one that specifies testable propositions and lays out a set of mediators and moderators of the relation between television viewing and judgments—then we can be much more confident that the observed relations represent true rather than spurious effects (Hawkins & Pingree, 1990; Shrum, 2002). For example, a testable model should provide a series or set of conditions under which a particular effect does or does not hold. The power of this model, then, is in the pattern of results that is produced across studies. Thus, even though a particular study may have alternative explanations that cannot be completely addressed, these alternative explanations would have to address the entire pattern of results to effectively refute the findings.

In the remainder of this chapter, we discuss our efforts in developing such a model. We first provide a brief overview of the model that has been developed to date and then offer an extension of this model. In doing so, we discuss some recent data that support key portions of this extension.

HEURISTIC PROCESSING MODEL OF CULTIVATION EFFECTS

The heuristic processing model of cultivation effects (Shrum, 1996, 1999c, 2002; Shrum et al., 1998) represents an initial attempt at developing a model of the mental processes that underlies cultivation effects. Figure 10.1 provides a flow diagram of the model. A more detailed account of the components of this model can be found in the literature just cited. For our purposes, we simply want to highlight certain features of the model, particularly with respect to the assumptions, general propositions, and limitations.

Assumptions of the Model

Types of Cultivation Judgments. To understand both the contribution and the limitations of the model, it is necessary to understand that a variety of dependent variables (judgments) have been used to test for cultivation effects. Hawkins and Pingree (1982) first noted that the types of judgments used to test for cultivation effects could conveniently be categorized into two groups: demographic and value-system measures. These measures have also been termed first-order and second-order measures, respectively (Gerbner, Gross, Morgan, & Signorielli, 1986). *Demographic* or *first-order measures* pertain to those that relate to the facts of television and the social world—those aspects of the television world that can

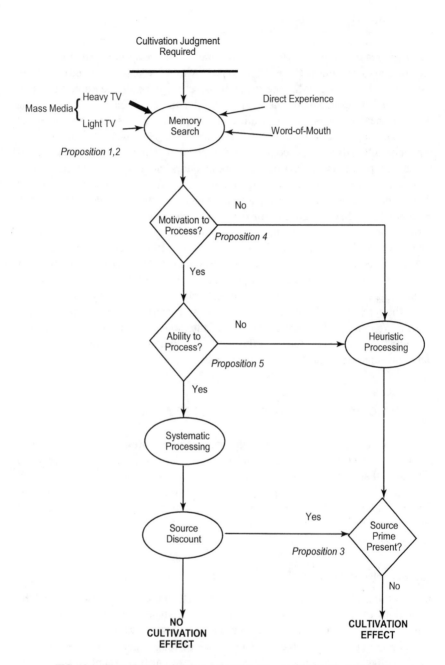

FIG. 10.1 Flow diagram of the heuristic processing model of cultivation effects. Circles represent mental processes. The thicker arrow from Heavy TV to Memory Search indicates a greater contribution to the search process. From *Media Effects: Advances in Theory and Research* (2nd ed., p. 87), by J. Bryant & D. Zillmann (Eds.), Mahwah, NJ: Lawrence Erlbaum Associates. Reprinted with permission.

be objectively compared with the same aspects of the real world. Examples include asking respondents to estimate the percentage of Americans who are involved in a violent crime; the percentage of the American workforce that consists of lawyers, doctors, or police officers; the percentage of marriages that end in divorce; and so forth. *Value-system* or *second-order measures* pertain to the values, attitudes, and beliefs that might be cultivated from television content. Examples include asking respondents if they are afraid to walk alone at night, measuring their level of mistrust, their acceptance of violence, their belief that their spouse would be unfaithful, or their level of materialism.

What makes this distinction interesting is that, according to Hawkins and Pingree's (1982) review of the literature up to that point, the size and reliability of the cultivation effect tends to vary as a function of the type of judgments. The cultivation effect tends to be observed more strongly and more often for first-order (demographic) than for second-order (value-system) beliefs. There are at least two nonmutually exclusive explanations for this pattern of findings. One explanation is that only one type of judgment—judgments related to the prevalence of particular constructs that occur often on television—is influenced by television viewing. Judgments related to values and attitudes that might be developed from the lessons of television, however, are simply not affected by amount of viewing. A second explanation is that the judgments differ in terms of the processes involved in constructing them. This possibility implies at least two important things: Television may influence each of the two types of judgments in different ways, and different factors may mediate or moderate the relation between television viewing and the two types of judgments.

Cultivation Judgments As Psychological Judgments. If one scrutinizes the types of judgments that have been classified as first- or second-order judgments in terms of how psychologists categorize them, it is apparent that they differ in fundamental ways. First-order judgments for the most part consist of judgments of probability or set size (Shrum, 1995). Examples include estimating risk (e.g., risk of crime) and estimating the number or percentage of instances in which a particular category (e.g., millionaire) occurs within a larger, superordinate category (e.g., Americans). Second-order judgments typically consist of attitude, value, or belief judgments. Examples include beliefs related to trust, the extent to which the world is a mean and violent place, and whether achievement is reflected in product ownership, just to name a few. Viewed this way, it is quite possible that first- and second-order judgments differ in terms of the way in which they are constructed. Moreover, decades of research in social and cognitive psychology have detailed the processes involved in constructing these judgments, which is useful in determining the role that certain types of inputs (e.g., television information) may play in this process.

A Process Model of First-Order Cultivation Judgments

How Are the Judgments Constructed?   In attempting to construct a process model for cultivation effects, it seemed reasonable to start with first-order (set-size and probability) judgments, given that those are the types of judgments for which cultivation effects have tended to be more robust and consistent. So how are those types of judgments constructed? Research by Tversky and Kahneman (1973; see also Kahneman & Tversky, 1982) suggests that these types of judgments are often made through the application of particular heuristics, or rules of thumb. Specifically, judgments of set size and probability tend to be based on the application of the availability heuristic (Tversky & Kahneman, 1973) or the simulation heuristic (Kahneman & Tversky, 1982). In using the *availability heuristic*, people base their judgments of set size or probability on how easy a relevant example comes to mind: The easier it is to recall, the higher the estimate. Thus, people tend to estimate that words in the English language that start with the letter *K* occur more often than words that have *K* as the third letter (Tversky & Kahneman, 1973, Study 3), even though the opposite is in fact the case. This result is presumably because words tend to be organized in memory according to their first letter, and thus words that start with *K* are more easily recalled. Similarly, 80% of people tend to estimate that accidents account for more deaths than do strokes, even though strokes account for about 85% more deaths than do accidents (Lichtenstein, Slovic, Fischhoff, Layman, & Combs, 1978). Again, this is presumably because accidents are easier to recall or imagine than strokes.

When judging set size or probability, a relevant example may not be available in memory (i.e., present in memory) or, if available, not particularly accessible (i.e., not easily retrieved). Thus, the availability heuristic cannot be applied. In these instances, people may resort to basing their estimates on the ease with which a relevant example can be imagined. This is an example of the *simulation heuristic*. Supporting this notion, research has shown that when people are induced to imagine a particular event such as winning a contest (Gregory, Cialdini, & Carpenter, 1982) or contracting a disease (Sherman, Cialdini, Schwartzman, & Reynolds, 1985), they provide higher estimates of the probability that they will experience these events compared with people who are not induced to imagine such events, and these relations are mediated by ease of imagining (Sherman et al., 1985).

Relation to Media Consumption.   The studies just noted, along with numerous others, clearly document that accessibility of relevant examples or ease of construction of a scenario influences estimates of set size and probability. Those with more accessible examples or greater ease of construction provide higher estimates. This has been shown to occur in both experimental studies and field studies. But what influences this accessibility? Clearly, in the experimental studies, accessibility is manipulated. But what of the field studies of Lichtenstein et al. (1978)? Why did people tend to greatly overestimate the number of deaths caused by accidents but greatly underestimate deaths caused by strokes? Lichtenstein et al. speculated

that accessibility is influenced by media coverage, suggesting that media publicity of such dramatic events as accidents and homicides increases accessibility of these examples relative to less dramatic and publicized causes of death such as strokes. This speculation was supported by a content analysis of newspaper articles showing just such differences in coverage (Combs & Slovic, 1979).

These studies suggest that media consumption may influence the accessibility of constructs that are commonly portrayed. It follows, then, that differences in media consumption (all other things being equal) may influence levels of accessibility of relevant constructs. If so, then for judgments of set size and probability, if the availability or simulation heuristic is used, then heavier media consumers should provide higher estimates of set size or probability than lighter media consumers. In fact, this is exactly what cultivation theory predicts.

Constructing the Process Model. From this point, it is a fairly simple leap to the development and testing of a process model of cultivation. Such a model predicts that heavier television viewing will make relevant examples more accessible in memory than lighter viewing (Proposition 1) and that this enhanced accessibility will result in higher estimates, indicating a mediating role of accessibility (Proposition 2). Note, however, that the notion that television examples would be used in the construction of these judgments is not necessarily intuitive. When estimating the prevalence of lawyers or police officers in the workforce, it is unlikely that people would consciously use an example of a TV lawyer or police officer to construct this judgment. Thus, if such TV examples are indeed used in constructing real-world judgments, then people are likely unaware of the source of these examples (because they are made fairly quickly) and thus do not discount the television examples as an invalid source (Proposition 3). Finally, conditions that facilitate or inhibit the use of judgmental heuristics such as availability and simulation should correspondingly increase or decrease the cultivation effect. These conditions include motivation to process information, which should inhibit the cultivation effect (Proposition 4) and lack of ability to process information, which should facilitate the cultivation effect (Proposition 5). Approximately a dozen studies have validated and replicated each of these key propositions (for a review, see Shrum, 2002).

Addressing Second-Order Cultivation Judgments

As noted elsewhere (Shrum, 1995, 2002), the psychological process model shown in Figure 10.1 is mute with respect to second-order judgments such as attitudes and values. This is unfortunate because, as Gerbner et al. (2002) have noted, it is the extrapolation or symbolic transformation of the television message into more general perspectives and ideologies that is perhaps more interesting and better captures the concept of cultivation theory than a focus on simple perceptions and beliefs that are captured by first-order measures. For this reason, it seems useful

to extend the process model to include second-order judgments such as attitudes and values.

In developing the model for first-order judgments, we first started with the question of how such judgments are made, working backward to understand how television information might influence these judgments. In applying this approach to second-order judgments, it quickly becomes apparent that first- and second-order judgments are made quite differently. For one, judgments of set size and probability are virtually always memory based (Hastie & Park, 1986). That is, when asked to form a judgment about the probability of being involved in a violent crime or the incidence of millionaires in the United States, people would not be likely to have such answers stored in memory. Rather, they would construct them by recalling relevant examples or scenarios. Thus, first-order judgments are likely constructed at the time the judgment is required (e.g., responding to a research query; playing Trivial Pursuit). For this reason, we would expect that memory for these examples would correlate with both the independent (TV viewing) and dependent (judgments) variables (Hastie & Park, 1986). In fact, that is what the studies have consistently shown (Busselle & Shrum, in press; Shrum, 1996). This process also implies that conditions operating at the time of judgment would be more likely to impact the TV–judgment relation than would conditions operating at the time of encoding or viewing. Consistent with this notion, judgment conditions such as time pressure (Shrum, 1999a), task involvement (Shrum, 2001), and source discounting (Shrum et al., 1998) have been shown to moderate the cultivation effect. Conversely, conditions or variables operating at the time of viewing (e.g., attention while viewing, intention to view, perceived reality of television, need for cognition) have been shown to have virtually no effect on either the magnitude of first-order judgments or memory for TV information (Busselle & Shrum, in press; O'Guinn & Shrum, 1997; Shrum, 1996, 2001; Shrum et al., 1998).

In contrast, the construction of values, attitudes, and beliefs is likely made in a different manner. It is of course possible that attitudes and beliefs could be constructed in a memory-based fashion. When asked to provide an attitude toward a particular object, people may attempt to recall relevant information (both cognitions and affect) and then construct their attitude in real time. This would likely occur when people do not have a readily accessible attitude or belief to provide when a request for attitude expression is made. If they did have an attitude or belief readily accessible, they would instead simply retrieve their prior constructed attitude or belief and report it (Hastie & Park, 1986; see also Carlston, 1980; Lichtenstein & Srull, 1985, 1987; Lingle & Ostrom, 1979).

But consider the types of attitudes and beliefs that are typically measured in cultivation research. These measures assess the extent to which people believe the world is a violent place, are afraid to walk alone at night, approve of violence by police, believe crime is the most important political issue, do not trust others, and so forth. These types of beliefs are commonly used in everyday life. Thus, they are likely to already exist for most people, having been formed long ago

and reinforced or updated on a consistent basis. This is even more so the case for constructs such as personal values. By definition, values are stable and enduring beliefs that everyone possesses and that serve as guides to behavior over the course of a lifetime (Rokeach, 1973). Thus, they are formed at a relatively early age and then changed (either made stronger or altered) as new information comes in. This process of constructing judgments on the basis of incoming information (as opposed to retrieved information) is what Hastie and Park (1986) term an online judgment.

If it is true that these types of judgments are formed in an online fashion, important implications are made for the role that television viewing might play in the formation of those judgments. In particular, it suggests that these types of judgments are likely made (developed, reinforced, or altered) during the viewing process. If so, it also implies that conditions operating during viewing may affect the influence of television information rather than conditions operating at the time the judgment is required by some external situation (e.g., being asked by a researcher). Note that this is essentially the opposite of the process involved with first-order (memory-based) cultivation judgments, which depend on recall at the time the judgment is required and thus should be affected by conditions present at that time rather than at the time of viewing.

Supportive Evidence.   The notion that second-order cultivation judgments might be influenced by conditions at the time of viewing is a proposition that was addressed in a recent study (Burroughs et al., 2002). In that study, we investigated the relation between television viewing and the consumer value of materialism. Materialism is commonly viewed as the value placed on the acquisition of material objects, such as expensive cars, homes, and clothes (Richins & Dawson, 1992). Because content analyses have consistently shown that the world portrayed on television tends to be more affluent and materialistic than the real world (Hirschman, 1988; Lichter et al., 1994; O'Guinn & Shrum, 1997), we expected that, consistent with cultivation theory, these materialistic messages would be internalized by viewers, resulting in higher levels of materialism for those who viewed relatively more television in general. However, we expected this positive relation between television viewing and materialism to be moderated by certain factors that might affect the processing of the message during viewing. These factors included the degree to which viewers tend to be attentive while viewing and the extent to which viewers tend to elaborate on the television message while viewing. We expected that those who pay more attention while viewing would be more persuaded by the television message than those who pay less attention, and we also expected that those who elaborate more on the message (those higher in need for cognition; Cacioppo & Petty, 1982) would also be more affected than those who elaborate less.

The results were as expected. We found that level of television viewing was related to materialism: The more people viewed television, the more materialistic they were. However, also as expected, this relation was moderated by the two

process variables. Specifically, the positive relation between television viewing and materialism was stronger for those who paid more attention to the program while viewing than for those who paid less attention and stronger for those higher in need for cognition than for those lower in need for cognition.

Implications for Model Development and Causality

The moderating role of attention while viewing and need for cognition is consistent with our theorizing that the process of cultivation for second-order cultivation judgments tends to occur during viewing. The variables of attention and need for cognition were intended to capture processes that were taking place during the viewing process. As such, it is highly unlikely that such variables would moderate the cultivation effect if in fact the judgments were memory based, at least in the pattern we observed. This last phrase is an important qualifier. It is possible that greater elaboration and greater attention could indeed have an effect on the extent to which television information is used in a memory-based judgment. However, as has been shown in previous studies (Shrum, 2001; Shrum et al., 1998) the effect should be just the opposite of the one we observed: Greater attention and elaboration should lead to more source discounting (discounting the television information because it is not veridical) and thus reduce rather than inflate the cultivation effect.

The pattern of results we observed also has important implications for causality. As we noted earlier, correlational results are always open to alternative explanations of causal paths. However, the pattern of moderating effects that we observed are difficult to explain in reverse causality or third-variable terms. In particular, attention and elaboration are process variables that necessarily occur during rather than prior to viewing, making a reverse causality explanation untenable. And, although it is still possible that some third variable is driving the TV–materialism relation, that variable would also have to account for the two moderating effects we observed. Given that constraint, it is unclear what that third variable might be.

Limitations of the Study

There is one important limitation to the results of Burroughs et al. (2002). That limitation pertains to the use of need for cognition as a surrogate measure of elaboration during viewing. It could certainly be argued that those higher in need for cognition would not enjoy such a cognitively easy task as television viewing. Moreover, if they did view, they might be more prone to counterarguing than support arguing. In fact, Burroughs et al. found that need for cognition was indeed negatively correlated with television viewing. However, we would argue that for those who are high in need for cognition who do decide to view frequently, a continual counterarguing of the television message would be a particularly miserable experience. Rather, we expect that those high in need for cognition who view frequently are the ones who enjoy watching television and thus would be more

likely to suspend disbelief and elaborate extensively than those high in need for cognition who are lighter viewers. Our pattern of results is consistent with that notion: It is the people who are both heavy viewers and high in need for cognition that exhibit the highest levels of materialism.

CONCLUSION

The arguments that we have presented in this chapter for the processes involved in the construction of second-order cultivation judgments are just that—arguments. Although we have discussed some empirical findings that support our reasoning, there is still quite a bit of work to do in terms of fleshing out the entire process. Ideally, one would end up with a process model for second-order judgments that is similar to the one shown in Figure 10.1 for first-order judgments, one that specifies testable propositions that address the processes that mediate and moderate the effect of television viewing on judgments. Doing so would provide a major step in establishing the causal impact that television viewing has on the gamut of human judgment and behavior.

REFERENCES

Bargh, J. A. (1997). The automaticity of everyday life. In. R. S. Wyer (Ed.), *The automaticity of everyday life: Advances in social cognition* (Vol. 10, pp. 1–61). Mahwah, NJ: Lawrence Erlbaum Associates.

Bryant, J., Carveth, R. A., & Brown, D. (1981). Television viewing and anxiety: An experimental investigation. *Journal of Communication, 31*(1), 106–119.

Bryant, J., Zillmann, D. (Eds.). (2002). *Media effects: Advances in theory and research* (2nd ed., p. 87). Mahwah, NJ: Lawrence Erlbaum Associates.

Burroughs, J. E., Shrum, L. J., & Rindfleisch, A. (2002). Does television viewing promote materialism? Cultivating American perceptions of the good life. In S. Broniarczyk & K. Nakamoto (Eds.), *Advances in consumer research* (Vol. 28, pp. 442–443). Provo, UT: Association for Consumer Research.

Bushman, B. J., & Anderson, C. A. (2001). Media violence and the American public: Scientific facts versus media misinformation. *American Psychologist, 56*(6–7), 477–489.

Busselle, R. W., & Shrum, L. J. (in press). Media exposure and the accessibility of social information. *Media Psychology.*

Cacioppo, J. T., & Petty, R. E. (1982). The need for cognition. *Journal of Personality and Social Psychology, 42*, 116–131.

Carlston, D. E. (1980). The recall and use of traits and events in social inference processes. *Journal of Experimental Social Psychology, 16*, 303–328.

Combs, B., & Slovic, P. (1979). Newspaper coverage of causes of death. *Journalism Quarterly, 56*, 837–849.

DeFleur, M. L. (1964). Occupational roles as portrayed on television. *Public Opinion Quarterly, 28*, 54–74.

Dixon, T., & Linz, D. (2000). Overrepresentation and underrepresentation of African Americans and Latinos as lawbreakers on television news. *Journal of Communication, 50*, 131–154.

Gerbner, G., & Gross, L. (1976). Living with television: The violence profile. *Journal of Communication, 26*(2), 173–199.

Gerbner, G., Gross, L., Morgan, M., & Signorielli, N. (1980). The "mainstreaming" of America: Violence profile no. 11. *Journal of Communication, 30*(3), 10–29.

Gerbner, G., Gross, L., Morgan, M., & Signorielli, N. (1986). Living with television: The dynamics of the cultivation process. In J. Bryant & D. Zillmann (Eds.), *Perspectives on media effects* (pp. 17–40). Hillsdale, NJ: Lawrence Erlbaum Associates.

Gerbner, G., Gross, L., Morgan, M., & Signorielli, N. (1994). Growing up with television: The cultivation perspective. In J. Bryant & D. Zillmann (Eds.), *Media effects: Advances in theory and research* (pp. 17–41). Hillsdale, NJ: Lawrence Erlbaum Associates.

Gerbner, G., Gross, L., Morgan, M., Signorielli, N., & Shanahan, J. (2002). Growing up with television: Cultivation processes. In J. Bryant & D. Zillmann (Eds.), *Media effects: Advances in theory and research* (2nd ed., pp. 43–67). Mahwah, NJ: Lawrence Erlbaum Associates.

Gregory, L. G., Cialdini, R. B., & Carpenter, K. M. (1982). Self-relevant scenarios as mediators of likelihood estimates and compliance: Does imagining make it so? *Journal of Personality and Social Psychology, 43*, 89–99.

Hastie, R., & Park, B. (1986). The relationship between memory and judgment depends on whether the judgment task is memory-based or on-line. *Psychological Review, 93*, 258–268.

Hawkins, R. P., & Pingree, S. (1982). Television's influence on constructions of social reality. In D. Pearl, L. Bouthilet, & J. Lazar (Eds.), *Television and behavior: Ten years of scientific progress and implications for the eighties* (Vol. 2, pp. 224–247). Washington, DC: Government Printing Office.

Hawkins, R. B., & Pingree, S. (1990). Divergent psychological processes in constructing social reality from mass media content. In N. Signorielli & M. Morgan (Eds.), *Cultivation analysis: New directions in media effects research* (pp. 33–50). Newbury Park, CA: Sage.

Head, S. W. (1954). Content analysis of television drama programs. *Quarterly of Film, Radio, and Television, 9*, 175–194.

Hirsch, P. (1980). The scary world of the nonviewer and other anomalies: A reanalysis of Gerbner et al.'s findings on cultivation analysis. *Communication Research, 7*, 403–456.

Hirschman, E. C. (1988). The ideology of consumption: A structural–syntactical analysis of "Dallas" and "Dynasty." *Journal of Consumer Research, 15*, 344–359.

Hughes, M. (1980). The fruits of cultivation analysis: A reexamination of some effects of television watching. *Public Opinion Quarterly, 44*, 287–302.

Kahneman, D., & Tversky, A. (1982). The simulation heuristic. In D. Kahneman, P. Slovic, & A. Tversky (Eds.), *Judgment under uncertainty: Heuristics and biases*. New York: Cambridge University Press.

Lichtenstein, M., & Srull, T. K. (1985). Conceptual and methodological issues in examining the relationship between consumer memory and judgment. In L. F. Alwitt & A. A. Mitchell (Eds.), *Psychological processes and advertising effects: Theory, research and application* (pp. 113–128). Hillsdale, NJ: Lawrence Erlbaum Associates.

Lichtenstein, M., & Srull, T. K. (1987). Processing objectives as a determinant of the relationship between recall and judgment. *Journal of Experimental Social Psychology, 23*, 93–118.

Lichtenstein, S., Slovic, P., Fischhoff, G., Layman, M., & Combs, B. (1978). Judged frequency of lethal events. *Journal of Experimental Psychology: Human Learning and Memory, 6*, 551–578.

Lichter, S. R., Lichter, L. S., & Rothman, S. (1994). *Prime time: How TV portrays American culture*. Washington, DC: Regnery Publishing.

Lingle, J. H., & Ostrom, T. M. (1979). Retrieval selectivity in memory-based impression judgments. *Journal of Personality and Social Psychology, 37*, 180–194.

Morgan, M., & Shanahan, J. (1996). Two decades of cultivation research: An appraisal and meta-analysis. In B. R. Burleson (Ed.), *Communication yearbook 20* (pp. 1–45). Newbury Park, CA: Sage.

Newcomb, H. (1978). Assessing the violence profiles of Gerbner and Gross: A humanistic critique and suggestion. *Communication Research, 5,* 264–282.

Ogles, R. M. (1987). Cultivation analysis: Theory, methodology and current research on television-influenced constructions of social reality. *Mass Comm Review 14*(1, 2), 43–53.

O'Guinn, T. C., & Shrum, L. J. (1997). The role of television in the construction of consumer reality. *Journal of Consumer Research, 23,* 278–294.

Oliver, M. B. (1994). Portrayals of crime, race, and aggression in "reality based" police shows: A content analysis. *Journal of Broadcasting & Electronic Media, 38,* 179–192.

Richins, M. L., & Dawson, S. (1992). A consumer values orientation for materialism and its measurement: Scale development and validation. *Journal of Consumer Research, 19,* 303–316.

Rokeach, M. (1973). *The nature of human values.* New York: Free Press.

Shanahan, J., & Morgan, M. (1999). *Television and its viewers: Cultivation theory and research.* New York: Cambridge University Press.

Sherman, S. J., Cialdini, R. B., Schwartzman, D. F., & Reynolds, K. D. (1985). Imagining can heighten or lower the perceived likelihood of contracting a disease: The mediating effect of ease of imagery. *Personality and Social Psychology Bulletin, 11,* 118–127.

Shrum, L. J. (1995). Assessing the social influence of television: A social cognition perspective on cultivation effects. *Communication Research, 22,* 402–429.

Shrum, L. J. (1996). Psychological processes underlying cultivation effects: Further tests of construct accessibility. *Human Communication Research, 22,* 482–509.

Shrum, L. J. (1999a). *The effect of data-collection methods on the cultivation effect: Implications for the heuristic processing model of cultivation effects.* Paper presented at the meeting of the International Communication Association, San Francisco, CA.

Shrum, L. J. (1999b). The relationship of television viewing with attitude strength and extremity: Implications for the cultivation effect. *Media Psychology, 1,* 3–25.

Shrum, L. J. (1999c). Television and persuasion: Effects of the programs between the ads. *Psychology & Marketing, 16,* 119–140.

Shrum, L. J. (2001). Processing strategy moderates the cultivation effect. *Human Communication Research, 27,* 94–120.

Shrum, L. J. (2002). Media consumption and perceptions of social reality: Effects and underlying processes. In J. Bryant & D. Zillmann (Eds.), *Media effects: Advances in theory and research* (2nd ed., pp. 69–95). Mahwah, NJ: Lawrence Erlbaum Associates.

Shrum, L. J., & Bischak, V. D. (2001). Mainstreaming, resonance, and impersonal impact: Testing moderators of the cultivation effect for estimates of crime risk. *Human Communication Research, 27*(2), 187–215.

Shrum, L. J., Wyer, R. S., & O'Guinn, T. C. (1998). The effects of television consumption on social perceptions: The use of priming procedures to investigate psychological processes. *Journal of Consumer Research, 24,* 447–458.

Smythe, D. W. (1954). Reality as presented by television. *Public Opinion Quarterly, 18,* 143–156.

Tversky, A., & Kahneman, D. (1973). Availability: A heuristic for judging frequency and probability. *Cognitive Psychology, 5,* 207–232.

Van den Bulck, J. (2003). Is the mainstreaming effect of cultivation an artifact of regression to the mean? *Journal of Broadcasting & Electronic Media, 47*(2), 289–295.

Volgy, T., & Schwarz, J. (1980). Television entertainment programming and sociopolitical attitudes. *Journalism Quarterly, 57,* 150–155.

Zillmann, D. (1980). Anatomy of suspense. In P. H. Tannenbaum (Ed.), *The entertainment functions of television* (pp. 133–163). Hillsdale, NJ: Erlbaum.

CHAPTER ELEVEN

Paths From Television Violence to Aggression: Reinterpreting the Evidence

George Comstock

Syracuse University

Entertainment provides at least three gratifications: a respite from the anxieties and pressures of everyday life; the opportunity to compare oneself with the demeanor, possessions, and behavior of others; and a means of keeping up with what is transpiring in the world. These gratifications have been particularly well documented in the case of television (Comstock & Scharrer, 1999), where a variety of measures of stress and interpersonal conflict predict greater affinity for or consumption of television; where viewers tend to watch those on the screen like themselves in gender, age, or ethnicity more attentively (which would make comparisons more meaningful); and where there is a common belief that something can be learned from all types of programming and keeping abreast embraces both events in the world at large and the varied portrayals and depictions offered by the medium in news, sports, and entertainment programming. There are also less-positive consequences of attending to entertainment, with one of the most investigated by the social and behavioral sciences the facilitation of aggressive and antisocial behavior by violent television and film portrayals.

The empirical evidence on the influence of violent television entertainment on aggression, bolstered by an extraordinary seven meta-analyses with varying emphases, often has been interpreted as supporting the view that attitudes serve as the link between exposure to violent programs and behavior. The evidence, in

fact, gives equal support to the hypothesis that the link is the availability of genres of behavior in the minds of viewers—that is, the readiness by which they may be retrieved—rather than dispositions toward behavior.

From this latter perspective, television violence is processed by young viewers in a manner similar to advertising within the elaboration likelihood model (ELM; Cacioppo & Petty, 1985; Petty & Cacioppo, 1990). The factors that seemingly promote favorable evaluations of aggressive behavior instead govern the salience of such behavior. Violent portrayals operate like television commercials, which most of the time, because they are low in persuasive argumentation, affect consumers by maintaining the salience of particular brands among purchase options (Comstock & Scharrer, 1999).

The research on television violence and aggressive and antisocial behavior has been voluminous but has been generally assigned to a sphere of scientific endeavor quite distinct from consumer psychology. This is more a product of myopia and an inclination to honor the apparent boundaries of paradigms than it is one of distinctiveness among theories or any interest in decidedly different types of outcomes. In fact, it is a quick and comfortable journey that leads face-to-face with consumer psychology if one travels the backward loop from Bandura's (1986) social cognitive theory to the health belief model (Becker, 1974). The health belief model was derived from social learning theory, an earlier version of what Bandura now calls social cognitive theory. The health belief model essentially argues that behavior related to health—such as food preferences, cigarette and alcohol consumption, seat belt use, and cancer examinations—can be changed by manipulating beliefs about personal risk, the availability of effective means of risk reduction, and the ease of access to and social acceptability of these means of risk reduction. It has been the conceptual model for such large-scale federally financed interventions as the Stanford cardiovascular field experiments (Farquar et al., 1977, 1990), in which persuasive campaigns, using the mass media and counseling by physicians, were employed to encourage individuals to behave in ways that would reduce the risk of cardiovascular mishap. Social cognitive theory, of course, is the underpinning for much of the experimental research on young children's increased aggressiveness as a consequence of exposure to violent portrayals (e.g., Bandura, Ross, & Ross, 1963a, 1963b). The health belief model makes it clear that social cognition is a theory of persuasion, although one that emphasizes behavior, modeling of that behavior by attractive persons, relevance achieved through attributes of the portrayal that encourage identification, and, in its application to the area of television violence and aggression, persuasion that is unintended. Thus, the connection between consumer psychology and television violence is not limited to the frequent consumption of media content that is a vehicle for commercials but extends to the fundamentals of theory, specifically, in the present case, the analogy provided by the peripheral or heuristic path of dual-processing theories such as the ELM.

THE MOST USEFUL GATEWAY

At this point in time, the most useful gateway to the evidence on television violence and aggressive and antisocial behavior is through meta-analyses (Comstock & Scharrer, 2003). Meta-analysis estimates the magnitude of the relationships among variables. These estimates are more reliable and more valid than those produced by a single study (Hunt, 1997). It thereby enhances the quality and veracity of evidence.

The role of meta-analysis, and its appeal, is aptly conveyed by the title of Morton Hunt's (1997) account of its development and uses, *How Science Takes Stock*. It has become an important tool for drawing inferences when several and often many empirical studies exist on the same topic. The essence of meta-analysis is the estimating of the size of the relationship between two variables. Typically, there is an exhaustive search for unpublished as well as published studies. This is directed at the file drawer problem—published studies alone may result in an overestimate of the magnitude of a relationship because studies showing larger, statistically significant outcomes are more likely to be published (Rosenthal, 1979). In turn, studies can be scored on various dimensions for quality and for ecological validity (conditions that parallel everyday life) so that the analysis eventually can focus on the studies that have the strongest claims for generalizing beyond their particular sets of data. In meta-analysis jargon, the goal is to estimate the *effect size*—the magnitude of the association between two variables. Despite this language, there is nothing about meta-analysis that ensures that the independent variable contributes to or in any way is causally related to the dependent variable. This is an inference that is left to the analyst. The benefits of meta-analysis are the use of all retrievable data to estimate the magnitude of a relationship, the greater reliability and validity that result from the enlarged N, and the ability to code studies for any and every conceivable attribute so that the analyst can focus on those with particular characteristics or qualities. For example, in the case of violent television portrayals and aggressive or antisocial behavior, the analyst could isolate those experiments where a portrayal of justified aggression was the treatment and compare the effect size for the dependent variable with effect sizes for other treatments. The estimate based on several experiments would have greater reliability and validity than the estimate from the original 1963 experiment by Berkowitz and Rawlings (i.e., if the additional experiments were equivalent as a group in quality and ecological validity to the original). In effect, studies are treated analogously to respondents in a survey. The quality and validity of interpretation depends on the representativeness of the sample (in the case of meta-analysis, a census) and the selection of questions addressed to the sample (in the case of meta-analysis, the studies). The basic calculation is as follows:

$$\text{Effect Size} = \frac{\text{Mean}_t - \text{Mean}_c}{ESD}$$

Where t = treatment, c = control, and ESD = estimate of the standard deviation. Because the standard deviation represents the same proportion of cases for all normal distributions, this produces an effect size that can be pooled with others for an aggregate estimate. The formula obviously fits only experimental designs, but procedures have been developed to estimate the equivalent for surveys and other designs. In addition, procedures also have been developed to estimate the statistical significance of any effect size and fail-safe numbers—the number of additional outcomes with null results that would be necessary to reduce the obtained estimate to null. Thus, meta-analysis in its current form makes it possible for the confidence of the analyst to rest not only on the magnitude of the effect size but also on the estimated probability that an outcome is attributable to sampling variability and the estimated quantity of null results that would have to be uncovered to overturn an observed effect size.

Nevertheless, meta-analysis is not a substitute for interpretation. The fretful analyst still must decide whether the outcomes of experiments are generalizable to everyday circumstances and whether positive correlations between two variables in survey data represent the operation of a third variable or causation, as well as the direction of causation.

In the case of television and film violence and aggressive and antisocial behavior, interpretation is confronted with a large array of data—seven quantitative aggregations of study outcomes. The most comprehensive (Paik & Comstock, 1994) presents almost 1,150 instances in which an effect size was calculated. Furthermore, the outcomes of individual studies sometimes may supply information that clearly adds to, extends, and qualitatively enriches rather than is merely represented in a meta-analysis. As a result, meta-analysis should not be thought of as a means by which all scientific questions are answered but as a source of particularly reliable and valid estimates of the relationships among variables that may be importantly augmented or qualified by the outcomes of particular studies.

In the present instance, the meta-analytic data lead to a number of conclusions unambiguously thoroughly supported by empirical evidence. In addition, the examination of the outcomes of a particularly compelling study leads to a surprise that suggests a revision in theory.

Andison (1977), in a pioneering effort, simply categorized the outcomes of 67 experiments and surveys as to the direction and size of the relationship between violence viewing and aggressive or antisocial behavior. Hearold (1986) was the first to apply the now widely accepted meta-analytic paradigm in which the standard deviation is the criterion for assessing the magnitude of the relationship between variables to the literature on media and behavior. A student of Eugene Glass at the University of Colorado (who is credited with developing meta-analysis in the 1970s in an attempt to quantitatively discredit H. J. Eysenck's claims that psychotherapy was ineffective) examined more than 1,000 relationships (drawn from 168 separate studies) between exposure to anti- and prosocial portrayals and anti- and

prosocial behavior.[1] Wood, Wong, and Cachere (1991) examined 23 experiments in and out of the laboratory in which the dependent variable was "unconstrained interpersonal aggression" among children and teenagers. Allen, D'Alessio, and Brezgel (1995) aggregated the data from 33 laboratory-type experiments in which the independent variable was exposure to sexually explicit video or film portrayals and the dependent variable was aggression. Hogben (1998) confined himself to 56 coefficients drawn from studies measuring everyday viewing but included a wide array of aggression-related responses, including, in addition to aggressive or antisocial behavior, hostile attitudes, personality variables, and, in one case (Cairns, Hunter, & Herring, 1980), the content of invented news stories. Bushman and Anderson (2001) tracked the correlation between exposure to violent television or film portrayals in experimental and nonexperimental designs in 5-year intervals over a 25-year period. Paik and Comstock (1994), in a comprehensive updating of Hearold's assessment of the relationship between exposure to television violence and aggressive and antisocial behavior, included 82 new studies for a total of 217 that produced 1,142 coefficients between the independent and dependent variables.[2]

These data represent the behavior of many thousands of persons ranging in age from preschool to adulthood, an assortment of independent and dependent variables, and a variety of research methods. For example, Paik and Comstock (1994) included the full range of ages, a variety of types of programming and nine categories of behavior, and laboratory-type experiments, field experiments, time series, and surveys. These are all typically positive features of meta-analyses, which, as surveys of a literature, take on the characteristics of the area of inquiry in contrast to the more limited (and limiting) attributes of a single study.

---

[1]The meta-analytic paradigm made its first public appearance in the 1976 presidential address by Glass (1976) at the annual meeting of the American Educational Research Association in San Fransisco. This justifiably places him foremost among the pioneers of the method. However, at about the same time Robert Rosenthal at Harvard was at work on a similar scheme (Rosenthal & Rubin, 1978). Neither knew of what the other was doing (Hunt, 1997), an example of the frequent independence of innovations from the ventures of specific innovators.

[2]Paik and Comstock (1994) focused on the most substantial portion of the Hearold (1986) meta-analysis. Hearold examined all possible combinations of antisocial and prosocial portrayals and behavior, including the effect size between exposure to prosocial portrayals and antisocial behavior and the effect size between exposure to antisocial portrayals and prosocial behavior (although the data on these pairings expectedly was not voluminous). However, she did not include erotica or pornographic portrayals among the independent variables, and she included among her antisocial dependent variables such outcomes as stereotyping, passivity, and feelings of powerlessness. Aggressive portrayals and behavior nevertheless made up the largest number of independent and dependent variables. Paik and Comstock confined themselves to aggressive portrayals and outcomes, except for including erotica and pornographic portrayals among their independent variables. Thus, they updated the major portion of Hearold's analysis and extended it in terms of coverage by including erotica and pornographic portrayals and in terms of method by including estimates of statistical significance and fail-safe numbers.

These analyses irrefutably confirm that there is a positive correlation between exposure to violent television and movie portrayals and engagement in aggressive or antisocial behavior. This holds for the data from experiments and for the data from surveys. All seven of the quantitative aggregations of data can be invoked on behalf of this outcome including the four not confined to a narrow focus on particular measures of exposure or quite specific outcomes (such as unconstrained interpersonal aggression)—the initial pioneering effort by Andison (1977), Hearold (1986), Bushman and Anderson (2001), and Paik and Comstock (1994). However, interpretation quickly strides to center stage because this datum is not very informative about the processes responsible for the relationship. Experiments unambiguously document causation within their circumstances, but it is a matter of judgment whether their outcomes can be generalized to other circumstances, and positive correlation coefficients within surveys document association in everyday life but by themselves are insufficient to infer causation (Cook & Campbell, 1979).

INTERPRETING THE EVIDENCE

The case for causation is quite strong. It rests on two factors readily observable in the meta-analyses. The first is the consistency of the outcomes for the experimental designs, where the positive effect sizes are quite robust ($r = .40$ in Paik & Comstock 1994), statistical significance is readily achieved (p exceeds four digits in Paik & Comstock), and fail-safe numbers are huge (over 700,000 in Paik & Comstock). The second is the confirmation by the survey designs—where the effect sizes are more modest but respectable ($r = .19$ in Paik & Comstock), while statistical significance and fail-safe numbers (the quantity of null findings necessary to reduce a coefficient to statistical insignificance) remain impressive—that the condition necessary to infer causation in everyday life exists. This condition is quite explicit: a positive correlation between everyday violence viewing and everyday aggressive or antisocial behavior (i.e., a correlation outside the laboratory) that stoutly resists explanation other than by some causal contribution of viewing to behavior. The meta-analyses supply the correlation. Other studies supply the additional evidence. Thus, the experiments begin with evidence of causation, and the surveys confirm that this outcome is generalizable to everyday life.

The reverse hypothesis (Belson, 1978), though superficially promising, is particularly disappointing. This is the proposition that the positive correlation is explained by the seeking out of violent entertainment by those prone to aggressiveness. Admittedly, there are some sets of data in which aggressiveness predicts subsequent violence viewing, although the literature is quite mixed as to the regularity or pervasiveness of such on outcome (Comstock & Scharrer, 1999). In fact, the analysis that supplies some of the strongest evidence against the reverse hypothesis also provides some data consistent with it. The difficulty is that the reverse hypothesis fails woefully as a complete explanation for the correlation.

The most convincing evidence comes from the reanalysis by Kang (1990) of the NBC panel data on elementary school children (Milavsky, Kessler, Stipp, & Rubens, 1982).[3] This repeated measures surveying of the same sample over a 3.5-year period permitted the calculation of coefficients representing earlier viewing and later behavior or earlier behavior and later viewing, permitting inferences about which was affecting the other. Kang found eight statistically significant coefficients for a viewing-to-behavior effect but only four for a behavior-to-viewing effect, out of a total of 15 pairings of earlier and later measurement. Moreover, there was only one instance of reciprocal association (viewing predicted behavior and behavior predicted viewing within the same span of time). These data are wholly inconsistent with the reverse hypothesis as a comprehensive explanation. The behavior variable in the NBC data was interpersonal aggression—hitting, fighting, stealing, name calling. Belson (1978) in his survey of about 1,600 London teenage males extends the dismissal of the reverse hypothesis to seriously harmful behavior. He statistically manipulated his data so that he could compare directly the plausibility of the direct and the reverse hypothesis. He concluded that there was no support for the reverse hypothesis and strong support for the direct hypothesis that violence viewing increased the committing of seriously harmful acts (such as attempted rape, false report of a bomb threat, and use of a tire iron, razor, knife, or gun in a fight) among a subsample with a high propensity for delinquent behavior (p. 390, Table 12.13).

The impression given by Bandura and colleagues (Bandura et al., 1963a, 1963b), and often repeated in textbooks, after early experiments with nursery school children is that males are more likely to be affected. Meta-analysis demurs. Girls as well as boys appear to be affected. In Paik and Comstock (1994), effect sizes are similar for boys and girls in the data from the method that represents everyday events—surveys. Only in experiments are effect sizes clearly greater for males. Whether this false impression is attributable to entertainment history (aggressive females on the screen are now more frequent), social change (childrearing is probably now somewhat more accepting in regard to the expression of aggression by girls), norms (the Stanford nursery school surely was a campground of gender role convention), or the preponderance of males as subjects in the experiments (they outnumber females by about 6 to 1) is a matter of speculation. What is not is that meta-analysis has supplied a corrective. Meta-analysis also leads to the conclusion that effects do not diminish with age, although they are largest among the very young. In Paik and Comstock, effect sizes displayed an upward shift among those

---

[3]The NBC panel study involved the collection of data from elementary and high school samples over a 3.5-year period in two cities, one in the Midwest and one in the Southwest. There were six points of data collection, which led to 15 wave pairs of earlier and later measurement (I-II, I-III, I-IV, etc.). The focus was on earlier television violence exposure and later aggressive behavior. The lag time between measurements varied from 3 months to more than 3 years. The elementary school N for the shortest period was 497 and for the longest period, 112, with attribution reducing the N as the time lags became longer.

of college age, although otherwise there was a modest decline from preschool to adulthood with increasing age. Thus, it is not justified to conclude that the effects of television violence on aggressive and antisocial behavior are limited to the very young, or that they decline as cognitive ability increases to understand what is transpiring on the screen, to separate fantasy from reality, and to make distinctions between stirring acts and devious motives. Again, this is a pattern that becomes more readily recognizable in meta-analyses because single studies typically are quite restrictive in the range of ages included.

The experiments that began to accumulate in 1963 with the work of Bandura, Berkowitz, and their colleagues (Bandura et al., 1963a, 1963b; Berkowitz & Rawlings, 1963) drew attention to the possibility that exposure to violent portrayals increased aggressive and antisocial behavior. However, they also were rather starkly limited to immediate effects. Surveys began to address the possibility of effects over time by attempting to represent earlier viewing in the measure of exposure (McLeod, Atkin, & Chaffee, 1972a, 1972b), and Eron and Lefkowitz and colleagues (Lefkowitz, Eron, Walder, & Huesmann, 1972, 1977) reported a statistically significant correlation between violence viewing at about age 8 years and aggressive behavior a decade later after controlling for aggression in the earlier time period (and, thus, its correlates, including any otherwise unmeasured causes of the behavior) as part of the 1972 U. S. Surgeon General's inquiry into television violence. This was the beginning of the production of data sets that seemingly show an effect over time. The most recent is from Johnson and colleagues (Johnson, Cohen, Smailes, Kasen, & Brook, 2002), who report statistically significant correlations between television viewing at age 14 years and aggressive and antisocial behavior at ages 16 and 22 years with the reverse hypothesis encountering the usual inhospitality among the data with the pattern about the same for those both high and low initially in aggressive and antisocial behavior. However, the clearest documentation of effects over time occurs in the NBC panel data, where it is possible to distinguish between longitudinal effects and cumulative effects.

NBC's original analysis by Milavsky et al. (1982), found that there were two instances in which effects increased with the passage of time. In one case, the coefficients among the elementary school sample became larger as the number of months between measurements increased, with the largest clustered among the five coefficients representing the longest time spans. In the other, the coefficients among the same elementary school sample became somewhat larger when there were no statistical controls for the influence of earlier viewing, implying that there was an aggregative influence of violence viewing. Two reanalyses of the NBC panel data provide further evidence of effects over time. Cook, Kendzierski, and Thomas (1983) concluded that there was evidence of increasing coefficients with the passage of time among both the elementary school sample and the teenage sample and for several different measures of aggressive and antisocial behavior. Kang (1990) found that five of his statistically significant eight viewing-to-behavior coefficients were clustered among the longest time spans, whereas three of his four

behavior-to-viewing coefficients were clustered among the shortest time spans. These analyses suggest that there are longitudinal effects and cumulative effects. The former probably represents the influence of earlier viewing on behavior that has become newly relevant or newly within the range of the individual. The latter indicates that influence accumulates. Thus, the data supports the developmental interpretation (Eron & Huesmann, 1987) that earlier viewing establishes traits that will persist and perhaps become even more pronounced while confining the reverse hypothesis largely to the short term.

Milavsky and colleagues (Milavsky et al., 1982) seized on socioeconomic status as a possible explanation for positive coefficients in their panel data. They argued that the substantial representation of young people from households of low socioeconomic status (SES) led to samples where television viewing—and thus exposure to violent portrayals—and aggressive behavior would be correlated. Alas, SES proves inadequate to producing the required artifact. Socioeconomic status consistently has been judged as unable to fully explain positive associations between violence viewing and aggressive and antisocial behavior (Belson, 1978; Chaffee, 1972; Comstock & Scharrer, 1999). Furthermore, in the case of the NBC data, Cook et al. (1983) teased out a truly embarrassing rejoinder—the pattern that held for the males of increasing coefficients as time spans increased, alleged by Milavsky and colleagues as an artifact of socioeconomic status, was duplicated with middle-class girls.

The recorded effects are not trivial in seriousness or size. The effect sizes in Paik and Comstock (1994) for interpersonal aggression, the category of behavior for which the evidence is the strongest because it has been examined more often than any other type of antisocial behavior, are in the medium range by Cohen's (1988) frequently employed criteria (Rosenthal, Rosnow, & Rubin, 2000). Interpersonal aggression includes hitting, fighting, name calling, and stealing and ordinarily would constitute an experience that most victims would prefer to avoid. Other seriously harmful or criminal outcomes have much smaller effect sizes, but they are statistically significant and represent the infliction of greater harm than merely hitting, fighting, name calling, or stealing. The Belson data (Belson, 1978) provide a particularly striking example of a nontrivial outcome. He found in his London sample of teenage males that the viewing of violent television entertainment predicted the committing of significantly more seriously hurtful (and decidedly criminal) acts than were committed by those like them in every other measured respect (other than the greater viewing of violence), and there was no evidence that this could be attributed to the reverse hypothesis. Similarly, Johnson and colleagues (2002) found that greater television viewing (which would imply greater exposure to violent portrayals) at an earlier age predicted more frequent assaults or physical fights resulting in injury among 16- and 22-year-old males with the plausibility of the reverse hypothesis diminished (as pointed out earlier) by the occurrence of the same pattern for those scoring lower as well as higher in aggressiveness at the earlier time period.

Taking advantage of the Federal Communication Commission's (FCC) television station license freeze in the late 1940s and early 1950s to conduct a quasi-experimental time series with switching replications (Cook & Campbell, 1979), a group led by the methodologist Thomas Cook (Hennigan et al., 1982) found consistent evidence across two different samples (cities and states) and at two points in time (early and late introduction of television) that television's introduction was followed by a significant rise in larceny theft. This is an outcome that has enjoyed two distinct interpretations: that it should be attributed to relative deprivation accelerated by the materialistic emphases of the medium (Hennigan et al., 1982) and that it represents emulation of television's antisocial emphases in a manner that apprehension would be unlikely and sanctions modest (Comstock, 1991).

In the Paik and Comstock (1994) meta-analysis, coefficients were mostly in the medium range (by Cohen's criteria) for simulated aggressive behavior (such as aggressive inclination measured by questionnaire or performance on an aggression machine) and minor aggression (such as violence done to an object or physical aggression against a person that would fall under the law's radar), although sometimes they were in the large range.[4] They were smaller when illegal activities were the dependent variable and became progressively smaller as the seriousness of the offense increased. Even so, criminal violence against a person achieved statistical significance and scored a fail-safe number just shy of 3,000. The issue of the possible triviality of the effect sizes for television violence viewing and aggressive and antisocial behavior is addressed somewhat differently by Bushman and Anderson (2001). They compiled a selection to compare with the effect size for all observations in the Paik and Comstock (1994) meta-analysis (p. 481, Figure 2). The $r. = .31$ for media violence and aggression compares favorably in terms of magnitude with those for such pairings as passive smoking and lung cancer, calcium intake and bone mass, and homework and academic achievement. In their own cumulative meta-analysis, Bushman and Anderson found stable, statistically significant correlations for experimental designs from 1975 to 2000, and for the ecologically most valid data, the nonexperimental designs representing real-life aggression or antisocial behavior, Bushman and Anderson found statistically significant correlations that have increased in magnitude over the past 25 years. In contrast, in a parallel content analysis of major news media, they uncovered a decline in the frequency

---

[4]Paik and Comstock (1994) divided outcomes into three categories: simulated aggression, minor aggressive behavior, and illegal activities. In effect, they created a scale of increasing social consequence in terms of the validity of the dependent variable. The first included use of an aggression machine and self-report of aggressive inclination, play with aggressive toys, and miscellaneous simulated aggressive behavior. The second included physical aggression against an object, verbal aggression, and physical aggression against a person below the threshold of serious harm. The third included burglary, grand theft, and seriously harmful violence against a person. Self-report of aggressive inclination was largely represented by responses indicating what the individual would do in hypothetical situations. Thus, it was analogous to the expression of a norm, value, or attitude—a disposition—rather than an intention to behave in the future in a particular way in a specific situation.

that reports linked television and film violence with an undesirable behavioral outcome (they record a sizable negative correlation of $r = -.68$ between average effect sizes and the average ratings of news reports for their fealty to the scientific evidence over six data points between 1975 and 2000). They conclude, with considerable exasperation at the performance of the news media, that "regardless of preference for experimental or non-experimental methods, it has been decades since one could reasonable claim that there is little reason for concern about media violence effects" (p. 485).

Finally, based on Paik and Comstock (1994), the U. S. Surgeon General's recently released report on youth violence (U. S. Department of Health and Human Services, 2001) identifies greater exposure to television violence between the ages of 6 and 11 years as an early risk factor for the committing of criminal violence equivalent to a felony between the ages of 15 and 18 years (p. 58, Box 4–1). The effect size ($r. = .13$) was categorized as falling into the small range, and the report concluded that the effect sizes for both aggression in general and physical aggression—apparently using slightly more liberal criteria than Cohen—achieved the large range. However, about three fourths of the near 20 factors identified as posing early risks for later violence also fell into the small category.

Young people are particularly vulnerable to the influence of television and film violence when they have attributes that predict greater exposure to violent portrayals or greater likelihood of engaging in aggressive or antisocial behavior (Comstock & Scharrer, 1999; U. S. Department of Health and Human Services, 2001). Five such attributes are low socioeconomic status, rigid or indifferent parenting, unsatisfactory social relationships, low psychological well-being, and a predisposition for antisocial behavior. Although there are no data that directly document such interactions, there is data clearly linking these factors to either the independent or dependent variables, and thus logically they would appear to increase vulnerability. Exposure to television and to television violence is inversely associated with socioeconomic status (Comstock & Scharrer, 1999; Thornton & Voigt, 1984). When parent-child communication is open and constructive (in contrast with families where communication is rigid, many topics are avoided, differences in opinion are discouraged, and orders rather than explanations by parents are the rule), there typically is less television viewing by children and less exposure to violent television entertainment (Chaffee, McLeod, & Atkin, 1971; McLeod et al., 1972b). In addition, a variety of delinquent behavior is inversely associated with parental interest in the whereabouts of children and teenagers (Thornton & Voigt, 1984). Psychological discomfort and social conflicts predict greater exposure to television—those under stress, lonely, anxious, in negative moods, or in conflict with others apparently find the medium a satisfying escape and thus score higher in viewing or attraction to television (Anderson, Collins, Schmitt, & Jacobvitz, 1996; Canary & Spitzberg, 1993; Comstock & Scharrer, 1999; Kubey & Csikszentmihalyi, 1990; Maccoby, 1954; Potts & Sanchez, 1994). It is clear that the predisposed—those scoring higher in antisocial behavior or possessing attributes

that are correlates of antisocial behavior—are most likely to be affected. Surveys (Belson, 1978; Robinson & Bachman, 1972), experiments (Josephson, 1987; Celozzi, Kazelskis, & Gutsch, 1981), and a meta-analysis (Paik, 1991) all record associations that are greater among or limited to the predisposed. We doubt that it is a necessary condition because results are so consistent for general populations in surveys and experiments, but, if it is, then it is also very widespread. Thus, television violence is most likely to add to the burdens of those who already face considerable challenge in coping with everyday life, and this becomes particularly clear when it is acknowledged that the kind of behavior likely to be increased by violent portrayals is also the kind likely to lead to conflicts with others and clashes with the law.

Two independent analyses concur that among the independent variables responsible for effects on aggression one of the most powerful is violent erotica. Both Paik and Comstock (1994), who examined erotic as well as violent portrayals, and Allen, D'Alessio, and Brezgel (1995) who examined only erotic portrayals, although proceeding somewhat differently (as is usually the case in these matters) and producing somewhat different effect sizes (as would be expected), report effect sizes for violent erotica that are among the highest recorded.

The data also provide an important contribution to the debate over whether it is the sex (Weaver, 1991) or the violence (Donnerstein, Linz, & Penrod, 1987) that is responsible. Effect sizes for violent erotica are consistently higher than they are for erotica without violence. However, coefficients for erotica without violence are consistently positive. When Allen and colleagues (Allen et al., 1995), following the schema developed by the Attorney General's Commission on Pornography (1986), divided their independent variables into portrayals of nudity without sex, erotica (sex without violence), and violent erotica, they found for the first an inverse effect size and for the latter two positive and increasing effect sizes. The answer, then, is that it is both the sex and the violence, with the two creating a powerful joint stimulus.

The inverse effects for nudity and the weaker effects for erotica presumably derive from the absence of cues that would facilitate aggression, including depiction of the participants in sexual behavior as meriting callousness, derision, or contempt. It is tempting to argue that the inverse and weaker effects represent the lower levels of arousal induced, but the finding of Allen and colleagues (Allen et al., 1995) that throughout self-reported arousal was inversely (if modestly) correlated with aggression precludes such a rash inference.

The data bestow considerable confidence that the patterns observed are not the products of methodologically inferior or ecologically questionable undertakings. In neither the early meta-analysis of Hearold (1986) nor the more recent one by Paik and Comstock (1994) does the introduction of measures of study quality and ecological validity alter conclusions with one noteworthy exception. Hearold found that when she confined her analysis to the studies scoring high in methodological quality (which would give the data particular credibility) the outcomes were

symmetrical for antisocial and prosocial portrayals. Antisocial portrayals were associated with a positive effect size for antisocial behavior and a negative effect size for prosocial behavior. Prosocial portrayals were associated with a positive effect size for prosocial behavior and a negative effect size for antisocial behavior. One clear implication is the imposition of a double jeopardy by violent children's programming: greater likelihood of antisocial behavior and lesser likelihood of prosocial behavior by the young viewer.

Hearold (1986) also examined another design element—the matching in experiments of treatment and outcome variables. These experiments involved pure modeling, with the outcomes undeterred by the requirement that the subjects generalize from one situation to another. She found that this design element doubled effect sizes for both antisocial and prosocial behavior. There are two implications. One is that commercial entertainment has less effect than might otherwise be the case because it often fails to match the situations in which viewers find themselves. The other is that experiments with these characteristics should not be taken as offering an effect size likely to be duplicated in everyday life, except when portrayals and behavioral options exactly match.

DISAPPOINTMENT AND SURPRISE

There is also an element that is both disappointing and surprising. Often, exposure to violent portrayals has been a predictor of an attitudinal disposition favorable to aggressive or antisocial behavior, and, often, these outcomes have occurred in experimental designs. As a consequence, exposure in these cases can be said to be the cause of the disposition. For example, in the Paik and Comstock (1994) meta-analysis, a substantial number of the outcomes categorized under the rubric "aggressive intent" ($r = .33$, medium magnitude by Cohen's criteria) consisted of responses indicating what the individual would do in hypothetical situations. Such measures represent attitudes or dispositions rather than clear-cut intentions in regard to specific circumstances. Thus, meta-analysis (and the many individual studies encompassed) provides evidence of a causal link between violence viewing and dispositions. Nevertheless, there is little direct evidence that dispositions are a key and necessary link between the independent and dependent variables—exposure to violent portrayals and aggressive or antisocial behavior.

There is a data set that permits an examination of this issue and possesses attributes that give it unusual credibility. Belson's (1978) sample of London male teenagers was very large (about 1,600) and is the only probability sample in the literature (as a result, it has the inferential nicety of clearly representing a larger population). Belson's measurement was meticulous and statistical analysis assiduous. The respondents were personally interviewed by a conservatively attired male in a clinical setting. Boys were given false names to emphasize the confidentiality of the investigation, and the names were used throughout to encourage forthright

responses. The interviews were unusually lengthy—about 3.5 hours. This is the equivalent of almost 1,000 days of interviewing, an apt reflection of the scale of this enterprise. When it came to aggressive and antisocial behavior, they were asked to indicate whether, within the past 6 months, they had committed an act printed on a card by placing the card in a location clearly designated as representing "Yes," "No," or "Not sure." The intent was to reduce guile resulting from shame or embarrassment by eliminating the need for the respondent to speak about what he had done. The interviewer then engaged in forceful probes in regard to a "Not sure" and the frequency with which a confessed act had been committed. The labeling of these acts as to their seriousness was based on the rating of adult judges. Thus, the aggressive and antisocial outcome measures were sensitive, probing, and rooted in normative social judgments and presumably minimized both guile and conformity to interviewer expectancies. Thus, the data have a strong claim to representing real-world patterns.

Among the variables included in the Belson (1978) survey were a number of items representing attitudinal dispositions—norms, values, and beliefs. He included them as possible outcomes associated with exposure to violent television entertainment. This makes it possible to embark on the path of theory testing and possible revision. I begin with Belson's findings and then turn to a brief examination of the evidence supporting the popular view that there is an attitudinal or dispositional link between viewing and behavior. Finally, I attempt to resolve any conflicts between the two bodies of evidence—in this case, by positing an alternative path connecting violence viewing to aggressive and antisocial behavior. Belson obtained direct measures of four dispositions—antisocial attitudes, approval of violence, hostile personality traits, and willingness to commit violence—as well as a dimension of behavior with a dispositional aspect, social contagion (antisocial behavior in the company of others). Reliability was high for the first four, which were multiitem scales with 10 or more items for each disposition, whereas the latter represented a variety of antisocial acts. The first four directly represent attitudes, norms, and values. The fifth has a dispositional aspect because it represents indirectly the attitudes, norms, and values implied by the expressed beliefs and behavior of peers. None of these outcomes was predicted by the viewing of violent television entertainment. Thus, there was no evidence of a dispositional link between viewing and behavior.

Much of the research that has been central in the investigation of the relationship between exposure to television and film violence and aggressive and antisocial behavior would seem to assign a central place to attitudes, norms, and values. Both Bandura's (1986) social cognition and Berkowitz's (1984, 1990) neoassociationism give considerable weight to the categorizing of acts according to their effectiveness, social approval, and appropriateness for the circumstances. Both theories hold that portrayals with these characteristics are more likely to influence behavior. Such categorizing would seemingly depend on cognitive processes whose terminal state would be a disposition. The conclusion of Eron and Huesmann (1987), in

interpreting a positive correlation in survey data between childhood violence viewing and adult aggressiveness, is representative of many others writing on television violence and antisocial behavior:

> It is not claimed that the specific programs these adults viewed when they were 8 years old still had a direct effect on their behavior. However, the continued viewing of these programs probably contributed to the development of certain attitudes and norms of behavior and taught these youngsters ways of solving interpersonal problems which remained with them over the years. (p. 196)

Interpretation thus faces a quandary. The Belson (1978) survey provides strong evidence that attitudes, norms, and values are not invariably a link in real life in the causal chain between exposure and behavior. Numerous experiments also provide convincing evidence that aggression and antisocial behavior are increased when certain factors are present that would seem to operate through cognitive processes—portrayals that depict behavior as effective, socially approved, and appropriate for the viewer, as well as circumstances that place the viewer in the market for some behavioral guidance. These are the contingencies that Comstock and Scharrer (1999) refer to as efficacy, normativeness, pertinence, and susceptibility. They represent, respectively, the degree to which a portrayed behavior is perceived as effective, as evidenced by reward or, for those intrinsically pleasurable, lack of punishment; as socially accepted, approved, or conventional; as relevant to the viewer, such as a perpetrator of the same age or gender or a victim resembling a potential real-life target; and the degree to which the viewer is motivated or rendered vulnerable to being affected by the portrayal.[5]

The Belson (1978) data clearly falsify the hypothesis that certain attitudes and norms (to use the phrasing of Eron and Huesmann, 1987) are a necessary link in the causal chain. The challenge is equally clear. If we accept the Belson finding, we must explain the role that these four factors have other than constituting a link through dispositions. The alternatives—draw a line through the Belson data, impugn the experiments—are not scientifically permissible.

The interpretation that conforms to both sets of evidence is that these factors promote the incorporation and accessibility of the portrayed behavior. Behavioral

---

[5]Susceptibility is a factor that has been found often to play a role in the influence of communication. In the case of aggressive or antisocial behavior, it is typically represented by frustration or provocation and in experiments often induced by the rude or insulting behavior of the experimenter. However, it also has been found to operate in other contexts. For example, in the Stanford cardiovascular field experiment (Farquar et al., 1977, 1990) those who scored higher in risk proneness were more influenced by persuasive appeals intended to reduce behavior that contributed to cardiovascular disorder, and in the area of agenda setting (Comstock & Scharrer, 1999) those scoring higher in the need for orientation are more likely to be influenced by the emphases of media coverage in regard to the issues and topics they perceive as important. In each of these three instances, the influence of messages is somewhat contingent on individual motives, needs, and interests.

classes or genres would be influenced because we would expect some generalization, although the effect would be greatest when there was a match between the portrayal and behavioral options. The function of these factors is to govern the salience of classes or genres of behavior in the repertoire of the individual. In terms of the theory of a link between perception and behavior, offered by Dijksterhuis and Bargh (2001), these factors determine the significance or validity as a guide to behavior extended to the behavior portrayed. Efficacy, normativeness, pertinence, and susceptibility would act as gatekeepers, to use communication research jargon.

From this perspective, observation and attitudes, norms, and values often act as competitors rather than the coconspirators they are usually taken for. Attitudes, norms, and values may remain stable while the likelihood of a change in behavior increases. Good people (at least, those with constructive thoughts) may behave badly without any sign of a change in expressed dispositions. This lowers the predictive power of attitudes, norms, and values, which have a notoriously weak resistance to the demands of situational circumstances (Eagly & Chaiken, 1993; Terry & Hogg, 2000) and heightens the predictive power of observation. Efficacy, normativeness, pertinence, and susceptibility become conditions on which the latter, rather than the former, rest.

This revision of theory addresses two nagging puzzles. One is the quite frequent occasion when attitudes, norms, and values, and behavior part ways. The other is the similarly frequent occasion when the enormity of an act seems beyond a contribution by the media. We expect people to be consistent in thought and behavior, and we expect heinous acts to be outside the influence of observation or perception. The revision asserts that there are routes to behavior other than through dispositions (although they sometimes may be crucial) and that role of the media may be modestly confined to gatekeeping but on that account sometimes crucial.

The data support the view that one route by which entertainment affects behavior is analogous to peripheral processing in the ELM. Accessibility or salience is a key element. However, it would be premature to conclude that this is the sole route by which behavioral effects occur. Attitudes, norms, and values surely sometimes play a role. One would occur when these cognitive dispositions and accessibility coincide, which would increase the likelihood of an effect; this would be a special case of susceptibility in operation. Another is when thoughtful motivation enters, such as Bandura's (1986) famous example of a well-contrived (and financially successful) airline bomb extortion attempt following the televising of a movie depicting such a caper. This analysis obviously fits quite well with the general aggression model (GAM) proposed by Anderson and Bushman (2002), where cognitive processes may have an influence but are not a necessary element. The present analysis, however, addresses the specific question of whether attitudes, norms, and values—that is, cognitive elements—are a necessary part of any causal chain where exposure to violent portrayals predicts aggressive or antisocial behavior (as in the Belson data), as much research suggests, and the conclusion is that they are not.

The Belson (1978) data do not support a role for direct effects of attitudes, norms, and values. However, they are consistent with a role for cognitive dispositions through effects on accessibility and salience. In addition, the Belson data have nothing conclusive to say about the possibility that attitudes, norms, and values held by others may create an environment more or less favorable to modes of behavior made accessible or salient by the media. Thus, attitudes, norms, and values remain key concepts in explaining the effects of violent portrayals on aggressive and antisocial behavior although they are not a necessary mediating link between exposure and behavior.

REFERENCES

Allen, M., D'Alessio, D., & Brezgel, K. (1995). A meta-analysis summarizing the effects of pornography II: Aggression after exposure. *Human Communication Research, 22*(2), 258–283.

Anderson, C. A., & Bushman, B. J. (2002). Human aggression. *Annual Review of Psychology, 53*, 27–51.

Anderson, D. R., Collins, P. A., Schmitt, K. L., & Jacobvitz, R. S. (1996). Stressful life events and television viewing. *Communication Research, 23*(3), 243–260.

Andison, F. S. (1977). TV violence and viewer aggression: A cumulation of study results. *Public Opinion Quarterly, 41*(3), 314–331.

Attorney General's Commission on Pornography. (1986). *Final report*. Washington, DC: U. S. Government Printing Office.

Bandura, A. (1986). *Social foundations of thought and action: A social cognitive theory*. Englewood Cliffs, NJ: Prentice Hall.

Bandura, A., Ross, D., & Ross, S. A. (1963a). Imitation of film-mediated aggressive models. *Journal of Abnormal and Social Psychology, 66*(1), 3–11.

Bandura, A., Ross, D., & Ross, S. A. (1963b). Vicarious reinforcement and imitative learning. *Journal of Abnormal and Social Psychology, 67*(6), 601–607.

Becker, M. H. (Ed.). (1974). The health belief model and personal health behavior. *Health Education Monographs, 2*(4), 324–473.

Belson, W. A. (1978). *Television violence and the adolescent boy*. Westmead, UK: Saxon House, Teakfield.

Berkowitz, L. (1984). Some effects of thoughts on anti- and prosocial influences of media events: A cognitive-neoassociationistic analysis. *Psychological Bulletin, 95*(3), 410–427.

Berkowitz, L. (1990). On the formation and regulation of anger and aggression: A cognitive-neoassociationistic analysis. *American Psychologist, 45*(4), 494–503.

Berkowitz, L., & Rawlings, E. (1963). Effects of film violence on inhibitions against subsequent aggression. *Journal of Abnormal and Social Psychology, 66*(3), 405–412.

Bushman, B. J., & Anderson, C. A. (2001). Media violence and the American public: Scientific facts versus media misinformation. *American Psychologist, 56*(6–7), 477–489.

Cacioppo, J. T., & Petty, R. E. (1985). Central and peripheral routes to persuasion: The role of message repetition. In L. F. Alwitt & A. A. Mitchell (Eds.), *Psychological processes and advertising effects:Theory, research and application* (pp. 91–111). Hillsdale, NJ: Lawrence Erlbaum Associates.

Cairns, E., Hunter, D., & Herring, L. (1980). Young children's awareness of violence in Northern Ireland: The influence of Northern Irish television in Scotland and Northern Ireland. *British Journal of Social and Clinical Psychology, 19*, 3–6.

Canary, D. J., & Spitzberg, B. H. (1993). Loneliness and media gratification. *Communication Research, 20*(6), 800–821.

Celozzi, M. J., II, Kazelskis, R., & Gutsch, K. U. (1981). The relationship between viewing televised violence in ice hockey and subsequent levels of personal aggression. *Journal of Sport Behavior, 4*(4), 157–162.

Chaffee, S. H. (1972). Television and adolescent aggressiveness (overview). In G. A. Comstock & E. A. Rubinstein (Eds.), *Television and social behavior: Television and adolescent aggressiveness* (Vol. 3, pp. 1–34). Washington, DC: U. S. Government Printing Office.

Chaffee, S. H., McLeod, J. M., & Atkin, C. K. (1971). Parental influences on adolescent media use. *American Behavioral Scientist, 14*, 323–340.

Cohen, E. E. (1988). *Children's television commercialization survey.* Washington, DC: National Association of Broadcasters.

Comstock, G. (1991). *Television and the American child.* San Diego, CA: Academic Press.

Comstock, G., & Scharrer, E. (1999). *Television: What's on, who's watching, and what it means.* San Diego, CA: Academic Press.

Comstock, G., & Scharrer, E. (2003). The contribution of meta-analysis to the controversy over television violence and aggression. In Gentile, D. A. (Ed.). *Media Violence and Children.* Westport, CT: Praeger.

Cook, T. D., & Campbell, D. T. (1979). *Quasi-experimentation: Design and analysis issues for field settings.* Chicago: Houghton Mifflin.

Cook, T. D., Kendzierski, D. A., & Thomas, S. A. (1983). The implicit assumptions of television research: An analysis of the 1982 NIMH report on television and behavior. *Public Opinion Quarterly, 472*, 161–201.

Dijksterhuis, A., & Bargh, J. A. (2001). The perception-behavior expressway: Automatic effects of social perception on social behavior. In M. P. Sanna (Ed.), *Advances in Experimental Social Psychology* (Vol. 33, pp. 1–40). San Diego, CA: Academic Press.

Donnerstein, E., Linz, D., & Penrod, S. (1987). *The question of pornography: Research findings and policy implications.* New York: Free Press.

Eagly, A. H., & Chaiken, S. (1993). *The psychology of attitudes.* Orlando, FL: Harcourt.

Eron, L. D., & Huesmann, L. R. (1987). Television as a source of maltreatment of children. *School Psychology Review, 16*(2), 195–202.

Farquar, J. W., Fortmann, S. P., Flora, J. A., Taylor, C. B., Haskell, W. L., Williams, P. T., et al. (1990). Effects of communitywide education on cardiovascular disease risk factors: The Stanford Five-City Project. *Journal of the American Medical Association, 264*(3), 359–365.

Farquar, J. W., Maccoby, N., Wood, P. D., Alexander, J. K., Breitrose, H., Brown, B. W., Jr., et al. (1977) Community education for cardiovascular health. *Lancet, 1*, 1192–1195.

Glass, G. V. (1976). Primary, secondary, and meta-analysis of research. *Educational Researcher, 5*, 3–8.

Hearold, S. (1986). A synthesis of 1043 effects of television on social behavior. In G. Comstock (Ed), *Public communication and behavior* (Vol. 1, pp. 65–133). New York: Academic Press.

Hennigan, K. M., Heath, L., Wharton, J. D., Del Rosario, M. L., Cook, T. D., & Calder, B. J. (1982). Impact of the introduction of television on crime in the United States: Empirical findings and theoretical implications. *Journal of Personality and Social Psychology, 42*(3), 461–477.

Hogben, M. (1998). Factors moderating the effect of television aggression on viewer behavior. *Communication Research, 25*, 220–247.

Hunt, M. (1997). *How science takes stock.* New York: Russell Sage.

Johnson, J. G., Cohen, P., Smailes, E. M., Kasen, S., & Brook, J. S. (2002). Television viewing and aggressive behavior during adolescence and adulthood. *Science, 295*, 2468–2471.

Josephson, W. L. (1987). Television violence and children's aggression: Testing the priming, social script, and disinhibition predictions. *Journal of Personality and Social Psychology, 53*(5), 882–890.

Kang, N. (1990). *A critique and secondary analysis of the NBC study on television and aggression.* Unpublished doctoral dissertation, Syracuse University, Syracuse, NY.

Kubey, R., & Csikszentmihalyi, M. (1990). *Television and the quality of life: How viewing shapes everyday experience*. Hillsdale, NJ: Lawrence Erlbaum Associates.

Lefkowitz, M. M., Eron, L. D., Walder, L. O., & Huesmann, L. R. (1972). Television violence and child aggression: A followup study. In G. A. Comstock & E. A. Rubinstein (Eds.), *Television and social behavior: Vol. 3. Television and adolescent aggressiveness* (pp. 35–135). Washington, DC: U. S. Government Printing Office.

Lefkowitz, M. M., Eron, L. D., Walder, L. O., & Huesmann, L. R. (1977). *Growing up to be violent: A longitudinal study of the development of aggression*. Elmsford, NY: Pergamon.

Maccoby, E. E. (1954). Why do children watch television? *Public Opinion Quarterly, 18*(3), 239–244.

McLeod, J. M., Atkin, C. K., & Chaffee, S. H. (1972a). Adolescents, parents, and television use: Adolescent self-report measures from Maryland and Wisconsin samples. In G. A. Comstock & E. A. Rubinstein (Eds.), *Television and social behavior: Television and adolescent aggressiveness* (Vol. 3, pp. 173–238). Washington, DC: U. S. Government Printing Office.

McLeod, J. M., Atkin, C. K., & Chaffee, S. H. (1972b). Adolescents, parents, and television use: Self-report and other-report measures from the Wisconsin sample. In G. A. Comstock & E. A. Rubinstein (Eds.), *Television and social behavior: Television and adolescent aggressiveness* (Vol. 3, pp. 239–313). Washington, DC: U. S. Government Printing Office.

Milavsky, J. R., Kessler, R., Stipp, H. H., & Rubens, W. S. (1982). *Television and aggression: A panel study*. New York: Academic Press.

Paik, H. (1991). *The effects of television violence on aggressive behavior: A meta-analysis*. Unpublished doctoral dissertation, Syracuse University, Syracuse, NY.

Paik, H., & Comstock, G. (1994). The effects of television violence on antisocial behavior: A meta-analysis. *Communication Research, 21*(4), 516–546.

Petty, R. E., & Cacioppo, J. T. (1990). Involvement and persuasion: Tradition vs. integration. *Psychological Bulletin, 107*(3), 367–374.

Potts, R., & Sanchez, D. (1994). Television viewing and depression: No news is good news. *Journal of Broadcasting and Electronic Media, 38*(1), 79–90.

Robinson, J. P. & Bachman, J. G. (1972). Television viewing habits and aggression. In G. A. Comstock & E. A. Rubinstein (Eds.), *Television and social behavior: Television and adolescent aggressiveness*. (Vol. 3, pp. 372–382). Washington, DC: U. S. Government Printing Office.

Rosenthal, R. (1979). The "file drawer problem" and tolerance for null results. *Psychological Bulletin, 86*, 638–641.

Rosenthal, R., Rosnow, R. L., & Rubin, D. B. (2000). *Contrasts and effect sizes in behavioral research: A correlational approach*. New York: Cambridge University Press.

Rosenthal, R., & Rubin, D. B. (1978). Interpersonal expectancy effects: The first 345 studies. *Behavioral and Brain Sciences, 3*, 377–415.

Terry, D. J., & Hogg, M. A. (Eds.). (2000). *Attitudes, behavior, and social context*. Mahwah, NJ: Lawrence Erlbaum Associates.

Thornton, W., & Voigt, L. (1984). Television and delinquency. *Youth and Society, 15*(4), 445–468.

U. S. Department of Health and Human Services. (2001). *Youth violence: A report of the Surgeon General*. Rockville, MD: U. S. Department of Health and Human Services, Centers for Disease Control and Prevention, National Center for Injury Prevention and Control, Substance Abuse and Mental Health Services Administration, Center for Mental Health Services, National Institutes of Health, National Institute of Mental Health.

Weaver, J. (1991). Responding to erotica: Perceptual processes and dispositional implications. In J. Bryant & D. Zillmann (Eds.), *Responding to the screen: Reception and reaction processes* (pp. 329–354). Hillsdale, NJ: Lawrence Erlbaum Associates.

Wood, W., Wong, F., & Cachere, J. (1991). Effects of media violence on viewers' aggression in unconstrained social interaction. *Psychological Bulletin, 109*(3), 371–383.

CHAPTER TWELVE

Between the Ads: Effects of Nonadvertising TV Messages on Consumption Behavior

Maria Kniazeva

University of San Diego

Research on the impact of nonadvertising television programs (e.g., series, soap operas, TV movies) on consumption behavior cannot boast the recognition gained by inquiries into the effects of television advertising. The latter research obviously has been built on the assumption that such effects exist and explores variables contributing to the effectiveness of this influence. The research on the influence of nonadvertising television exposure on consumer attitudes and behavior appears to be fragmented and overlooked in the marketing discipline. The major question, "Are the entertaining programs a powerful engine for change in daily consumption activity?" still seems to need further inquiry.

If we turn to experts in the search for answers, we can find strong advocates of the real effects of nonadvertising television programs on consumption behavior. For example, activists of the international organization Soap Operas for Social Change credit soap operas with generating demand for goods like sewing machines and condoms (Williams, 2001). Though the reported effects were witnessed in developing countries, they support the TV producers' general belief that nonadvertising television programs can encourage positive behavioral changes. The logical question is, to what extent have such claims and hopes been supported theoretically? This is the question that this chapter aims to address.

This chapter focuses specifically on the effects of nonadvertising television programs on consumption behavior and discusses these effects in terms of the psychological processes of encoding, interpretation, and memory. The objective is to analyze how researchers in different fields have conceptually defined and

empirically identified the effects of television viewing on consumers' attitudes toward goods and services and consumer behavior in the marketplace. This research is a response to invitations to investigate the link between marketing and nonadvertising media that has repeatedly sounded in the marketing discipline in recent years. Specifically, Lehmann (1999) urged researchers to broaden their current narrow focus on mass advertising by considering the cumulative effect of marketing and media on consumer welfare. John (1999) welcomed efforts to understand the influence of subtle messages delivered by television. Hirschman and McGriff (1995), who represented an initial step in employing marketing skills toward the application of televised images to addressing social problems, expressed hope that studies like this will lessen destructive consumer behavior. Varey (1999) argued that studying the effects, and not just the effectiveness, of media should help in dealing with the consequences of the wholesale marketization of society.

In light of these academic calls, it is timely to review the existent body of research on the impact of nonadvertising media on consumption behavior. To fill this need, this chapter offers an analysis of reported findings on how and why nonadvertising television has been found to influence consumption behavior. The presented literature review of the academic research conducted in the past 20 years examines the most popular and the most controversial media channel—television. Commercial advertising is excluded from the scope of this work due to the substantial attention that television advertising has already received in marketing literature. In this way, attention is diverted from the omnipresent and often annoying and intrusive commercial messages that prompt audiences to resist and neglect them to those equally ubiquitous but subtle and hidden messages to which customers deliberately expose themselves during the programs.

Specifically, this chapter investigates how television messages are encoded by producers and interpreted by receivers and presents the findings under several headings. After providing a brief historical overview of the phenomenon of television, I illuminate theoretical explanations for the effects of TV on consumption behavior. Second, I summarize a set of empirical evidence of these effects, including both immediate and long-term effects. Third, I analyze research of cultural texts. Finally, I discuss public policy implications, identify some unanswered questions, and suggest directions for future research. In the overall discourse, two major streams of inquiry become visible: one exploring nonadvertising television's effects as emotional enhancers of commercials and the other examining these effects as cognitive enhancers of commercials. Both types of enhancers are seen as mediating the impact of television viewing on consumption behavior.

"OLD" MEDIA UNDER NEW ATTACKS

The mass arrival of television in 1946 is often termed revolutionary, and after the 1949 debut of the TV set in Sears Roebuck catalog, it took only 14 years for the American public to recognize that they received more of their news from television

than from newspapers. Moreover, surveys indicate that since the 1980s, more than two thirds of Americans have regarded TV not only as their primary but also their preferred source of news, and more than half believe it is the most credible source (Dennis, 1989). On the other hand, there were just 3 years between the first sounds of gunshots from televised westerns in the 1955–1956 season and the first formal complaint about TV violence by a U.S. senator. Published in *Reader's Digest* under the title "Let's Get Rid of Tele-Violence" (Kefauver, 1958), this article presumed a direct link between the rising rates of juvenile crime and television viewing and virtually opened up the still ongoing debates about the controversial impact of television on its viewers and society as a whole. (For reviews, see Comstock [this volume] and Shrum [this volume].)

Today, television is attacked by public health specialists for the potential health risks that media exposure presents to children and adolescents, by sociologists for being a time waster and social isolator (Tonn & Petrich, 1998), and by social scientists and public policy officials for the prevalence of violent content. Many of the sins attributed to television's influence have either direct or indirect links with consumption behavior. Materialism, compulsive buying, smoking, and the antisocial consumption of drugs and alcohol are the "sins" that are referred to most often. The overall situation seems to be so critical that the American Academy of Pediatrics (AAP) suggested that pediatricians eschew televisions in their waiting rooms, provide guidance about media use in the home to parents and children during pediatric visits, and take a media history from patients by asking them about their TV viewing habits (Hogan, 2000). These steps were included in a 5-year, nationwide education campaign, Media Matters, launched by the AAP in 1997 with the purpose to protect youth from the potential harm of media messages and images. Thus, regardless of the dominant character of television, societal attitudes regard this medium as both a threat and an opportunity, a conflict that is rooted in the recognition of TV as a powerful message sender.

STUDYING TV: UNREALISTIC ATTEMPT?

Despite (and perhaps because of) the pervasiveness of television, studying its effects has never been considered an easy task. Yet at the dawn of television, scholars predicted not only the overwhelming popularity of an audiovisual communication channel but also the difficulty of grasping the effects of TV on people's lives. The word *totality* best explains the phenomenon, which resulted from the intervention of TV in personal, political, and social lives. Some scholars even expressed concern over the prospects of possible studies: "Since it [television] has affected the totality of our lives, . . . it would be quite unrealistic to attempt systematic or visual presentation of such influence" (McLuhan, 1964, p. 317). Instead, what seemed a more feasible way of studying these effects was suggested—"to present TV as a complex *gestalt* of data gathered almost at random" (McLuhan 1964, p. 317). Forty years later, however, it is evident that research on the impact of television viewing on

people's lives, including their consumption behavior, has been conducted in two major directions: One stream of research uses quantitative methods and focuses on responses that are outwardly observable; the second approach is characterized by qualitative research. Both directions have the same goal: explaining the effects of TV on various aspects of life. The studies include careful analysis of what is offered on the screen and of how this translates into viewers' daily activities beyond the screen.

Research on the impact of nonadvertising televised messages on behavior of viewers has been conducted in several disciplines and is presented by scholars of communications (e.g., Gerbner, Gross, Morgan, Signorielli, & Shanahan, 2002), psychology (e.g., Bandura, 1994), sociology (e.g., Fox & Philliber, 1978), child development (e.g., Potts, Doppler, & Hernandez, 1994), and preventive medicine (e.g., Cooper, Roter, & Langlieb, 2000). The authors agree in defining the place of television in the individual decision-making and judgmental process. The shared theoretical framework assumes two important factors employed by the viewers: direct and indirect experiences. *Direct experience* refers to past activities in which an individual was personally engaged, whereas *indirect experience* includes activities experienced by other people but of which the consumer is aware through two possible sources—a social network, mass media, or both. Thus, indirect experience can be gained through friends, relatives, and neighbors and through television, print media, and radio. But to what extent do nonadvertising messages conveyed by television really matter in an individual's consumption behavior? In the search for the answer to this general question, a substantial body of knowledge has been collectively generated.

Scholars have analyzed statistical descriptions of the audience, engaged in contextual analysis of the television messages and images, offered theoretical explanations and empirical evidence of the mechanism of television's influence, and claimed to find immediate and long-term effects of television watching on the audience. Their findings suggest that after the shift in the public's preference from a print to a visual culture occurred, the artificial reality perpetually portrayed on the TV screen started serving as a subliminal frame of reference for the viewers in their consumption activity while affecting both "good" consumption (e.g., making the right lifestyle choices, developing healthy eating patterns) and "bad" consumption (e.g., smoking, consuming alcohol, doing drugs, practicing overconsumption). These findings are analyzed in the rest of the chapter.

THEORETICAL EXPLANATION FOR THE EFFECTS OF TV ON CONSUMPTION BEHAVIOR

A determined attempt to offer a theoretical explanation for the effects of nonadvertising TV on consumption behavior is what unites the majority of the reported studies. Current research pursuing this goal can be grouped into the examination

of consumption associative and consumption nonassociative television viewing and their effects. Thus, research that explores the explicit consumption context of the television messages or the feelings produced by watching the portrayals of certain products, goods, and services directly associated with their use by the characters of a TV program can be termed under the rubric consumption associative viewing. Examples include the works by Hirschman and Thompson (1997), O'Guinn and Shrum (1997), and Shrum, Wyer, and O'Guinn (1998). In turn, research that is consumption context independent and does not focus on the depicted consumer products and their perception by TV viewers can be termed as research into consumption nonassociative viewing. This stream of research explores overall emotions elicited by the program and examines TV programs as emotional enhancers of the advertisements. Examples include the works by Goldberg and Gorn (1987), Murry, Lastovicka, and Singh (1992), and Murry and Dacin (1996).

Consumption Nonassociative Viewing

The main objective of the consumption nonassociative research is to define which factors facilitate the greater effectiveness of commercials embedded in the program. The scholars engaging in this research mostly have tested what is considered to be conventional advertising wisdom that asserts the following scheme: If the program elicits positive emotions, the viewer will like the program; liking the program, in turn, leads to a positive attitude toward the advertisement; and this attitude is followed by a positive attitude toward the brand advertised. In accordance with this theory, there is empirical evidence that commercials are more effective when placed in happy rather than in sad programs. Thus, building on previous mood research that suggested that the effects of the elicited mood may be evidenced for at least 15–20 min, Goldberg and Gorn (1987) exposed their participants to advertisements embedded in a happy episode about frogs trained to improve their self-image and in a sad episode about the killing of a young child. The authors then asked their participants (among other questions) about their likelihood of purchasing the products advertised in the embedded commercials and demonstrated the difference in responses. Those seeing the happy episode felt happier while watching the commercials than did those who saw the sad episode. The happy episode viewers also demonstrated a stronger intention to purchase the advertised products than did viewers of the sad episode.

However, it has been also argued that these program-elicited feelings do not directly influence attitudes toward the advertisement and brands but rather that viewer attitudes toward the program are what matter (Murry et al., 1992). Thus, dramas that elicit sadness may result in a positive attitude toward the advertisement similar to that produced by the positive-emotion programs, provided that the viewer likes the drama. Going further in this line of research, Murry and Dacin (1996) proposed and proved the hypothesis that "negative emotions elicited by a program will diminish program liking only if viewers believe the program to be either too realistic or personally relevant" (p. 441). This leads to the conclusion that negative

moods elicited by TV viewing are not a threat to the positive attitude toward advertisements and advertised brands when the individual does not feel personally threatened.

Consumption Associative Viewing

Whereas the research into consumption nonassociative viewing mostly explores nonadvertising television programs as emotional enhancers, the study of consumption associative viewing mostly regards TV programs as cognitive enhancers. This stream of research, as well as the previous one, also refers to a relation between advertising and media, which it characterizes as symbiotic. Some of the most sound recent theory-building work was offered by Hirschman and Thompson (1997), who argued that advertising, though certainly a powerful influence on consumption, is not a dominant voice and is being supplanted by mass media nonadvertising messages and images that largely define consumers' beliefs and behavior. The strength of these subtle messages lies in their informal, unobtrusive nature because such mass media texts are not viewed with the same cultivated skepticism as actual advertisements.

By examining the mediating role of nonadvertising forms of media on advertising, Hirschman and Thompson (1997) expanded prior multidisciplinary research that ascertained that media enhance the effectiveness of some advertising by portraying certain products as more appealing than others. In that role, media sort reality into meaningful social categories that provide a frame of reference from which consumers interpret their daily lives (Miller, 1988; Schiller, 1989). This theoretical framework was further developed when Hirschman and Thompson defined three interpretive strategies employed by consumers of televised messages in their relationships with the mass media. First is the inspiring and aspiring mode that is present when a media image is interpreted as representing an ideal self to which the consumer can aspire. The second mode is rather oppositional to the first: Labeled by the authors as deconstructing and rejecting, it refers to consumer relationships with the mass media that are characterized by overt criticism of the artificial and unrealistic quality of the media representation. The third mode is tailoring and personalizing; termed identifying and individualizing, it occurs when consumers negotiate their personal goals and self-perceptions in relation to idealized images presented in the media.

Proposing that consumers' relationships with nonadvertising forms of mass media are an essential aspect of the perceived meaning they derive from advertisements, the authors implied that the process of decoding messages portrayed on the screen is not a completely random and unpredictable affair. Moreover, they emphasized the interactive nature of television, which requires viewers who consume the TV images to actively construct the meanings associated with depicted goods and services. In line with this conclusion, a number of studies have been designed to test whether television consumption can be argued to alter the

perception of reality and subsequently affect consumer behavior (e.g., O'Guinn & Shrum, 1997; Shrum et al., 1998).

Television and the Perception of Reality

Several authors have claimed a causal relationship between viewing television programs and the formation of beliefs about social reality. According to their findings, heavy viewers of television do differ from light viewers in their perception of the real world, which in their mental construction closely reflects that portrayed on the screen. Thus, a positive relation between TV viewing and materialism was found (see Shrum, Burroughs, & Rindfleisch, this volume). Specifically, heavy viewers were found to overestimate the ownership of expensive products to a greater extent than did lighter viewers (O'Guinn & Shrum, 1997). Heavy viewers also overestimate the rate of crime (Gerbner, Gross, Morgan, & Signorielli, 1980a) and drug and alcohol consumption in society (Shrum & O'Guinn, 1993). They negatively view the elderly as unhealthy and financially poor and perceive women as aging faster than men (Gerbner, Gross, Morgan, & Signorielli, 1980b). These works have employed Gerbner's cultivation theory (Gerbner et al., 2002), which begins with an analysis of the aggregated messages embedded in television as a system and compares them with answers received in response to surveys designed to measure the correlation between televised images and viewers' perceptions of the real world. Cultivation theory suggests that heavy exposure to television results in largely viewing the world the way it is depicted on the screen. Thus, the overrepresented possession of certain goods on television (luxury cars, cell phones, nice houses) leads to a perception of a similar level of possession in the real world and subsequently to a distorted picture of reality.

In several attempts at exploring the mechanism by which concepts of the social reality of consumption are constructed, scholars examined the effects of television on perceptions of affluence (Fox & Philliber, 1978; O'Guinn & Shrum, 1997; Shrum, 2001; Shrum, O'Guinn, Semenik, & Faber, 1991) and reported a significant relationship between the two variables. Their findings supported the general hypothesis that heavier viewers of television perceive greater affluence in America than do lighter viewers. This included perceptions related to the ownership of swimming pools, convertible automobiles, use of maids, and the percentage of millionaires.

Cultivation theory, though widely accepted and tested by scholars, elicits some criticism for not providing a thorough explanation of its mechanism and not considering other variables (e.g., people's socioeconomic situation or education) that also could lead to the social judgments and beliefs expressed by participants of studies (Fox & Philliber, 1978; McGuire, 1986). In response to this criticism, some research implicates the availability heuristic as a psychological mechanism responsible for the effects of television viewing on judgmental processes (Shrum, 2001). The availability heuristic refers to a mode of information processing that

links judgments of frequency or probability of occurrence with ease of recall. The availability heuristic was developed by decision scientists Tversky and Kahneman (1973), who suggest that people estimate the prevalence of patterns and events based on how easy it is for them to retrieve the related information from memory. According to the availability heuristic, heavy viewers of TV should have more information received from television accessible in memory because they are exposed to a higher number of televised messages than are light viewers. These messages are stored in the memory over time, and when it comes to making judgments and decisions, heavy viewers of TV retrieve the accumulated information (Shrum et al., 1998). For this reason, heavy viewers should have relevant images (those frequently sent through the media channel) more accessible in memory. Thus, the application of the availability heuristic is seen as responsible for viewers' estimates of the real frequency and probability of events portrayed on the screen, which may explain the psychological mechanism of the cultivation effect.

In addition to the role television plays in consumer socialization, there has been some empirical evidence that it can play a role in consumer acculturation as well. The idea that the televised world is perceived as a close model of the real one and is turned to as a reference point for understanding society's values and beliefs was evident in Reece and Palmgreen's (2000) inquiry into the motives for watching television by foreigners. In a study of Asian Indian graduate students enrolled at American universities, the authors distinguished the motives of acculturation and reflection on values from among eight motives. Having conducted a survey of the convenience sample of 99 students, scholars argued that those subjects who wanted to learn more about current issues in their host country, understand the ways in which American people behave and think, and make American friends spent more time in front of the TV. The respondents also reported substantial exposure to host media back home. This led to assumptions that they were aware of what to expect on the screen and were prepared to decode the images encoded in news and sports coverage and situation comedies and movies—programs defined as preferred in the search for valuable cultural information. Furthermore, the participants of the study were found to deliberately turn to indirect televised experience in the search for answers about real-life experiences in the host country.

Lifestyle-Related Product Choices

The conceptual research into the effects of TV also suggests that consumers' incorporation of television-mediated images of reality into their perceptions of how others live and consume is used during the making of lifestyle-related product choices. Thus, Englis and Solomon (1997) noted that images of affluence transmitted via mass media become objects of desire for many who aspire to this quasi-mythical lifestyle. Conversely, some symbolical images associated with lifestyles that consumers tend to avoid are being stored as a negative mental set of objects. Moreover, the authors strongly assert that these pervasive consumption-rich images replete in

mass media are no mere shadows playing across the screen of popular culture but become equally or even more important than actual behavior observed when consumers subconsciously engage in the construction of lifestyle meanings. Englis and Solomon have argued that these intangible lifestyle meanings are powerful social constructions developed in the minds of consumers and should not be regarded by marketers as secondary. After conducting several studies on consumers' cognitive processing of media and marketing information and their consumption behavior, the scholars suggested a model that assigned the central role of generating and modifying lifestyle imageries to channel intermediaries—those including commercial vehicles (e.g., advertising), popular culture (e.g., television), and media hybrids. Overall, Englis and Solomon stressed that lifestyles should not be understood solely in terms of the actual patterns of behavior that marketers typically measure and use to cluster consumers.

The Promising Future of Hybrids

The use of messages embedded in television programs and labeled hybrids seems to have raised more ethical concerns than conceptual attention. These messages are paid for by the sponsor but are not explicitly identified as being such. A relatively new genre of marketing communication is growing (Balasubramanian, 1994) and is represented by product placements, infomercials, and program tie-ins. It is believed that hybrid messages avoid key disadvantages inherent in commercial advertising (i.e., a sponsor is identified and consumers can view the message with skepticism) and benefit from key advantages provided by commercial advertising, such as the sponsor's total control over the message content and its format. As a result, consumers perceive hybrid messages without any of the resistance they may practice while dealing with explicitly purchased messages. Conceptually, product placement hybrids appear to play a role in influencing consumer behavior similar to that of any other embedded product messages. Thus, Balasubramanian identified several theories on which the expected effects of impacting consumers are built: attribution theory (Mills & Jellison, 1967), the classical conditioning principle (Gorn, 1982), and the modeling paradigm (Bandura, 1994). Attribution theory assumes that television viewers perceive portrayed products without any reporting bias that could be attributed to a paid message. The classical conditioning principle assumes a positive paired-association enhancing product perception when a favorable endorser image (unconditional stimulus) and a product (conditional stimulus) wisely match each other. The modeling paradigm assumes that models demonstrating positive consequences of product used reinforce the process of persuasion.

Public policy officials invite researchers to employ the powerful persuasive potential of hybrid messages for conveying noncommercial messages designed to promote socially desirable consumption behavior. They call for embedding into television programs not so much products as social concepts and argue that the positive effects of such practices have been empirically supported.

GRASPING TELEVISION EFFECTS

The empirical study of television effects is defined by an approach that prompts or analyzes responses that are outwardly observable. These responses may be grouped into those characterized by immediate effects and those defined by long-term impacts. Whereas the studies of immediate effects are usually conducted in the laboratory setting where the researchers experimentally induce the expected effects, the research on long-term effects usually aims at identifying the correlation between television viewing and observable changes in attitude and consumption behavior. Both approaches seem to have had strong advocates. Thus, the proponents of long-term effects find strong support in the cultivation theory proposed by Gerbner et al. (2002). They argue that despite the time, energy, and money invested, the conceptualization of television's effect as a short-term individual change has not produced research that helps understand the distinctive features of television. To them, these features include massive, long-term, and common exposure of large and heterogeneous publics to centrally produced, mass distributed, and repetitive systems of stories (Gerbner et al., 2002).

Another theoretical model of the mass media's effects on individual decision-making can be found in the works of Tyler (Tyler, 1984; Tyler & Cook 1984), who has extensively tested the impersonal impact hypothesis proposed in prior research. According to this hypothesis, decisions are based on the judgments people make. These judgments, in turn, should be divided between those on a personal and those on a societal level. Moreover, the researchers should clearly separate them because the media messages may produce contradictory and independent societal and personal judgments. Thus, the individual, influenced by presumably overrepresented violence on the TV screen, may perceive a similar rate of crime in the surrounding society. However, when it comes to personal judgment, the viewer may not think there is an increasing danger and a high likelihood of being personally affected by crime. For this reason, the decision making and following behavior may not always be ruled by television exposure, even if the viewer is a heavy viewer.

The impersonal impact hypothesis suggests that the impersonal nature of mass media is less effective in influencing personal concerns than in influencing societal concerns. Furthermore, compared with the second type of indirect experience—a social network—mass media is also the least effective in impacting personal judgments. Consequently, mass media is argued to primarily influence judgments only on a general level. However, recently this theory has been questioned because of the implications that it poses for the processes involved in the construction of the different judgments. Shrum and Bischak (2001) point to several definitional and analytical ambiguities about the relation between type of risk judgment (personal/societal) and experience modality (direct/indirect). They argue that the definitions of personal risk and mass media representations are not clear and leave room for different interpretations. Shrum and Bischak also suggest that the types of

analysis used to test the impersonal impact hypothesis ignore the assessment of interaction between direct experience and media information. Thus, further research on the impersonal impact hypothesis is invited.

Long-Term Effects

Evidence of long-term effects of nonadvertising television has been proclaimed by several authors. DeJong and Winsten (1990) credited 80 network television episodes broadcast during two seasons for more responsible public alcohol consumption and the tendency to perceive the concept of a designated driver as a social norm. Evans et al. (1981) reported that social modeling films can help deter smoking in adolescents. An example of the probable positive effect of a media campaign on the population's beliefs and healthy behavior in respect to cardiovascular diseases (CVD) was offered in Finnegan, Viswanath, and Hertog's (1999) interpretive analysis proposing a causal relationship between the two. The authors referred to an overall decline in smoking in the country and a parallel increase in public opinion that smoking causes heart disease and cancer. They interpreted the positive outcome and evidence of the secular trend in CVD-related beliefs, knowledge, and behavior as due to the strong influence of national media that had offered numerous heart disease stories, including about 5–10 per month on three TV networks alone. Their analysis suggested the potential strength of media influence when the media are guided by organized activity geared not only toward building an individual's awareness but also toward creating an encouraging environment. This activity, known in the marketing discipline as social marketing and based on agenda-building models of communication, provides for a unified approach to influencing social, behavioral, and policy change, where television as a powerful media channel takes a leading role.

Immediate Effects

There also exists a strong feeling among communication theorists that televised influence is best defined in terms of the content people watch rather than the amount of television viewing (Hawkins & Pingree, 1982). The studies in support of content's predominance are usually conducted in controlled laboratory settings. A series of them have been designed to empirically test the immediate effects of television influence on behavior. An example is a study that investigated the impact of risk taking by characters in television programs on children's willingness to take physical risk (Potts et al., 1994). This problem has not only medical aspects but also a number of social ones because risk-prone behavior, especially when prompted in immature children and vulnerable teenagers, may later have direct links to such antisocial consumption behavior as drug and alcohol use. Potts, Doppler, and Hernandez assigned a group of 50 children ages 6 to 9 years, to three experimental conditions—television stimulus programs with infrequent physical risk taking, programs with frequent risk taking, and no TV stimuli. Their results

indicated that children exposed to high-risk TV programs self-reported higher levels of willingness to take risk than did those exposed to low- or no-risk TV programs. The authors interpreted their results as "evidence of a small effect that may accumulate into a larger effect across the many hours of TV viewed routinely by most children" (p. 328). Moreover, they argued that even relatively innocuous and humorous animated cartoons may result in a previously unidentified impact on children via the observational learning process because risk-taking television characters are rarely punished and even glamorized.

It is clear that for ethical reasons laboratory studies cannot be designed to elicit strong effects proving the negative influence of television watching. The body of research exploring negative impact is more inclined to apply survey and observational and interpretive methods. Consequently, the findings are usually suggestive. The typical example is a study by Distefan, Gilpin, Sergeant, and Pierce (1999) that explored whether movie stars who smoke on and off screen may encourage adolescents to start smoking. After running a multivariate statistical analysis of data gathered in the 1996 California Tobacco Survey of more than 6,000 teenagers, the authors claimed that the suggestive influence of movie star smoking on their fans' tendency to start smoking was evident and only slightly weaker than the influence of smoking by friends and family members. Though the findings did not establish that smoking portrayed in films directly leads adolescents to smoke, the study supported the idea of a reversed causal order in that adolescents accepting smoking tend to favor actors and actresses associated with smoking. The results prompted Distefan et al. to send the alarming message that stars have the potential to be much more powerful role models for youth smoking behavior than parents and teachers, a claim that certainly has public policy implications and supports the use of televised appeals by stars to prompt desirable consumption behavior.

In this light, Hirschman and McGriff's (1995) study provided a novel empirical attempt to examine possible therapeutic uses of motion pictures in drug reha-bilitation programs. The study, designed to apply marketing theory and method toward assisting the treatment of addiction as a social problem, was conducted in a real-life setting. Recovering alcoholics and drug addicts were exposed to films that they viewed on a television monitor and were then asked to fill out a ques-tionnaire while evaluating the accuracy of the portrayal of addiction on the screen and the ability of the films to stimulate their recovery. Having analyzed the data, the authors concluded that two factors defined certain films' stronger constructive effect: The stories were not overly graphic or violent, and the films modeled not only addiction but also a path to recovery. In contrast, the more extreme portrayals of addiction tended to stimulate neutral or negative response in some viewers who did not identify themselves with the portrayed images and thus led the viewers to reject an intended positive message. With this experiment, for which four films with addiction stories were carefully chosen, Hirschman and McGriff enhanced the trend of research into cultural texts, including those presented on television screens, which leads directly to the next stream of research.

RESEARCH ON CULTURAL TEXTS

The methodological practice of examining the content of television programs has been termed telethnography and applied to explorations of the televised presentation of products and their surrounding consumption environment (Sherry 1995; Wells & Anderson, 1996). It is argued that the method provides rich data for understanding the mental images attached by customers to products and services. In addition, these meanings are vital to understanding the exchange value of the products in the marketplace. Consequently, thorough analysis of product classes (e.g., automobiles, credit cards, breakfast cereals) allows for developing effective promotional campaigns (Hirschman & Thompson, 1997).

In one of the first attempts to explore the domain of televised narratives under the marketing angle, Hirschman (1988) explored the ideology of consumption encoded within two, (at the time) immensely popular television series, *Dallas* and *Dynasty*. She investigated the messages the series transmitted about consumption, how prominent characters behaved as consumers, and what their consumption behavior signified. Through the hybrid structural-syntactical method, Hirschman explored the symbolic meanings of products and the ways in which they were linked to actions and outcomes in a televised series. Her findings proposed that popular television programs are strong vehicles of consumption ideology, which also serve as vehicles of consumers' projective self-reflection.

It is in a proposed model of the dynamic relationships between consumption practices and cultural texts that Hirschman, Scott, and Wells (1998) presented a method of interpreting the symbolism of consumption practice and its symbolic depiction on the screen. They used data on coffee drawn from advertising and television programming and incorporated a broad historical and sociological perspective into their discursive model. Their main theoretical conclusion was not limited to highlighting the power of television programs that constantly inform consumers' beliefs and affect their behavior. To Hirschman, Scott, and Wells, it is important to remember that these effects are not isolated because they cooccur in media time adjacent to television commercials and thus are worth being included in the set of variables influencing consumers' perception of products and services. The model also encouraged cross-cultural research application and examination of how specific product categories are portrayed in other cultures.

Exploration in this area has been implemented in some marketing studies. Thus, a content analysis of consumption imagery in music television shown in the United States (MTV) and Sweden (MTV-Europe) suggested that the American sample of videos contains more consumption imagery and presents a higher frequency of brand mentions than those videos to which Swedish viewers are exposed (Englis, Solomon, & Olofsson, 1993). Thus, only 14.9 percent of the Swedish sampled videos contained brand mentions versus 38.9 percent of the videos sampled in the United States, Moreover, the findings revealed several differences in consumption imagery as a function of musical genre. Thus, rap videos consisted of more

dark-side consumption images (alcohol, weapons, and drugs), heavy metal favored band-related products, and dance music conveyed more fashion messages. Considering music television to be an important agent of adolescent socialization, the authors highlighted the importance of studying consumption-relevant content of music to better predict and understand the effects of music on consumers, particularly young consumers.

DISCUSSION AND PUBLIC POLICY IMPLICATIONS

Though it is often claimed that most of the inquiry into media's effects has so far been behavioral and focused on responses that are outwardly observable (Walsh, 2000), the careful review of research on the effects of nonadvertising television on consumption behavior has demonstrated that this topic also has been marked by the incorporation of analysis of cultural texts and strong attempts at theory building. All these areas of research provide strong evidence that television functions "to survey the environment for us, to socialize us into society and culture, and to entertain and sell us things" (Finnegan et al., 1999, p. 50). But, because of its ubiquity, TV makes it really difficult to distinguish those effects caused solely by television viewing, and the functions of television can be indeed compared to the "invisible operation of bacteria" (McLuhan, 1964, p. 320).

Methodologically, the main challenge researchers face today is that there is presumably no authentic control group—people not affected by the phenomenon of television. For this reason, studies are often criticized for employing a nonrepresentative sample. In addition, there is no clear agreement among scholars on the definitions of light and heavy viewers. Most research refers to calculations of the number of hours that the respondents self-report TV watching. This way the boundary between heavy and light viewing remains arbitrary and vague, and an individual who may only watch sports programs can easily be referred to as a heavy viewer.

Another challenging point is the choice of methods. Whereas some scholars favor purely empirical studies, believing that laboratory-run experiments can test the power of TV influence on its audience and thus arm the public with scientifically proven evidence, others question the limitedness of such studies. Thus, Brown and Cantor (2000) have argued that "any experimental manipulation may be just a drop in the bucket compared with the massive exposure to the same kind of content" (p. 3) in everyday lives and that often the focus of research interest lies in long-term attitude or behavioral change rather than short-term effects.

Seen in this light, it seems especially suitable that marketing researchers studying television effects have experimented with methods themselves and have included in their operational set such methods as telethnograpy (Sherry, 1995), the hybrid structural-syntactical method (Hirschman, 1988), historical discourse (Hirschman et al., 1998), and the application of grounded theory (Hirschman &

Thompson, 1997). This range of methods has helped explore not only immediate but also long-term effects of exposure to television on consumption behavior.

The recognition by scholars of the importance of studying nonadvertising television is only the first step. The next step should be the exploration of differential effects of TV messages and images on viewers. It is evident now that early models of mass media effects assumed a homogeneous audience and that invitations to conduct differential effects research and explore selective exposure more systematically have become more pronounced lately (Brown & Cantor, 2000; Roe, 2000; Walsh, 2000). Scholars have called for an examination of the mediating effects of such variables as education, gender, socio economic status, family life, ethnicity, and cognitive development and for exploration of which attributes make messages more powerful and influential for different groups. They propose that television's impact is often disputed not because it is not always visible but because effects often accumulate over time and are obscured by the individual differences of the viewers.

Previous research indicates that gender is one of the most fundamentally differentiating factors in media use in terms of both quantity and content preferences (Roe, 2000). Thus, boys are more likely than girls to have a television in their bedrooms, they tend to spend more time in front of the TV, and they prefer watching action, crime, sports, science fiction, and war programming, whereas girls rate music, talk shows, and soaps higher. Only comedy seems to attract equal attention. It is also known that boys watch more animated cartoons (Huston, Wright, Kerkman, & Peters, 1990), that African American and Hispanic youngsters are more likely than White peers to have TV sets in their bedrooms, and that TV viewing is the most substantial during early childhood and declines in middle adolescence (Roberts, 2000). These data provide a valuable starting point for further inquiry.

Many researchers have already empirically highlighted the importance of exploring mediating variables. Granting media's influence, including that of television, for positive change in the public's attitude toward smoking and health disease prevention, several scholars from different countries have provided evidence that not all sociodemographic groups have benefited equally from media information (Brannstrom & Lindblad, 1994; Dennis, 1989; Finnegan et al., 1999). According to these scholars' findings, people with fewer years of formal education or of lower socioeconomic status demonstrated only modest improvements in risk knowledge, which suggests that the phenomenon of a knowledge gap in information does not seem to be reduced by media.

Though age differences in information processing have long been reported, it is especially important to recall the studies with a consumption context. Thus, it has been claimed that young children demonstrate a better ability to process audiovisual televised information than solely audio transmissions (Peracchio, 1992), and the elderly better process consumer information learned from television than from print media (Cole & Houston, 1987).

Hirschman and Thompson (1997), in their study of motivational relationships between viewers and televised messages, reported to have discovered age- and

gender-based differences in the interpretations of television's appeal. According to their findings, older people seem to express a more inspirational relationship with media images and more often refer to some of them as an ideal self to which they can aspire. The scholars also discerned a major difference between men's and women's interpretations of media messages with regard to the perceived need to resist them on the basis of being unreal and artificial. Whereas many of their female participants described themselves as resisting the distorting influences of televised messages, the male participants reported their ability to stand outside these influences.

Another potential area for future research was pointed out by Englis and Solomon (1997), who believe that the role of cultural gatekeepers, including television, is overlooked with regards to symbolic encoding. According to these researchers, the process of how media select and design consumption imagery that is passed on to consumers through media channels needs more examination. Similarly, the process of how consumers decode product messages also deserves more exploration.

Shrum et al. (1998) found that the order of data collection might affect the results and that it matters what is measured first—television viewing or the estimates. Consequently, more research is needed to test how the order of data collection may affect the results. In terms of data collection, it could also be especially appropriate, given the nature of media research, to respond to Lehmann's (1999) challenge to marketers to explore nontraditional ways of gathering data and not to ignore facts reporting—data widely accessible to the public and offered in news reports. Such examples of potential data collection could be presented by a print media story about a new trend evident among singers. This particular story goes that singers introduce lucrative clothing lines while singing lyrics that mention which brands are hot and recording music videos that show how to wear these clothes (Herman-Cohen, 2001). Another story describes barbers in Afghanistan who were jailed for providing local males with popular haircuts styled after the American actor Leonardo DiCaprio (Wallwork, 2001). These real-life television effects were not prompted in the laboratory setting, but scholars nevertheless could try to incorporate them in their research conducted in controlled settings.

Since the advent of television in 1946, researchers have actively speculated on the role of television in influencing people's behavior, attitudes, and knowledge. The phenomenon of television is still full of contradiction. It is depicted as a threat and as an opportunity, it can promote and deter behavior, it can encourage positive and negative attitudes, it can lead to socially desirable and avoidable effects, it can advocate consumption or abstention from consumption, and television viewing itself can be intimate and social, global and local, innocent and evil, passive and active, cheap and expensive. Because of this conflicting nature, television poses numerous public policy implications; after half a century of research scholars recognize they still know little about the extent or consequences of television's

influence (Brown & Cantor, 2000), and public health specialists are unclear about how best to advise parents and children about media use in the home (Hogan, 2000). Public policy officials ask scholars to study the effects of TV portrayals of tobacco, alcohol, and illicit drug use, urge parents to be more involved in children's media exposure, and encourage viewers to resist the potentially harmful impact of television.

In a changing media environment that embraces new channels of communication, the "old" media of television has not yet been relegated to secondary status. In light of the increasing tendency to simultaneously use multiple media, television still remains a powerful shaper and mirror of consumers' minds, lives, and experiences. The disturbing prediction is that because of information overload we may witness the decline of credible fact (Braman, 1993), and for this reason it will become "harder to distinguish between what is on-screen and in reality" (Walsh, 2000, p. 72), what is experience and what is fiction. Thus, the characters in television programs and the products they will use will even more define the consumers' perception of their surrounding environment.

This review of the body of knowledge accumulated by research on the effects of television on consumption behavior suggests that both marketers and public policy officials need a working knowledge of televised messages to be able to communicate their goods and ideas. Because television viewing is argued to have a strong impact on the associations consumers have with lifestyles, both aspired and avoided, the media gatekeepers' choices revealed on the screen should be constantly monitored for information about current and future consumption trends. This task becomes particularly necessary in light of assertions that producers of TV programs "read" from present consumer behavior—a conclusion that leads to a two-tiered perspective on the encoding and decoding of lifestyle information from media sources (Englis & Solomon, 1997). In addition, this behavior also demands the investigation of whether the strength of nonadvertising television effects depends on viewers' involvement with the program (Murry & Dacin, 1996).

Many research questions that go unanswered have direct links to public policy issues. Thus, what implications appear at the societal level, and is it good or bad for the public when TV viewers perceive the real world as a more affluent place than it is in reality (O'Guin & Shrum, 1997)? Does the heavy TV exposure of children and teenagers make them socially savvy or more materialistic and greedy? Does it teach them the value of money and how to spend it (Brown & Cantor, 2000)? Does TV promote compulsive and violent behavior by portraying risk-taking television characters (Potts et al., 1994)? Though television violence has probably received more scrutiny than any other area (see Comstock, this volume), hot debates about the possible contribution of television violence to antisocial behavior haven't so far been explicitly linked to consumer behavior. Assuming there are causal relationships between the violent images abundant on TV and the aggressive behavior of their recipients, it is worth exploring how consumption behavior changes in a crime-ridden society, town, or neighborhood. There is a

need to examine both immediate effects (demand on guns, violent toys, or crime-preventive goods and services, including locks, insurance) and long-lasting effects (lifestyles, values, etc.).

The final and perhaps most socially important question is whether the reported findings can be used to reduce the antisocial consequences of televised messages and enhance their positive potential. Can academic studies, as some researchers optimistically hope (Hirschman, 1991), contribute to solving destructive social problems based on compulsive and addictive consumer behavior?

ACKNOWLEDGMENTS

The author thanks John Graham, Alladi Venkatesh, Judy Rosener, and Connie Pechmann for the strong support that she found during the work on the earlier versions of this chapter. She also greatly appreciates helpful guidance she received from L. J. Shrum during the work on this chapter.

REFERENCES

Balasubramanian, S. K. (1994). Beyond advertising and publicity: Hybrid messages and public policy issues. *Journal of Advertising, 23*(4), 29–46.
Bandura, A. (1994). Social cognitive theory of mass communication. In J. Bryant & D. Zillmann (Eds.), *Media effects: Advances in theory and research* (pp. 61–90). Hillsdale, NJ: Lawrence Erlbaum Associates.
Braman, S. (1993). Harmonization of systems: The third stage of the information society. *Journal of Communication, 43*(3), 133–40.
Brannstrom I., & Lindblad I. (1994). Mass communication and health promotion: The power of the media and public opinion. *Health Communication, 6*(1), 21–36.
Brown, J. D., & Cantor J. (2000). An agenda for research on youth and the media. *Journal of Adolescent Health, 27*(2), 2–7.
Cole, C. A., & Houston, M. J. (1987). Encoding and media effects on consumer learning deficiencies in the elderly. *Journal of Marketing Research, 24*, 55–63.
Cooper, C. P., Roter, D. L., & Langlieb, A. M. (2000). Using entertainment television to build a context for prevention news stories. *Preventive Medicine, 31*(3), 225–231.
DeJong, W., & Winsten, J. A. (1990). The use of mass media in substance abuse prevention. *Health Affairs, 9*(2), 30–46.
Dennis, E. (1989). *Reshaping the media: Mass communication in an information age.* Newbury Park, CA: Sage.
Distefan, J. M., Gilpin, E. A., Sargent, J. D., & Pierce, J. P. (1999). Do movie stars encourage adolescents to start smoking? *Preventive Medicine, 28*, 1–11.
Englis, B. G., & Solomon, M. R. (1997). Where perception meets reality: The social construction of lifestyles. In L. R. Kahle & L. Chiagouris (Ed.), *Values, lifestyles and psychographics* (pp. 25–44). Mahwah, NJ: Lawrence Erlbaum Associates.
Englis, B. G., Solomon, M. R., & Olofsson, A. (1993). Consumption imagery in music television: A bi-cultural perspective. *Journal of Advertising, 22*(4), 21–33.
Evans, R. I., Rozelle, R. M., Maxwell, S. E., Raines, B. E., Dill, C. A., & Guthrie, T. J. (1981). Social modeling films to deter smoking in adolescents: Results of a three-year field investigation. *Journal of Applied Psychology, 66*(4), 399–414.

Finnegan, J. R., Jr., Viswanath, K., & Hertog, J. (1999). Mass media, secular trends, and the future of cardiovascular disease health promotion: An interpretive analysis. *Preventive Medicine, 29*(6), 50–58.

Fox, S., & Philliber, W. (1978). Television viewing and the perception of affluence. *Sociological Quarterly, 19*, 103–112.

Gerbner, G., Gross, L., Morgan, M., & Signorielli, N. (1980a). Aging with television: Images on television drama and conceptions of social reality. *Journal of Communication, 30*, 37–47.

Gerbner, G., Gross, L., Morgan, M., & Signorielli, N. (1980b). The "mainstreaming of America": Violence profile no. 11. *Journal of Communication, 30*, 10–29.

Gerbner, G., Gross, L., Morgan, M., Signorielli, N., & Shanahan, J. (2002). Growing up with television: The cultivation perspective. In J. Bryant & D. Zillmann (Eds.), *Media effects: Advances in theory and research* (pp. 43–67). Mahwah, NJ: Lawrence Erlbaum Associates.

Goldberg, M. E., & Gorn, G. J. (1987). Happy and sad TV programs: How they affect reactions to commercials. *Journal of Consumer Research, 14*, 387–403.

Gorn, G. J. (1982). The effects of music in advertising on choice behavior: A classical conditioning approach. *Journal of Marketing, 46*, 94–101.

Hawkins, R. P., & Pingree, S. (1982). Television's influence on constructions of social reality. In D. Pearl (Ed.), *Television and behavior: Ten years of scientific progress and implications for the eighties* (pp. 224–247). Washington, DC: U. S. Government Printing Office.

Herman-Cohen, V. (2001, March 19). Whose music are you wearing? *Los Angeles Times*, pp. E1, E3.

Hirschman, E. C. (1988). The ideology of consumption: A structural syntactical analysis of *Dallas*. *Journal of Consumer Research, 15*, 344–359.

Hirschman, E. C. (1991). Secular morality and the dark side of consumer behavior: Or how semiotics saved my life. In R. H. Holman & M. R. Solomon (Eds.), *Advances in Consumer Research* (pp. 1–4). Provo, UT: Association for Consumer Research.

Hirschman, E. C., & McGriff, J. A. (1995). Recovering addicts' responses to the cinematic portrayal of drug and alcohol addiction. *Journal of Public Policy and Marketing, 14*(1), 95–107.

Hirschman, E. C., Scott, L., & Wells, W. D. (1998). A model of product discourse: Linking consumer practice to cultural texts. *Journal of Advertising, 27*, 33–50.

Hirschman, E. C., & Thompson, C. J. (1997). Why media matter: Toward a richer understanding of consumers' relationships with advertising and mass media. *Journal of Advertising, 26*, 43–60.

Hogan, M. (2000). Media matters for youth health. *Journal of Adolescent Health, 27*(2), 73–76.

Huston, A. C., Wright, M. C., Kerkman, D., & Peters, S. M. (1990). Development of television viewing patterns in early childhood: A longitudinal investigation. *Developmental Psychology, 26*, 409–420.

John, D. R. (1999). Consumer socialization of children: A retrospective look at twenty-five years of research. *Journal of Consumer Research, 26*, 183–213.

Kefauver, E. (1958). Let's get rid of tele-violence. *Reader's Digest*, 23–25.

Lehmann, D. R. (1999). Consumer behavior and Y2K. *Journal of Marketing, 63*, 14–18.

McGuire, W. J. (1986). The myth of massive media impact: Savagings and salvagings. In G. Comstock (Ed.), *Public communication and behavior* (pp. 173–257). New York: Academic Press.

McLuhan, M. (1964). *Understanding media: The extensions of man*. New York: McGraw Hill.

Miller, M. C. (1988). *Boxed in: The culture of TV*. Evanston, IL: Northwestern University Press.

Mills J., & Jellison, J. M. (1967). Effects on opinion change of how desirable the communication is to the audience the communicator addressed. *Journal of Personality and Social Psychology, 6*, 98–101.

Murry, J. P., Jr., & Dacin, P. A. (1996). Cognitive moderators of negative-emotion effects: Implications for understanding media context. *Journal of Consumer Research, 22*, 439–447.

Murry, J. P., Jr., Lastovicka, J. L., & Singh, S. N. (1992). Feeling and liking responses to television programs: An examination of two explanations for media-context effects. *Journal of Consumer Research, 18*, 441–451.

O'Guinn, T. C., & Shrum, L. J. (1997). The role of television in the construction of consumer reality. *Journal of Consumer Research, 23*, 278–294.

Peracchio, L. A. (1992). How do young children learn to be consumers? A script processing approach. *Journal of Consumer Research, 18*, 425–440.

Potts, R., Doppler, M., & Hernandez, M. (1994). Effects of television content on physical risk taking in children. *Journal of Experimental Child Psychology, 58*, 321–331.

Reece, D., & Palmgreen, P. (2000). Coming to America: Need for acculturation and media use motives among Indian sojourners in the US. *International Journal of Intercultural Relations, 24*(6), 807–824.

Roberts, D. F. (2000). Media and youth: Access, exposure, and privatization. *Journal of Adolescent Health, 27*(2), 8–14.

Roe, K. (2000). Adolescents' media use: A European view. *Journal of Adolescent Health, 27*(2), 15–21.

Schiller, H. I. (1989). *Culture Inc.* New York: Oxford University Press.

Sherry, J., Jr. (1995). Bottomless cup, plug-in drug: A telethnography of coffee. *Visual Antropology, 7*, 351–370.

Shrum, L. J. (2001). Processing strategy moderates the cultivation effect. *Human Communication Research, 27*(1), 94–120.

Shrum, L. J., & Bischak, V. D. (2001). Mainstreaming, resonance, and impersonal impact. Testing moderators of the cultivation effect for estimates of crime risk. *Human Communication Research, 27*(2), 187–215.

Shrum, L. J., & O'Guinn, T. C. (1993). Process and effects in the construction of social reality: Construct accessibility as an explanatory variable. *Communication Research, 20*, 436–471.

Shrum, L. J., O'Guinn, T. C., Semenik, R. J., & Faber, R. J. (1991). Process and effects in the construction of normative consumer beliefs: The role of television. In R. H. Holman & M. R. Solomon (Eds.), *Advances in consumer research* (pp. 755–763). Provo, UT: Association for Consumer Research.

Shrum, L. J., Wyer, R. S., Jr., & O'Guinn, T. C. (1998). The effects of television consumption on social perceptions: The use of priming procedures to investigate psychological processes. *Journal of Consumer Research, 24*, 447–458.

Tonn, B. E., & Petrich, C. (1998). Everyday life's constraints on citizenship in the United States. *Futures, 30*(8), 783–813.

Tversky, A., & Kahneman, D. (1973). Availability: A heuristic for judging frequency and probability. *Cognitive Psychology, 5*, 207–232.

Tyler, T. R. (1984). Assessing the risk of crime victimization: The integration of personal victimization experience and socially transmitted information. *Journal of Social Issues, 40*(1), 27–38.

Tyler, T. R., & Cook, F. L. (1984). The mass media and judgments of risk: Distinguishing impact on personal and societal level judgments. *Journal of Personality and Social Psychology, 47*(4), 693–708.

Varey, R. J. (1999). Marketing, media, and McLuhan: Rereading the prophet at century's end. *Journal of Marketing, 63*, 148–159.

Wallwork, L. W. (2001, February 25). Lockup for long locks. *Parade Magazine*, 2.

Walsh, D. A. (2000). The challenge of the evolving media environment. *Journal of Adolescent Health, 27*(2), 69–72.

Wells, W. D., & Anderson, C. L. (1996). Fictional materialism. In K. Corfman & J. Lynch (Eds.), *Advances in consumer research 23*, Provo, UT: Association for Consumer Research, 120–126.

Williams, C. J. (2001, April 24). Entertained into social change. *Los Angeles Times*, pp. A1, A6, A7.

CHAPTER THIRTEEN

Media Factors That Contribute to a Restriction of Exposure to Diversity

David W. Schumann
University of Tennessee

The theme of this book, blurring the lines of media, is significantly large to span such topics as product placement within various media forms (e.g., television, movies, videogames) and genre (e.g., drama, sports), the impact of media-based product exposure on different audience segments (e.g., age, gender, ethnicity), media cultivation of personal values and self-image, and individual difference and situational factors posited to moderate these media-related effects. It naturally follows that nearly all of the phenomena explored in these chapters reflect two forms of stimulus processing: apparent or subliminal (see Erdelyi & Zizak, this volume). *Apparent processing* is the mental processing that occurs at the conscious level, whereas *subliminal processing* denotes the mental processes that occur at the subconscious or preconscious level (e.g., see Bargh, 2002). But what happens when no processing occurs as a result of simply not exposing oneself to a stimulus, or when minimal processing occurs as a result of a conscious or subconscious choice?

Within our daily lives, as a result of limited processing capacity or limited time or energy constraints, we often select to enhance our exposure to certain stimuli, while at the same time we limit or restrict our exposure to other stimuli (e.g., Lynch & Srull, 1982; Shiffrin, 1976). The stimuli we do process are typically triggered by a need to fulfill certain motivations or by the nature of the situations in which we find ourselves. We will naturally be led to process certain stimuli, while limiting or eliminating exposure to other stimuli. Although the typical questions posed by social scientists concern the nature of the stimuli being processed (for examples in

consumer information search, see Beatty & Smith, 1987; Punj & Staelin, 1983), perhaps an equally important question concerns the nature and consequence of what is not being processed or what is minimally being processed. It is proposed here that much of this minimized or missing stimuli is of a diverse nature. Thus, this exposure trade-off process creates a naturally occurring restriction of exposure to diversity.

I previously put forth a model as a framework for designating and examining the internal and external antecedent conditions and the subsequent consequences that result from restricting exposure to diversity (Schumann, 2002). This chapter reviews the phenomenon of restricting exposure to diversity, reviews the important relationships in the aforementioned model, and provides specific attention to describing relevant media factors that influence the phenomenon.

RESTRICTING EXPOSURE TO DIVERSITY

What does restricting exposure to diversity mean? The definition employed here is as follows: "the purposeful or non-purposeful restriction of exposure to available messages about the characteristics, culture, values, beliefs, points-of-view including worldviews, preferences, and behaviors of those who we believe may be different from us."

Not only will the subject of exposure restriction center around people, but this phenomenon is also viewed as it might apply to objects that are unfamiliar to us (e.g., international brands of products). Restricting exposure concerns the basic processing strategies that employ mental categorization in a manner that is consistent with, and reinforces, one's self-identity. *Self-identity* refers to notions of the present self as well as what one aspires to be.

Let's take an example. When the question "Do you know anyone who only listens to conservative talk radio or who just reads liberal or conservative columnists or who just views the liberal news networks?" is asked of groups, inevitably a significant number of people raise their hands and even point to themselves. We each have a tendency to focus on messages that reinforce the kind of person we perceive ourselves to be or to whom we aspire to be compared. As such, we may miss a significant amount of information about those individuals in groups who are not like us or about unfamiliar objects.

PRECEDENT FOR THE CONCEPT

Over the past 60 years, the notion of restricting exposure to diversity has been discussed. Theodore Newcomb (1947), in referring to the autistic person as one who is motivated by a focus on her/himself, suggested that mutual avoidance precludes opportunities for acquiring information that might disconfirm perceptions of the

other's motives and character. He also reflected that misperceptions and distrust between groups are fed by a lack of contact between members of different social categories.

Gordon Allport (1954), in his seminal book titled *The Nature of Prejudice*, stated that human groups tend to stay apart from each other. He explained this phenomenon in terms of basic motivational principles to include ease, least effort, congeniality, and pride in one's own culture. Allport noted that people who stay separate have few channels of communication. Also in the prejudice literature, Stephan and Stephan (1984) propose and support a model whereby a lack of contact between groups promotes ignorance, which in turn promotes anxiety and frustration, assumed dissimilarity, and stereotyping.

Atkin (1985), in expanding the notion of selective exposure beyond reduction of cognitive dissonance, suggested that selective exposure can reconfirm one's beliefs, values, attitudes, and behaviors and fulfill one's sought-after affective states. In a similar vein, from the recent debate between trait theorists (e.g., Wiggins 1973, 1997) and situationalists (e.g., Mischel, 1968, 1990) over the differential impact on behavior, the point was made that we actively choose situations that reflect and reinforce our self-concepts (Ickes, Snyder, & Garcia, 1997; Snyder, 1981; Swann, 1987; Swann & Read, 1981; Tesser, 1988; Tesser & Paulhus, 1983). Thus, we are likely to place ourselves in situations and expose ourselves to information that reflects our values and present or aspired lifestyle. In point of fact, Ickes and his colleagues (Ickes et al., 1997) found that people tend to avoid dispositionally incongruent situations (e.g., Furnham, 1981). In selected situations where incongruity exists, people tend to resolve the incongruity to favor their personality (Srull & Karabenick, 1975; Watson & Baumal, 1967).

There are also external forces that are proposed to facilitate exposure restriction. James Turow, in his book titled the *Breaking Up America* (1997), spoke about how advertisers have segmented the market, with one result being a significant reduction of exposure to messages aimed at other target markets. He states, the following:

> I noticed that media were increasingly encouraging people to separate themselves into more and more specialized groups and to develop distinctive viewing, reading, and listening habits that stressed differences between their groups and others... marketers look for splits in the social fabric and then reinforce and extend the splits for their own ends. (p. ix)

More recently, Cass Sunstein, a legal scholar writing in the political science arena, revealed his concern regarding the interactive element of the Internet. In his book titled *Republic.com*, Sustein (2001) suggests that our increasing ability to control (filter) the news- and issues-related verbiage we receive via interactive electronic media (i.e., Internet) may likely cause a restriction of exposure to other points of view. This one-sided exposure, he warns, will likely lead to a break down in practiced democracy.

Finally, Todd Gitlin, a media sociologist, writing in his 2001 book titled *Media Unlimited*, states the following:

> An unavoidable consequence of all the flashes and shouts for attention, all the message casters casting their messages simultaneously more or less in the same direction, is clutter and cacophony. As a result, when we pay attention to any particular signal, we must pay inattention elsewhere. Coping, in other words, demands a willed myopia. Everyone learns not only to see but not to see—to tune out and turn away. (pp. 118–119)

ANTECEDENTS AND CONSEQUENCES

What drives this tendency to restrict exposure to diversity and what are the consequences of the phenomenon? A comprehensive model is offered here that denotes the internal and external antecedents that predict the level of exposure to diversity as well as a set of ordered consequences resulting from the phenomenon. Its major components are reviewed in the next sections (see Fig. 13.1a; 13.1b).

Internal Antecedents

The internal antecedents in the model reflect the motivations, fulfillment strategies, inclinations to restrict or expand one's experience, and self-directed exposure leading to a level of exposure to diversity. A model must begin somewhere, and this model commences by enumerating five motivational states thought to contribute to differentiated levels of exposure to diversity. Borrowed from Maslow (1954) and Erikson (1980), these motives include: (1) basic needs, (2) social needs, (3) emotional needs, (4) instrumental needs, and (5) ego-sustaining needs. Although the first four are viewed as contributing to the fifth, each individually has the potential to lead to a restricting of exposure. Consider the following examples for each in turn.

To fulfill Maslow's basic needs of security or safety, one might quickly settle on selecting a solution to a threat. This solution may come as a result of previous experience where a specific solution worked in the past to end the threat. Thus, rather than exploring other avenues of response, the tendency to immediately default to the known solution eliminates the need to expose oneself to other options that may be different from those considered in the past.

In fulfilling affective needs, individuals often attempt to manage their feeling states. For example, a candy bar or an ice cream cone may instantly change the mood of a child (or adult). Likewise, a shopping spree may be just what the doctor ordered to remove one from a funk. Perhaps, for some, boredom can be eleviated through the selection of a certain genre of television programming

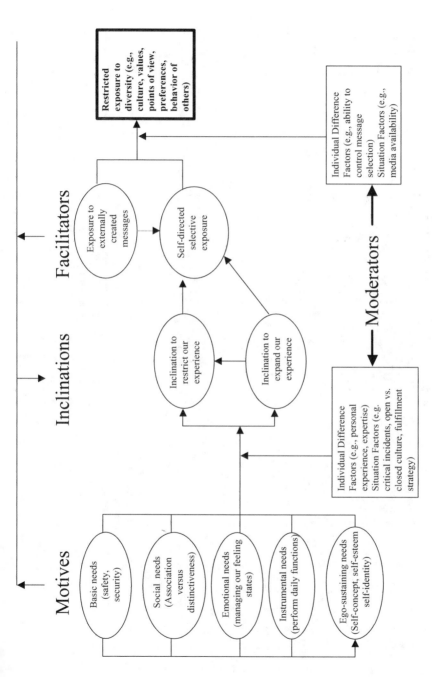

FIG. 13.1a Antecedent factors and relationships. From "Media and Market Segmentation Strategies as Contributing Factors to Restricted Exposure to Diversity: A Discussion of Potential Societal Consequences," by D. W. Schumann, 2002. Reprinted with permission.

237

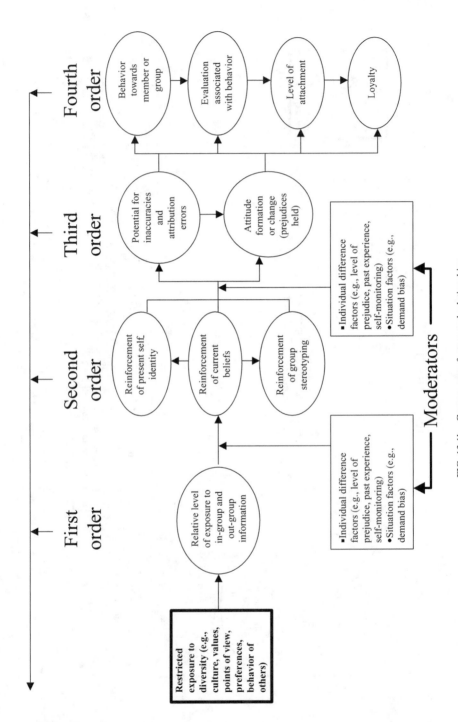

FIG. 13.1b Consequence factors and relationships.

238

(e.g., watching a sitcom). There are many ways in which people change or alter their affective feeling states (for more on this topic, see Gardner, Schumann, & Walls, 2002). But in many cases, tried and true solutions are repeated. One learns that one's motivation to alter a mood can be fulfilled in a specific way, and thus other means of altering a mood state are often ignored or not considered. Although people may claim they look to buy something different for a change of pace, what they buy is rarely radically different from that which has been purchased in the past. In most cases, one just doesn't stray very far from that which has a sense of familiarity.

Instrumental needs reflect the motivation to complete tasks. In many cases, we resign ourselves to what we know in defining how we carry out a task. We also tend to place ourselves in common situations that call for an existing problem-solving script. When faced with a new task, we first consider what problem-solving information is available from our existing schema. If that fails to provide an adequate solution, some people give up altogether, whereas some begin to think out of the box. It is here that diverse solutions are often considered. Thus, critical situations and how we handle failure are thought to be important moderating factors.

Finally, these four motives contribute to a fifth motivation—the need to feel good about oneself. Enhancing one's self-esteem or self-concept can be accomplished through interacting with a certain set of people who make one feel good or repeatedly placing oneself in situations where one's expertise can be demonstrated and even be useful. An example of these latter situations can be found in our professional career activities, where our expertise is often needed and appreciated and our self-concept is typically enhanced.

Based on the nature of the need (interacting with one or more prescribed moderating variables as noted in the model), individuals are likely to have an inclination to either expand their experience or restrict it. Indeed, the expansion of experience may itself be restrictive. For example, when individuals seek to expand their knowledge, they might only look in known places. On the other hand, when people seek to expand their knowledge, this objective has the potential to lead to an increase in exposure to diversity. However, in most cases, even an expansion of knowledge will eventually cease or diminish, and the inclination to restrict new knowledge will take over as one considers eventual actions. Possible moderators that guide inclination type (i.e., restrict or expand experience) include individual difference factors, such as personal experience and expertise, as well as situational factors, such as a critical incident (which might lead to an inclination to expand knowledge; e.g., Americans reading the Koran after the September 11th tragedy), an open or closed culture, or the need fulfillment strategy (hedonic vs. instrumental).

Finally, on the internal antecedent path, the inclination to restrict or extend experience will lead to the level of self-directed selective exposure. Atkin (1985) noted two explanations for selective exposure that are consistent with the antecedent notions discussed previously. He posits that selective exposure results from either a guidance orientation (e.g., novices searching for information) or a reinforcement

orientation. The reinforcement orientation is believed to explain selective exposure as used to reduce dissonance (Festinger, 1957), reaffirm one's position or behavior, or seek positive affect. Because of the tendency to seek experiences that reinforce self-identity, individuals will more likely selectively expose themselves to stimuli consistent with that reinforcement and thus increase the potential for restricting exposure to diversity.

External Antecedents

The internal antecedents previously described focus on the individual as a contributor to restricting one's own exposure to diversity, but there are also several identified external mechanisms that serve as possible antecedents to the phenomenon. One important contributor is found in the actions of market segmentation, both in terms of strategy and the tools employed by marketers to better target products and services to likely users. Market segmentation is typically viewed in a positive light for several reasons: It matches products (programs) with consumer needs and desires, it reduces the costs associated with promotion and distribution (theoretically passed on to the consumer), it reduces the time the consumer spends in search and purchase activity, it enhances the collection of more accurate and timely market data, and it keeps undesired segments away from the product.

However, market segmentation may have a negative side that is rarely considered (for exceptions, see Schumann, 1999; Turow, 1997). One consequence of market segmentation is the tactical focus on audience-related stimuli, while minimizing or negating exposure to other stimuli. Through means such as direct marketing and positioning of product advertising within specific media formats, individuals are bombarded with opportunities to view images that reflect their lifestyles, existing values, and opinions. Target marketing strategies purposely minimize exposure of the target audience to other, diverse alternatives.

A set of media-related factors are also identified because they contribute to restricting exposure to diversity. These are reviewed in depth later in this chapter.

Consequences

The model offers a set of ordered consequences based on the intergroup bias literature (for comprehensive reviews, see Brewer & Miller, 1996; Hewstone, Rubin, & Willis, 2002). The intergroup bias literature suggests that individuals naturally support groups they either presently belong to or to which they aspire membership (in-groups), and will either ignore, stereotype, or denigrate those in groups in which they do not perceive themselves as members (out-groups). There is a long-standing literature based in social psychology that provides strong support for the in-group bias, while providing clear, yet moderated, evidence for an out-group bias.

The first consequence of restricting exposure to diversity is an imbalance that favors attention to in-group information as opposed to out-group information. Individuals will likely take in significantly larger amounts of in-group information

while minimizing encoding of out-group information. This one-sided exposure is believed to reinforce self-identity, currently held beliefs, and stereotypes about out-groups (second-order consequences). In turn, these reinforcements are posited to affect the belief system and increase the potential for inaccuracies (i.e., Judd & Park, 1993) and a host of attribution errors. The latter would include attribution of outcome to behavior (Ross & Sicoly, 1979), adaptation of a self-serving attribution error to groups (Pettygrew, 1979), the potential to overestimate the frequency with which out-group members act in stereotypical fashion (illusory correlation: Chapman, 1967; Chapman & Chapman, 1969), the probability of reaching a false concensus (Ross, Greene, & House, 1977), and the probability of a self-fulfilling prophecy (Jussim, Eccles & Madon, 1996; Mertin, 1957).

These inaccuracies and attribution errors may contribute to the formation of attitudes based on prejudicial beliefs. These beliefs and attitudes will in turn lead to actions or behaviors that are arguably restricted by the lack of exposure to out-group information. Selection of options will be limited. The end result is an individual who, either through his or her own means or through external facilitators, is making choices with a relatively narrow set of options. Satisfaction with choices is based on a limited set of comparison standards; thus, there may be little opportunity to develop attachments or loyalty.

MEDIA FACTORS THAT INFLUENCE RESTRICTION OF EXPOSURE TO DIVERSITY

The model reviewed previously refers to certain external antecedents that include various media-related factors. The following sections address six characteristics of today's media environment that are thought to influence the restriction of exposure to diverse peoples, information, and points of view.

The Media Stimulation Curve

The media stimulation curve is a graduated curve of media stimulation (note Fig. 13.2). The x-axis reflects the various ages of humankind. The y-axis could contain any one of three stimulation-related exposure variables: amount, types, and variation. The nature of the relationship curve will be similar in all cases. That is, over time the amount of stimulation, the types of stimulation, and the variation in stimulation that the human race has been exposed to has increased dramatically at an exponential rate. This is an intuitive notion, and one can easily surmise that the angle of the curve has dramatically angled upward over time. This change in the angle has become most pronounced during the 20th century.

Media forms have been the key facilitator of this shifting curve dating back to Guttenberg's introduction of the printing press in 1455. This single event created an availability of information that was unprecedented at the time. In the 1800s the

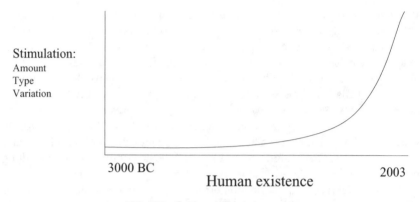

Stimulation:
Amount
Type
Variation

3000 BC   2003
Human existence

FIG. 13.2   Graduated stimulation curve.

ability to capture and reproduce pictures again increased the amount, type, and variation of stimuli to which one was exposed. In the early 1900s, the combination of radio and moving pictures (i.e., movies) created another leap forward in the mass communication of information and images. But none of the previous inventions matched the remarkable impact that resulted from the technical ability to televise, or send images over the airways. In recent times market segmentation has moved televised programming to the schools (i.e., Channel 1), airports, doctors' offices, and retail establishments, to name just a few targeted locations. To capture this upward curve in the present we must now consider the influence of computing and the Internet. Today, with multiple types of media, we are bombarded by various forms, changing formats, and increased variation of stimulation, the vast majority of which we now take for granted or tune out; one can imagine the impact that today's amount and variation of stimuli would have had on a human being 100 years ago, let alone a person living a thousand years ago or earlier.

A specific example of this graduated curve is commercial television. As commercial television made its early debut in the late 1940s, audiences for the first time were exposed on a regular basis to visually oriented, motion-based commercial messages about products. These early commercial messages were often pitched by celebrities and would typically last between 1 to 2 min, with any one image or scene lasting up to the full amount of time allotted for the commercial. For example, it was not unusual for the product to be demonstrated employing the same camera shot and angle for between 20 s and 2 min. Today, the average commercial lasts between 10 and 15 s, with single camera shots moving at an incredible pace, sometimes shifting literally each second (in some cases less than a second) of viewing.

This evolutionary change in the rate of exposure to the amount, types, and variation of stimulation has also brought about changes in how humans process this stimulation. While one might logically argue that such stimulation has increased our potential exposure to diversity, and it clearly has, the graduated curve also suggests that if we were able to process most of this stimulation, at best it would be at a very

shallow level, or subliminally, and we would likely filter most of it out very quickly. However, what is more likely is that we select (either intentionally or unintentionally) to ignore much of the stimuli that we are exposed to today (Gitlin, 2002).

Simplicity of Message

A second media-related facilitator that restricts exposure to diversity lies in the nature of the messages that are forthcoming in today's media environment. Building off of the previously discussed graduated curve of stimulation, along with the notion of reduced commercial time, comes a parallel reduction in the length and thus the depth of the message. In today's fast-paced media environment, the rule is to be extremely concise. This plays out in the commercial environment in the form of reduced product descriptions, sound bites, and catch phrases; increased use of fine print for required messages; and enhanced use of graphics to convey the message.

If one considers the print media over the past century, one is quick to note that advertising has evolved from a significant use of detailed information within any given ad to a greater reliance on graphics as a means to project the message. In the broadcast industry, this reduced wording has come as a result of the shrinking length of commercials. Today we listen to and are accustomed to hearing sound bites and catch phrases (e.g., BASF's "We don't make the products; we make them better" or United Airlines's "Fly the friendly skies"). The purpose of these concise messages is to present a proposition statement, often reflecting a relationship between the consumer and a product, or a brand and a key attribute. It is left up to the consumer to search for a deeper level of information. Although the search for more detail becomes the responsibility of the consumer, whether such search is undertaken depends on many factors. As a condition to elaborative message processing, Petty and Cacioppo (1981, 1986) in their elaboration likelihood model ask whether a person is motivated to or able to process the message. These questions are especially applicable here. Does the consumer have time to search? Will this search activity require a sacrifice in time and energy and draw attention away from other desired (leisure) or necessary (work) activities? Does the consumer have access to the more detailed information? Is the need for more information viewed as important? Is the consumer able to process detailed and complex information? In today's fast-paced world where sound bites are prominent in the media environment, the question arises as to the degree to which the consumer is reinforced to seek more detailed information. Does this reduced message strategy cause the consumer to seek more information? This is an empirical question, the answer to which will require future research. However, the hypothesis offered here is that such reduction in message length and depth creates an environment where exposure to diverse information is constrained and a person's existing beliefs as well as one's existing stereotypes persist.

Because of the increased governmental regulation of certain industries, there appears to be an enhanced use of fine print in advertising. More than not, this

fine print may be required, as in the case of pharmaceutical advertising, but it is also used to downplay certain negative product attributes (e.g., pricing in the high-end automobile market). Fine print, in and of itself, discourages further reading. Because of its inhibiting and complex nature, many consumers miss significant information, some of which might not have been considered in the past. Thus the consumer's knowledge base is restricted due to inhibited exposure.

It could be argued that a greater awareness of Freud's (1924/1969) teachings regarding relationships, dreams, and subconscious images, combined with Watson's application of behaviorism to advertising strategies on Madison Avenue (Buckley, 1989), were catalysts to a revolutionary change in promotional tactics. Advertising strategy, once loaded down with verbiage, evolved in the 1930s and 1940s to a greater dependence on images as a means to convey and reinforce message content. These images depicted people using products in different settings. The images reinforced certain attributes and how products could be used to produce beneficial (or, in the case of public service announcements, negative) outcomes. The pairing of product and celebrity became a norm. Before the dangers of tobacco were known and publicized, professional athletes and medical personal were used to promote the product.

Images have the unique property of forcing the viewer to generate descriptions, often accessing existing memory to do so. During the period of mass marketing that was created after the end of World War II and with the advent of television, audiences were exposed to many diverse images. However, as marketing has evolved and market segmentation has become a sophisticated science, today's images are targeted, and, as noted previously, these images are often reflections of our unique lifestyle and needs. It is posited here that the act of targeting images to certain segments, by its very nature, restricts exposure to diverse images that are unfamiliar to the viewer.

Stereotype Reinforcement

Continued use of stereotyping in programming and commercials restricts exposure to other dimensions of a person or object. There is a wealth of research that has considered stereotyping employed in advertising. In reviewing the literature on the topic, I found that most of these stereotypes reflect four categories: age group, ethnicity, gender, and level of attractiveness. Within each category, studies generally addressed the nature of an individual's role (e.g., Bristor, Lee, & Hunt, 1995; Cheng, 1997; Elliot, 1995; Gilens, 1996; Signorielli, McLeod, & Healy, 1994), behavior (Hansen & Osborne, 1995; Power, Murphy, & Coover, 1996), perceptions and beliefs (Ford & LaTour, 1996; Strutton & Lumpkin, 1993), product association (Allan & Coltrane, 1996; Downs & Harrison, 1985; Mazis, Ringold, Perry, & Denman, 1992; Taylor & Lee, 1994), and the environmental setting (Culley & Bennett, 1976; Swayne & Greco, 1987). For example, Taylor and his colleagues (Taylor & Lee, 1994; Taylor, Lee, & Stern, 1995; Taylor & Stern, 1997) conducted

a thorough examination of the depicted roles that Asians play within advertising. They found that Asian models appeared more frequently in the popular business press and science publications (vs. women's or general interest magazines), were more likely to be associated with technology-based products (vs. nontechnology-based products), appeared in ads more often in business contexts, were depicted more typically as co-workers, and were seldom seen in ads containing family or social settings.

Use of stereotyped images and messages in the media has the potential to serve as a reinforcing agent, encouraging continued individual stereotypes among the audience. In maintaining the stereotype, other characteristics of a person or object may be omitted or only partially presented. This is especially true in print advertising, where only one image is presented. If that image reinforces a stereotype, it is not likely introducing other nonstereotype or counterstereotype information. Thus, the exposure to stereotypes in the media environment may preclude the opportunity to learn new things about dissimilar people and objects.

Value Reinforcement

Segmented media programming is purposely targeted to capture subsets of the viewing population. ESPN targets the male sports fan, BET targets the African American viewer, MTV targets the adolescent audience, PBS targets the highly educated, HGTV targets the upscale female population, and so on. Likewise, women's magazines target females in different age groups, *Sports Illustrated* targets men (with attempts to target females and children through *SI for Women, SI for Kids*), *Savoy* and *Ebony* target African American readers, and so on. There are special interest magazines for the science oriented (*Scientific American, Science, Popular Science*), for the endurance athlete (*Runner's World, Triathlete*), for the automobile enthusiast (*Car and Driver, Hot Rod*), and for the computer jock (*PC World, Wired*). Each of these media outlets may reflect different, or in some cases overlapping, market segments (e.g., Morris 2002). A market segment can be defined in terms of the uniqueness of its held values and the specific value it seeks. Segmented programming and focused periodicals do their best to reinforce these group value systems while minimizing or eliminating exposure to the values of other groups.

It has also been argued that value reinforcement may come from media-driven agendas. For example, in countries where the mass communication enterprise is in the direct hands of the state, monopolistic control over the media is reflected in official censorship and the promotion of the goals of the state. On the other hand, for non-state-controlled media (which includes a large percentage of Western civilization), a debate rages between political liberals and conservatives regarding the projected bias in the news. Some argue the bias reflects the large media conglomerates' control and profit motive (see Chomsky, 2002; Herman & Chomsky, 2002), whereas some argue that the bias is due to either a liberal orientation (see Baker, 1994; Goldberg, 2002) or a conservative orientation as reflected in radio

and television talk shows (e.g., *Russ Limbaugh, The O'Reilly Factor*). Regardless of the position one takes, there is increasing evidence that media reporting of the news and media programming is highly value laden, resulting in specific selection of images and news based on targeted audience requirements.

News As Biased Entertainment

Building on the conclusion offered in the last section, several media scientists have noted that today's news has moved away from objectivity toward a biased form of entertainment based on audience segmentation (for a review of studies supporting this point, see MacGregor, 1997). A visit to any online bookstore search engine will reveal a significant number of recent books questioning the topic of biased news reporting, some from whistle-blowers from within the industry. This potential bias can perhaps be attributed the media's facilitation of desired motivational states, which are reinforced through varied types of programming (Gitlin, 2001). Today's presentation of the news contains programming and messages that are believed to be of interest to the identified viewer of a single specific news program. The NBC national news format is in fact different from FOX, which in turn is different from the presentation one would get from CNN or the BBC. Coverage of international stories varies greatly between *Newsweek* or *Time*, and the *Economist*.

These differences are based in part on the nature of the audience who selects these news outlets, how the audience wants news presented, and the types of stories the audience wants to hear (MacGregor, 1997). To retain the audience, news must be presented in a fashion that plays to what the audience wants and needs. One only has to return to the murder trial of O. J. Simpson to study the way a news story attracts an audience. During that time, because of early recognition by the media that continuance of such a story would guarantee high ratings/readership, a great deal of other news, perhaps judged by the news agency as not as controversial or attractive, was never aired. The trial was a major media event, reported by more than 1,000 journalists reporting via 121 video paths, including 14 satellite uplinks, 80 miles of sound and vision cable, and 650 phone lines (*"That Simpson Trial in Full,"* 1995). The murder, the trial, and the reporting and news discussion that continued afterwards took well over a year. There have been other trials involving celebrities, so why did this one attract such a large audiences? What was the makeup of the audience? These questions are intriguing, and further understanding of audience attractiveness to this new way of promoting a continuing news story over time deserves further empirical examination.

News stories involve presented images (often highly graphic) and carefully crafted writing. In many cases, the collection of images and writing is not well grounded because studies of reporting behavior suggest shortcuts and biased information searches (reviewed in MacGregor, 1997). Images and words are brought together by media professionals in an attempt to convey a story. Each story has a plot that is written in such a way as to keep the audience interested. Thus, the

news focuses on stories the news media believe their target audience wants to be exposed to and omits what they subjectively believe their viewers do not want to see or hear. To the point, decisions are made that impact the degree to which the audience is exposed to diverse points of view.

One further point needs to be made. Gitlin (2002) provided anecdotal evidence that the media audience tends to accept as truth whatever is printed and broadcasted. In a news environment that includes talk show opinion, we need to examine how well the audience discriminates between objective-based and subjective-based "truths"? We have been conditioned to view the media as objective, yet there is much evidence to suggest what is reported is often flawed because news reporting plays to what the audience wants to hear or see (MacGregor, 1997).

Desensitization of Media and Message, One-Sidedness, and Demographic Restriction

Today's commercial and media environments are arguably very cluttered. Consumers are exposed to thousands of product images and verbiage daily. In addition, media forms carrying the images and verbiage are exploding. The traditional sources of print and broadcasting are rapidly expanding. Transportation advertising still appears in trains, buses, taxicabs, subways, and so forth but now also appears as we drive the highways, such as on large moving billboards that take the form of 18-wheelers. The location of televised programming has expanded from the home to doctor's offices, grocery stores, airports, and even in our schools. With the advent of the Internet it is possible to transmit commercial messages online to our computers, our PDAs (personal digital assistant), and even to our connected cell phones. Internet sites, now numbering in the hundreds of millions, have the opportunity to promote and persuade. Promotional signage of all types (e.g., billboards, grocery store aisles, shopping carts) continues to be ever present in our travel and shopping environments. Direct marketing invades our privacy at home with cold calling, targeted mailers, and samples that come through the mail. This is a constant bombardment, as Gitlin (2001) terms it, a media torrent. The consumer can't possibly process all the messages they are exposed to. Traditional folklore suggests that out of the thousands of commercial messages one is exposed to daily, only a dozen or so break through to the attention level. This suggests that although messages and media forms may be novel initially, with significant levels of repetition, we become desensitized to them over time (e.g., Schumann et al., 1991). This desensitization suggests that a significant number of messages are never processed.

On top of a clutter environment exists a one-sidedness in the promotion of culture through mass communication sources. One only has to visit abroad to see the contrast in media distribution. American television shows are popular throughout the world. American products are promoted in every culture. American television influences what is broadcast globally. Right or wrong, other populations compare their culture with the culture of the United States.

Finally, within the United States, ethnic-based television has taken hold in the larger markets, but many cities have restricted cultural programming. For example, in the mid-size cities in the Southeast, it is still the case that there are no basic Hispanic or Asian television or radio stations. Yet on the West Coast they are plentiful. This targeted media strategy has an important consequence. Individuals who live in the Southeast are rarely exposed to the Hispanic or Asian cultures via the media. The only program from abroad that receives geographically wide exposure in this country is arguably Great Britain's BBC News. While we receive the world's news from CNN's global broadcasting offices, unless it is a strategic move to focus on a single event, the audience sees only short clips of the global news at best. In sum, the growth of media clutter, one-sided promotion of culture, and restricted demographic-based exposure all contribute to a limiting of exposure to diverse cultures and diverse points of view.

CONCLUSION

Media segmentation (as does market segmentation) focuses on the individual or the in-group. The presentation of messages and illustrations typically reflects an in-group member's own lifestyle and values. The commercial environment presents a "me" as owning certain products, doing certain activities, having certain values, socializing with certain people. But it also infers a "they" as being different in their choice of products, activities, and friends (Turow, 1997). We target products based on ethnic groups, age groups, and gender, and, even within these large demographic groups, we find segregation. For example, a visit to an American public high school will reveal that today's teenagers reinforce a segregation of groups through their informal but obvious group dress codes. Thus, it could be argued that media factors and market segmentation strategies reinforce social segregation.

There are a number of interesting research questions that fall out of this question regarding the degree to which individuals restrict their exposure to diversity. One could identify how and when targeted media programming and commercials reinforce self-identity. How do targeted media programming and associated advertising influence in-group and out-group perceptions? How do stereotypes employed in media programming and commercial communication form and reinforce out-group perceptions and personal stereotyping? With children? To what extent do we tend to focus our share of controlled exposure to messages via interactive media in ways that reinforce our self-identity and restrict exposure to out-group information? What inaccuracies and attribution errors occur as a result of restricted exposure and stereotyping? Extending this inquiry to include elements of market segmentation, one could ask whether market segmentation results in significantly less exposure to other groups in our society. Does market segmentation serve to enhance insecurity or fear toward out-groups? What impact do market segmentation strategies have on the formation or reinforcement of prejudicial attitudes

toward out-groups? How do market segmentation strategies alter our cognitive schemas? What are the long-term costs of market segmentation on society? This chapter has sought to present the phenomenon of restricting exposure to diversity. As such, several media factors were discussed that are thought to contribute to the phenomenon. It is hoped that this discussion will lead to further empirical investigation of the phenomenon.

REFERENCES

Allan, K., & Coltrane, S. (1996). Gender displaying television commercials: A comparative study of television commercials in the 1950s and 1980s. *Sex Roles, 35*(3), 185–203.

Allport, G. W. (1954). *The nature of prejudice*. Reading, MA: Addison-Wesley.

Atkin, C. K. (1985). Informational utility and selective exposure to entertainment media. In D. Zillmann & J. Bryant (Eds.), *Selective exposure to communication* (pp. 63–91). Hillsdale, NJ: Lawrence Erlbaum Associates.

Baker, B. (1994). *How to identify, expose and correct liberal media bias*. Alexandria, VA: Media Research Center.

Bargh, J. A. (2002). Losing consciousness: Automatic influences on consumer judgment, behavior, and motivation. *Journal of Consumer Research, 29*(2), 280–285.

Beatty, S. E., & Smith, S. M. (1987). External search effort: An investigation across several product categories. *Journal of Consumer Research, 14*(1), 83–95.

Brewer, M. B., & Miller, N. (1996). *Intergroup relations*. Buckingham, UK: Open University Press.

Bristor, J. M., Lee, R. G., & Hunt, M. R. (1995). Race and ideology: African-American images in television advertising. *Journal of Public Policy & Marketing, 14*(1), 48–59.

Buckley, K. W. (1989). *Mechanical man*. New York: Guilford Press.

Chapman, L. J. (1967). Illusory correlation in observational report. *Journal of Verbal Learning and Verbal Behavior, 6*, 151–155.

Chapman, L. J., & Chapman, J. P. (1969). Illusory correlation as an obstacle to the use of valid psychodiagnostic signs. *Journal of Abnormal Psychology, 74*, 271–280.

Cheng, H. (1997). "Holding up half of the sky"? A sociocultural comparison of gender role portrayals in Chinese and U. S. Advertising. *International Journal of Advertising, 16*, 295–319.

Chomsky, N. (2002). *Media control: The spectacular achievements of propaganda*. New York: Seven Stories Press.

Culley, J. D., & Bennett, R. (1976). Equality in advertising: Selling women, selling Blacks. *Journal of Communication, 36*, 160–174.

Downs, A. C., & Harrison, S. D. (1985). Embarrassing age spots or just plain ugly? Physical attractiveness stereotyping as an instrument of sexism on American television commercials. *Sex Roles, 13*(2), 9–19.

Elliot, M. T. (1995). Differences in the portrayal of blacks: A content analysis of general media versus culturally targeted commercials. *Journal of Current Issues and Research in Advertising, 17*(1), 75–86.

Erikson, E. H. (1980). *Identity and the life cycle*. New York: Norton.

Festinger, L. (1957). *A theory of cognitive dissonance*. Evanston, IL: Row-Peterson.

Ford, J. B., & LaTour, M. S. (1996). Contemporary female perspectives of female role portrayals in advertising. *Journal of Current Issues and Research in Advertising, 18*(1), 81–94.

Freud, S. (1924/1969). *A general introduction to psychoanalysis*. New York: Pocket Books.

Furnham, A. (1981). Personality and activity preference. *British Journal of Social Psychology, 20*, 57–68.

Gardner, M., Schumann, D. W., & Walls, S. (2002). Managing our affective states through consumption activity. In S. E. Heckler & S. Shapiro (Eds.), *Proceedings of the Society for Consumer Psychology* (pp. 189–204). Society for Consumer Psychology.

Gilens, M. (1996). Race and poverty in America: Public misperceptions and the American news media. *Public Opinion Quarterly, 60*, 515–541.

Gitlin, T. (2001). *Media unlimited*. New York: Metropolitan Books.

Goldberg, B. (2002). *Bias: A CBS insider exposes how the media distort the news*. Washington, DC: Regnery Publishing.

Hansen, F. J., & Osborne, D. (1995). Portrayal of women and elderly patients in psychotropic drug advertisements. *Women and Therapy, 16*(1), 29–141.

Herman, E. S., & Chomsky, N. (2002). *Manufacturing consent: The political economy of the mass media*. New York: Pantheon Books.

Hewstone, M., Rubin, M., & Willis, H. (2002). Intergroup bias. *Annual Review of Psychology, 53*, 575–604.

Ickes, W., Snyder, M., & Garcia, S. (1997). Personality influences on the choice of situations. In R. Hogan, J. Johnson, & S. Briggs (Eds.), *Handbook of personality psychology* (pp. 165–195). New York: Academic Press.

Judd, C. M., & Park, B. (1993). Definition and assessment of accuracy in social stereotypes. *Psychological Review, 100*, 109–128.

Jussim, L., Eccles, J., & Madon, S. (1996). Social perception, social stereotypes, and teacher expectations: Accuracy and the quest for the powerful self-fulfilling prophecy. In M. P. Zanna (Ed.), *Advances in experimental social psychology* (Vol. 28, pp. 281–388). San Diego, CA: Academic Press.

Lynch, J. G., Jr., & Srull, T. K. (1982). Memory and attentional factors in consumer choice: Concepts and research methods. *Journal of Consumer Research, 9*(1), 18–36.

MacGregor, B. (1997). *Live, direct and biased?* London: Arnold.

Maslow, A. H. (1954). *Motivation and personality*. New York: Harper.

Mazis, M. B., Ringold, D. J., Perry, E. S., & Denman, D. W. (1992). Perceived age and attractiveness of models in cigarette advertisements. *Journal of Marketing, 56*, 22–37.

Mertin, R. K. (1957). *Social theory and social structure*. New York: Free Press.

Mischel, W. (1968). *Personality and assessment*. New York: Wiley.

Mischel, W. (1990). Personality dispositions revisited and revised: A view after three decades. In L. A. Pervin (Ed.), *Handbook of personality theory and research* (pp. 111–134). New York: Guilford Press.

Morris, M. (2002, October). *Classic "and" cool?: The marketing of luxury goods to the urban market*. Presentation at the Association for Consumer Research Conference, Atlanta, GA.

Newcomb, T. (1947). Autistic hostility and social reality. *Human Relations, 1*, 69–86.

Petty, R. E., & Cacioppo, J. T. (1981). *Attitudes and persuasion: Classic and contemporary approaches*. Dubuque, IA: Brown.

Petty, R. E., & Cacioppo, J. T. (1986). *Communication and persuasion: Central and peripheral routes to attitude change*. New York: Springer.

Pettygrew, T. F. (1979). The ultimate attribution error: Extending Allport's cognitive analysis of prejudice. *Personality and Social Psychology Bulletin, 5*, 461–476.

Power, J. G., Murphy, S. T., & Coover, G. (1996). Priming prejudice: How stereotypes and counterstereotypes influence attribution of responsibility and credibility among ingroups and outgroups. *Human Communication Research, 23*(1), 36–58.

Punj, G., & Staelin, R. (1983). A model of consumer information search behavior for new automobiles. *Journal of Consumer Research, 9*(4), 366–380.

Ross, L., Greene, D., & House, P. (1977). The "false consensus effect": An egocentric bias in social perception and attribution processes. *Journal of Experimental Social Psychology, 13*, 279–301.

Ross, L., & Sicoly, F. (1979). Egocentric biases in availability and attribution. *Journal of Personality and Social Psychology, 37*, 322–336.

Schumann, D. W. (1999, February). *The transmission of prejudice: What do our marketing strategies really reinforce? Presidential address.* Presented at the Conference of the Society for Consumer Psychology, St. Petersburg, FL.

Schumann, D. W. (2002, June). Media and market segmentation strategies as contributing factors to restricted exposure to diversity: A discussion of potential societal consequences. Keynote address to the 21st Annual Advertising and Consumer Psychology Conference, New York.

Schumann, D. W., Grayson, J., Ault, J., Hargrove, K., Hollingsworth, L., Ruelle, R., & Seguin, S. (1991). Shopping cart signage: Is it an effective advertising medium? *Journal of Advertising Research, 31*(1), 17–22.

Shiffrin, R. M. (1976). Capacity limitations in information processing, attention and memory. In W. K. Estes (Ed.), *Handbook of learning and cognitive process* (Vol. 4, pp. 177–236). Hillsdale, NJ: Lawrence Erlbaum Associates.

Signorielli, N., McLeod, D., & Healy, E. (1994). Gender stereotypes in MTV commercials: The beat goes on. *Journal of Broadcasting and Electronic Media, 38*(1), 91–101.

Snyder, M. (1981). On the influence of individuals on situations. In N. Cantor & J. F. Kihlstrom (Eds.), *Personality, cognition, and social interaction* (pp. 309–329). Hillsdale, NJ: Lawrence Erlbaum Associates.

Srull, T., & Karabenick, S. A. (1975). Effects of personality-situation locus of control congruence. *Journal of Personality and Social Psychology, 32*, 617–628.

Stephan, W. C., & Stephan, C. W. (1984). The role of ignorance in intergroup relations. In N. Miller & M. B. Brewer (Eds.), *Groups in contact* (pp. 229–250). New York: Academic Press.

Strutton, D., & Lumpkin, J. R. (1993). Stereotypes of Black in-group attractiveness in advertising: On possible psychological effects. *Psychological Reports, 73*, 507–511.

Sunstein, C. (2001). *Republic.com.* Princeton, NJ: Princeton University Press.

Swann, W. (1987). Identity negotiation: Where two roads meet. *Journal of Personality and Social Psychology, 53*, 1038–1051.

Swann, W., & Read, S. J. (1981). Self-verification processes: How we sustain our self-conceptions. *Journal of Experimental Social Psychology, 17*, 351–372.

Swayne, L. E., & Greco, A. J. (1987). The portrayal of older Americans in television commercials. *Journal of Advertising, 16*(1), 47–54.

Taylor, C. R., & Lee, J. Y. (1994). Not in *Vogue*: Portrayals of Asian Americans in magazine advertising. *Journal of Public Policy & Marketing, 13*(2), 239–245.

Taylor, C. R., Lee, J. Y. & Stern, B. B. (1995). Portrayals of African, Hispanic, and Asian Americans in magazine advertising. *American Behavioral Scientists, 38*(4), 609–621.

Taylor, C. R., & Stern, B. B. (1997). Asian-Americans: Television advertising and the "model minority" stereotype. *Journal of Advertising, 26*(2), 49–60.

Tesser, A. (1988). Toward a self-evaluation maintenance model of social behavior. In L. Berkowitz (Ed.), *Advances in experimental social psychology* (Vol. 21). New York: Academic Press, 181–227.

Tesser, A., & Paulhus, D. (1983). The definition of self: Private and public self-evaluation management strategies. *Journal of Personality and Social Psychology, 44*, 672–682.

That Simpson trial in full. (1995, November). *International Broadcasting*, p. 19.

Turow, J. (1997). *Breaking up America: Advertisers and the new media world.* Chicago: University of Chicago Press.

Watson, D., & Baumal, E. (1967). Effects of locus of control and expectation of future control upon present performance. *Journal of Personality and Social Psychology, 6*, 212–215.

Wiggins, J. S. (1973). *Personality and prediction: Principles of personality assessment.* Reading, MA: Addison-Wesley.

Wiggins, J. S. (1997). In defense of traits. In R. Hogan, J. Johnson, & S. Briggs (Eds.), *Handbook of personality psychology* (pp. 95–115). New York: Academic Press.

III. INDIVIDUAL DIFFERENCES IN MEDIA USAGE AND THEIR ROLE AS MEDIATORS AND MODERATORS OF MEDIA EFFECTS

CHAPTER FOURTEEN

The Need for Entertainment Scale

Timothy C. Brock
Stephen D. Livingston
Ohio State University

What I am claiming here is not that television is entertaining but that it has made entertainment itself the natural format for the representation of all experience.

(Postman, 1986, p. 87)

Measuring individual differences in social-psychological variables has proved fruitful in consumer psychology. Well-known measures assess cognitive styles and motivations toward having various types of personal and social experiences. For example, the past 20 years of research have produced the development of scales measuring self-monitoring (Snyder, 1987), the need for cognition (Cacioppo & Petty, 1982), dispositional transportation into stories (Green & Brock, 2000; Green, Garst, & Brock, this volume), and the need for affect (Maio & Esses, 2001). Such individual-difference measures have served moderating functions that facilitate explanation in a variety of domains in persuasion and interpersonal relationships.

A heretofore neglected factor may be individuals' need for entertainment (NEnt). Postman's (1986) claim assumed, without proof, that the trend to present "all subject matter as entertaining" (p. 87) stemmed from individual recipients' changed manner of processing information (p. 107). In dissent from Postman's broad psychological transformation assumption, we propose instead that people likely differ in their habitual seeking of experiences and consumption of products from which they derive entertainment. If such differences could be identified and

255

scaled, their role in moderating consumers' experience of media could be fruitfully explored. The benefit to consumer behavior theory is reflected in the impetus for the current volume: Entertainment media have increasingly become venues that foster the persuasiveness of public narratives (Green & Brock, 2000; Green, Garst, & Brock, this volume). If people do indeed differ in their drive toward entertainment media, then arguably those who seek out entertainment more frequently may be more susceptible to the public narratives that often comprise media persuasion. Message acceptance processes may be facilitated by NEnt: The couching of a persuasive message within a fictional narrative (e.g., Prentice, Gerrig, & Bailis, 1997; Wheeler, Green, & Brock, 1999) could have a differential impact depending on the magnitude of the recipients' disposition to seek out and consume entertainment. NEnt may not only moderate the impact of messages in entertainment contexts but also lead to addiction-like dependency, and it could impede the primary purpose of other societal functions, such as education.

ENTERTAINMENT INTO ADDICTION

In a *Scientific American* article about the stylistic tricks of television, Kubey and Csikszentmihalyi (2002) showed how TV functions physiologically like a habit-forming drug and includes severe withdrawal symptoms: "Families have volunteered or been paid to stop viewing, typically for a week or a month. Many could not complete the period of abstinence. Some fought, verbally and physically. . . . When the TV habit interferes with the ability to grow, to learn new things, to lead an active life, then it does constitute a kind of dependence" (p. 80). We propose that people who are high in NEnt may be more susceptible to the addictive enslavement of passive forms of entertainment, such as TV.

SITUATIONAL PRESS FOR ENTERTAINMENT: CLASSROOM EXAMPLE

More generally, we propose that any situation in which people feel themselves to be members (perhaps a sole member) of a relatively passive audience is a situation in which NEnt can be evoked. Such situations are not limited to official entertainment (TV, movies, sports spectacles) but would also include school, church, and airport waiting lounges: "How television stages the world becomes the model for how the world is properly to be staged. It is not merely that on the television screen entertainment is the metaphor for all discourse, it is that off the screen (in classrooms) the same metaphor prevails" (Postman, 1986, p. 92). People high in NEnt may carry that need and express that need in all realms of their lives (school, church, etc.). An interesting testable implication is that NEnt could moderate the evaluation of teachers and instructors. Given that most instructors do not perform as well as

professional entertainers, their evaluations may be misleadingly reduced by students for whom NEnt is high in the classroom and other audience-type situations.

MEDIA THEORIES AND NEED FOR ENTERTAINMENT

That people may differ in their NEnt and that these differences may drive recourse to entertainment modalities is entirely consistent with leading media theories, such as uses and gratification (Rubin, 1994, 2002), cultivation (Gerbner, Gross, Morgan, & Signorielli, 1986; Gerbner, Gross, Morgan, Signorielli, & Shanahan, 2002), agenda setting (McCombs & Shaw, 1972), knowledge gap (Tichenour, Donohue, & Olien, 1970), and diffusion of innovation (Rogers, 1995). Unfortunately, a survey of the literature (e.g., Bryant & Zillmann, 2002; Rubin, 1994, 2002; Zillmann & Bryant, 1994; Zillmann & Vorderer, 2000) did not yield a global measure of entertainment need (for a review, see Oliver, 2002); it did not provide a measure that featured relatively passive receipt of entertainment stimuli (e.g., cinema, books, television, theater) in contrast with active recreational pursuits (e.g., sailing, snowmobiling, playing tennis). Of course, one challenge inherent in studying entertainment motivation is definitional. As noted by Zillmann and Bryant (1994), entertainment, in its broadest sense, could be defined as any situation or activity from which a person derives pleasure. Such a definition could include anything from watching a film to playing sports to spending time with loved ones.

We decided to limit the scope of our studies to experiences in which recipients receive exogenous stimuli in a largely passive way (e.g., TV, radio, film, print, theater, and sport spectacles). Fortunately, for our purposes, these kinds of media are among the most amenable to direct study by consumer psychologists. We expected that the bulk of our respondents would primarily define entertainment in terms of largely passive modalities, even without being prompted to do so.[1]

ENTERTAINMENT: SOVEREIGN INDUSTRY, SOVEREIGN NEED

In *The Entertainment Economy*, Wolf (1999) coined the term *entertainmentization* to convey that entertainment is the largest and fastest growing industry (see also Zillmann & Vorderer, 2000) and that the bulk of commercial ventures, to succeed,

---

[1] Although TV is provided for the recipient—so the recipient is completely passive—actual use may entail somewhat energetic activity. According to Wolf (1999), "The inertia of the TV viewer in the days of programming scarcity has been replaced by the hyperactivity of the TV users in these days of programming glut. A viewer watches what is offered, a user chooses to watch or not to watch. A *Los Angeles Times* poll showed that 40 percent of male viewers zapped commercials as soon as they came on. It's a well-known joke in broadcasting that 'Men don't want to know what's on television, they want to know what else is on!'" (p. 255).

must entertain along with their other functions:

Modern mass media—that is, television—were born with the baby-boom generation. From its first formative years, the evolution of media impacted the development
of this generation and was in turn influenced by the wants and desires of this new
economic colossus—a whole generation of consumers who were socialized by what
they saw on the tube. A common consumer culture leapfrogged national and cultural
boundaries and then, as boomers had children and now grandchildren, the process
has, if anything, been accelerated. When the game console and the computer screen
are added to the TV screen, together with all the implications of the Internet, I
see an endless appetite for entertainment content: something to connect us emotionally with products, something to provide us with information in a stimulating
way. The bottom line is that *we have come to expect that we will be entertained all
the time*. . . . Products and brands that deliver on this expectation succeed. Products
that do not will disappear. Entertainment has become the unifying force of modern
commerce, as pervasive as currency. (p. 72; emphasis added)

HOW STRONG AND UBIQUITOUS IS THE NEED
FOR ENTERTAINMENT?

Prior to developing a Need for Entertainment scale, we surveyed 115 undergraduates from Ohio State University and Georgia Southern University with a question
about the role of TV in their lives (Mazzocco, Brock, & Brock, 2003). We prefaced
the focal TV question with a warm-up question, as follows:

Imagine that, although actually a citizen of Pennsylvania [South Carolina], you have
always been considered a citizen of Ohio [Georgia] and that a new Pennsylvania
[South Carolina] program offers a one-time tax-free "bounty from surplus" to persons who can prove they are Pennsylvanians [South Carolinians]. As you can easily provide such proof, you are considering applying for the Pennsylvania [South
Carolina] gift if it is sufficiently generous. What amount of cash would you require
to continue your life, publicly (and correctly) identified as a Pennsylvanian [South
Carolinian]?

_____

(write in amount in dollars)

The top of Fig. 14.1 shows a histogram with the raw results. Respondents
perceived more than negligible inconvenience in correcting their state citizenship
to get the cash gift: Only 13 people were willing to change for no money at all. Yet
more than half of the respondents were willing to switch back from their current
citizenship state to their true citizenship state for less than $10,000.

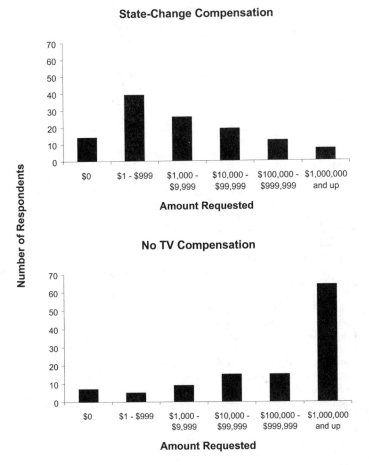

FIG. 14.1 Money requested as compensation to change statehood (top) and to forego television (bottom).

Respondents next answered a similarly worded question, with the focus now placed on the cessation of TV viewing:

Imagine that there is a tiny invisible sensor (worn on an earring or watchband), which reliably detects TV watching by the wearer and which reliably tracks the wearer's normal daily movement. If the wearer watches TV or if the sensor is any way tampered with, a control station with global transponding is notified. What amount of cash would you require to cease watching TV for the rest of your life? (If you "cheated"—by watching TV—the entire cash sum, plus compounded interest, would be legally seizable from you and all your assets).

_____

(write in amount in dollars)

TABLE 14.1
Initial Need for Entertainment Questionnaire

For each of the statements below, please indicate whether or not the statement is characteristic of you or of what you believe. If the statement is extremely uncharacteristic of you or what you believe (*not at all like you*), please place a "1" on the line to the left of the statement. If the statement is extremely characteristic of you or of what you believe (*very much like you*), please place a "5" on the line to the left of the statement. You should use the following scale as you rate the statements below.

1	2	3	4	5
Extremely	*Somewhat*	*Uncertain*	*Somewhat*	*Extremely*
unlike me	*unlike me*		*like me*	*like me*

Answer all questions as accurately as you can, but please remember that there are no right or wrong answers. We are interested in your perceptions.

1.____When traveling, I get very bored unless there is something entertaining to do.
2.____I tend to use computers for work much more than for games. (R)
3.____I am very selective about how I spend my free time. (R)
4.____Because they entertain millions of people, professional athletes are paid fair wages for their performances.
5.____Watching television for an extended period of time makes me restless. (R)
6.____Previews of upcoming movies and television programs generally make me very interested in seeing these shows.
7.____When reading a newspaper, I tend to look at the comics before anything else.
8.____**Entertainment is the most enjoyable part of life.**
9.____**I tend not to seek out new ways to be entertained. (R)**
10.____**I spend a lot of money on entertainment expenses.**
11.____I prefer to "make my own fun," rather than be entertained by others. (R)
12.____**I do not spend much time during the week on entertaining activities. (R)**
13.____**It is a waste of tax money to fund entertainment programs. (R)**
14.____I hardly ever check my watch when I am at a performance.
15.____When Friday approaches, I find that I often think about how I will spend my leisure time.
16.____I find it much easier to learn things when they are taught in an entertaining way.
17.____Watching television is a poor use of free time. (R)
18.____As far as my choice of entertainment is concerned, anything will do.
19.____Entertainers play an important role in our society.
20.____If I don't get to engage in the sort of entertaining activities that I prefer, then I tend to feel uncomfortable.
21.____It is human nature to need entertainment.
22.____I prefer work-related activities to entertaining activities. (R)
23.____**I enjoy being entertained more than my friends do.**
24.____Cultures that emphasize work responsibilities to the exclusion of entertainment are unhealthy.
25.____I prefer to read magazines such as *People* or *Entertainment Weekly*.
26.____**I need some entertainment time each and every day.**
27.____Laugh tracks foster enjoyment of television comedy programs.
28.____I prefer being entertained, instead of having to entertain myself.
29.____I would rather read a fictional story than something related to work or school.
30.____**My idea of entertainment is a situation where everything is done for me.**
31.____I feel really guilty when I put off work in order to do something entertaining. (R)
32.____**I prefer to be entertained in ways that don't require any effort on my part.**
33.____I find that I like most movies.
34.____**Entertainment is an unnecessary luxury. (R)**

(*continued*)

TABLE 14.1

(continued)

35.____ I feel like my time spent on entertainment purposes is generally wasted. (R)
36.____ Exciting rides are the best thing about amusement parks.
37.____ If I don't have enough fun in the evening, I find it hard to function properly the next day.
38.____ I become easily bored on long trips.
39.____ I think life should be spent being entertained.
40.____ I spend most of my free time seeking out entertainment.
41.____ I do not find satisfaction after being entertained for many hours in a row. (R)
42.____ Entertainment is an example of a need that is usually fulfilled without genuine satisfaction. (R)
43.____ Very little of my money is spent on entertainment. (R)
44.____ I am always on the lookout for new forms of entertainment.
45.____ I like to take an active role in my entertainment activities. (R)
46.____ Entertainment is something you do when you're too lazy to do anything else. (R)
47.____ I find parades to be boring. (R)
48.____ I like being part of a crowd of spectators.
49.____ I could be described as an "entertainment-oholic."
50.____ The government would be better off encouraging people to be more productive instead of always seeking out entertainment. (R)
51.____ I like to watch tropical fish swim in tanks.

Note. Boldface items comprise the reduced (19-item) Need for Entertainment questionnaire. (R) denotes reverse-coded items.

The bottom of Fig. 14.1 shows the results from this question. Evidently, respondents were not very willing to forego TV. Only eight people said they were willing to stop watching TV for no money at all. Indeed, for more than half of the respondents a fortune in compensation, at least one million dollars, was required. In fact, the mean amount requested to forego TV, admittedly distorted by several outliers, was 23 billion dollars. The conclusion appears inescapable that, to the extent that TV viewing is correlated with the need for entertainment, NEnt may be an extremely powerful force in many people.

STUDY 1 AND STUDY 2: SCALE DEVELOPMENT AND FACTOR STRUCTURE

We initially generated dozens of potential scale items. Discarding those items that seemed double-barreled or that lacked apparent face validity, we were left with a total of 51 items. Participants were asked to rate, on a scale of 1 to 5, the extent to which the items were characteristic of themselves (see Table 14.1). When assembling the scale, we tried to construct subsets of items that addressed various underlying themes of interest, such as entertainment drive, entertainment utility, and entertainment passivity.

Among problematic issues was selectivity in choices of entertainment. If we presumed that individual differences in NEnt indeed exist, would people high in this need be particularly selective about the types of entertainment they seek? Put another way, would high NEnt motivate drive reduction such that individuals indiscriminately consumed whatever products are available (i.e., akin to eating whatever is immediately available if one is particularly hungry), or would it instead be associated with discriminating tastes in entertainment (i.e., such that qualities of specific entertainments are key to fulfilling the need). We therefore included items (with occasional reverse scoring) that addressed such issues (e.g., "If I don't have enough fun in the evening, I find it hard to function properly the next day").

We were also interested in whether NEnt might be reflected in reports of experience. Items that attempted to address experience included those that concerned entertainment consumption (e.g., "I spend a lot of money on entertainment expenses" and "When reading a newspaper, I tend to look at the comics before anything else"). Items such as "Entertainment is an unnecessary luxury" and "It is a waste of tax money to fund entertainment programs" assessed evaluative disposition toward entertainment.

SAMPLES, PROCEDURES, AND ADDITIONAL INSTRUMENTS

We employed two large samples. The first sample consisted of 389 Ohio State University undergraduates who filled out questionnaires at the beginning of an academic quarter as part of a mass prescreening procedure. These 389 participants also completed the Need for Cognition scale (Cacioppo & Petty, 1982).

The second sample consisted of 282 Ohio State University undergraduate participants in a large laboratory experiment in which the principal task was to react to the reading of texts, presented in either narrative and rhetorical formats and, within each format, in strong or weak versions. The participants in the second sample also completed the Need for Cognition scale (Cacioppo & Petty, 1982), a measure of dispositional transportation (Green & Brock, 2000; Green, Garst, & Brock, this volume), the Vividness of Visual Imagery Scales (Babin & Burns, 1998), and the Tellegen Absorption Index (Tellegen, 1982). Thus, the contexts and tasks of the participants in each sample were quite different.

Analytical Approach: Factor Analyses

We conducted a factor analysis of the first sample and then observed whether the emerging factor structure replicated in the second sample. We investigated the consistency and reliability of the emerging 19-item reduced NEnt scale and its degree of association with the other measured variables.

Factor analyses were conducted using maximum likelihood extraction, with quartimax rotation, a type of rotation that assumes orthogonality. From the total

administration of 51 items, initial analyses attempted to extract 12 factors and were then followed by analyses with successively smaller numbers of factors. Items that did not load at above .20 on a single factor were deleted and the factor solution was rerun. This procedure was followed until 19 items were left that loaded well and differentially on three factors.

Entertainment Drive: Factor 1. The first factor consisted of 12 items with substantial loadings that reflected a drive toward or motivation toward entertainment (see Table 14.2). The items did not load notably on Factors 2 and 3. Importantly,

TABLE 14.2
Factor 1 (Drive for Entertainment) Loadings on Need for Entertainment
in Studies 1 and 2

Item	Factor 1		Factor 2		Factor 3	
	Study 1[a]	Study 2[b]	Study 1[a]	Study 2[b]	Study 1[a]	Study 2[b]
Entertainment is the most enjoyable part of life.	**0.57**	**0.50**	0.10	0.14	0.16	0.22
I tend not to seek out new ways to be entertained. (R)	**0.25**	0.19	0.19	0.18	−0.10	**−0.25**
I spend a lot of money on entertainment expenses. [M > F]	**0.54**	**0.62**	0.17	0.06	0.07	−0.04
I do not spend much time during the week on entertaining activities. (R)	**0.44**	**0.38**	0.25	0.25	0.10	−0.19
I enjoy being entertained more than my friends do.	**0.48**	**0.38**	0.04	−0.03	0.09	0.13
I need some entertainment time each and every day. [M > F]	**0.53**	**0.40**	0.24	0.37	−0.02	0.08
If I don't have enough fun in the evening, I find it hard to function properly the next day. [M > F]	**0.38**	**0.38**	−0.11	−0.21	0.10	0.06
I think life should be spent being entertained.	**0.67**	**0.55**	0.00	0.03	0.22	0.24
I spend most of my free time seeking out entertainment.	**0.75**	**0.71**	−0.01	−0.08	0.03	0.08
Very little of my money is spent on entertainment. (R)	**0.51**	**0.54**	0.24	0.11	0.08	−0.21
I am always on the lookout for new forms of entertainment.	**0.54**	**0.42**	0.16	0.12	−0.20	−0.27
I could be described as an "entertainment-oholic."	**0.72**	**0.66**	0.04	−0.07	0.04	0.15
Items loading highest on factor	12	11	0	0	0	1

Note. Boldfacing indicates highest factor loading of an item.
[a]$N = 389.$
[b]$N = 282.$

factor loadings generally replicated, for 11 of the 12 items, on the drive factor in the second sample. Factor 1 items included "Entertainment is the most enjoyable part of life"; "I tend not to seek out new ways to be entertained" (reverse scored); "I spend a lot of money on entertainment expenses"; "I enjoy being entertained more than my friends do"; and "I could be described as an 'entertainment-oholic'." Although one of these items, "I tend not to seek out new ways to be entertained" (reverse scored), did not replicate its loading on Factor 1 in the second sample, we decided to retain it in the emergent 19-item scale. In our opinion, the item both fundamentally reflects the nature of the drive factor and happens to be useful in determining response biases (e.g., acquiescent responses) because it is the functional opposite of another item, "I am always on the lookout for new forms of entertainment," that loaded well and reliably on Factor 1 across both samples.

As indicated in Table 14.2 males had reliably higher mean scores than females for three Factor 1 items: spending money on entertainment, daily need for entertainment, and inability to function without entertainment. These mean gender differences replicated across the two samples.

Entertainment Utility: Factor 2.   The second factor consisted of four items with substantial loadings that seemingly reflected attitudes toward the general utility of entertainment. (See Table 14.3.) Importantly, factor loadings generally

TABLE 14.3
Factor 2 (Utility of Entertainment) Loadings on Need for Entertainment in Studies 1 and 2

Item	Factor 1 Study 1[a]	Study 2[b]	Factor 2 Study 1[a]	Study 2[b]	Factor 3 Study 1[a]	Study 2[b]
It is a waste of tax money to fund entertainment programs. (R)	0.19	0.18	**0.37**	**0.28**	0.10	−0.18
Entertainment is an unnecessary luxury. (R)	0.28	0.05	**0.64**	**0.67**	−0.02	−0.17
I feel like my time spent on entertainment purposes is generally wasted. (R)	0.25	−0.01	**0.64**	**0.61**	−0.08	−0.11
Entertainment is something you do when you're too lazy to do anything else. (R)	0.13	0.05	**0.55**	**0.38**	−0.16	−0.26
Items loading highest on factor	0	0	4	4	0	0

Note. Boldfacing indicates highest factor loading of an item.
[a] $N = 389$.
[b] $N = 282$.

replicated, for each of the four items, on the utility factor in the second sample. Attitudes toward the utility of entertainment were reflected in items such as "It is a waste of tax money to fund entertainment programs" (reverse scored) and "Entertainment is an unnecessary luxury" (reverse scored).

Entertainment Passivity: Factor 3.   The third factor consisted of three items with substantial loadings that reflected preference for passivity in entertainment. (See Table 14.4, Columns 7 and 8.) Importantly, factor loadings replicated on the passivity factor in the second sample. Factor 3 items included "My idea of entertainment is a situation where everything is done for me" and "I like to take an active role in my entertainment activities" (reverse scored).

Correlational Evidence and Scale Parameters

Factor 1 (Drive) was moderately positively associated with Factor 2 (Utility) in both samples—the reliable correlations were .39 and .17. However, Factor 1 had near zero association with Factor 3 (Passivity) in both samples. Factors 2 and 3 were reliably inversely associated in both samples: −.12 and −.33.

Table 14.5 shows that, for Studies 1 and 2, substantial Cronbach alphas, in the .7 to .8 range, were obtained in both samples for the entire scale and for the Factor 1 subscale. The mean scores were just above the middle of the 5-point scale. Correlational evidence showed that NEnt was reliably inversely related to Need for Cognition, an outcome that supported our passive bias in defining NEnt and in generating initial items. In particular, the strongest inverse correlations with Need for Cognition occurred for the third factor (Passivity). Finally, NEnt was only weakly associated with dispositional transportation and not at all with imagery propensity or absorption.

Discussion

Need for Entertainment appeared to have a sensible and replicating factor structure with satisfactory reliabilities for the overall scale and at least the largest (12-item) subscale. Importantly, in both large samples, NEnt was inversely associated with Need for Cognition, a measure of how much a person enjoys active problem solving and active critical thinking. These inverse correlations were particularly strong for the third factor (passivity) and therefore were consistent with our anticipated passive bias in the meaning to respondents of entertainment. Finally, NEnt appears to occupy a distinctive niche in that it was only weakly associated with dispositional transportation and not at all with imagery propensity or absorption (see Table 14.6). In the next studies, we further examined the passive assumption by measuring respondent's self-definition of entertainment (Study 3) and by assessing the impact of an investigator-provided definition of entertainment (Study 4).

TABLE 14.4
Factor 3 (Passivity of Entertainment) Loadings on Need for Entertainment in Study 1 Through Study 3

Item	Factor 1			Factor 2			Factor 3		
	Study 1[a]	Study 2[b]	Study 3[c]	Study 1[a]	Study 2[b]	Study 3[c]	Study 1[a]	Study 2[b]	Study 3[c]
My idea of entertainment is a situation where everything is done for me.	0.20	0.22	0.21	−0.06	−0.25	−0.06	**0.78**	**0.64**	**0.67**
I prefer to be entertained in ways that don't require any effort on my part.	0.13	0.15	−0.01	−0.02	−0.06	−0.01	**0.71**	**0.64**	**0.81**
I like to take an active role in my entertainment activities. (R)	0.34	0.26	−0.52	0.14	0.13	−0.13	**0.39**	**0.35**	**0.60**
Items loading highest on factor	0	0	0	0	0	0	3	3	3

Note. Boldfacing indicates highest factor loading of an item.
[a] $N = 389$.
[b] $N = 282$.
[c] $N = 60$.

TABLE 14.5
Need for Entertainment Means, Reliabilities, and
Associations With Other Variables: Study 1

	M	SD	α	NC[a]
Entire scale (19 items)	3.15	.51	.81	−.24**
Drive (12 items)	3.11	.66	.83	−.19**
Utility (4 items)	3.93	.72	.68	−.01
Passivity (3 items)	2.31	.74	.62	−.34**

Note. The last column contains values of *r*.
[a] NC = Need for Cognition; see text.
** $p < .01$, two-tailed.

TABLE 14.6
Need for Entertainment Means, Reliabilities, and Associations With Other
Variables: Study 2

	M	SD	α	NC[a]	Imagery[b]	Transportation[c]	Absorption[d]
Entire Scale (19 items)	3.19	.44	.72	−.22**	.03	−.17**	.01
Drive (12 items)	3.18	.61	.83	−.19**	.00	−.15*	.02
Utility (4 items)	3.84	.73	.68	.09	.02	−.04	.08
Passivity (3 items)	2.34	.73	.62	−.33**	.02	−.12	−.13*

Note. The last four columns contain values of *r*.
[a] NC = Need for Cognition.
[b] Imagery = Vividness of Visual Imagery Scale.
[c] Transportation = Dispositional Transportation.
[d] Absorption = Tellegen Absorption Index. See text.
* $p < .05$, two-tailed. ** $p < .01$, two-tailed.

STUDY 3: RESPONDENTS' DEFINITIONS OF ENTERTAINMENT

Though the results of the first two studies were promising, we became concerned with two matters of construct validity. First, we wanted to confirm that our participants were defining the construct of entertainment in the same way that we intended, that is, in a largely passive manner. Second, we wanted to try to differentiate NEnt from a seemingly related construct—sensation seeking. Previous research has shown that sensation seeking can affect the selection of specific entertainment, such as music (Litle & Zuckerman, 1986) and film (Schierman & Rowland, 1985). However, though sensation seeking may impact particular entertainment preferences, it has not been shown to impact the overall amount of sought entertainment in the way that we believe NEnt should.

Method and Procedure

To explore the meaning of entertainment for respondents, 60 Ohio State University undergraduates (introductory psychology pool) completed all sections of a booklet

consisting of three parts: (1) the 19-item NEnt questionnaire (i.e., the bold-face items in Table 14.1), (2) questions designed to elicit a personal definition of entertainment, and (3) the 39-item Sensation-Seeking Scale Form V (Zuckerman, 1994, 1996). In the second part, participants read the following:

> You just answered some questions about "entertainment." In the space below, please define what "entertainment" meant to you when you were answering the questions on the previous page: [followed by a rectangular space measuring 2″ × 4″]
>   What experiences or activities are good examples that illustrate your personal definition of "entertainment"? Please list up to four answers in the spaces below. [followed by four blank lines]

Results

Although we regard a sample of 60 participants as too small for conclusive factor analyses, we again observed the third factor (Passivity). The factor loadings can be seen in the 4th, 7th, and 10th columns of Table 14.4.

We coded respondents' definitions into three categories: passive ($N = 43$), active ($N = 12$), and unclear or ambiguous ($N = 5$). Two verbatim examples of a passive definition were "a show being put on for you: watching TV, listening to music, going to the movies" and "TV, movies, theater, etc.; something that keeps you entertained, usually observing."

Two verbatim examples of an active definition were "entertainment—something you do for pleasure: hunting, fishing, backpacking" and "entertainment is interacting with others and making sure that all parties involved are having a good time. I consider entertainment activities physical and therefore not something lazy people do: volleyball, swimming, dance." A verbatim example of an unclear definition was "I see entertainment as anything in life really. Just common everyday experiences entertain me: people, life, experiences." In sum, only about 20% of the respondents personally defined entertainment in a clearly nonpassive fashion.

But did people who defined entertainment in an active fashion differ from the others? Table 14.7 shows the mean scores for the entire sample and, separately, for passive, active, and unclear self-definers. None of the mean differences for NEnt scores between these subsamples reached statistical significance. However, sensation-seeking scores were higher for the active subsample ($M = 3.51$) than for the passive subsample ($M = 2.99$), $t(53) = 3.404$, $p < .001$.

Finally, at the level of the entire sample, we observed a reliable moderate correlation between the total NEnt score and sensation seeking, $r = .34$, $p < .01$. The correlation between the passivity factor of NEnt and sensation seeking was unreliable, however ($r = -.11$, ns).

Discussion

The present sample was drawn from the same introductory psychology pool as the samples used in Study 1 and Study 2. Therefore, because only approximately 1 out

TABLE 14.7
Need for Entertainment Means As a Function of Self-Definition of Entertainment
(Passive, Active, or Unclear): Study 3

Sample Analyzed	n	Total NEnt		NEnt Passivity Subscale		SSS-V[a]	
		M	SD	M	SD	M	SD
Entire Sample	60	3.27	.42	2.20	.79	3.11	.51
Passive Self-Definition	43	3.25	.44	2.25	.74	2.99	.47
Active Self-Definition	12	3.37	.44	2.11	1.07	3.51	.46
Unclear Self-Definition	5	3.19	.21	2.07	.43	3.18	.47

Note. NEnt = Need for Entertainment.
[a] SSS-V = Zuckerman Sensation Seeking Scale (Form V).

of 5 respondents defined entertainment in an active fashion, we might infer that the bulk of the respondents (i.e., 70% or more) from the earlier samples (Studies 1 and 2) were defining entertainment in a similar fashion: as being entertained, relatively passively, by some exogenous performance or spectacle. Replication of the passivity factor in the present sample reinforced this interpretation.

Regardless of how respondents here defined entertainment, their mean scores on the total NEnt scale, on the passivity subscale, and on the sensation-seeking scales were not differentially affected. The observed association with sensation seeking was moderate; this result, like the correlational evidence of Studies 1 and 2, again suggests that NEnt, as scaled here, is distinctive. NEnt is not measuring sensation seeking or absorption or dispositional transportation.

STUDY 4: IMPACT OF PRIMING PASSIVITY OF ENTERTAINMENT

To further examine the definitional issue we asked Ohio State University undergraduates ($N = 28$) from the same introductory psychology pool as Studies 1, 2, and 3 to first self-define entertainment (cf. the second part of the questionnaire from Study 3) and then complete the 19-item version of the NEnt scale. The NEnt scale in Study 4 now included the following in its instructions: "For the purpose of the task on this page, define 'entertainment' in terms of passive activities—such as movies, TV, watching sports, reading books, etc.—where something is done for you." As in Study 3, participants then completed the Sensation-Seeking scale.

In corroboration of Study 3, the responses of most ($N = 22$) participants were codable as passive (see Study 3). We compared mean scores on total NEnt and on Factor 3 (Passivity) across four samples: Study 1, Study 2, Study 3, and the present study (Study 4) in which a passive definition of entertainment was primed. The means for total NEnt were 3.15, 3.19, 3.27, and 3.11, respectively, for the four samples. These means did not differ statistically. The means on the passivity factor

(Factor 3) were 2.31, 2.34, 2.20, and 2.37, respectively. These means also did not differ statistically.

In sum, priming with a passive definition did not affect NEnt scores. This result is not surprising considering that the majority of respondents—in the current study and in Study 3—spontaneously defined being entertained in a passive-recipient fashion. Recall that participants in Study 4 defined entertainment as their first step. We used our coding of definitions to divide participants at the median into highs and lows in coded passivity. The total NEnt scores for those high ($M = 3.16$) and low ($M = 2.94$) in passivity did not differ statistically. Because the bulk of respondents spontaneously define being entertained in passive-recipient fashion, we believe that it may be superfluous to provide such a definition in future administrations of the NEnt scale.

Finally, we again observed a positive correlation between total NEnt and sensation seeking ($r = .13, ns$). Although this correlation was not statistically significant, and as such we cannot claim true replication of the effect from Study 3, it should be noted the comparatively small sample size in Study 4 would not likely have provided sufficient power to detect small effects.

SCALE STATUS, SOCIAL IMPLICATIONS, AND CONCLUSIONS

Magnitude of need for entertainment may be a fundamental determinant of how media are processed. Our working assumption is that dispositional NEnt drives expectations, framing, and receptivity with respect to all public media communications. Measurement of NEnt may therefore account for blurring of the lines in media as well as help explain how attitudes and behaviors can be influenced by presentations that are largely intended to entertain. Indeed, to the extent that one's NEnt is being satisfied, advocacies presented within narrative modes may be more influential than advocacies presented in rhetorical modes.

The factor structure of NEnt appeared robust across two large data collections. The three factors (see Tables 14.2, 14.3, and 14.4) are sensible and meaningfully related to one another. The present NEnt scale is not specific about kind of entertainment. Similarly, the well-known Need for Cognition scale (Cacioppo & Petty, 1982) is nonspecific: The Need for Cognition scale does not stipulate targets for cognitive effort, such as crossword puzzles or auto mechanics. The results of our NEnt studies suggest that the bulk of our respondents adopted a passive definition of being entertained; they were thinking about TV, movies, and so on when the scale was administered. In future applications of the NEnt scale, we recommend using the 19-item version. Of course, it would be wise to check a small subsample (as in Studies 3 and 4) to verify that being passively entertained is indeed salient for the majority of respondents.

We have not yet taken a position on whether NEnt might be better conceptualized as a trait or as an evaluative disposition. Whether this distinction (need vs. trait

vs. disposition) is important can be settled empirically by the ability of the scale and its constituent factors to fruitfully account for variance that has been hitherto unexplained.

Concurrent with the work specifically concerning NEnt, we are also conducting research in the domain of narrative persuasion (e.g., Green, Garst, & Brock, this volume). These laboratory experiments attempt to contrast the underlying mechanisms of narrative-based and rhetoric-based persuasion. Recent theories on this topic (for a review, see Green, Strange, & Brock, 2002) led us to suspect that NEnt might serve in a moderating role in narrative persuasion. If persuasive messages can be framed within an entertaining medium (e.g., a fictional story), then perhaps individuals who are particularly concerned with entertainment (i.e., individuals high in NEnt) will be more likely to attend to and accept the conclusions of such messages. In this way, NEnt might serve as a moderator of narrative persuasion (but would not moderate rhetorical persuasion), analogous to how Need for Cognition serves as a moderator of rhetorical persuasion (but does not moderate narrative persuasion; see Green & Brock, 2000). The present reliable inverse relationships (Studies 1 and 2) between NEnt and Need for Cognition are consistent with their proposed differential moderating roles in narrative versus rhetorical persuasion.[2]

Social Replacement Implications of Differences in Need for Entertainment

Entertainment As Birth Control?   The role of entertainment in substituting for other kinds of interpersonal relationships has been explicitly recognized in India:

> In a mark of frustration over India's perennially stalled family planning efforts, the country's health minister has come up with a proposal to distribute television sets to the masses to keep their minds off procreation. The minister suggested last month to the Indian Parliament that entertainment is an important component of the population policy. To drive down birth rates, he said, we want people to watch television. Members of the opposition scoffed at the idea—but only because it would be expensive. (Holden, 2001, p. 1987)

Aging and Emotional Well-Being.   An exception to the general overall decline in function with aging is thought to be emotion, specifically, the greater saliency

---

[2]Indeed, the role of individual differences in moderating the impact of entertaining facets of persuasive messages has gained some recent recognition. Conway and Dubé (2002) demonstrated that masculine sex-role orientation predicts greater intent to adopt the recommendations of a persuasive message with humorous content than of the same message without humorous content when the message addressed a threatening health-related topic. Given that we found reliable gender differences in certain aspects of NEnt (see Studies 1 and 2), we might be able to explain such sex-role orientation effects as epiphenomena of NEnt in the persuasive context. Although this is admittedly speculative, we see such experimental paradigms as potential opportunities to demonstrate the power of NEnt across theoretical and disciplinary boundaries.

and improved regulation of emotion. According to developmental authorities at Stanford, "emotional well being, when it does suffer, declines only at the very end of life" (Carstensen & Charles, 1998, p. 144). It turns out that emotional well-being in the second half of life stems, unsurprisingly, from improved satisfaction with real interpersonal relationships. NEnt may moderate the preservation and fostering of real interpersonal relationships. One testable implication is that high NEnt may thwart real interpersonal relationships to the extent that NEnt drives usually solitary behaviors such as watching TV. High NEnt may therefore diminish emotional well-being, an outcome of real interpersonal relationships that does not have to undergo a significant decline in older people.

Reduction of Democracy's Wellsprings.   Need for Entertainment may moderate democratic processes. Putnam (2000) compellingly showed that TV viewing undermines the social skills and bonding that contribute to social capital, the wellspring of democracy. Thus, NEnt may be inversely related to participation in the town-meeting types of activities, with their emphasis on social, face-to-face, and give-and-take and inversely related to active decision-making behavior carried out in the real world, such as voting. High levels of NEnt may drive behaviors that are fundamentally inimicable to Toquevillian democracy (Green, 2000; Green & Brock, 1998; Putnam, 2000). We concur with Wolf (1999):

> Most people are less likely to look to the family dinner table or the office water cooler for real interpersonal contact. More and more, if you are looking for common ground with family and colleagues, it will be *a shared entertainment experience* [italics added], a few stolen moments in an America Online chat room, a book you know everybody else is reading. . . . Entertainment products put the mass audience on the same wavelength and, while engaging the emotions, they replace the sense of shared community that is disappearing in regular life. (p. 38)

Conclusion

The present research has made preliminary strides toward identifying and scaling individual differences in the preference for seeking out entertaining products and experiences. We agree with Singhal and Rogers (2002) that "never before in history has so much entertainment been so readily accessible to so many people for so much of their leisure time" (p. 119). Further systematic investigations and evaluations of need for entertainment are therefore both worthwhile and timely. We take seriously Postman's warning (1986, p. 155) that spiritual devastation is coming from an enemy with a smiling face. We contend not only that individuals may differ in their need for entertainment but that measurement of such differences will provide a more nuanced and more correct understanding of the implications of this need.

ACKNOWLEDGMENTS

Continuing research on this topic is supported by a Social Sciences and Humanities Research Council of Canada Doctoral Fellowship awarded to the second author. We are grateful to Philip Mazzocco and Shari Lewis for their assistance. We are indebted to feedback garnered from a conference presentation of portions of this chapter at the Advertising and Consumer Psychology 21st Annual Meeting, May 2002, in New York.

REFERENCES

Babin, L. A., & Burns, A. C. (1998). A modified scale for the measurement of communication-evoked mental imagery. *Psychology and Marketing, 15*, 261–278.

Bryant, J., & Zillmann, D. (Eds.). (2002). *Media effects: Advances in theory and research* (2nd ed.). Mahwah, NJ: Lawrence Erlbaum Associates.

Cacioppo, J. T., & Petty, R. E. (1982). The need for cognition. *Journal of Personality and Social Psychology, 42*, 116–131.

Carstensen, L. L., & Charles, S. T. (1998). Emotion in the second half of life. *Current Directions in Psychological Science, 7*, 144–149.

Conway, M., & Dubé, L. (2002). Humor in persuasion on threatening topics: Effectiveness is a function of audience sex-role orientation. *Personality and Social Psychology Bulletin, 28*, 863–873.

Gerbner, G., Gross, L., Morgan, M., & Signorielli, N. (1986). Living with television: The dynamics of the cultivation process. In J. Bryant & D. Zillmann (Eds.), *Perspectives on media effects* (pp. 17–40). Hillsdale, NJ: Lawrence Erlbaum Associates.

Gerbner, G., Gross, L., Morgan, M., Signorielli, N., & Shanahan, J. (2002). Growing up with television: Cultivation processes. In J. Bryant & D. Zillmann (Eds.), *Media effects: Advances in theory and research* (2nd ed., pp. 43–68). Mahwah, NJ: Lawrence Erlbaum Associates.

Green, M. C. (2000). *Choice of real versus ersatz social interaction in the formation of social capital: Laboratory and longitudinal approaches.* Unpublished doctoral dissertation, The Ohio State University, Columbus.

Green, M. C., & Brock, T. C. (1998). Trust, mood, and the outcome of friendship determine preference for real versus ersatz social capital. *Political Psychology, 19*(3), 527–544.

Green, M. C., & Brock, T. C. (2000). The role of transportation in the persuasiveness of public narratives. *Journal of Personality and Social Psychology, 79*, 701–721.

Green, M. C., Strange, J. J., & Brock, T. C. (Eds.). (2002). *Narrative impact: Social and cognitive foundations.* Mahwah, NJ: Lawrence Erlbaum Associates.

Holden, C. (2001). Birth control by remote. *Science, 293*, 1987.

Kubey, R., & Csikszentmihalyi, M. (2002). Television addiction is no mere metaphor. *Scientific American, 286*, 74–80.

Litle, P., & Zuckerman, M. (1986). Sensation seeking and music preferences. *Personality and Individual Differences, 7*, 575–577.

Maio, G. R., & Esses, V. M. (2001). The need for affect: Individual differences in the motivation to approach or avoid emotions. *Journal of Personality, 69*, 583–615.

Mazzocco, P. J., Brock, T. C., & Brock, G. J. (2003). *Money needed to live as a descendant of slaves: Reparations in the court of public opinion.* Unpublished manuscript, Columbus, OH.

McCombs, M. W., & Shaw, D. L. (1972). The agenda-setting function of the mass media. *Public Opinion Quarterly, 36*, 176–187.

Oliver, M. B. (2002). Individual differences in media effects. In J. Bryant & D. Zillmann (Eds.), *Media effects: Advances in theory and research* (2nd ed., pp. 507–524). Mahwah, NJ: Lawrence Erlbaum Associates.

Postman, N. (1986). *Amusing ourselves to death.* New York: Penguin.

Prentice, D. A., Gerrig, R. J., & Bailis, D. S. (1997). What readers bring to the processing of fictional texts. *Psychonomic Bulletin and Review, 4,* 416–420.

Putnam, R. D. (2000). *Bowling alone: The collapse and revival of American community.* New York: Simon & Schuster.

Rogers, E. M. (1995). *Diffusion of innovation* (4th ed.). New York: Free Press.

Rubin, A. M. (1994). Media uses and effects: A uses-and-gratifications perspective. In J. Bryant & D. Zillmann (Eds.), *Media effects: Advances in theory and research* (pp. 417–436). Hillsdale, NJ: Lawrence Erlbaum Associates.

Rubin, A. M. (2002). The uses and gratifications perspective of media effects. In J. Bryant & D. Zillmann (Eds.), *Media effects: Advances in theory and research* (2nd ed., pp. 525–548). Mahwah, NJ: Lawrence Erlbaum Associates.

Schierman, M. J., & Rowland, G. L. (1985). Sensation-seeking and selection of entertainment. *Personality and Individual Differences, 6,* 599–603.

Singhal, A., & Rogers, E. M. (2002). A theoretical agenda for entertainment-education. *Communication Theory, 12*(2), 117–135.

Snyder, M. (1987). *Public appearances/private realities: The psychology of self-monitoring.* New York: Freeman.

Tellegen, A. (1982). *Brief manual for the Differential Personality Questionnaire.* Unpublished manuscript, University of Minnesota, Minneapolis.

Tichenour, P. J., Donohue, G. A., & Olien, C. N. (1970). Mass media flow and differential growth in knowledge. *Public Opinion Quarterly, 34,* 159–170.

Wheeler, S. C., Green, M. C., & Brock, T. C. (1999). Fictional narratives change beliefs: Replications of Prentice, Gerrig, & Bailis (1997) with mixed corroboration. *Psychonomic Bulletin and Review, 6,* 136–141.

Wolf, M. J. (1999). *The entertainment economy: How mega-media forces are transforming our lives.* New York: Times Books.

Zillmann, D., & Bryant, J. (1994). Entertainment as media effect. In J. Bryant & D. Zillmann (Eds.), *Media effects: Advances in theory and research* (pp. 437–461). Hillsdale, NJ: Lawrence Erlbaum Associates.

Zillmann, D., & Vorderer, P. (Eds.). (2000). *Media entertainment: The psychology of its appeal.* Mahwah, NJ: Lawrence Erlbaum Associates.

Zuckerman, M. (1994). *Behavioral expressions and biosocial bases of sensation seeking.* New York: Cambridge University Press.

Zuckerman, M. (1996). Item revisions in the Sensation Seeking Scale Form V (SSS-V). *Personality and Individual Differences, 20,* 515.

CHAPTER FIFTEEN

People and "Their" Television Shows: An Overview of Television Connectedness

Cristel A. Russell
San Diego State University

Andrew T. Norman
Drake University

Susan E. Heckler
The University of St. Thomas

Recently, the realization that individual variations exist among audience members has prompted a more in-depth consideration of the television experience. Using a combination of qualitative and quantitative methodologies, researchers have started to explore how television viewers build relationships, loyalty, and connections with "their" shows, with the characters portrayed in the story lines, and with fellow audience members. In this chapter, we review the existing work on these more complex conceptualizations of television consumption and provide an overview of *Television Connectedness*. We present a conceptual model illustrating the types of relationships represented by connectedness and propose a series of theoretical propositions relating connectedness to various aspects of the psychology of the consumption of television programming.

Television audience measurement began many years ago to support the sale of advertising space and to determine the success of programming strategy. For more than 3 decades now, Nielsen has dominated television ratings at the national and local levels with its measures of the audience size of network shows via its *people meters*—electronic set-top boxes that are placed in 5,000 homes around the country (Nielsen Media, 2002). This and other traditional audience measures are often limited to bulky, global TV-watching frequency that only consider sizes of audience segments and measure an audience as only a homogenous sample in terms of viewing intensity (Beville, 1988). However, empirical evidence shows that people define *watching* as everything from "eating a snack while looking at

the TV" to "sitting in a room where the TV set is on, but not looking at the screen or listening" (Clancey, 1994, p. 4) to instances when they might be intensely connected with the programs and the characters in them (Russell & Puto, 1999). Although these consumption experiences are clearly different, such differences are not captured by quantity audience measures.

We believe that viewers of current and popular television series, such as *Friends, ER,* or *The Drew Carey Show,* actually vary greatly in the ways in which and the extent to which they feel any relationship with the television programs they watch. Some viewers may become very connected to a program—visiting *The Drew Carey Show*'s Web site to see how they fare as a fan by playing the *Drew or False* trivia game, asking their hairstylist to recreate *Friends*' Rachel's latest hair color and style, or spending all of their extra cash to dress like the characters on *The Practice.* Others may be regular viewers, enjoying the entertainment of the show but not noticing or remembering many specifics about the characters or the show's story lines. Still others may watch a program "just because it's on" or simply to "pass the time away...when I'm bored" (Rubin & Perse, 1987, p. 258).

Given this potential variation across audience members, the traditional reliance on the overall amount of television watching or audience size as a measure of television consumption seems to ignore important qualitative distinctions in the experience. Specifically, such measures do not account for the fact that audience size is not necessarily related to audience evaluation (Barwise & Ehrenberg, 1987). Additionally, the quantity of television watching does not account for variances in how people watch and the motivations for watching television (Clancey, 1994), emotional/affective responses to television programs (Pavelcheck, Antil, & Munch, 1988), and the nature and strength of the overall individual–show relationships (Russell & Puto, 1999).

CONCEPTUALIZING TELEVISION CONSUMPTION

Existing literature, particularly in the mass communications discipline, provides insights into the different facets of the consumption of TV programming. The uses and gratifications paradigm of communications research, for instance, has identified many benefits that viewers might seek from their television experience. In their research on the consumption of television news, Levy and Windahl (1984) stressed the need for entertainment–parasocial interaction, surveillance, and interpersonal utility. Rubin and Perse's (1987) research on soap operas identified five viewing motives: desire for exciting entertainment, desire to pass time, voyeurism, escapist relaxation, information, and social utility. Lee and Lee (1995) also identified commitment to viewing, mood improvement, informational benefit, social learning, and social grease as some of the key descriptors of viewers' motivations

for consumption of TV programs. Although these approaches have been instrumental in identifying the motivations behind television consumption, they have yet to effectively demonstrate the effects of television on viewers beyond those explained by measures of overall television viewing.

Important insights on television consumption also emerged with the advent of qualitative research methods in the fields of media and cultural studies. Ethnographic researchers, such as Morley (1980) and Livingstone (1990), offered rich accounts of television audiences by exploring how viewers interpret and interact with television programs. Qualitative methods also served to understand how subcultures of consumption develop around television programs, with their rituals, paraphernalia, and participation in collective activities, such as fan groups, conventions, and gatherings on the Internet (Kozinets, 2001).

Collectively, existing research suggests that when conceptualizing the consumption of television programs we should recognize that the experience of television extends beyond the actual viewing experience and involves pre- as well as postexposure phases (Levy & Windahl, 1984). Indeed, in addition to addressing responses that occur during the viewing of a program, such as the emotional arousal or the informational benefits (Lee & Lee, 1995), or even active interactions with the program (Whetmore & Kielwasser, 1983), television consumption involves key activities that take place before watching a program, such as selection and anticipation (Perse, 1990), as well as ways that viewers might use a program after they watch it, such as for its social utility (Morley, 1980). Therefore, it is more important to think of viewers' interactions with television along more complex dimensions than quantity or regularity and to recognize that viewers' relationships with television programs may vary in type and intensity. The contributions of the research serve as the basis for our efforts to define and measure connectedness and its implications.

WHAT IS CONNECTEDNESS?

In an attempt to provide a complex and qualitatively rich view of television audience experiences, connectedness research has identified different types of relationships that develop between viewers and their programs. Russell and Puto (1999) initially introduced connectedness as a multidimensional construct that captures the extent to which a television program influences the personal and social aspects of the viewer's life. Through a qualitative assessment of focus groups, in-depth interviews, and Internet fan forums, they demonstrated that connectedness captured a TV program's contribution to a viewer's self and social identity beyond the mere watching experience. In more recent research, a scale of connectedness has been developed and validated (Russell, Norman, & Heckler, 2004) that focuses on the relationships that individual viewers develop with TV shows and the characters

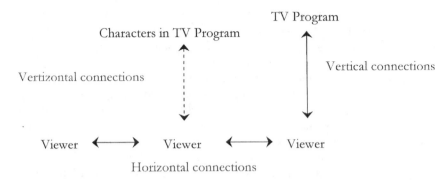

FIG. 15.1   Connections within television consumption.

in those shows. The instrument measures the intensity of the relationships that individuals develop with their television show and thus concentrates on the relationships between the viewer, the program itself, and the characters portrayed in the program.[1]

Overall, this research on connectedness proposes that several types of connections develop with television programs. Russell et al. (2004) established that connectedness can involve connections drawn from self–show relationships as well as those developed with the characters in the show. Russell and Puto (1999) also emphasized the social embeddedness of the television experience and the importance of relationships within the community of viewers. Fig. 15.1 captures these different types of connections and provides a model of the connections that exist within the realm of television consumption. In this model, vertical connections reflect the relationships between viewers and their programs, parasocial (or vertizontal) connections are those that emerge between viewers and the characters in the show, and horizontal connections are those that represent the social relationships between viewers (Frenzen & Davis, 1990). We discuss each dimension in more detail in the following sections.

Vertical Connections: Viewer–Program

Vertical connections are established between an individual viewer and the program itself. Such relationships may be facilitated in various ways. For example, it is common for dedicated viewers of a program to view each and every episode that airs. People typically rearrange their schedules or record episodes of their show to ensure that it is not missed. At the highest levels of connectedness, not only do viewers go out of their way to see each episode but also their emotions might be adversely affected if they miss an episode. In a similar manner, viewing the

---

[1]The scale is available from the first author.

program elevates the mood state of these viewers. Additionally, as relationships with the program develop, viewers characteristically perceive the show as being well written or produced and recommend the show to others. More extreme viewer–program connections may also be manifested in the collection of objects that relate to the show, such as books or pictures.

Horizontal Connections: Viewer–Viewer

Horizontal, or viewer–viewer, relationships form among viewers of the same program. Even at lower levels of connectedness, this type of connection reflects the role of television as a "lubricant to interpersonal communications" (Lee & Lee, 1995, p. 14), providing a way to create or reinforce relationships with others. Indeed, people often watch certain television shows because of their social utility (Rubin & Perse, 1987). Horizontal connections are characterized by more than merely using a program as a topic of conversation. This type of relationship supports the idea that a program can contribute to viewers' social identity (Russell & Puto, 1999). In our research, focus group participants often commented on their favorite programs as being integral to their relationships with friends, family members, and acquaintances. Favorite programs are often watched regularly by groups of individuals and serve as social bonds to others. More highly connected viewers may even become a part of a community of consumption that forms around a television show, whether this is an informal membership to a club or a more formal affiliation with a fan club or regular viewing group.

Vertizontal Connections: Viewer–Character

The vertizontal dimension of the connectedness framework captures the parasocial interactions that viewers establish with the characters. We coined the term *vertizontal* to capture the notion that it entails both characteristics of the vertical dimension, because characters are part of the program, and features of the horizontal dimension, because connected viewers often think of the characters in their shows as real people who live on similar timescales as they do (Fiske, 1992) and with whom they can relate and interact (Newton & Buck, 1985). This type of connection is therefore more than just a character application of the viewer–program relationship (i.e., "I never miss the program because I want to see my favorite character"). Rather, it is characterized by the influence that characters in a program have on a viewer's cognitions, attitudes, and behaviors. Highly connected viewers commonly apply or relate material from the program to situations in their own lives. Such viewers also adopt gestures, facial expressions, and vocal characteristics of the characters on their shows. In addition, aspiration is evident when a viewer seeks out hair and clothing styles worn by their favorite characters and connects with them as if they were real (i.e., "I wish I could be a part of the show" or "I get ideas for my life from the characters in the show").

FURTHER EXPLORATION OF CONNECTEDNESS—THEORETICAL PROPOSITIONS

The conceptual model of the connections within television consumption heretofore presented allows us to develop propositions relating television connectedness to various aspects of the psychology of the consumption of television programming. This next section highlights several key propositions that include an antecedent, correlates, and consequences of connectedness.

Time As an Antecedent to Connectedness

At the core of the construct of connectedness is the notion of relationships. A highly connected viewer has a deeper, more intimate relationship with a show, the characters in the show, and other viewers of the show. Therefore, understanding how connectedness develops can be examined using the literature on relationship development. The transactional philosophy of relationships views them as nonsteady states that are constantly changing (Werner & Baxter, 1994). Time is considered an integral part of the events that shape a relationship, regardless of whether the relationship is growing stronger or deteriorating. A commonly accepted approach to relationship development establishes that relationships pass through a series of stages as they progress from lower to higher levels of intimacy (Davis, 1973; Kelley et al., 1983; Levinger, 1983). Although there is no specified length or even range of time required to pass through each stage, some amount of time is necessary as each stage is experienced. Thus, deeper relationships take more time to form than shallow ones because they have gone through more stages.

If one thinks of a highly connected individual as having a close relationship with a TV show, then what is "close"? One author (Kelley et al., 1983) defines a close relationship in terms of duration of time where the causal connections between the involved parties are strong, frequent, and diverse. Duration is considered one of the primary properties of a close relationship, such that close relationships have endured a considerable length of time. Although the duration of time alone is not sufficient to establish a relationship (various factors affect whether and how relationships are formed), it is a necessary prerequisite. The proposition that time is crucial in fostering connectedness is captured in the following excerpt from one of our interviews: "If you don't keep up with what's going on with these shows, you turn it on and it doesn't mean anything; but if you can keep up on a couple of different shows, it's easier."

The basic concept of time passage applies to all three types of connections in our model. Vertical connections develop through continuous viewing of the show, as has been documented in previous research on repeat viewership (Ehrenberg & Wakshlag, 1987; Sherman, 1995). Specifically, Sherman established that television programs with a continuing story line establish a basis for history and therefore

have higher levels of repeat viewing than those that do not. Similarly, as viewers get to know the characters over time, they become more connected to them. Finally, as viewers' individual connectedness levels increase, they may also engage in more horizontal relationships and share their appreciation and attachment for the show with other viewers. Therefore, we propose that, overall, deeper and more intense levels of connectedness require the passage of time.

Correlates of Connectedness

Gender. The nature of connectedness, and especially the vertizontal dimension, also imply that gender differences may exist. Indeed, feminist theory suggests that female reading style is defined as stronger engagement with a work (Bleich, 1978; Rosenblatt, 1978), and male style is considered detachment (Friestad & Wright, 1994). Female engagement is based on the idea that women are more willing to accept fictional characters as realistic people who act in their own right, whereas men are presumed to look for the reason why the author put them there and made them act the way they do. Similarly, previous research has shown that men and women interpret television programs differently and that women are more likely to invest themselves in and identify with the characters (Stern & Russell, 2001). This in turn is likely to trigger stronger parasocial connections with the characters and overall levels of connectedness. We thus expect that women will be more likely to engage with the programs and characters in the programs, therefore generating higher levels of connectedness than men.

Susceptibility to Interpersonal Influence. In a similar vein, individuals who are high in susceptibility to interpersonal influence (Bearden, Netemeyer, & Teel, 1989) may be more prone to perceive the characters in their programs as referent others and thus develop stronger vertizontal connections with them. If an individual is highly susceptible to the influence of a person in a given situation, that individual will also be more susceptible to the influence of the characters in a program to which they are connected because they perceive those characters as referent others. Therefore, we propose that susceptibility to interpersonal influence will be correlated with connectedness.

Imaginal Ability. The very nature of the vertizontal dimension suggests that certain personality characteristics may make some individuals more prone to engaging in such parasocial interactions. For instance, highly imaginative individuals would be more likely to expand their favorite television characters' lives to other activities or settings. They might even go as far as writing fictional stories about them, as has been documented in previous research (e.g., Jenkins, 1994). One participant we interviewed was actually deeply involved in such fan fiction. She discussed the process through which she and other connected viewers create and

publish *fanzines* (i.e., fan-created fiction stories):

> Some fans produce songvids. People take existing footage from shows and choose a theme or song, and recut it and do their own videos and tell their own stories. It's illegal and underground, but most producers realize that they can't control it. . . . They had no money, so they relied on their scripts instead of special effects. I took some of the producers to lunch during a convention and showed them some of my fanzines, and [they] were very happy to take them. For [them] it was evidence of continuing fan loyalty.

As is clearly the case in this quote, we propose that imaginal ability will be related to connectedness. This is a particularly interesting proposition because previous studies on the relationship between imaginal styles and television use have usually found no association between positive constructive daydreaming and television use (McIlwraith & Schallow, 1983; Schallow & McIlwraith, 1986–1987). What we are proposing instead is that individuals who are high in imaginal ability will be more likely to develop connections to a show because that show provides them opportunities for letting their imagination run wild.

Optimum Stimulation Level. It has long been known that humans can be classified by their need for novel, arousing, or stimulating experiences. The property of optimum stimulation level (OSL) characterizes individuals in terms of their general response to environmental stimuli (Hebb, 1955; Leuba, 1955). This concept holds that every individual seeks to maintain a certain level (or optimum level) of stimulation. When environmental inputs provide stimulation that exceeds the optimum level, a person will try to reduce stimulation by seeking less arousing inputs. When stimulation from the environment falls below the optimum level, a person will seek to increase it. Attempts to increase stimulation have been shown to result in more exploratory behavior (Berlyne, 1960) and the willingness to engage in more risk-taking behavior (Raju, 1980; Zuckerman, Kolin, Price, & Zoob, 1964).

In a media context, a correlation has been established between OSL or sensation seeking and television-viewing motivations. In short, people whose level of arousal exceeds their OSL will seek out less exciting, more relaxing programs to reduce their levels of stress or anxiety (Conway & Rubin, 1991). In terms of viewing motivations, people who are attempting to reduce their level of stimulation will watch television to pass time, escape, or relax. It also follows that if a person trying to reduce stimulation is more likely to explore less and take fewer risks, then such a person would be more likely to stay with programs that are familiar to them rather than switch from program to program.

We propose that OSL and sensation seeking are related to connectedness. As a person becomes highly connected to a show, they not only watch with greater frequency, but they also become more familiar with the show's content and come to know the program and its characters on a deeper level. Low OSL individuals would

remain more committed to that which they know and not take the risk to switch to another show with which they are unfamiliar. In the same manner, we propose that a person with a high OSL would be more likely to sample various programs, watching many different shows occasionally because such individuals have a need for new and, in the novel sense, more stimulating experiences. In short, a person with a low OSL will more likely develop a high level of connectedness with one or more shows relative to a person with a high OSL. This proposed relationship is supported in a more traditional product context by the finding that individuals with high OSLs are more likely to engage in brand switching to satisfy a need for change and variety, whereas those with low OSL are more likely to remain loyal to the brands they consume (Raju, 1980).

Additionally, because low levels of OSL correspond to low risk-taking behavior, the relationship between OSL and connectedness should be affected by the level of perceived risk in switching programs. The perception of risk should be greater as the time spent watching television in general decreases. For individuals who spend little time watching television, television viewing time is a scarce resource. Therefore, for individuals with a low OSL that are highly connected to a television program and those who spend little time watching TV should perceive watching any show other than their show as a greater risk than those who watch a great deal of TV. The latter type of individual would have plenty of time to watch the show with which they are connected and still have time to explore other programs without that exploratory behavior posing the risk of missing the show to which they are connected.

We do recognize a possible exception to this proposed relationship between OSL and connectedness. The very nature of connectedness is based on a relationship that is deeper and more intimate. Although this does not necessarily imply that this relationship will be more stimulating, it is possible that a high connection to a show could satisfy the need for stimulation. OSL research defines *stimulating* as inputs that are novel, unfamiliar, risky, or satisfying to the curious. To the extent that such inputs arouse the senses or emotions, they are stimulating (Berlyne, 1960; Hebb, 1955; Leuba, 1955; Mehrabian & Russell, 1974). We thus recognize that a person with a high OSL might satisfy their need for stimulation through a strong connection with a television program, thus arousing the senses or emotions. However, because OSL tends to be based more on arousal from that which is new and unfamiliar, we believe that high connectedness will account for very little in the way of satisfying the need for stimulation across populations.

Consequences of Connectedness

Development of the Self-Concept. The literature on individual–brand relationships (Fournier, 1998) has theorized that, as such relationships form, people link brand associations to various aspects of the self (Escalas, 2002). The self can be defined by various components, and it has been stated that the most salient

aspect of the self at any given moment is the working self-concept (Markus & Kunda, 1986). Although each individual's self-concept consists of many different roles, aspects, and characteristics, brand associations may become linked to the mental representations that individuals hold of themselves (Krugman, 1965). The extent to which a person uses a brand to construct, cultivate, and express his or her self-concept defines the concept of self–brand connections (Escalas & Bettman, 2000).

One of the main factors that has been linked to the development of self–brand connections is the extent to which individuals engage in narrative processing in relation to the brand (Escalas, 2004). Narrative processing is characterized by the presence of a structure that provides temporal and relational organization and a basis for causal inferencing. In a consumer context, not only does the structure of narrative processing facilitate in the generation of brand associations but also narrative thought is likely to facilitate the integration of brand information from the marketing environment with brand experiences. Because people tend to create their self-identify through narratives about themselves, narrative thought is also likely to create a link between brand associations and experiences and a person's self-concept (Polkinghorne, 1991).

It is relatively simple to conceive of a television show as a brand. TV shows are developed and marketed with specific target audiences in mind. There are many TV shows in a given genre or program category. TV shows consist of names, symbols, features (characters and settings), and characteristics (underlying moods engendered or personality traits that can be applied). Considering a TV program as a brand, we propose that narrative thought facilitates the formation of show-related associations and the creation of a link between a television program and a person's self-concept. As people think about a brand or a television show in narrative form, they become more connected to a show, and show associations are more likely to be used to cultivate and express their self-concept.

Identification and Social Comparison.   As connected viewers interact with their favorite TV characters, the influence they may receive from them resembles that triggered from traditional interpersonal relationships (Perse & Rubin, 1990). Indeed, as the TV characters exceed their textual existence, they become referent others to the connected viewers, providing them with a source of identification (Harwood, 1999; McCracken, 1986), of social comparison (Richins, 1991), and even of inspirational goals that connected viewers choose to work toward (Hirschman & Thompson, 1997). This process is especially powerful with fictional characters because the dramatic nature of TV programming elicits expressions of feeling and verisimilitude instead of counterargumentation (Deighton, Romer, & McQueen, 1989).

Such parasocial relationships develop with characters in TV shows because viewers find them personally relevant and can therefore identify with them.

This personal relevance can be triggered in many different ways: Age group, professional situation or interest, marital or familial situation all contribute to initiating this process of identification (e.g., Harwood, 1999). For instance, in our interviews, we found that medical school students developed deeper connections to the characters in *ER* because they represented the hospital environment in which they aspired to work. Similarly, a young woman reported liking the series *Lifeworks* because she could relate to the situations in the life of the main character—a mom going back to school. The process of identification may also happen as a projection in the past or in the future. One interviewee explained that her mother and stepfather watched *Home Improvement* to "make up for missing those family times." Yet another informant felt a connection to the character Kramer of *Seinfeld* because he used to have hair like him "back in the good old days."

In sum, connectedness triggers a process of identification and social comparison with the characters.

Product Placement Effectiveness. Because of this process of social comparison, connectedness has consequences when evaluating the effectiveness of marketing efforts placed within TV programs, particularly product placements. Russell and Puto (1999) found that highly connected viewers were not only more likely to pay attention to and to be interested in the brands portrayed in their shows but also that they responded more positively to product placement efforts. The following inquiry in an Internet chat room where connected viewers of *Mad About You* meet and chat about their show clearly illustrates this type of influence:

> I just recently saw the rerun where Jamie and Paul buy the tea-colored couch (or is it a loveseat?) for their apartment. Does anyone know if that couch . . . is available at a store or where to get something similar? I would love to find something like it.

Similar Internet postings provide insights into the motivations for such requests. Viewers explain, sometimes at length, how much they relate to or aspire to a character's lifestyle and even emulate it. For instance, connected viewers of *Sex and the City* proudly announced that they were throwing a party for the season premiere and would serve "cosmopolitans and tartinis," products that have become symbolic of the characters' lifestyle on the show.

Because they identify with and compare themselves to television characters, connected viewers are very attentive to the surroundings of their characters and get ideas for their own lives from the lifestyles they vicariously experience through television programs. Many TV program Web sites have capitalized on this phenomenon and provide links to stores where such viewers can order the furniture or clothes they have observed in their television shows. Therefore, as initially proposed by Russell and Puto (1999), we anticipate that connectedness will increase the effectiveness of product placement.

Community Building. Our connectedness research acknowledges that the television watching experience is often a social endeavor because viewers watch TV with friends and family or talk about the programs with others. The relational uses of television include the facilitation of communication based on the show and the use of the television set as a source of interpersonal contact or avoidance (Lull, 1980). Whether viewers engage in joint consumption, watching their shows with their friends and family, or whether the consumption experience is discussed with other viewers at a later point, TV series generate a great amount of word-of-mouth communication and even become a catalyst for community building.

This horizontal embeddedness (Frenzen & Davis, 1990) of the television consumption experience can indeed be such that subcultures of consumption may form around TV shows (Schouten & McAlexander, 1995). These subcultures can form casually among existing social circles as well as formally in the case of fan clubs or specialized chat rooms on the Internet (Kozinets, 2001). Regardless of the nature of the subculture, the joint experience of watching or discussing a program with others can increase the emotional experience through the appraisal of another person's presence and emotional contagion (Jakobs, Fisher, & Manstead, 1997) and thus makes TV programs an important locus of interpersonal influence (Reingen, Foster, Brown, & Seidman, 1984). One respondent we interviewed describes, in his own words, the meaning of such in- and out-groups:

> It was a community bonding thing too. Finding people that had the same interest and quoting it with them. The whole Comedy Central lineup has a following. There's a sort of pleasure derived from finding people with similar sense of shared culture. You share the same cultural reference points. The *Simpsons* itself is very intertextual. If people were getting the same jokes that I was, it means they've seen the same sort of things. Like, the first time the grad students went out to a bar, we played the 6 degrees of Kevin Bacon. In a perverse way, it's fun when you quote things and people don't know what you're talking about. It's community building, like in high school quoting teen comedies.

Clearly, in this excerpt, we sense how television programs can foster a cultural identification among viewers, especially during the developmental phase of the teenage years (Arnett, 1995). Many of our respondents talked about being horizontally connected as requiring a "unique know," as exemplified in the following example of a group of friends connected to the NBC Must See lineup on Thursday nights:

> I've got a large circle of friends and maybe we can't always watch the shows, but we make sure that we get the tape recorder going. I have to actually divi out my tapes, and then I wait for people to watch them and then talk to them.

Because the horizontal dimension refers to social interactions among viewers of the same program, it is likely to be affected by personality characteristics related

to socialization. For instance, introverted individuals may be less likely to admit their connections to certain programs or characters publicly and resort to private consumption or anonymous forums for discussion, as can be observed in Internet chat rooms.

Regardless of the mechanisms viewers use to participate in communities of consumption, we propose that connectedness will lead to the development of such communities.

IMPLICATIONS OF OUR CONNECTEDNESS RESEARCH

A recent *Advertising Age* article urged advertisers to reconsider their media placement strategies because "at a time when America is running from advertising as fast as it can click, advertising return-on-investment depends on a new definition of 'prime time.' To be designated prime time, a medium must be capable of riveting its audience—and that connection must be measured" (Rossi, 2002, p. 16). Clearly, our research efforts echo this call by documenting the need to think of television audiences not in terms of numbers but in terms of levels of connectedness. As we discussed, certain programs may carry relatively small audiences but these audiences may be strongly connected to them, the characters within them, and the other audience members.

At a time of increasing audience fragmentation, a connected audience may indeed be more important than a large audience. As we discussed in this chapter, connected viewers are committed to their shows and invest in them a great deal of time, effort, emotion, and passion. Connected audiences are equivalent to loyal customers, who come back for more, season after season, and who are dedicated to their show and characters to the point where the shows help define who the viewers are, how they behave, and even what they consume and whom they interact with.

Our framework of connectedness suggests many venues for research in the realm of television consumption. An area of further investigation involves the interplay between the different types of relationships developed with and involving TV programs. Although all three types of relationships can certainly coexist, it is conceivable, for example, that certain individuals only watch a show to develop horizontal linkages with other viewers of the show or that certain viewers develop parasocial relationships with their characters as a substitute for real relationships with others, maybe because they do not want to publicly admit that they watch the program.

Implications in terms of marketing practices are evident. At a time of increasingly blurred lines between content and promotion, connectedness is an important predictor of the influence received from consumption portrayals in the television programs, such as product placements (Russell, 2002). Technological evolutions within the television industry also prompt television researchers to anticipate further changes in the nature of television consumption. For instance, Forrester

predicts explosive growth of interactive television, stating that over 60 million U. S. households will be able to interact with their TV programming by 2005 (Lee, 2002). These technologies will make it easier for television viewers to blend their Internet and television experiences together, for instance, allowing them to chat online with coviewers as they watch the show or even instantaneously place orders for items they notice on the sets of those shows. This opens many possibilities for research of how such changes will affect the consumption of television.

REFERENCES

Arnett, J. J. (1995). Adolescents' use of media for self-socialization. *Journal of Youth and Adolescence, 24*, 519–534.

Barwise, T. P., & Ehrenberg, A. S. C. (1987). The liking and viewing of regular TV series. *Journal of Consumer Research, 14*, 63–70.

Bearden, W. O., Netemeyer, R. G., & Teel, J. E. (1989). Measurement of consumer susceptibility to interpersonal influence. *Journal of Consumer Research, 15*, 473–481.

Berlyne, D. E. (1960). *Conflict, arousal, and curiosity*, New York: McGraw-Hill.

Beville, H. M. (1988). *Audience ratings: Radio, television, and cable*, Hillsdale, NJ: Lawrence Erlbaum Associates.

Bleich, D. (1978). *Subjective criticism*. Baltimore: The Johns Hopkins University Press.

Clancey, M. (1994). The television audience examined. *Journal of Advertising Research, 34*, 1–11.

Conway, J. C., & Rubin, A. M. (1991). Psychological predictors of television viewing motivation. *Communication Research, 18*, 443–464.

Davis, M. S. (1973). *Intimate relations*. New York: Free Press.

Deighton, J., Romer, D., & McQueen, J. (1989). Using drama to persuade. *Journal of Consumer Research, 16*, 335–343.

Ehrenberg, A. S. C., & Wakshlag, J. (1987). Repeat-viewing with people-meters. *Journal of Advertising Research, 27*, 9–14.

Escalas, J. E. (In press). Narrative processing: Building consumer connections to brands. *Journal of Consumer Psychology. 14*(1).

Escalas, J. E., & Bettman, J. R. (2000). Using narratives to discern self-identity related consumer goals and motivations. In C. Huffman, S. Ratneshwar, & D. G. Mick (Eds.), *The why of consumption: contemporary perspectives on consumer motives, goals and desires* (pp. 237–258). New York: Routledge.

Fiske, J. (1992). *Television culture*. London: Methuen.

Fournier, S. (1998). Consumers and their brands: Developing relationship theory in consumer research. *Journal of Consumer Research, 24*, 343–373.

Frenzen, J., & Davis, H. L. (1990). Purchasing behavior in embedded markets. *Journal of Consumer Research, 17*, 1–12.

Friestad, M., & Wright, P. (1994). The persuasion knowledge model: How people cope with persuasion attempts. *Journal of Consumer Research, 21*, 1–32.

Harwood, J. (1999). Age identification, social identity gratifications, and television viewing. *Journal of Broadcasting and Electronic Media, 43*, 123–136.

Hebb, D. O. (1955). Drives and the C.N.S (central nervous system). *Psychological Review, 62*, 243–254.

Hirschman, E. C., & Thompson. C. J. (1997). Why media matter: Toward a richer understanding of consumers' relationship with advertising and mass media. *Journal of Advertising, 26*, 43–60.

Jakobs, E., Fisher, A. H., & Manstead, A. S. (1997). Emotional experience as a function of social context: The role of the other. *Journal of Non-Verbal Behavior, 21*, 103–130.

Jenkins, H., III. (1994). *Star Trek*: Fan writing as textual poaching. In H. Newcomb (Ed.), *Television: The critical view* (pp. 448–473). New York: Oxford University Press.

Kelley, H. H., Berscheid, E., Christensen, A., Harvey, J. H., Huston, T. L., Levinger, G., et al. (1983). Analyzing close relationships. In H. H. Kelley (Ed.), *Close relationships* (pp. 20–67). New York: W. H. Freeman.

Kozinets, R. V. (2001). Utopian enterprise: Articulating the meanings of *Star Trek's* culture of consumption. *Journal of Consumer Research, 28*, 67–88.

Krugman, H. E. (1965). The impact of television advertising: Learning without involvement. *Public Opinion Quarterly, 30*, 349–356.

Lee, B., & Lee, R. S. (1995). How and why people watch TV: Implications for the future of interactive television. *Journal of Advertising Research, 35*, 9–18.

Lee, J. (2002, April 4). Interactive TV is finally here, sort of. *The New York Times*, p. G1.

Leuba, C. (1955). Toward some integration of learning theories: The concept of optimal stimulation. *Psychological Reports, 1*, 27–33.

Levinger, G. (1983). Development and change. In H. H. Kelley (Ed.), *Close relationships* (pp. 315–359). New York: W. H. Freeman.

Levy, M. R., & Windahl, S. (1984). Audience activity and gratification: A conceptual clarification and exploration. *Journal of Broadcasting and Electronic Media, 11*, 51–78.

Livingstone, S. M. (1990). *Making sense of television: The psychology of audience interpretation.* Oxford, UK: Pergamon Press.

Lull, J. (1980). The social uses of television. *Human Communication Research, 6*, 197–209.

Markus, H., & Kunda, Z. (1986). Stability and malleability of the self-concept. *Journal of Personality and Social Psychology, 51*, 585–866.

McCracken, G. (1986). Culture and consumption: A theoretical account of the structure and movement of the cultural meaning of consumer goods. *Journal of Consumer Research, 13*, 71–84.

McIlwraith, R., & Schallow, J. (1983). Adult fantasy life and patterns of media use. *Journal of Communication, 33*, 78–91.

Mehrabian, A., & Russell, J. (1974). *An approach to environmental psychology.* Cambridge, MA: MIT Press.

Morley, D. (1980). *The "nationwide" audience: Structure and decoding.* London, UK: British Film Institute.

Newton, B. J., & Buck, E. B. (1985). Television as a significant other. *Journal of Cross-Cultural Psychology, 16*, 289–311.

Nielsen Media. (2002). *What TV ratings really mean* [On-line]. Available: www.nielsenmedia.com

Pavelchak, M. A., Antil, J. H., & Munch, J. M. (1988). The Super Bowl: An investigation into the relationship among program context, emotional experience, and ad recall. *Journal of Consumer Research, 15*, 360–367.

Perse, E. M. (1990). Audience selectivity and involvement in the newer media environment. *Communication Research, 17*, 675–697.

Perse, E. M., & Rubin, A. M. (1990). Chronic loneliness and television use. *Journal of Broadcasting and Electronic Media, 34*, 37–53.

Polkinghorne, D. E. (1991). Narrative and self-concept. *Journal of Narrative and Life History, 1*, 135–153.

Raju, P. S. (1980). Optimum stimulation level: Its relationship to personality, demographics, and exploratory behavior. *Journal of Consumer Research, 7*, 272–282.

Reingen, P. H., Foster, B. L., Brown, J. J., & Seidman, S. B. (1984). Brand congruence in interpersonal relations: A social network analysis. *Journal of Consumer Research, 11*, 771–783.

Richins, M. L. (1991). Social comparison and the idealized images of advertising. *Journal of Consumer Research, 18*, 71–83.

Rosenblatt, L. (1978). *The reader, the text, the poem: The transactional theory of the literary work.* Carbondale: Southern Illinois University Press.

Rossi, D. (2002). Rethink "prime time." *Advertising Age, 73,* 16.

Rubin, A. M., & Perse, E. M. (1987). Audience activity and soap opera involvement. *Human Communication Research, 14,* 246–268.

Russell, C. A. (2002). Investigating the effectiveness of product placements in television shows: The role of modality and plot connection congruence on brand memory and attitude. *Journal of Consumer Research, 29,* 306–318.

Russell, C. A., Norman, A. T., & Heckler, S. E. (2004). *The consumption of television programming: Development and validation of the connectedness scale. Journal of Consumer Research, 31*(2).

Russell, C. A., & Puto, C. P. (1999). Rethinking television audience measures: An exploration into the construct of audience connectedness. *Marketing Letters, 10,* 387–401.

Schallow, J., & McIlwraith, R. (1986–1987). Is television viewing really bad for your imagination? Content and process of TV viewing and imaginal styles. *Imagination, Cognition and Personality, 6,* 25–42.

Schouten, J. W., & McAlexander, J. H. (1995). Subcultures of consumption: An ethnography of the new bikers. *Journal of Consumer Research, 22,* 43–61.

Sherman, S. M. (1995). Determinants of repeat viewing to prime-time public television programming. *Journal of Broadcasting and Electronic Media, 39,* 472–482.

Stern, B. B., & Russell, C. A. (2001). Paradigms regained: Humanities theory and empirical research. In M. Gilly & J. Meyers-Levy (Eds.), *Advances in consumer research* (Vol. 28, p. 177). Valdosta, GA: Association for Consumer Research.

Werner, C. M., & Baxter, L. A. (1994). Temporal qualities of relationships: Organismic, transactional, and dialectical views. In M. L. Knapp & G. R. Miller (Eds.), *Handbook of interpersonal communication* (2nd ed., pp. 323–379). Newbury Park, CA: Sage.

Whetmore, E. J., & Kielwasser, A. P. (1983). The soap opera audience speaks: A preliminary report. *Journal of American Culture, 6,* 110–116.

Zuckerman, M., Kolin, E. A., Price, L., & Zoob, I. (1964). Development of a sensation seeking scale. *Journal of Consulting Psychology, 28,* 477–482.

CHAPTER SIXTEEN

The Interplay Among Attachment Orientation, Idealized Media Images of Women, and Body Dissatisfaction: A Social Psychological Analysis

Dara N. Greenwood
Paula R. Pietromonaco
University of Massachusetts at Amherst

Social psychologists have focused on the powerful impact of the social environment on human behavior and motivation (Milgram, 1965; Zimbardo, 1972), whereas personality psychologists have long emphasized the power of individual dispositions (McCrae & Costa, 1996). Although social and personality psychologists engaged in a heated debate in the 1970s about the relative importance of person versus situation variables for understanding behavior, social-cognitive formulations (Bandura, 1978; Mischel & Shoda, 1995) have reconciled the two positions by emphasizing the dynamic interplay between what individuals bring to the situation and the situational context itself.

Along similar lines, researchers who study the cluttered environment of the mass media have encountered their own variation of the person versus situation debate. Some communication theorists argue that sheer exposure to the mass media uniformly affects how individuals construct and understand social reality (Gerbner, 1969; Signorelli & Morgan, 1990), whereas others endorse a more selective-effects model (Harris, 1999, p. 17) that conceptualizes media use as a function of the individual needs and gratifications that motivate viewing (Rosengren, 1974; Rubin, 1983). Thus, the former perspective focuses more on the effects of media impact (e.g., situation variables) and the latter focuses more on the dispositional factors that shape viewing choices (e.g., person variables). As with the person-situation debate in social and personality psychology, however, it makes sense to integrate the two perspectives. For example, although the cultivation theory of media effects

describes how media function as one large gravitational force, the model is qualified by an acknowledgment that "the angle and direction of the 'pull' depends on where groups of viewers and their styles of life are with reference to the line of gravity" (Gerbner, Gross, Morgan, Signorielli, & Shanahan, 2002, p. 49). Research on media violence clearly illustrates the usefulness of applying both person and situation approaches. Specifically, although studies have documented the generalized impact of violent content on the majority of viewers (Comstock, this volume; Paik & Comstock, 1994), it is clearly important to understand which young boys who play violent video games, for example, are likely to bring a gun to school and to intentionally harm their peers. In this vein, much work has focused on which individual difference variables moderate responses to violent media content. Characteristics such as hypermasculinity (Scharrer, 2001), aggression (Bushman, 1995), and sensation seeking (Zuckerman, 1996) in men have been associated with the tendency to enjoy and be more influenced by media violence. Ultimately, each perspective on media influence is incomplete without the other; it is only by examining the roles of the person, the situation, and their interaction that we may begin to clarify the complex relationship between media content and media effects.

One of the most widely researched media domains in recent years, whose causal explanation lies somewhere in the murky waters between person and situation, is the association of idealized images of female beauty and the body image disturbances that plague young girls and women. This line of research follows from the observation that parallel and marked increases have occurred in both a slender media ideal of female beauty and in the proportion of young girls and women who experience anything from normative discontent with their bodies (Rodin, Silberstein, & Striegel-Moore, 1985) to fatal eating disorders. As with the impact of violent media content, not all women who are exposed to idealized female images in the mass media develop body preoccupation and eating disorders. It is therefore crucial to understand which women may be most vulnerable; how the media and commercial industry may transform relational concerns into appearance concerns, thereby fueling the anxieties of all young women as they negotiate and struggle to achieve an idealized body type; and how particular individual vulnerabilities interact with the information and images presented in the media.

In the first part of this chapter, we briefly review the literature on media exposure and eating disorders and focus on a person variable that may be useful in understanding the nature of this association. Specifically, we propose that a young woman's relational style, as captured by measures of adult attachment orientation (Hazan & Shaver, 1987), may heighten her vulnerability to be influenced by idealized images of female beauty. We then outline some preliminary data pointing toward an interaction among attachment style, media perceptions, and body image concerns. Next, relevant to the overall theme of this volume, we focus on the increasingly ambiguous lines between fantasy and reality and between entertainment and fashion that may lead young women to experience their attachment needs as

body image concerns. Specifically, young women may be encouraged to feel connected to celebrities' personal lives through interview shows and entertainment magazines and even to think of such celebrities as their friends, when, in fact, the relationships are inherently one-sided. These feelings of identification and idealization may then manifest in an attempt to emulate the impossibly perfect and slender appearance of both the fictional characters portrayed by the celebrities and the celebrities themselves. Finally, we examine the social comparison processes that may underlie these vulnerable young women's ambivalent response to media images and ultimately lead them to feel intensely dissatisfied with their own appearance.

MEDIA AND BODY IMAGE

The majority of research examining the relationship between media exposure to idealized female forms and body image concerns has revealed that greater exposure leads to greater body image concerns, but the causal nature and direction of this association remains unclear. Most studies have documented a correlational relationship between the two (Harrison & Cantor, 1997; Stice & Shaw, 1994) and thus cannot determine causality. However, even studies that have experimentally manipulated media exposure have difficulty pinning down causality because such exposure appears to negatively impact those women already preoccupied with eating and weight (Hamilton & Waller, 1993; Heinberg & Thompson, 1995; Posovac, Posovac, & Posovac, 1998). Thus, these correlational data leave open the questions of how and why those individuals become particularly vulnerable. Further, although some researchers have attempted to identify an underlying psychological mechanism linking media to eating disorders by postulating the risk factor of ideal body type internalization (Heinberg & Thompson, 1995; Stice, Schupak-Neuberg, Shaw, & Stein, 1994), this explanation does not provide an answer for why some people are more likely to internalize this ideal than others.

One notable study (Harrison, 1997) has helped to address the question of why some women are more vulnerable, suggesting that self-selected exposure to media images may be the surface manifestation of a more active relationship with idealized images. In this study, women who were more interpersonally attracted to thin media personalities were more likely to evidence eating disorder symptoms, and this relationship held even after the researchers controlled for individual differences in the frequency and quality of media consumption. Harrison concluded, "Young women's patterns of disordered eating . . . are related not only to the types of media that they expose themselves to, but *also the way they perceive and respond to specific mass media characters*" (Harrison, 1997, p. 494, emphasis added). Thus, a more active, relational process may help explain the media—eating disorders link. However, the question still remains: Which women are interpersonally attracted

to thin characters? We propose that women's attachment orientations—the characteristic way in which they think about themselves in relation to others—may shape how they perceive and respond to idealized media images of women. We first provide an overview of adult attachment theory and then explain how individual differences in attachment orientations might influence responses to unrealistic media portrayals of women.

OVERVIEW OF ADULT ATTACHMENT THEORY

Adult attachment theory (Bartholomew & Horowitz, 1991; Hazan & Shaver, 1987), derived from Bowlby's (1969, 1973) formulation of the attachment of infants to their primary caregiver, suggests that children build internal working models of themselves in relation to others on the basis of the responsiveness, availability, and sensitivity of early caregivers. These internal working models are thought to include sets of beliefs, expectations, and goals about the self in relation to others that shape the way in which people think about, respond to, and negotiate their social worlds.

The precise content of individuals' working models is determined by the nature of their experiences with important others throughout the life course. Through positive early experiences with caregivers, people acquire a sense of felt security (Sroufe & Waters, 1977) that enables them to feel protected and valued by others, even when they are alone. If people fail to acquire felt security, they may develop unstable, negative views of self in relation to others. In childhood, experiences with primary caregivers are thought to be central to the development of working models, whereas experiences with peers and romantic partners may contribute to and modify working models in adolescence and adulthood (Zeifman & Hazan, 1997). Research on attachment in adults has focused on adult children's orientations toward their relationships with parents (e.g., Main, Kaplan, & Cassidy, 1985) as well as other close relationships, such as those with best friends and romantic partners (e.g., Bartholomew & Horowitz; 1991; Collins & Read, 1990). (The extent to which specific continuity exists across these developmental stages remains open for empirical and theoretical debate and is beyond the scope of this chapter.)

Individual differences in adult attachment style are captured by two dimensions—models of self and models of others—which yield four adult attachment patterns: secure, preoccupied, fearful-avoidant, and dismissing-avoidant (Bartholomew & Horowitz, 1991). Adults who evidence a secure pattern hold a positive view of themselves and others, and they report low levels of anxiety and avoidance of intimacy in interpersonal relationships. They are able to trust and depend on their partners to care for them and comfort them in times of distress. Adults with an insecure pattern, in contrast, experience some difficulty negotiating anxiety, avoidance of intimacy, or both, in close relationships. Specifically, adults showing a preoccupied pattern hold negative views of self and positive views of

others, and they score low on avoidance of intimacy but high on anxiety. They are eager to seek out and form close relationships but have trouble trusting that their partner truly cares for them and will be there for them in times of need. Adults who show the fearful-avoidant or dismissing-avoidant pattern both view others in a negative way and score high on avoidance of intimate relationships, but they differ from one another in their reported views of self and in their levels of anxiety. Whereas fearful-avoidant individuals hold a negative model of self and steer clear of intimacy because they fear rejection, dismissing-avoidant individuals appear to hold a positive view of self, and they claim that they are content without close partnerships. However, the latter reports may reflect defensive denial (Fraley, Davis, & Shaver, 1998).

In addition to describing working models as beliefs about self and other, some researchers have taken a more dynamic route, endeavoring to assess adult attachment in terms of underlying motivational and behavioral processes. Pietromonaco and Feldman Barrett (2000) posit that the four attachment styles may be distinguished from one another by two related processes: the degree to which the need for felt security is activated and the extent to which interpersonal relationships are used to regulate this need. For example, the attachment system of secure adults may be activated only in times of objective distress, during which these adults will attempt to gain comfort by seeking the support of close others in their lives. The attachment system of dismissing avoidants, on the other hand, may be (defensively) deactivated, preventing them from either consciously experiencing attachment distress or relying on others for support. In contrast to secure and dismissing-avoidant individuals, those with preoccupied and fearful-avoidant styles may experience a hyperactivated attachment system. Having less stable and less positive views of self, they may interpret many situations as threatening to their esteem (Pietromonaco & Feldman Barrett, 2000). The difference between these styles exists, therefore, not in their heightened need for felt security but in the way they cope with this chronic state of arousal. Fearful-avoidant individuals, afraid of rejection, may feel conflicted about depending on others in times of distress. Preoccupied individuals, however, may depend excessively on various others in their lives to gain validation and reassurance. This reliance on others is in line with their tendency to idealize others and devalue themselves.

Adult attachment theory provides a framework for understanding why some women may be especially vulnerable to the deleterious effects of idealized media images. First, although most attachment research focuses on the degree to which adults use actual others in the service of obtaining felt security, new evidence suggests that imagined others, such as those found in the mass media, also may address attachment needs. Women with a preoccupied attachment orientation, who tend to rely more on others to serve attachment needs (Feldman Barrett & Pietromonaco, 2002), then, also may use imagined others in the interest of obtaining felt security. Second, this use of imagined others may render women with a preoccupied attachment orientation especially sensitive to the idealized ultra-thin images projected by

the media and thus more susceptible to eating disordered behavior. This hypothesis fits with clinical and developmental research (O'Kearney, 1996; Ward, Ramsay, & Treasure, 2000) indicating that women with disordered eating patterns are more likely to evidence a preoccupied attachment style. In the next two sections, we discuss how attachment orientations might be connected to media relationships as well as to eating disorders.

Attachment and Media Relationships

> Modern media now engages old brains. . . . There is no switch in the brain that can be thrown to distinguish between the real and mediated worlds. People respond to simulations of social actors and natural objects as if they were in fact social, and in fact, natural. (Reeves & Nass, 1996, p. 12)

Believing the mass media to be an inherently social domain, communications researchers have developed a measure of parasocial interaction (Rubin, Perse, & Powell, 1985), or the degree of perceived closeness experienced by individuals with their favorite television characters. They also have begun to examine how adult attachment orientations might shape the nature of relationships with media images. Although only two studies have been conducted on the topic (Cohen, 1997; Cole & Leets, 1999), preliminary evidence suggests that people with a preoccupied attachment orientation may engage in more intense parasocial interaction than those with either a secure or avoidant orientation. In explanation of this finding, researchers speculate that television characters may provide individuals who show a preoccupied attachment pattern with the reliable, if illusory, feelings of intimacy that they crave in their real-life relationships (Cole & Leets, 1999). As further support for the idea that parasocial goals may reflect real-life relationship goals, individuals with an avoidant orientation were least likely to engage in parasocial relationships (Cole & Leets, 1999).

In addition to providing a direct means of obtaining felt security by functioning as surrogate attachment figures, media characters also may provide felt security indirectly, by enabling vicarious identification with highly valued icons. The phenomenon of deriving pleasure from identification with an idealized other has piqued the interest of both psychodynamic and social cognitive theorists. Rauch (1987), who takes a psychodynamic perspective, suggests that feeling connected to idealized media images may feed a primitive desire to replicate the original parent-child bond, noting that "the subject's need for love and recognition by an other is substituted by an imaginary unified identity derived from the image" (p. 33). This feeling of oneness, derived from actual or imagined closeness with an idealized other, has also been captured by social psychologists (e.g., Aron, Aron, & Smollan, 1992). Aron et al. designed a visually based scale that measures the degree of close self-other overlap, "hypothesized to tap people's *sense* of being interconnected with another" (p. 598). Finally, work on possible selves (Markus & Nurius, 1986) indicates that feelings of self-other overlap may prove to be motivational

in daily life; by fantasizing that we are idealized versions of ourselves, we have the opportunity to simulate and rehearse for various future roles. Following this line of reasoning, attaching to and identifying with idealized images in the mass media may allow insecurely attached individuals to experience, albeit briefly, the felt security that eludes them in their own lives.

Attachment and Eating Disorders

Within the clinical literature, girls and women who have a preoccupied attachment style are overrepresented in eating disordered populations. Both quantitative and qualitative studies have documented striking parallels between the psychological patterns underlying attachment insecurity and body image and eating concerns. Empirical studies have found a link between insecure attachment and relational anxieties in adult relationships and eating disorder symptoms (Brennan & Shaver, 1995; Evans & Wertheim, 1998; Friedberg & Lyddon, 1996; Sharpe et al., 1998). Although two extensive reviews of the literature (O'Kearney, 1996; Ward et al., 2000) caution that the findings do not support a direct, causal relationship between insecure attachment and eating disorders, researchers note that "the overwhelming message from the research literature is of abnormal attachment patterns in eating disorder populations" (Ward et al., 2000, p. 45).

The clinical profile of bulimic individuals, in particular, resembles that of a person with a preoccupied attachment orientation. As mentioned earlier, preoccupied individuals tend to idealize others and seek their approval, while at the same time devaluing themselves and having a low awareness for their own needs and boundaries. Similarly, researchers (Friedberg & Lyddon, 1996; Guidano, 1987) have noted that both anorexic and bulimic individuals have trouble separating their own emotions from those around them and that bulimic individuals, in particular, tend to be overly idealizing of others and concerned with receiving social approval while lacking a sense of self-worth. Although insecure attachment may be linked to psychopathology in general, and thus it may be premature to link specific attachment styles to specific eating disorder symptoms (see Ward et al., 2000), the constellation of findings on attachment, media, and eating disorders merits further exploration.

PUTTING IT ALL TOGETHER: ATTACHMENT
STYLES, MEDIA, EATING DISORDERS

Given the overlap in the literatures on adult attachment style, media consumption, and eating disorders, it is surprising that no one, to our knowledge, has attempted to integrate all three domains of inquiry. Research on media and attachment has yet to incorporate the problem of eating disorders, and research on media and eating disorders has yet to use attachment style as a potentially useful individual risk factor. Finally, research on attachment and eating disorders has yet to include media consumption into the hypothesized etiological models. In an effort to connect the

various associations reviewed thus far, we propose that a preoccupied attachment style may motivate individuals to use idealized images in the interest of obtaining a temporary sense of felt security. This security may manifest as a sense of imagined closeness to, and vicarious identification with, idealized television icons. However, given the inevitable failure of two-dimensional images to generate actual attachment security, and given the ultra-thin body type that currently presides over the television landscape, emotional engagement with television role models may ultimately perpetuate feelings of both relational anxiety and body dissatisfaction.

Preliminary Empirical Investigation

We conducted a study to begin to examine the links between attachment, media consumption, and body image concerns. We predicted that women with a preoccupied attachment style would identify with, idealize, and feel closest to favorite female television characters and, because the majority of female television stars tend to have ultra-thin body types, we predicted that these feelings of identification, idealization, and closeness to a favorite female television character would be associated with greater body image concerns. Participants were 132 women at the University of Massachusetts who were surveyed about their attachment styles, media viewing habits and favorite characters, and body image concerns. Attachment styles were assessed using a multi-item measure (Brennan, Clark, & Shaver, 1998) including both anxiety (e.g., "I worry about being abandoned"; "I need a lot of reassurance that I am loved by my partner") and avoidance subscales (e.g., "I get uncomfortable when a romantic partner wants to be very close"; "I prefer not to show my partner how I feel deep down"). Media questions (adapted from Harrison, 1997; Rubin et al., 1985) were designed to target feelings of identification with (e.g., perceived similarity to) idealization of (e.g., wanting to act/look like), and feelings of closeness with favorite television characters. Finally, body image disturbance was assessed using McKinley and Hyde's (1996) Objectified Body Consciousness Scale and included subscales for body shame (e.g., "When I'm not the size I think I should be, I feel ashamed") and body surveillance (e.g., "During the day, I think about how I look many times").

In keeping with our original assumption about the body types of female characters, the majority of selected female characters (coded following Harrison, 1997) were indeed ultra-thin compared with average or heavy characters. (Unexpectedly, just over half of our sample chose men as favorite characters. However, to focus on our specific hypotheses, the analyses reported in this chapter include only those choosing favorite female characters). It bears mentioning that in TV-land, being average is, of course, a relative phenomenon. For example, although Rachel of *Friends*, the most popularly chosen female character, was coded as ultra thin, characters such as Phoebe of *Friends* and Elaine of *Seinfeld* were coded as average. Moreover, choosing an ultra-thin, female character was significantly linked to both appearance idealization and body shame. Specifically, we found that women who chose an ultra-thin character reported a significantly greater desire to look like that character and higher levels of body shame/surveillance.

Our first prediction, that preoccupied women would report greater attachment-relevant feelings toward a favorite character, was supported. Women scoring higher in attachment anxiety and lower on avoidance (i.e., who fit the profile for the preoccupied attachment pattern) reported the greatest perceived identification with, feelings of closeness to, and wanting to be like and look like a favorite female character. Our second prediction, that these attachment-relevant feelings would be associated with greater body image concerns, was partially supported. Specifically, one variable—wanting to look like a favorite female character—was significantly associated with greater body shame/surveillance. Finally, to replicate previous research, we wanted to test the relationship between attachment style and body concerns. Although we did not obtain the expected interaction of high anxiety and low avoidance, greater attachment anxiety was associated with more body shame/surveillance. When we entered the media variable of appearance idealization into the same regression equation, both attachment anxiety and wanting to look like a favorite character remained significant predictors of body shame/surveillance. The continued significance of both variables suggests that attachment orientation and the desire to look like a favorite media character do not cancel each other out but contribute independently to feelings of body anxiety.

Our findings highlight the underlying relational processes in the media—eating disorders equation. Women with a preoccupied attachment style were most likely to report a constellation of attachment-relevant feelings for their favorite female character. Furthermore, one of these feelings, wanting to look like a favorite character, was significantly associated with body shame. Although we cannot determine causality from these cross-sectional, correlational data, the findings are consistent with the possibility that attachment needs may drive relational engagement with media figures, which, in turn, may exacerbate body image concerns. Understanding the psychological motivations that may provoke preoccupied women to attach to specific media characters is only one part of the story. To understand how using specific media characters in the interest of attachment needs ultimately may lead to greater body image concerns, it is also necessary to examine the way in which the media encourages us to view these super-slim, glamorous stars as parasocial, deceptively accessible friends as well as fashion icons.

THE ROLE OF THE MASS MEDIA

The mass media has begun to blur some critical lines—between the self and other, fiction and reality, and entertainment and fashion—which may facilitate the process by which women with a preoccupied attachment style feel close to and desire to emulate their favorite television icons. Indeed, the very success of a media or commercial endeavor often depends on how seamlessly individuals are able to weave their own lives into those lived by fictional characters on television and in magazines. Moreover, the media and commercial industries also thrive on degree of perceived closeness, identification, and idealization of the real-life people behind

the characters. Ultimately, the more accessible and engaging media characters and personalities are, the more convincing they may be as role models. As research on the concept of transportation in narratives suggests, the more absorbed people are in a story, the more likely they are to hold story-consistent beliefs and positive views of the leading characters (Green & Brock, 2000; Green, Garst, & Brock, this volume). To the extent that the media effectively transports viewers, young women may be more likely to perceive ultra-thin and seemingly perfect female characters as positive role models and attempt to emulate them. However, as we discuss later, it is this attempted emulation of an unattainable and unrealistic body type that may make women with a preoccupied attachment style most vulnerable to body shame.

The very title of the NBC hit sitcom *Friends* is one illustration of a fuzzy boundary created between viewers and the inherently social domain of the media world. *Friends* describes more than the characters' relationships with one another; it describes the relationship that viewers are repeatedly asked to cultivate with the six young characters as we consider them to be our friends. Further, we may also compare the dynamics of our own group of friends to the televised version and wonder who among them is the wisecracking but loveable Chandler or the ditzy but creative Phoebe. Indeed, the ease with which viewers can relate to the cast has been heralded as the reason why *Friends* has continued to hold viewers' attention while other long-running series have lost their momentum. In a *New York Times* article titled "What 'Friends' Has Going for it . . . That 'Ally Mcbeal' and the 'X-Files' Didn't Have," the author explains that, compared with the other two shows, *Friends* was able to "maintain the essential connection between the viewers and the characters on screen" (James, 2002, B5).

But our feelings of empathy and connection to television stars is hardly limited to the fictional characters they play; we also are invited to get to know the actors and actresses behind the characters we see daily in the reliable world of syndication. In a sense, we are given two friends for the price of one. Celebrity magazines and entertainment news and interview programs allow us to experience an illusory intimacy with our favorite characters and the actors who play them. We are enticed to buy magazines featuring a favorite character with promises of gaining access to the details of their personal lives. For example, Courtney Cox Arquette, known for her role as Monica on *Friends* appeared on the cover of *Redbook* with the caption, "The gutsy *Friends* star on how she put a tragic year behind her and opened her heart to love. PLUS: Her secret marriage vow" (June 2002). Just as we delight in being privy to the emotional lives of our actual friends and acquaintances, so we are thrilled to hear the inside scoop on seemingly unattainable Hollywood stars. Furthermore, there is no shortage of this inside scoop with various interview shows appropriately titled, *Intimate Portraits* (Lifetime) or *Revealed with Jules Asner* (E!). Magazine writers repeatedly rely on the language of friendship to construct a sense of shared reality between the reader and a featured celebrity. For example, a recent *Seventeen* magazine cover featured Sarah Michelle Gellar of *Buffy the Vampire Slayer* fame with the caption "Stuff she only tells her best friend" (July 2002). Although these ostensibly exclusive and intimate portraits

extend to males as well as females, it is the media access to female celebrity lives that dovetails so easily and conveniently with the ubiquitous commercial industry of fashion and cosmetics.

The extent to which we are given information about celebrities personal lives and feelings is matched only by the extent to which we are given updates about their latest fashion exploits and cosmetic endorsements. We are continually invited to "go behind the scenes and into their closets" (*People Weekly*, 2002, p. 2), as once again the language of intimacy and friendship is used to promote a common bond between the reader and the featured celebrity. A full page in *CosmoGirl* features the clothing style of the young "Vintage vixen" Christina Ricci with the caption, "You and Ms. Ricci share a fashion philosophy: Thrift stores are a girl's best friend" (2000, p. 86). The page details exactly where to purchase various look-alike articles of clothing and accessories as well as how much they will cost. The use of female stars as fashion billboards is not limited to their real-life personas, however. Young women are repeatedly shown exactly how to emulate their favorite television and movie characters by purchasing a similar style of wardrobe. Sometimes they are told exactly where and for how much they may buy their own version of the skimpy styles worn by favorite characters. Consider for example, the following caption from *US* magazine ("The Sweetest Things," 2002).

> The Sweetest Things: In the looking-for-love comedy *The Sweetest Thing*, best friends Cameron Diaz, Christina Applegate and Selma Blair share more than laughs—they also share a hip, sexy girl's sense of style. Here's how to get their looks with a little help from *Us*. (p. 64)

Less common, but perhaps more alarming, women are sometimes given the opportunity to purchase exactly the same wardrobe worn by celebrity characters. A recent article in the *New York Times* encourages appearance emulation: "In Hand-Me-Downs, Dress Like a Star" (Rothman, 2002, D3). Apparently, in preparation for a new season, wardrobe departments sell the previous season's outfits at more reasonable prices than might otherwise be expected. The article featured the cast from *Sex and the City* and explained how various "flirty dresses" worn by the characters could be purchased at a store in Hollywood. In explanation of the motive behind this type of glamorous vintage shopping, the author notes, "For some . . . the lure is getting designer clothes at fire-sale prices. For others, it is about owning a piece of the dream" (p. D3).

The idea of mixing celebrity with consumerism is not new. As Denise Mann (1992) explains in *Private Screenings: Television and the Female Consumer*:

> By encouraging viewers at home to identify with media celebrities whose lives mirror their own, a new form of celebrity worship is invoked and new form of cultural hegemony is validated—one which constructs women as "consumer allies" by aligning the values of home and family with popular media representations of celebrities. (p. 60)

What is new is the proliferation of single female characters selling a stereotyped image of sex appeal, instead of a stereotyped image of domestic family values. What is also new, and highly relevant to the point of this chapter, is the ultra-thin body type that is a virtual prerequisite for fitting into that wardrobe. Finally, it is worth noting that despite the prevalence of less traditionally feminine roles, such as vampire slayers (*Buffy the Vampire Slayer*) and secret agents (*Alias*) that might intuitively lead to athletic or corporate sponsorship, female celebrities, more often than not, end up as figureheads for appearance-oriented products. For example, Sarah Michelle Gellar (Buffy), whose character rescues the maiden in distress rather than being one herself (Garcia, 2000), does not advertise for martial arts programs but Maybelline. Young girls and women who identify with and admire Buffy as a powerful, feminist role model are ultimately left with a supermodel for a persuasive icon. Young women with a preoccupied attachment orientation, in particular, may find that the only way to feel close to and identify with their favorite female TV star is to attempt to emulate her physical appearance. Their anxiety may thus manifest in an endless pursuit of material consumption that serves the economy at the expense of young women's mental and physical well-being.

SOCIAL COMPARISON PROCESSES: ASSIMILATION AND CONTRAST

The individual difference variable of attachment style as well as the provocatively appealing media environment may, in combination, propel women into body anxiety and disordered eating. But what specific social psychological processes might underlie the route by which preoccupied young women move from inspired idealization to defeated self-objectification? How might we explain, from an empirical and theoretical standpoint, the sequential ambivalence associated with attaching to an ultra-thin female icon, vividly captured by this testimonial obtained by Naomi Wolf (1991) in her socially significant, if controversial, book, *The Beauty Myth*:

> [Women's magazines] give me a weird mixture of anticipation and dread, a sort of stirred-up euphoria. Yes! Wow! I can be better starting from right this minute! Look at her! Look at her! But right afterward, I feel like throwing out all my clothes and everything in my refrigerator and telling my boyfriend never to call me again and blow torching my whole life. (p. 62)

We propose that this double-edged reaction to idealized images might be explained in terms of two different social comparison processes: assimilation and contrast.

Research on the relationship between media exposure and eating disorders has typically referenced the process of social comparison (Festinger, 1954) to explain why exposure to ultra-thin images negatively impacts women's body esteem. The generally accepted theory is that girls and women engage in an upward contrast between themselves and an idealized and unrealistic female body type (Botta,

1999; Cattarin, Thompson, Thomas, & Williams, 2000; Cash, Cash, & Butters, 1983; Wilcox & Laird, 2000). This comparison leads to feelings of body shame and dissatisfaction, which may result from a glaring discrepancy between actual and ideal possible selves (Markus & Nurius, 1986) in the domain of physical appearance. An upward comparison process may indeed explain the way in which media icons contribute to negative body esteem, but it cannot account for the initial feelings of euphoric identification suggested by the previous quote. The lesser known and more recently studied phenomenon of upward assimilation (Collins, 1996) may clarify the positive feelings associated with attaching to images of ultra-thin female celebrities.

Assimilative comparisons manifest in an expansion of self-concept to incorporate the attributes of the comparison target (Gardner, Gabrial, & Hochschild, 2002). Rather than a comparison based on divergent characteristics, as in the case of contrast comparisons, assimilative comparisons are based on points of similarity between the self and the target in question. It follows, then, that the tendency to assimilate with a target should increase as perceptions of similarity increase. Indeed, researchers have found that the more people identify with and connect to an idealized other, the more likely they are to experience assimilation (Brewer & Weber, 1994; Brown, Novick, Lord, & Richards, 1992; Stapel & Koomen, 2000). Further, assimilation with such a target also is more likely to occur to the extent that people experience the target as less distinct from themselves (Stapel & Winkeilman, 1998) and to the extent that they are not explicitly primed to make self-other comparisons (Pelham & Wachsmuth, 1995). These conditions for assimilation appear to be met both by the relational styles of preoccupied individuals and by the ubiquitous mass media environment.

Women with a preoccupied attachment style are highly motivated to feel connected, or even merged, with an idealized close other (Brennan et al., 1998). They are also more likely to experience unstable or negative views of self (Bartholomew & Horowitz, 1991; Pietromonaco & Feldman Barrett, 1997). Both of these sets of variables, self-other overlap (Gardner et al., 2002) and mutable/negative self views (Pelham & Wachsmuth, 1995; Stapel & Koomen, 2000), have been associated with greater assimilation tendencies. Additionally, women, in contrast to men, may experience chronic activation of an interdependent perspective (i.e., greater connection between the self and others), which may be more likely to lead to assimilation than to contrast in social comparison (Gardner et al., 2002). This reasoning helps to explain why, in our research, women with a preoccupied attachment orientation were the most likely to report feelings of identification, closeness, and desire to be and look like favorite fictional characters. But how might the media context or situation also contribute to the initial stage of assimilation?

As we noted earlier, the mass media environment promotes blurred boundaries between self and idealized fictional others and uses the language of intimacy and identification to inspire commercial and appearance emulation. Thus, the stage seems to be set for preoccupied women to experience a positive physical

identification with a glamorous icon. Indeed, Wilcox and Laird (2000) applied the concept of identification, if not assimilation, with an idealized media image as the process by which a young woman may experience "at least a brief moment of pleasure as she imagines that she too is, or could be, as slim and attractive as the model" (p. 279). They also find that the identification process is more likely to occur when women are less attentive (vs. more attentive) to their own personal cues and emotions. This idea fits nicely with our application of upward assimilation to the domain of media and body image, suggesting that low self-distinctiveness leads to a more positive identification. Further, when people are transported or absorbed (Green & Brock, 2000) by a story or character, they are less likely to be tuned in to any potential discrepancies between the self and other.

But what happens when the television is turned off and personal distinctions become more salient? Once people are jolted back from the idealized images reflected by the fictional realm of television and magazines to their own images, reflected in bathroom or dressing room mirrors, the second sequence of media influence, namely, the contrast comparison processes, may be activated with demoralizing affects. As Lockwood and Kunda (1997) point out, one condition of assimilation is the perceived attainability of a comparison target's success on a relevant domain (e.g., physical appearance). Given that idealized images on television and in magazines are, more often than not, the result of personal chefs and trainers, cosmetic surgeons, and high-tech, airbrushing and photoshop techniques, these looks are, by their very definition, unattainable (Kilbourne, 2000). Thus, young women may be blatantly confronted with their own failure to measure up to media standards of beauty and feel a resulting body shame. Young women with a preoccupied attachment style may be particularly vulnerable to these feelings because they may be more likely to assimilate and idealize in the first place. As shown in our own study, women higher in preoccupation reported greater desire to look like their favorite female characters, a variable that, in turn, predicted higher levels of body shame and surveillance.

The idea that both assimilation and contrast processes may be elicited by exposure to the mass media may help reconcile a contradictory set of findings in the literature on media exposure and body dissatisfaction. On the one hand, Cash et al. (1983) found that women were more likely to negatively contrast their appearance with an attractive peer than an attractive model. On the other hand, Posovac et al. (1998) found that young women's body image was more threatened by an attractive model than an attractive peer. The former study explains the finding by noting that "perhaps in the eyes of most of our subjects, peer beauty qualified as a more appropriate standard for social comparison than professional beauty" (p. 354). The latter study however, points out that "to the extent that images depict extreme attractiveness, females are more likely to perceive a discrepancy between self and the ideal" (p. 199). We propose that these seemingly competing findings and explanations may be more similar than they appear. As described earlier, today's media invites us to consider otherwise inaccessible characters and images to

be our friends and thus fools us into an imagined intimacy or parasocial rapport. It is then likely that we may also begin to react to television icons as peers, who typically represent appropriate target comparisons for physical appearance. However, the fictional characters that surround us are inherently unrealistic comparison targets, destined to cause frustration and disappointment when we fail to match up. Thus, both assimilation and contrast comparisons may be implicated in individual women's perceptions of themselves in relation to idealized media figures.

Young women with a preoccupied attachment style, characterized by a desire to merge with an idealized other as well as an unstable view of themselves, may be the most adversely affected by media images. Because they may be the most driven to assimilate with an idealized female character, they may also be the most disillusioned when that imagined assimilation dissolves into very real contrast. The relational anxieties that permeate the personal lives of preoccupied women may not only fail to be resolved through a media relationship but may also be compounded by an increase in body anxiety. Understanding how a young woman's attachment style interacts with the parasocial reality of the mass media has great potential to clarify the media exposure to body dissatisfaction link. Future research should continue investigating the particular associations that emerge among attachment style, media perceptions, and body image concerns and continue examining the intricate interplay between individuals and their social environment.

ACKNOWLEDGMENTS

Portions of this chapter were presented at the 21st Annual Advertising and Consumer Psychology Conference (May, 2002, New York). We thank Linda Isbell, Ronnie Janoff-Bulman, and L. J. Shrum for helpful comments on earlier versions of this work.

REFERENCES

Aron, A., Aron, E., & Smollan, D. (1992). Inclusion of other in the self scale and the structure of interpersonal closeness. *Journal of Personality and Social Psychology, 63*, 596–612.

Bandura, A. (1978). The self-system in reciprocal determinism. *American Psychologist, 33*, 344–358.

Bartholomew K., & Horowitz, L. M. (1991). Attachment styles among young adults: A test of a four-category model. *Journal of Personality and Social Psychology, 61*, 226–244.

Botta, R. (1999). Television images and adolescent girls' body image disturbance. *Journal of Communication, Spring*, 22–41.

Bowlby, J. (1969). *Attachment and loss: Vol. 1. Attachment.* New York: Basic Books.

Bowlby, J. (1973). *Attachment and loss: Vol. 2. Separation: Anxiety and anger.* New York: Basic Books.

Brennan, K. A., Clark C. L., Shaver, P. R. (1998). Self-report measurement of adult attachment: An integrative overview. In J. A. Simpson & W. S. Rholes (Eds), *Attachment theory and close relationships* (pp. 46–76). New York: Guilford Press.

Brennan, K. A., & Shaver, P. R. (1995). Dimensions of adult attachment, affect regulation, and romantic relationship functioning. *Personality & Social Psychology Bulletin, 21*(3), 267–283.

Brewer, M. B., & Weber, J. G. (1994). Self-evaluation effects of interpersonal vs. intergroup social comparison. *Journal of Personality and Social Psychology, 66,* 268–275.

Brown, J. D., Novick, N. J., Lord, K. A., & Richards, J. M. (1992). When Gulliver travels: Social context, psychological closeness, and self-appraisals. *Journal of Personality and Social Psychology, 62,* 717–727.

Bushman, B. J. (1995). Moderating role of trait aggressiveness in the effects of violent media on aggression. *Journal of Personality and Social Psychology, 69,* 950–960.

Cash, T. F., Cash D. W., & Butters, J. (1983). "Mirror mirror on the wall . . . ?": Contrast effects and self evaluations of physical attractiveness. *Personality and Social Psychology Bulletin, 9*(3), 351–358.

Cattarin, J. A., Thompson, J. K., Thomas, C., & Williams, R. (2000). Body image, mood, and televised images of attractiveness: The role of social comparison. *Journal of Social and Clinical Psychology, 19,* 220–239.

Cohen, J. (1997). Parasocial relations and romantic attraction: Gender and dating status differences. *Journal of Broadcasting and Electronic Media, 41,* 516–529.

Cole, T., & Leets, L. (1999). Attachment styles and intimate television viewing: Insecurely forming relationships in a parasocial way. *Journal of Social and Personal Relationships, 16*(4), 495–511.

Collins, N., & Read, S. (1990). Adult attachment, working models, and relationship quality in dating couples. *Journal of Personality and Social Psychology, 58,* 644–663.

Collins, R. L. (1996). For better or worse: The impact of upward social comparisons on self-evaluations. *Psychological Bulletin, 119,* 51–69.

Evans, L., & Wertheim, E. M. (1998). Intimacy patterns and relationship satisfaction of women with eating problems and the mediating effects of depression, trait anxiety, and social anxiety. *Journal of Psychosomatic Research, 44,* 355–365.

Festinger, L. (1954). A theory of social comparison processes. *Human Relations, 7,* 117–140.

Fraley, R. C., Davis, K. E., & Shaver, P. R. (1998). Dismissing-avoidance and the defensive organization of emotion, cognition, and behavior. In J. A. Simpson & W. S. Rholes (Eds.), *Attachment theory and close relationships* (pp. 249–279). New York: Guilford Press.

Friedberg, N. L., & Lyddon, W. J. (1996). Self-other working models and eating disorders. *Journal of Cognitive Psychotherapy, 10*(3), 193–203.

Garcia, L. (2000, Winter). A stake in vampires. *Wesleyan University Magazine,* 3–7.

Gardner, W., Gabrial, S., & Hochschild, L. (2002). When you and I are "we," you are not threatening: The role of self-expansion in social comparison. *Journal of Personality and Social Pyschology, 82,* 239–251.

Gerbner, G. (1969). Toward "cultural indicators": The analysis of mass mediated message systems. *AV Communication Review, 17*(2), 137–148.

Gerbner, G., Gross, L., Morgan, M., Signorielli, N., & Shanahan, J. (2002). Growing up with television: Cultivation processes. In J. Bryant & D. Zillman (Eds.), *Media effects: Advances in theory and research* (pp. 43–67). Mahwah, NJ: Lawrence Erlbaum Associates.

Go behind the scenes and into their closets. (2002, March 6). *People Weekly: Special Celeb Fashion Issue,* 25.

Green, M. C., & Brock, T. C. (2000). The role of transportation in the persuasiveness of public narratives. *Journal of Personality and Social Psychology, 79,* 701–721.

Guidano, V. F. (1987). *Complexity of the self: A developmental approach to psychopathology and therapy.* New York: Guilford Press.

Hamilton, K., & Waller, G. (1993). Media influences on body size estimation in anorexia and bulimia: An experimental study. *British Journal of Psychiatry, 162,* 837–840.

Harris, R. J. (1999). *A cognitive psychology of mass communication (3rd ed.).* Mahwah, NJ: Lawrence Erlbaum Associates.

Harrison, K. (1997). Does interpersonal attraction to thin media personalities promote eating disorders? *Journal of Broadcasting and Electronic Media, 41,* 478–500.

Harrison, K., & Cantor, J. (1997). The relationship between media consumption and eating disorders. *Journal of Communication, 47,* 40–67.

Hazan, C., & Shaver, P. (1987). Romantic love conceptualized as an attachment process. *Journal of Personality and Social Psychology, 52*, 511–524.

Heinberg, L. J., & Thompson, J. K. (1995). Body image and televised images of thinness and attractiveness: A controlled laboratory investigation. *Journal of Social and Clinical Psychology, 14*, 325–338.

James, C. (2002, May 20). What "Friends" has going for it . . . That "Ally Mcbeal" and "The X-Files" didn't have. *New York Times*, pp. B1, B5.

Kilbourne, J. (2000). *Killing us softly 3: Advertising's image of women* [Video]. Northampton, MA: Media Education Foundation.

Lockwood, P., & Kunda, Z. (1997). Superstars and me: Predicting the impact of role models on the self. *Journal of Personality and Social Psychology, 73*, 91–103.

Main, M., Kaplan, N., & Cassidy, J. (1985). Security in infancy, childhood, and adulthood: A move to the level of representation. *Monographs of the Society for Research in Child Development, 50*(1–2, Serial No. 209), 66–104.

Mann, D. (1992). The spectacularization of everyday life: Recyling Hollywood sars and fans in early television variety shows. In L. Spigel & D. Mann (Eds.), *Private screenings: Television and the female consumer* (pp. 41–69). Minneapolis: University of Minnesota Press.

Markus, H., & Nurius, P. (1986). Possible selves. *American Psychologist, 41*, 954–969.

McCrae, R. R., & Costa, P. T., Jr. (1996). Toward a new generation of personality theories: Theoretical contexts for the five factor model. In J. S. Wigens (Ed.), *The five-factor model of personality: Theoretical perspectives* (pp. 51–87). New York: Guilford Press.

McKinley, N. M., & Hyde, J. S. (1996). The objectified body consciousness scale: Development and validation. *Psychology of Women Quarterly, 20*, 181–215.

Milgram, S. (1965). Some conditions of obedience and disobedience to authority. *Human Relations, 18*, 57–76.

Mischel, W., & Shoda, Y. (1995). A cognitive-affective system theory of personality: Reconceptualizing situations, dispositions, dynamics, and invariance in personality structure. *Psychological Review, 102*, 246–286.

O'Kearney, R. (1996). Attachment disruption in anorexia nervosa and bulimia nervosa: A review of theory and empirical research. *International Journal of Eating Disorders, 20*, 115–127.

Paik H., & Comstock, G. (1994). The effects of media violence on anti-social behavior: A meta-analysis. *Communication Research, 21*, 516–546.

Pelham, B. W., & Wachsmuth, J. O. (1995). The waxing and waning of the social self: assimilation and contrast in social comparison. *Journal of Personality and Social Psychology, 69*, 825–838.

Pietromonaco, P. R., & Feldman Barrett, L. (1997). Working models of attachment and daily social interactions. *Journal of Personality and Social Psychology, 73*, 1409–1423.

Pietromonaco, P. R., & Feldman Barrett, L. (2000). The internal working models concept: What do we really know about the self in relation to others? *Review of General Psychology, 4*, 155–175.

Pietromonaco, P. R., & Feldman Barrett, L. (2003). *What can you do for me?: Attachment style and motives for valuing partners*. Manuscript under review.

Posovac, H. D., Posovac, S. S., & Posovac, E. J. (1998). Exposure to media images of female attractiveness and concern with body weight among young women. *Sex Roles, 38*, 187–201.

Rauch, A. (1987). I and the (m)other. Why the ego's narcissism can be exploited by the media. *Literature and psychology*, 27–37.

Redbook (June 2002). Cover.

Reeves, B., & Nass, C. (1996). *The media equation: How people treat computers, television, and new media like real people and places*. New York: Cambridge University Press.

Rodin, J., Silberstein, L. R., & Striegel-Moore, R. H. (1985). Women and weight: A normative discontent. In T. B. Sonderegger (Ed.), *Nebraska Symposium on motivation: Vol. 32. Psychoolgy and gender* (pp. 267–307). Lincoln: University of Nebraska Press.

Rosengren, K. E. (1974). Uses and gratifications: A paradigm outlined. In J. G. Blumler & E. Katz (Eds.), *The uses of mass communications: Current perspectives on gratifications research* (pp. 269–286). Beverly Hills, CA: Sage.

Rothman, C. (2002, May 31). In hand-me-downs, dress like a star. *The New York Times*, p. D3.

Rubin, A. M., Perse, E. M., & Powell, R. A. (1985). Loneliness, parasocial interaction, and local television news viewing. *Human Communication Research, 12*, 155–180.

Rubin, A. M. (1983). Television uses and gratifications: The interactions of viewing patterns and motivations, *Journal of Broadcasting, 27*, 37–51.

Scharrer, E. (2001). Men, muscles, and machismo: The relationship between television exposure and aggression in the presence of hypermasculinity. *Media Psychology, 3*, 159–188.

Seventeen (July 2002). Cover.

Sharpe, T. M., Killen, J. D., Bryson, S. W., Shisslak, C. M., Estes, L. S., Gray, N. et al. (1998). Attachment style and weight concerns in adolescent and pre-adolescent girls. *International Journal of Eating Disorders, 23*, 39–44.

Signorelli, N., & Morgan, M. (Eds.). (1990). *Cultivation anlaysis: New directionsi n media effects research*. Newbury Park, CA: Sage.

Sroufe, L. A., & Waters, E. (1977). Attachment as an organizational construct. *Child Development, 48*, 1184–1199.

Stapel, D. A., & Koomen, W. (2000). Distinctness of others, mutability of selves: Their impact of self evaluations. *Journal of Personality and Social Psychology, 79*, 1068–1087.

Stapel, D. A., & Winkeilman, P. (1998). Assimilation and contrast as a function of context-target similarity, distinctness, and dimensional relevance. *Personality and Social Psychology Bulletin, 24*, 634–646.

Stice, E., Schupak-Neuberg, E., Shaw, H. E. & Stein, R. I. (1994). Relation of media exposure to eating disorder symptomatology: An examination of mediating mechanisms. *Journal of Abnormal Psychology, 103*, 836–840.

Stice, E., & Shaw, H. E. (1994). Adverse effects of the media portrayed thin-ideal on women and linkages to bulimic symptomatolgy. *Journal of Social and Clinical Psychology, 13*, 288–308.

The sweetest things. (2002, May 6). *Us Magazine*, 64.

Vintage vixen. (2002, August). *CosmoGirl*, 89.

Ward, A., Ramsay, R., & Treasure, J. (2000). Attachment research in eating disorders. *British Journal of Medical Psychology, 73*, 35–51.

Wilcox, K., & Laird, J. (2000). The impact of media images of super-slender women on women's self esteem: Identification, social comparison, and self-perception. *Journal of Research in Personality, 34*, 278–286.

Wolf, N. (1991). *The beauty myth: How images of beauty are used against women*. New York: DoubleDay.

Zeifman, D., & Hazan, C. (1997). A process model of adult attachment formation. In S. Duck (Eds.), *Handbook of personal relationships* (2nd ed., pp. 179–195). Chichester, UK: Wiley.

Zimbardo, P. G. (producer). (1972). The Stanford prison experiment [Slide/tape presentation]. (Available from P. G. Zimbardo, Inc., P.O. Box 4395, Stanford, CA, 94305).

Zuckerman, M. (1996). Sensation seeking and the taste for vicarious horror. In J. B. Weaver & R. Tamborini (Eds.), *Horror films: Current research on audience preferences and reactions* (pp. 147–160). Mahwah, NJ: Lawrence Erlbaum Associates.

CHAPTER SEVENTEEN

Marketing Through Sports Entertainment: A Functional Approach

Scott Jones
Colleen Bee
Rick Burton
Lynn R. Kahle
University of Oregon

The central objectives of this chapter are to explore the factors that make sport a unique entertainment medium for marketing communications and to place the factors into a theoretical context. Sport is an important type of entertainment with some special characteristics that imply a need for a sophisticated understanding of how it operates psychologically. Sporting events are characterized by an inherent intensity that is central to its entertainment function, and the source of this intensity is the competition for a limited resource—winning. Sport fans seek to affiliate with teams and players characterized by associations that they view as desirable, such as winning. After addressing these issues, the chapter then turns to the unique psychological consequences derived through sport properties, such as compliance, identification, and internalization. Through this description of the sport product and sport fans, we focus on the reasons a company seeks to align with sport properties. Sponsorship, hospitality, endorsement, product placement, and the Internet are presented as tactics employed by marketing practitioners in an effort to market their product through sport.

THE UNIQUE NATURE OF THE SPORT PRODUCT

Sports are a compelling form of entertainment because of their unique nature. Sports products are "either the entertainment of competition or a product/service associated with the excitement of the event, or both" (Schaaf, 1995, p. 22). The

primary product of the sports industry is the sporting event (Shank, 1999). The sporting event may be distinguished as the primary product because all related products and services (e.g., licensed merchandise, stadium concessions, sponsorships, athletes) are contingent on the existence of the event.

A sporting event is characterized by a number of tangible and intangible features. The tangible features vary widely and include services ranging from food services to parking; however, the features that make the sporting event product unique are best described as intangibles. The appeal of the product rests on the uncertainty of the game's outcome, which can have a profound effect on the consumer who experiences sporting events as "a *hedonistic experience* [italics added] in which the event itself elicits a sense of *drama*" (Madrigal, 1995, p. 206).

The characterization of a sporting event as a hedonic experience is consistent with the research of Hirschman and Holbrook (1982). Hedonic consumption refers to the multisensory and emotive aspects of consumption. Sporting events provide multisensory images such as the sights, sounds, smells, and traditions of attending a live sporting event or watching the event on television. These multisensory images may be thought of as both historic and fantasy. For example, a person attending a Boston Red Sox game at Fenway Park may invoke historic memories of attending games as a child or entertain fantasies, such as how it may feel to witness the Red Sox's win a World Series, or both. In addition to the development of multisensory images, sporting events are sources of arousal of hedonic emotions, such as fear, hope, joy, and rage (Hirschman & Holbrook, 1982). Holbrook (1980) posited that the search for emotional arousal is a major motivation for the consumption of sporting events.

Within the hedonic framework, the dynamic interaction between consumer and producer is especially important because the reaction of the audience can influence the performance (Hirschman & Holbrook, 1982). Sport fans seek to enhance the perception that they are involved in the game's production. Further, fans may directly influence the outcome of the game by providing a hostile environment for one player or team (e.g., crowd noise, "getting inside an opponents head"). The research of Tutko and Richards (1971) supports the proposal that fans influence the emotions and motivations of players (Sloan, 1989). In this sense, sport fans play an important role by both attending and participating in the performance of a sporting event (Deighton, 1992).

Players, teams, and their fans share a common objective, a winning outcome; however, winning in sport is a limited resource. From the perspective of players and teams, just as many competitors fall short of the objective of winning as those who achieve it. From the perspective of the sport fan, the desire to associate with a winning outcome is a source for the hedonic components of the product. For example, the emotive aspects of the product reflect the highs and lows associated with winning and losing. Further, many of the multisensory fantasy images one may expect a sport fan to hold are related to successful on-field performance. Therefore, the competition for a successful outcome combined with the unscripted and

unpredictable nature of the outcome are key contributors to the drama associated with the sporting event product.

FANS SEEK TO AFFILIATE WITH SPORT HEROES AND PROPERTIES

Sport fans seek to affiliate with teams or players for a variety of reasons. For example, affiliation can be based on desirable associations that enhance self-concept or provide extrinsic rewards, such as public acknowledgment and support. Additionally, sport fans form associations as a result of their inherent beliefs about particular sports, teams, or players.

Kelman's (1958) functional theory recognizes three different levels of attitudinal motivations for affiliation: compliance, identification, and internalization. *Compliance* is the result of group or individual influence, in which case a sport fan gives in to influence because he or she gains rewards or avoids punishment. The second level of influence, *identification*, occurs when a fan wants to maintain or enhance his or her image through relationships with a sport hero or property. *Internalization* is the result of shared values and beliefs. In contrast to compliance and identification, it is more enduring and long term. We now consider each of these more carefully.

Compliance

Compliance is the least engaging level in functional theory (Kelman, 1961). In the context of sport, this influence could be the formation of affiliations with a particular sport, player, or team to gain public approval and acknowledgment. This influence could also result in a disassociation with a sport, player, or team to avoid negative consequences and public embarrassment. Due to the social nature of this influence, the individual is looking for a favorable reaction from another person or group. As the most superficial level of social influence, compliance-related change is only the result of public acknowledgment of the behavior. In this case, sport fans participate in this type of behavior (i.e., attend a game) because of their need for a favorable response, not necessarily because they truly believe or support the action. Additionally, this action will be exhibited only when the referent individual or group is present and observes the action (Kelman, 1958, 1974).

Compliance can have important implications for marketing. Much of the sport-centered hospitality aims to develop compliance into a marketing relationship. Often major corporations entertain clients at sporting events, hoping to use compliance in attendance as a vehicle to improve fan relationships (Kahle, Elton, & Kambara, 1997).

Identification

The desire to associate with winning is one reason why sport fans identify with sport properties. "While there are clearly aesthetic pleasures in merely watching a sport performance, the real intensity comes from identifying with an individual

or team as they strive to win" (Whannel, 1992, p. 200). Identification may be described as a psychological orientation of the self whereby individuals define themselves in terms of their group membership and derive "strength and a sense of identity" from the affiliation (Kelman, 1961, p. 64). Fans often view a team or a player as an extension of their self (Kahle, Duncan, Dalakas, & Aiken, 2001). It is this identification motive that often leads consumers to form psychological alliances with sport heroes and properties.

The desire to create an extension of the self through identification with a team or player provides a foundation for understanding many of the unique psychological processes associated with sport fans. Identification has been studied quite extensively in the context of sport fan affiliations. Studies have found that consumers of sport identify with their favorite teams and players to the extent that they attempt to proclaim affiliation even when they in no way had a hand in the team's success. Basking in Reflected Glory (BIRGing; Cialdini, Borden, Thorne, Walker, Freeman, & Sloan, 1976) refers to the tendency of individuals to display a connection with a winning team. Further, research by Wann and Branscombe (1990) discovered that fans with low team identification were more apt to disassociate themselves from a losing team. Snyder, Higgins, and Stucky (1983) describe an image-protection tactic through which a low-identification fan disassociates from a losing team. The researchers labeled this phenomenon as Cutting Off Reflected Failure (CORFing). This finding is held as support for the fair weather fan phenomenon.

A sport fan, however, may identify with any player or team characterized by associations the fan views as positive. Although the literature cited to this point has focused on an identification with winning, other research has demonstrated that winning is not a required antecedent for identification. The research of Fisher and Wakefield (1998) suggests that fans may identify with an unsuccessful team or player. Fans of unsuccessful teams focus on aspects of the team that are beneficial for their view of the self and ignore information about the team's poor performance. This type of identification motive helps to explain the loyalty fans display for teams traditionally associated with poor on-field performance, such as the Chicago Cubs baseball team and a number of collegiate athletic programs. In this case, fans seek to identify with positive team associations, such as perseverance.

Sport fans who closely identify with a team or player display substantial involvement and may personalize a team victory or defeat. The research of Hirt, Zillmann, Erickson, and Kennedy (1992) demonstrated that game outcome significantly affected both subjects' current mood state and their self-esteem. Additionally, "game outcome influenced subjects' estimates of not only the team's future performance but also their own future performance on a number of tasks" (Hirt et al., 1992, p. 735).

Identification can also be extended from a player or team to involvement in a consumption community (Shoham & Kahle, 1996; Shoham, Rose, Kropp, & Kahle, 1997). People develop identification with communities built around sport, providing a basis of participating in their lives.

Internalization

Kelman (1958) proposes that the third motivational component, internalization, is the result of shared values (cf. Homer & Kahle, 1988; Kahle, 1983, 1996). Sport fan affiliation through internalization is the result of deeply held beliefs that match the sport property. The content of the association between the sport fan and team or player is important to the individual, and he or she then adopts the behavior because of this significance. Internalized behavior is the deepest level of motivation and is less likely to be influenced by extrinsic rewards and image. Sport fans demonstrating internalized motives may value characteristics of sport, such as beauty, teamwork, patriotism, and heroism. Internalized fans view themselves as part of the sporting world. In a sense, they are the most intense consumers.

In summary, the consumption of sporting events is a hedonic experience that involves the consumption of drama. Drama is derived through competition for a limited resource—a winning outcome. Just as teams and players strive to win, many sport fans seek to affiliate with players and teams with positive associations, such as competitive success. Using Kelman's (1958) framework, affiliation can occur at three different levels: compliance, identification, and internalization. Each level implies different mechanisms that have different psychological sources, different arousal conditions, and different attitude change procedures.

One attraction of this functional theory is that it provides a framework for understanding the relation between fan choices and the fundamental perspectives on psychological theory. Each of the three functions corresponds to one of the macro theories of psychology. The importance of rewards and punishments in compliance echoes reinforcement theory (Skinner, 1974) and classic behaviorism (Watson, 1913). Contemporary psychoanalytic theory has moved from the psychosexual motivations that Freud preferred to perspectives such as the identification theory of Erikson (1968). Humanistic theory emphasizes internalization, authenticity, and actualization as the driving forces behind values and behavioral choices (Kahle, 1983, 1996; Rogers, 1961). Functional theory underscores the situational utility of macromotivational theories and provides a framework for thinking about the motivations of fans.

Research

Some research evidence is consistent with the assumption that Kelman's model is applicable to sports marketing. Kahle, Kambara, and Rose (1996) developed a model based on Kelman's theory to understand student attendance at college football games. They found three major paths to attendance motivation, consistent with Kelman's theory. At the two lower levels (compliance and identification), however, they observed a division between internal and external motives. Obligation (internal or private) and compliance (external or public) were two separate motivational constructs at the first level. They were antecedents of an intervening construct, camaraderie. Identification also split into a public or external factor,

called identification with winning, and a private or internal factor, called seeking self-defining experiences.

These two constructs were antecedents of seeking a unique self-expressive experience. At the internalization level, internal or private and external or public are fused and inseparable. Thus, the three motives that surfaced as directly antecedent to the decision to attend a sporting event were named internalization; seeking a unique, self-expressive experience; and camaraderie. Each motive implies different marketing communication efforts.

CONSEQUENCES OF SPORT FAN AFFILIATION

There are several consequences of affiliation by sport fans. These consequences include influences on hostility, biased information processing, and symbolic consumption.

Sporting events may lead to increases in hostility and aggressive behavior. The research of Goldstein and Arms (1971) suggests that fans' hostility was higher after watching a football game, regardless of whether their team won or lost. Goldstein and Arms's results are consistent with more recent research that questions the efficacy of catharsis referring to the release of energy through either participation in or the observation of aggressive behavior (Bushman, Baumeister, & Stack, 1999).

Sport fan affiliation influences information processing. A norm that is posited to exist among sport participants and fans encourages the acceptance of personal responsibility and discourages the externalization of failure. Grove, Hanrahan, and McInman (1991) found support for this norm, leading the authors to conclude this attribution has two functions. First, it permits attributers to present themselves in a positive light, regardless of the outcome of the sporting event. Second, in the case of success, "such an attribution would imply that winning was due to a relatively stable factor that was under personal control" (p. 96).

Further, the consumption of such products characterized by hedonic benefits requires substantial mental activity on the part of the consumer (Hirschman & Holbrook, 1982). Consequently, dual-processing information models suggest that information related to sporting events has a greater likelihood of undergoing cognitive processing (Petty, Unnava, & Strathman, 1991). In turn, an attitude toward a team or player developed through central processing is highly stable and resistant to change.

A final consequence of affiliation considered here is symbolic consumption. A product, such as a sporting event and the related teams and players, provides consumers with more than just functional benefits (Gardner & Levy, 1955; Park, Jaworski, & MacInnis, 1986). Sporting events are a source of social symbols that may influence self-definition (Solomon, 1983). Self-definition has been proposed as an organizing construct through which ordinary consumption activities may be understood (Kleine, Kleine, & Kernan, 1993). This self-definition may refer to

consumers' image of their self-construct or what they envision as their idealized self. Sport fans use products such as licensed apparel, bumper stickers, and affinity credit cards as symbols of their affiliation with a team or player. This symbolic consumption assists in fostering a positive self-concept (Branscrombe & Wann, 1991).

To this point the focus of this paper has been on the role of fans as consumers of the sporting event product; however, television companies and corporations each seek to benefit from affiliation with a given team or league extending the BIRG phenomena beyond sport fans. Perhaps the single largest cause of the growth of the professional sport industry has been television that enjoys a symbiotic relationship with sport. Sport helps to build television and other media audiences, whereas television exposure builds an audience for the sports industry (Wolfe, O'Sullivan, & Meenaghan, 1997). Television companies and sponsors help to enculturate the drama of sporting events within the lives of sport fans through a variety of marketing tactics, including game, player, and team promotions (Celsi, Rose, & Leigh, 1993; Shoham, Rose, & Kahle, 1998).

COMPANIES ALIGN WITH SPORT PROPERTIES

Companies seek to align themselves with sports properties for three primary reasons. First, sports properties deliver an attractive demographic. This demographic may be local, regional, national, or global. Minor league baseball and youth sport programs are examples of local outlets companies may use for local associations. On the opposite end of the spectrum, the Olympic Games and the Super Bowl provide global exposure for allying companies. For example, the organizers of the 2002 World Cup soccer tournament estimated that as much as half of the world's population viewed the championship game.

Further, the growth of women as spectators of sport has been significant in recent years. According to Burnett and Menon (1993), women account for roughly 40% of professional baseball, 39% of professional basketball, 37% of any racing event, 40% of golf, and 58% of skating event viewership. Although certain sporting events may be used to reach a large, heterogeneous demographic, many companies still use sport to target specific consumer segments. In this sense marketing through sporting events is much like magazine advertising; however, with sport the advertisement may include multimedia.

Second, companies associating themselves with sports properties often benefit from a rub-off effect. The associative network memory model (Anderson & Bower, 1973) proposes that knowledge is represented through a network of linked concept nodes that are strengthened each time two events occur together. Consequently, companies marketing through sport may encourage the development of associations between their brand and the associations of a given sport. In this sense, sport acts as an extrinsic cue (Olson & Jacoby, 1972), which may be used

to develop inferences regarding a product, brand, or company (Huber & McCann, 1982). These associations provide companies with the opportunity to link their brands with sports-related values, such as courage and accomplishment (Mael & Ashforth, 1995).

Third, sports properties provide companies and brands with marketing platforms that allow them to achieve strategic and tactical objectives. As Hunt and Morgan (1995, 1996) have argued, some firms enjoy superior financial performance because they currently occupy marketplace positions of competitive advantage resulting from a comparative advantage in resources. Once reached, however, this position of advantage is subject to constant attack as competitors seek to close the gap between themselves and the industry leader (Hunt & Morgan, 1995, 1996). "Resources that are not articulable, not observable in use, and not apprehensible are the longer-term sources of advantage" (Wright, 1994, p. 56). Because they depreciate relatively slowly and are extremely firm specific, the two most important intangible resources are company or brand image and reputation (Conner, 1991).

Consequently, when consumers develop associations with a brand through sport, the association may endure longer than other associations developed through promotion. By means of example, the alliance between Budweiser beer and the National Football League is an illustration of a company that has developed its association into a sustainable and distinct resource (Amis, Pant, & Slack, 1997). The alliance provides Budweiser with access to a large portion of their target market, including the coveted young male demographic. The brand's advertising campaigns tie in well with the multisensory images of American football. The exclusivity of the Super Bowl makes it a sponsorship agreement that is difficult to replicate. The unique historical conditions that have shaped the image (Barney, 1991) would render it very difficult, costly, and time-consuming for another beer company to match the association in the eyes of the consumer, even if Budweiser were to terminate its sponsorship (Bharadwaj, Varadarajan, & Fahy, 1993).

TACTICS FOR MARKETING THROUGH SPORT

Marketers use a variety of strategies and tactics to exploit alliances with sports properties. Marketers may align with leagues, teams, athletes, events, or fans, or align with all groups. Previous research has supported the idea that marketing through sport is an effective strategy. The five alliances most often developed between marketers and sport are sponsorships, hospitality, endorsements, product placement, and the Internet.

Sponsorships

Prior research has found sport sponsorship to increase brand affect and recall (Levin, Joiner, & Cameron, 2001), influence purchase intentions (Madrigal, 2000), and act as a vehicle for brand (re)positioning (Gwinner & Eaton, 1999). *Sponsorship* may include, but is not limited to, the right to use a logo, name, or trademark to

signify an association with a sporting event; the right to provide exclusive service to the event; and the right to conduct promotional activities, such as contests and advertising campaigns.

Two theories that have been applied to explain how marketing through sport may change consumer attitudes and beliefs are balance theory and the halo effect. Balance theory (Heider, 1958) envisions a triangular relationship between three elements: the endorser, the object of the endorsement, and the consumer. The theory specifies that people desire the relations between the three elements to be harmonious and that people may adjust their attitudes to achieve consistency (Lutz, 1991). For example, a belief is out of balance if a lowly valued object is linked with a highly valued object. In terms of sport sponsorship, companies hope that consumers will hold positive associations toward the sport, and, consequently, the consumer will form a positive attitude toward the company (Dean, 1999).

Further, in the case of sport sponsorship, once a link between the sponsoring company and the event has been created and a positive sentiment toward the event has resulted in a similar attitude toward the sponsor, a halo effect (Aronson, 1999) may then suggest to consumers that the sponsor's products are superior to those products of competitors (Dion & Berscheid, 1972). In the case of Olympic sponsors, achievement of a halo effect has been shown to require either a natural or interpreted perceptual fit between the sponsor's product or brand and the Olympics (Dean, 1999). Consequently, an effective way for a firm to increase perceived customer value is to exploit the halo effect and increase brand equity through an association with a sporting event, team, or player (Keller, 1993).

Hospitality

Hospitality in the context of sport is the provision of tickets, lodging, transportation, on-site entertainment, and special events for sponsors, clients, guests, and employees. Sporting events such as the Super Bowl, the NCAA men's Final Four, and the Daytona 500 auto race have become some of the largest social events in corporate America. Corporate use of sporting events is an important mechanism for relationship marketing and personal selling. For example companies may invite a potential client to attend a sporting event and use that time to develop a relationship or describe a product in detail that would not be tolerated during a regular sales call (Kahle et al., 1997). Few other marketing media allow communication on the personal level attained during the attendance of a sporting event. Additionally, the hospitality offered through sporting events provides companies with unique opportunities for compensating and rewarding employees.

Endorsements

Using sports figures as product endorsers has also been shown to be an effective marketing strategy. *Endorsement* is the use of a sport celebrity by a company to sell or enhance the image of the company, product, or brand. Product endorsement using sport celebrities has been found to impact attitude toward an advertisement

(Tripp & Jensen, 1994), increase the likelihood of consumers choosing a product or brand (Kahle & Homer, 1985; Kamins, Brand, Hoeke, & Moe, 1989), and increase the profitability of a firm (Agrawal & Kamakura, 1995). Product endorsements may be explicit ("I endorse this product") or implicit ("I use this product"). The use of athlete endorsements provides an opportunity for companies to associate with attributes not found in other types of celebrities. More specifically, winning, success, teamwork, and community are associations an athlete may offer that other forms of celebrity may not.

Product Placement

Product placement is also a popular strategy for marketing through sport. The users of products placed on television provide an implicit endorsement for the product. The research of Johar (1995) considers the development of false beliefs about a brand including "extrinsic sources, such as *brand usage* [italics added]" (p. 268). When consumers expend effort to process the implications of product placement, the strategy is likely to be more memorable than an explicitly stated endorsement (Slamecka & Graf, 1978). Consequently, when a consumer views an athlete or coach using a particular product, this implied endorsement might lead to greater recall of the brand.

The need to consider product placement strategies to capitalize on the association with sporting events is increasingly important given the technological advances of recent years. Products such as TIVO allows television viewers to omit commercials during taping. Thus, placing advertisements within the entertainment product itself is increasingly important. The search for new tactics for placing advertising within the sport product itself is evidenced by a recent boxing match featuring a casino's Web address painted on the back of one fighter (Borges, 2002).

Internet

The Internet and sports marketing connect quite naturally. The gross demographics within the United States are quite similar for these two communication methods, tending toward educated, affluent young males in each case (Kahle, Madrigal, Melone, & Szymanski, 1999; Kahle & Meeske, 1999). Sport fans often want detailed, specialized information immediately, and the Internet can fulfill that desire more quickly than any other mass medium. From fantasy leagues to individual athlete Web sites, from league information to details about esoteric sports (e.g., canoe polo), the Internet can provide extensive rules, statistics, descriptions, and participation opportunities.

LIMITATIONS OF MARKETING THROUGH SPORT AND SUMMARY

A discussion of the potential benefits associated with marketing through sport is not complete without an acknowledgment of some of the risk associated with the strategy. Companies seeking to associate with a sport property cannot be sure how

the target audience perceives the athlete, team, league, or specific event (Amis et al., 1997). This absence of control is an inherent risk when marketing through sport. For example, insensitive public remarks, an arrest, or a poorly organized event may prove detrimental to a closely associated sponsor. Additionally, companies seeking to align with specific teams or players run the risk of poor on-field performance, such as an extended losing streak, which can influence consumers' perception of the product. Further, the benefits of aligning with sport organizations are dependent on consumers establishing a link between the sporting event and the company. A link in the consumers' mind may not develop if the sponsorship or product placement goes unnoticed or the relationship does not make sense (McDaniel, 1999).

In summary, sporting events are characterized by an inherent intensity. The source of this intensity is the competition for a limited resource—winning. Sport fans seek to affiliate with teams and players characterized by associations they view as desirable. This affiliation with sport properties results in unique psychological consequences, such as compliance, identification, and internalization. Companies may benefit through an alliance with sport properties when positive associations that a consumer holds for the sport product are transferred to the company through their association. Sponsorships, hospitality, endorsements, product placement, and the Internet each represent effective tactics employed by marketing practitioners in an effort to market their product through sport.

REFERENCES

Agrawal, J., & Kamakura, W. A. (1995). The economic worth of celebrity endorsers: An event study analysis. *Journal of Marketing, 59*(3), 56–62.

Amis, J., Pant, N., & Slack, T. (1997). Achieving a sustainable competitive advantage: A resource-based view of sport sponsorship. *Journal of Sport Management, 11*, 80–96.

Anderson, J. R., & Bower, G. H. (1973). *Human associative memory.* New York: Halstead.

Aronson, E. (1999). *The social animal.* New York: Worth Publishers.

Barney, J. (1991). Firm resources and sustained competitive advantage. *Journal of Management, 17*, 99–120.

Bharadwaj, S. G., Varadarajan, P. R., & Fahy, J. (1993). Sustainable competitive advantage in service industries: A conceptual model and research propositions. *Journal of Marketing, 57*(4), 83–100.

Borges, R. (2002, March 3). Why erase ads? There is the rub. *The Boston Globe,* pp. C15.

Branscombe, N. R., & Wann, D. L. (1991). The positive social and self-concept consequences of sports team identification. *Journal of Sport and Social Issues, 15*(2), 115–127.

Burnett, J., & Menon, A. (1993). Sports marketing: A new ball game with new rules. *Journal of Advertising Research, 33*(5), 21–36.

Bushman, B. J., Baumeister, R. F., & Stack, A. D. (1999). Catharsis, aggression, and persuasive influence: Self-fulfilling or self-defeating prophecies? *Journal of Personality and Social Psychology, 76*(3), 367–376.

Celsi, R. L., Rose, R. L., & Leigh, T. W. (1993). An exploration of high-risk leisure consumption through skydiving. *Journal of Consumer Research, 20*, 1–23.

Cialdini, R. B., Borden, R. J., Thorne, A., Walker, M. R., Freeman, S., & Sloan, L. R. (1976). Basking in reflected glory: Three (football) field studies. *Journal of Personality and Social Psychology, 34*(3), 366–375.

Conner, K. R. (1991). A historical comparison of resource-based theory and five schools of thought within industrial organization economics: Do we have a new Theory of the Firm? *Journal of Management, 17*, 121–154.

Dean, D. H. (1999). Brand endorsement, popularity, and event sponsorship as advertising cues affecting consumer pre-purchase attitudes. *Journal of Advertising, 28*(3), 1–13.

Deighton, J. (1992). The consumption of performance. *Journal of Consumer Research, 19*, 362–372.

Dion, K. K., & Berscheid, W. E. (1972). What is beautiful is good. *Journal of Personality and Social Psychology, 24*(4), 285–290.

Erikson, E. H. (1968). *Identity: Youth and crisis.* New York: Norton.

Fisher, R. J., & Wakefield, K. (1998). Factors leading to group identification: A field study of winners and losers. *Psychology and Marketing, 15*(1), 23–40.

Gardner, B., & Levy, S. J. (1955). The product and the brand. *Harvard Business Review, 33*, 33–39.

Goldstein, J. H., & Arms, R. L. (1971). Effects of observing athletic contests on hostility. *Sociometry, 34*(1), 83–90.

Grove, J. R., Hanrahan, S. J., & McInman, A. (1991). Success/failure bias in attributions across involvement categories in sport. *Society for Personality and Social Psychology, 17*(1), 93–97.

Gwinner, K. P., & Eaton, J. (1999). Building brand image through event sponsorship: The role of image transfer. *Journal of Advertising, 28*(4), 47–58.

Heider, F. (1958). *The psychology of interpersonal relations.* New York: Wiley.

Hirschman, E. C., & Holbrook, M. B. (1982). Hedonic consumption: Emerging concepts, methods, and propositions. *Journal of Marketing, 46*, 92–101.

Hirt, E. R., Zillmann, D., Erickson, G. A., & Kennedy, C. (1992). Costs and benefits of allegiance: Changes in fans' self-ascribed competencies after team victory versus defeat. *Journal of Personality and Social Psychology, 63*(5), 724–738.

Holbrook, M. B. (1980). Some preliminary notes on research in consumer esthetics. In J. C. Olson (Ed.), *Advances in consumer research.* Vol. VII (pp. 104–108). Ann Arbor, MI: Association for Consumer Research.

Holbrook, M. B., & Hirschman, E. C. (1982). The experiential aspects of consumption: Consumer fantasies, feelings, and fun. *Journal of Consumer Research, 9*, 132–140.

Homer, P. M., & Kahle, L. R. (1988). A structural equation test of the value-attitude behavior hierarchy. *Journal of Personality and Social Psychology, 54*(4), 638–646.

Huber, J., & McCann, J. (1982). The impact of inferential beliefs on product evaluations. *Journal of Marketing Research, 19*, 324–333.

Hunt, S. D., & Morgan, R. M. (1995). The comparative advantage theory of competition. *Journal of Marketing, 59*(2), 1–15.

Hunt, S. D., & Morgan, R. M. (1996). The resource-advantage theory of competition: Dynamics, path dependencies, and evolutionary dimensions. *Journal of Marketing, 60*(4), 7–14.

Johar, G. V. (1995). Consumer involvement and deception from implied advertising claims. *Journal of Marketing Research, 32*(3), 267–280.

Kahle, L. R. (Ed.). (1983). *Social values and social change: Adaptation to life in America.* New York: Praeger.

Kahle, L. R. (1996). Social values and consumer behavior: Research from the List of Values. In C. Seligman, J. M. Olson, & M. P. Zanna (Eds.), *The psychology of values: The Ontario Symposium* (Vol. 8, pp. 135–151). Mahwah, NJ: Lawrence Erlbaum Associates.

Kahle, L. R., Duncan, M., Dalakas, V., & Aiken, D. (2001). The social values of fans for men's and women's university basketball. *Sport Marketing Quarterly, 10*(2), 156–162.

Kahle, L. R., Elton, M. P., & Kambara, K. M. (1997). Sports talk and the development of marketing relationships. *Sport Marketing Quarterly, 6*(2), 35–40.

Kahle, L. R., & Homer, P. M. (1985). Physical attractiveness of celebrity endorsers: A social adaptation perspective. *Journal of Consumer Research, 11*, 954–961.

Kahle, L. R., Kambara, K. M., & Rose, G. M. (1996). A functional model of fan attendance motivations for college football. *Sport Marketing Quarterly, 5*(3), 51–59.

Kahle, L. R., Madrigal, R., Melone, N. P., & Szymanski, K. (1999). An audience survey from the first gridiron cybercast. In D. W. Schumann & E. Thorson (Eds.), *Advertising and the World Wide Web* (pp. 275–286). Mahwah, NJ: Lawrence Erlbaum Associates.

Kahle, L. R., & Meeske, C. (1999). Sports marketing and the Internet: It's a whole new ball Game. *Sport Marketing Quarterly, 8*(2), 9–12.

Kamins, M. A., Brand, M. J., Hoeke, S. A., & Moe, J. C. (1989). Two-sided versus one-sided celebrity endorsements: The impact on advertising effectiveness and credibility. *Journal of Advertising, 18*(2), 4–10.

Keller, K. L. (1993). Conceptualizing, measuring, and managing customer-based brand equity. *Journal of Marketing, 57*(1), 1–22.

Kelman, H. C. (1958). Compliance, identification, and internalization: Three processes of attitude change. *Journal of Conflict Resolution, 2,* 51–60.

Kelman, H. C. (1961). Processes of opinion change. *Public Opinion Quarterly, 25*(1), 57–78.

Kelman, H. C. (1974). Further thoughts on the processes of compliance, identification, and internalization. In J. T. Tedeschi (Ed.), *Perspectives on social power* (pp. 125–171). Chicago: Aldine.

Kleine, R. E., III, Kleine, S. S., & Kernan, J. B. (1993). Mundane consumption and the self: A social-identity perspective. *Journal of Consumer Psychology, 2*(3), 209–235.

Levin, A. M., Joiner, C., & Cameron, G. (2001). The impact of sports sponsorship on consumers' brand attitudes and recall: The case of NASCAR fans. *Journal of Current Issues and Research in Advertising, 23*(2), 23–32.

Lutz, R. J. (1991). The role of attitude theory in marketing. In T. S. Robertson & H. H. Kassarjian (Eds.), *Handbook of consumer behavior* (pp. 317–339). Englewood Cliffs, NJ: Prentice Hall.

Madrigal, R. A. (1995). Cognitive and affective determinants of fan satisfaction with sporting event attendance. *Journal of Leisure Research, 27*(3), 205–227.

Madrigal, R. A. (2000). The influence of social alliances with sports teams on intentions to purchase corporate sponsors' products. *Journal of Advertising 29*(4), 13–25.

Mael, F. A., & Ashforth, B. E. (1995). Loyal from day one: Biodata, organizational identification, and turnover among newcomers. *Personnel Psychology, 48*(2), 309–334.

McDaniel, S. R. (1999). An investigation of match-up effects in sports sponsorship advertising: The implications of consumer advertising schemas. *Psychology and Marketing, 16*(2), 163–185.

Olson, J., & Jacoby, J. (1972). *Cue utilization in the quality perception process.* In *Proceedings of the Third Annual Conference of the Association for Consumer Research* (pp. 167–179). Iowa City, IA: Association for Consumer Research.

Park, C. W., Jaworski, B. J., & MacInnis, D. J. (1986). Strategic brand concept-image management. *Journal of Marketing, 50,* 135–145.

Petty, R. E., Unnava, R. H., & Strathman, A. J. (1991). Theories of attitude change. In T. S. Robertson & H. H. Kassarjian, (Eds.), *Handbook of consumer behavior* (pp. 241–280). Englewood Cliffs, NJ: Prentice Hall.

Rogers, C. R. (1961). *On becoming a person.* Boston: Houghton Mifflin.

Schaaf, D. (1995). *Sports marketing: Its not just a game anymore.* Amherst, NY: Prometheus Books.

Shank, M. D. (1999). *Sports marketing: A strategic perspective.* Upper Saddle River, NJ: Prentice Hall.

Shoham, A., & Kahle, L. R. (1996). Spectators, viewers, readers: Communication and consumption communities in sport Marketing. *Sport Marketing Quarterly, 5,* 11–19.

Shoham, A., Rose, G. M., & Kahle, L. R. (1998). Marketing of risky sports: From intention to action. *Journal of the Academy of Marketing Science, 26,* 307–321.

Shoham, A., Rose, G. M., Kropp, F., & Kahle, L. R. (1997). Generation X women: A sport consumption community perspective. *Sport Marketing Quarterly, 6*(4), 23–34.

Skinner, B. F. (1974). *About behaviorism.* New York: Knopf.

Slamecka, N. J., & Graf, P. (1978). The generation effect: Delineation of a phenomena. *Journal of Experimental Psychology: Human Learning and Memory, 4*(6), 592–604.

Sloan, L. R. (1989). The motives of sport fans. In J. H. Goldstein (Ed.), *Sports, games and play : Social and psychological viewpoints* (pp. 175–240). Hillsdale, NJ: Lawrence Elrbaum Associates.

Snyder, C. R., Higgins, R. L., & Stucky, R. J. (1983). *Excuses: Masquerades in search of grace.* New York: Wiley-Interscience.

Solomon, M. R. (1983). The role of products as social stimuli: A symbolic interactionism perspective. *Journal of Consumer Research, 10*(4), 319–329.

Tripp, C., & Jensen, T. D. (1994). The effects of multiple product endorsements by celebrities on consumers' attitudes and intentions. *Journal of Consumer Research, 20*(4), 535–548.

Tutko, T., & Richards, J. W. (1971). *Psychology of coaching.* Boston: Allyn & Bacon.

Wann, D. L., & Branscombe, N. R. (1990). Die-hard and fair-weather fans: Effects of identification on BIRGing and CORFing tendencies. *Journal of Sport and Social Issues, 14*(2), 103–117.

Watson, J. (1913). Psychology as a behaviorist views it. *Psychological Bulletin, 20,* 158–177.

Whannel, G. (1992). *Fields in vision: Television sport and culture transformation.* London: Routledge.

Wolfe, R., O'Sullivan, P., & Meenaghan, T. (1997, September). *Sport, media and sponsor: The shifting balance of power.* Conference Proceedings of the Fifth Congress of the European Association for Sport Management, Glasgow.

Wright, R. W. (1994, September). *The effects of tacitness and tangibility on the diffusion on knowledge-based resources.* Best Papers Proceedings, Fifty-Fourth Annual Meeting of the Academy of Management, Dallas, TX.

CHAPTER EIGHTEEN

Sensation Seeking and the Consumption of Televised Sports

Stephen R. McDaniel
University of Maryland

One would be hard-pressed to find a form of entertainment that has blurred its lines with marketing more than spectator sports. Over the years, marketers have become increasingly adept at using athletes, arenas, scoreboards, race cars, blimps, and the ads aired between the action as platforms to promote their brands by targeting sports fans. For instance, in recent years the ads aired during the Super Bowl telecast have become as important to some viewers as the event itself. Likewise, sports properties and the networks that cover them have become brands unto themselves, which has helped to provide them with new streams of revenue through brand extensions (e.g., ESPNzone restaurants, *ESPN Magazine*) and licensed merchandise. Despite the proliferation of what has come to be known as sport marketing, relatively little is known about the psychology that draws audiences to televised sports. This chapter focuses on research dealing with the personality trait of sensation seeking, which is a consumer's individual need for stimulation, and how this might be a factor in audience preferences for viewing certain types of televised sports.

Telecasts of sporting events are one of the most ubiquitous forms of television programming, yet little systematic research has been conducted on the consumption of such entertainment media (Bryant & Raney, 2000). Some studies have suggested that preferences for viewing televised sports are a function of gender and the levels of violence and aggression in different events (Sargent, Zillmann, & Weaver,

1998). However, no theories have been tested that would explain gender-based preferences for sports telecasts. Zuckerman's (1994) sensation-seeking paradigm offers face validity in this context because the trait has been shown to account for variance in need for stimulation among men and women. Most audience research on the sensation-seeking paradigm on television viewing has conceptualized sports telecasts as a homogenous form of programming and has failed to link the trait with its consumption (cf. Hirschman, 1987; Perse, 1996; Potts, Dedmon, & Halford, 1996; Rowland, Fotts, & Heatherton, 1989; Schierman & Rowland, 1985). Previously, only one study in this area accounted for variance in the content of sports telecasts and found some association between adolescents' sensation-seeking levels and viewing coverage of hockey and football games (Krcmar & Greene, 1999). However, recent studies have revisited this tension in the literature, that regarding the relationship between respondents' sensation-seeking levels, estimates of viewing interest, and audience viewing behaviors. These findings and their implications are reviewed herein.

Shapiro (2001) noted that television ratings for all of the major professional sports leagues in North America have declined appreciably over the past decade. This trend has obvious economic implications to sports organizations and those companies who purchase broadcast rights from them or who buy advertising time during such telecasts. Major networks also use sports programming to promote their prime-time programming (Eastman & Otteson, 1994). Because the sports entertainment industry has become more vertically integrated (Stotlar, 2000), understanding the various psychological factors that influence consumption of televised sports should be every bit as important to sport management as understanding what drives attendance at events (cf. Laverie & Arnett, 2000; Madrigal, 1995; Wakefield, 1995). Moreover, Weaver (2000) argued that, given the increasingly specialized nature of television programming and subsequent audience fragmentation, the television industry would be wise to move beyond mere demographic analysis and consider other characteristics, such as personality traits, in analyzing content preferences of viewers.

Although personality research may prove beneficial to the (sport) media industry, it is equally important for scholars to develop a body of academic research on television audiences that is similar in scope to the literature on other forms of consumer behavior, such as sports participation (Bryant & Raney, 2000; Shrum, 1999). Sensation-seeking theory would seem to offer a potentially fruitful approach to begin examining audience penchants for viewing different spectator sports because research suggests it has application in terms of segmenting and targeting consumers for advertising and promotions (Leone & D'Arienzo, 2000; McDaniel, 2001; Palmgreen, Donohew, Lorch, Hoyle, & Stephenson, 2001). Moreover, the trait has demonstrated predictive validity in helping to explain consumer preferences for different types of media and sport participation (Goma'-I-Feixanet, 2001; Krcmar & Greene, 1999; Litle & Zuckerman, 1986; Schroth, 1994; Shoham, Rose, & Kahle, 1998; Zuckerman, 1994).

RESEARCH ON THE CONSUMPTION OF SPORT AND MASS MEDIA

Gender Differences in Enjoyment of Televised Sports

Research on group differences in sport media audiences has suggested that people perceive unique characteristics in televised sporting events and this significantly influences the variance in their viewing preferences and enjoyment (Bryant & Raney, 2000; Bryant, Comisky, & Zillmann, 1981; Gan, Tuggle, Mitrook, Coussement, & Zillmann, 1997; Sargent et al., 1998). For example, Sargent et al. (1998) had college students evaluate 25 sports on several descriptive dimensions and then used cluster analysis to identify nine categories of sports that they subsequently fit into three broad groupings: combative sports, stylistic sports, and mechanized sports. Combative sports were noted to involve direct physical contact between performers and were further characterized as either violent sports (e.g., football, ice hockey) or aggressive sports (e.g., basketball, soccer). Stylistic sports, on the other hand, were characterized as those emphasizing beauty and movement (e.g., figure skating, gymnastics, tennis). Mechanized sports were categorized on the basis of involving the use of tools (e.g., auto racing, golf).

Sargent et al. (1998) applied the typology of televised sports derived from the cluster analysis to study viewing preferences for three different categories by gender. They found that male participants reported a significantly greater level of enjoyment from viewing combative sports than did their female counterparts, and women reported enjoying stylistic sports to a greater degree than did men. Males also reported significantly greater preferences for mechanized sports than did females, but the former did not report enjoying them as much as they did combative sports. Thus, it would appear that college-age audiences may make certain distinctions between sporting events on the basis of the levels of violence and aggression involved, and this impacts their programming tastes. Although the researchers provided post hoc theoretical conjecture regarding the gender differences in their findings, no empirical evidence was offered to support their suppositions. Consequently, they called for further research involving the study of individual differences on older, nonstudent populations, to aid in understanding preferences for viewing televised sports as audiences mature.

Sensation Seeking and the Sport Consumer

Zuckerman (1994) defined sensation seeking as a biologically based characteristic that describes individuals' preferences for and willingness to seek out "varied, novel, and intense sensations and experiences" (p. 27). The sensation-seeking construct has been posited to exist within a broader trait, called impulsive sensation seeking (ImpSS), where impulsiveness and sensation seeking are argued to be interconnected (Zuckerman, 1994). Sensation seeking is part of a psychological paradigm dealing with an innate drive in humans to maintain optimum levels of stimulation (OLS) or arousal (OLA). According to Zuckerman (1994), people seek

out stimuli (such as media) with the appropriate arousal potential (i.e., ability to excite their nervous system). This process helps them to maintain a state that is most comfortable for them based on their individual needs, which can vary according to the biochemistry of their central nervous systems. Studies involving scaled measures of the trait have consistently found significant gender and age effects, which have been attributed to differences in testosterone levels (Zuckerman, 1994). Males tend to report higher levels of sensation seeking than females, and sensation seeking declines over the course of the life cycle in both sexes. Over the years, sensation seeking has proven to be one of the most prolific areas of personality research, and scaled measures of the trait have been found to predict a variety of leisure behaviors, including media use and sports participation (Zuckerman, 1994).

A number of studies have suggested that a consumer's choice of sports activities can be related to sensation seeking, especially those involving risky or so-called extreme sports, such as mountain climbing or skydiving (Goma'-I-Feixanet, 2001; Jack & Ronan, 1998; Shoham et al., 1998; Zuckerman, 1994). Likewise, participants in contact sports have been found to have significantly higher levels of sensation seeking compared with those who reported playing noncontact sports (Schroth, 1994). Although spectator sports may not provide the same arousal as actual participation, Zuckerman (1994) wryly suggested that "for millions of people the excitement of watching their teams compete is the greatest thrill they have except for sex" (p. 156). Likewise, Zillmann (1991, p. 112) argued that television viewing can be highly arousing, depending on the content. Nevertheless, the preponderance of sensation-seeking research on sports-related phenomena deals with participants and not spectators (Zuckerman, 1994). In one of the few studies on need for stimulation and sport fan behavior (in a nonmediated context), Mustonen, Arms, and Russell (1996) examined the relationship between the sensation-seeking trait and propensity for crowd violence in adult male respondents who attended hockey games. Based on samples from both Finland and Canada, they found a moderate positive relationship between sensation seeking and the estimated likelihood that study participants would engage in crowd violence. Such a finding does not generalize to (home) viewing of sports telecasts, however, because the consumption context is different in terms of arousal potential and environmental stimuli, such as crowd noise (cf. Wann, Melnick, Russell, & Pease, 2001). Nevertheless, it suggests that sensation seeking could be a trait associated with males who follow contact sports such as hockey in the same way it predicts participation in contact sports. However, the majority of sensation-seeking research on preferences for viewing televised sports has not accounted for the differences between event telecasts in terms of such factors as the variance in violent and aggressive content.

Audience Research and the Sensation-Seeking Personality

Weaver (2000) noted that the influence of personality characteristics on the uses and effects of mass media has been an important consideration of mass communication research for many years. Likewise, personality research has a long history in

marketing research as well (Haugtvedt, Petty, & Cacioppo, 1992; Kassarjian & Sheffet, 1991). However, the main criticism of personality research in both the communication and marketing disciplines has been the general failure to position such work in a broader conceptual framework (Haugtvedt et al., 1992; Kassarjian & Sheffet, 1991; Weaver, 2000). Consequently, there have been calls for programmatic research, whereby a trait (e.g., sensation seeking) is linked with a theoretical framework (e.g., OLS or OLA) to help understand relevant forms of consumer behavior, such as media use or content preferences (Haugtvedt et al., 1992; Kassarjian & Sheffet, 1991; Weaver, 2000).

According to Zuckerman (1988), "sensation seekers prefer stimuli that . . . elicit strong emotional reactions" (p. 180). Given the characteristics of certain sporting events and the emotional dynamics of being an avid sports fan (cf. Cialdini, Borden, Thorne, Walker, Freeman, & Sloan, 1976), telecasts of athletic contests offer a relatively unique form of television programming that would seem to appeal to sensation seekers (Guttman, 1996). In addition to sports that involve violent and aggressive play, sports-related programming also provides drama that is not scripted, and the uncertainty of outcomes often serves to create suspenseful endings (Gan et al., 1997; Guttman, 1996).

In his review of research on television viewing and physiological arousal, Zillmann (1991) noted that televised sports have been found to significantly elevate viewers' arousal levels. More recent studies on sports fans have also found significant differences in their psychophysiological responses to mediated sport based on their level of involvement with an athlete or sports team. For example, Hillman, Cuthbert, Cauraugh, Schupp, Bradley, and Lang (2000) found subjects who were highly identified with a particular sports team exhibited significantly different physiological (i.e., heart rate and electrocortical) responses to photos of their favorite team compared with their responses to photos of a team that they didn't follow. Likewise, Bernhardt, Dabbs, Fielden, and Lutter (1998) reported finding significant changes in the testosterone levels of males who watched basketball and soccer contests as a function of whether or not their team won or lost (regardless of viewing the event in a mediated or nonmediated context). Other studies (cited in Zuckerman, 1994) have found the aforementioned types of physiological responses to be significantly related to the sensation-seeking trait, and this suggests that spectator sports may indeed provide a mechanism for fans to reach or maintain optimum stimulation levels. However, this notion warrants further investigation before such claims can be substantiated.

According to Perse (1996), the sensation-seeking paradigm offers media researchers a potentially valuable approach to understanding how and why people use television. Likewise, Krcmar and Greene (1999) argued that the trait could be the most relevant variable in investigating an audience's need for stimulation. In fact, a growing body of literature suggests that sensation seeking is significantly linked with audience preferences for certain types of television programs, while significantly influencing other viewing-related behaviors as well (Perse, 1996). For example, it has been reported that participants who exhibited higher levels

of sensation seeking tended to prefer music videos, daytime talk shows, comedy performances, action-adventure shows, and horror movies more than those characterized as low sensation seekers (Perse, 1996; Potts et al., 1996; Schierman & Rowland, 1985). On the other hand, low sensation seekers were found to prefer newscasts and dramas to a greater degree than high sensation seekers (Potts et al., 1996). In addition, high sensation seekers tended to view ritualistically, engage in other tasks while viewing, and change channels more often those exhibiting lower levels of the trait (Conway & Rubin, 1991; Perse, 1996; Potts et al., 1996; Rowland et al., 1989; Schierman & Rowland, 1985).

One potential limitation of existing sensation-seeking research on media preferences has been the fairly inconsistent classification of television content in most studies. For instance, researchers have distinguished between: situation comedies and stand-up comedies (Potts et al., 1996), dramas and soap operas (Perse, 1996), westerns and detective shows (Hirschman, 1987), and morning, daytime, and evening talk shows (Rowland et al., 1989). However, almost all of the previous research in this area has treated sports as a singular (homogenous) form of television programming. Meanwhile, other sport media research has suggested audiences perceive significant differences in levels of violence, aggression, and suspense in different event telecasts (cf. Bryant et al., 1981; Gan et al., 1997; Sargent et al., 1998). The failure to account for the variance in arousal potential of sports telecasts could explain why most of the studies in this area have not found a link between sensation seeking and preferences for viewing such content (cf. Hirschman, 1987; Perse, 1996; Potts et al., 1996; Rowland et al., 1989).

There is evidence to suggest that artificially limiting media content categories has been problematic in sensation-seeking research examining peoples' preferences for other types of media, such as music. For example, Zuckerman (1988) contended that the null findings of Glasgow and Cartier's (1985) study of the relationship between sensation seeking and music preferences were due to the latter researchers limitation of their study to classical music and to only two dimensions related to arousal. In a subsequent study, Litle and Zuckerman (1986) used a variety of music categories and found sensation seeking to be significantly related to preferences for certain music, such as rock and roll, which has the potential to arouse listeners. Their results also indicated that the trait was negatively related to liking other categories, such as Muzak, which tends to be more tranquil. Consequently, it seems plausible that previous studies examining sensation seeking and preferences for viewing televised sports may have been limited by some of the same issues noted by Litle and Zuckerman. The null findings concerning sports content may have been attributable to a lack of content specificity, which obscured the trait's influence on preferences for viewing coverage of certain types of events. Just as categories of music can differ in terms of their properties and subsequent potential to arouse listeners, different sporting events can also vary in terms of the levels violence or aggression involved (e.g., ice hockey vs. skating). And the violent or aggressive attributes of certain sports have been found to differentially

attract and stimulate audiences of televised sport (cf. Bryant et al., 1981; Gan et al., 1997; Sargent et al., 1998).

To date, the only work that has examined the association between sensation seeking and consumption of different types of sports telecasts has been that of Krcmar and Greene (1999). They investigated the relationship between the four individual subscales of the 40–item sensation-seeking scale (SSS form V) and self-reports of adolescents' exposure to coverage of events that were classified as either contact sports (using football and hockey as exemplars) or noncontact sports (using tennis and golf as exemplars). They found that the experience-seeking (ES) subscale was negatively related to male respondents' exposure to both contact and noncontact sports, with the disinhibition (DIS) dimension being positively related to the former type of programming. They also found that boredom susceptibility (BS) was the only subscale (negatively) related to viewing (contact) sports for females in the study.

Krcmar and Greene (1999) provided preliminary support for the notion that the sensation-seeking trait is related to viewing certain televised sporting events. However, it is important to note that their study did not examine the relationship between the global sensation-seeking construct and sport viewing preferences. Instead, the four subscales of the SSS form V were used individually and the reliabilities for two of them (ES and BS) were reported to be below alpha = .65 (Krcmar & Greene, 1999, p. 30). These results are similar to those of Ridgeway and Russell (1980), who previously noted concerns over the reliability levels of the individual subscales. In addition, Krcmar and Greene (1999) were limited in terms of the variety of sports programming content that was covered because the study did not include what Sargent et al. (1998) termed *violent aggressive sports*, such as basketball or soccer. Likewise, it did not include *stylistic sports*, such as gymnastics and figure skating, which are among the most popular spectator sports for women. Despite these arguable limitations, however, Krcmar and Greene's (1999) findings suggest that research investigating the link between sensation seeking and audience interest in viewing televised sports should not treat such programming as a homogenous form of content. Consequently, the varying degree to which different types of televised sporting events might appeal to audience segments (e.g., adult males or females) based on their optimum levels of stimulation was an area that warranted further examination.

RECENT RESEARCH ON SENSATION SEEKING
AND CONSUMPTION OF TELEVISED SPORTS

Building on the work of Sargent et al. (1998) and Krcmar and Greene (1999), a recent study found significant a relationship between sensation seeking and interest in viewing certain types of televised sports (McDaniel, 2002). The study focused on the two categories of sports telecasts found to be most popular with

male (combative sports) and female (stylistic sports) viewers in previous studies (Sargent et al., 1998).

Participants in the study ($n = 305$) indicated their viewing interest for event telecasts, using 5-point single-item scales. For example, NHL hockey, NFL football, NCAA Division I College football, and professional wrestling were all grouped into the violent-combative sports category. Likewise, the aggressive-combative sports category consisted of different types of men's and women's basketball (i.e., NCAA, NBA, and WNBA), and these scores were compiled to create an interest index for viewing that type of telecast as well. Reported interest levels for watching telecasts of figure skating, gymnastics, and men's and women's professional tennis were combined to create a viewing interest index for coverage of stylistic sports. The 19-item Impulsive Sensation Seeking scale (ImpSS) from the larger Zuckerman-Kuhlman Personality Questionnaire (ZKPQ) was used to gauge sensation seeking (cf. Zuckerman, 1994).

Consistent with previous research (cf. Kcmar & Greene, 1999), McDaniel (2002) used separate hierarchical regression analyses to examine the unique influence of ImpSS levels on viewing interest for each of the sport typologies. These analyses were run separately for men and women, while controlling for respondents' age, race, and enduring involvement (Zaichowsky, 1994) with spectator sports. The results suggest that reported levels of interest in viewing violent combative sports were a significant ($p < .05$) positive function of impulsive sensation seeking for both male and female participants. Moreover, interest in viewing telecasts of stylistic sports was found to be a significant ($p < .05$) negative function of the trait for females. However, ImpSS was not significantly ($p > .05$) related to interest in viewing aggressive-combative sports for either sex, nor was it related to interest in viewing stylistic sports for males.

In addition to examining the relationship between viewing interest and sensation seeking, the study also examined the relationship between ImpSS and parasocial interaction during consumption of spectator sports. *Parasocial interaction* has been defined in the communication literature as an interaction between media characters and audience members (Rubin & McHugh, 1987). McDaniel (2002) queried respondents as to whether they yelled at players, coaches, officials while watching televised sporting events. Analysis of variance suggested that those respondents who reported engaging in parasocial viewing reported significantly ($p < .05$) higher levels of estimated arousal while watching televised sports than those who reported not participating in such viewing behavior. Not surprisingly, the former group also found reported significantly ($p < .05$) higher mean levels of ImpSS than the latter group of respondents.

IMPLICATIONS OF THE SENSATION-SEEKING SPORTS FAN

The results of McDaniel (2002) departed from most of the previous studies on sensation seeking and the consumption of televised sports, which have not linked

the trait with viewing televised sports (cf. Hirschman, 1987; Perse, 1996; Potts et al., 1996; Rowland et al., 1989). McDaniel's (2002) findings are in line with those of Krcmar and Greene (1999), who found sensation seeking was related to viewing certain types of sporting event telecasts in high school and college audiences. Thus, it appears that audience preferences for televised sports may vary by personality and subsequent need for stimulation, similar to what has been found for other types of television programming (cf. Krcmar & Greene, 1999; Litle & Zuckerman, 1986; Perse, 1996; Potts et al., 1996; Rowland et al., 1989).

The findings reported by McDaniel (2002) are consistent with other sports media research, which has found that men and women differ significantly in terms of their proclivity for viewing televised events involving violent or aggressive content (Bryant et al., 1981; Sargent et al., 1998). Men reported significantly greater interest in viewing violent sports than women, and patterns of mean viewing interest were reversed concerning stylistic sports (McDaniel, 2002). It is still unclear when these preferences are formed, however, and if or how they change over the course of the life cycle (Sargent et al., 1998). Therefore, future research should attempt to add to the knowledge base in this area because this would inform the sport media literature and add to our overall understanding of the consumer behavior of sports fans.

McDaniel's (2002) findings support Weaver's (2000) contention that audience research should employ both group and individual difference measures when determining preferences for unique forms of programming, such as sports telecasts. The relationships between sensation seeking and interest in viewing violent and stylistic sports are also consistent with the notion of maintaining optimum levels of stimulation through media use (Zuckerman, 1988). Although reported interest in viewing violent aggressive sports, such as basketball, was not related to sensation seeking for men or women in the study, McDaniel found that the trait was positively related to interest in viewing violent combative sports for both sexes. Mean ImpSS scores were also found to be negatively related to interest in viewing the least violent type of sports (i.e., stylistic) for women. Therefore, the research does not tend to support sensation-seeking theory as an explanation for the gender-based differences in mean sports-viewing interest. The directionality of the relationships between ImpSS and women's interest in viewing violent combative and stylistic sports seems counterintuitive because they are significantly more interested in the former than the latter. The positive relationship between females' ImpSS levels and their interest in viewing violent combative sports also runs counter to the results of Krcmar and Greene (1999). However, McDaniel's findings concerning violent combative sports are similar to studies that have found significant positive relationships between scores on the SSS Form V and reported enjoyment of X-rated movies and horror films for both sexes (Litle & Zuckerman, 1986; Schierman & Rowland, 1985; Sparks, 1984, cited in Zuckerman, 1994).

Although McDaniel's (2002) results do not support sensation seeking as an explanation for gender-based differences in preferences for televised sports, they do not discount the potential value of such research in terms of promoting consumption of televised sports. For example, other research has suggested that the

trait has use in terms of targeting audiences (cf. Palmgreen et al., 2001). Therefore, we could extrapolate from his research on sports audiences and previous research on sensation seeking's impact on other aspects of audience behavior. This might help in targeting audiences of different sporting events with ads promoting other programming by mentioning prime-time shows or specials that are consistent with the OLS/OLA levels associated with the genre being promoted. For example, violent sports such as hockey and football telecasts could be used as media vehicles to target high sensation-seeking viewers with promotions for stand-up comedy programs or animated cartoons (cf. Potts et al., 1996). Mentioning television programs and sponsors within the telecasts of violent sporting events might also be a prudent strategy in light of research that has suggested viewers of these events (i.e., high sensation seekers) tend to channel surf (cf. Conway & Rubin, 1991; Perse, 1996; Potts et al., 1996; Rowland et al., 1989; Schierman & Rowland, 1985). Thus, they are less likely to see traditional advertising.

In addition to using sensation-seeking research in targeting sports audiences, broadcasters and advertisers might also use such information in designing their advertisements to make them more consistent with the type of programming in which it will run. For example, research has suggested that the trait is positively related to people's enjoyment of novel and complex imagery and rock music (Litle & Zuckerman, 1986; Zuckerman, 1994). Therefore, airing commercials that use intricate imagery (e.g., quick cuts) and driving music (e.g., hard rock) might be an effective approach to promoting sports such as hockey or football because appreciation for these types of media have also been positively associated with sensation seeking (Zuckerman, 1994).

Another difference between the current study and others on this topic is that it is the only work on audience preferences for televised sports to account for the notion of media affinity, through the use of the Zaichowsky (1994) Personal Involvement Inventory (PII). The involvement construct turned out to be the most influential predictor of viewing interest in almost all genres for respondents of both sexes, which is in line with the results of Conway and Rubin (1991). In addition, McDaniel (2002) departed from most work in this area, as did Krcmar and Greene (1999), by attempting to account for the differences in arousal potential between sports telecasts in terms of violent and nonviolent content (cf. Hirschman, 1987; Perse, 1996; Potts et al., 1996; Schierman & Rowland, 1985). Finally, the sample consisted of a broader age cohort than some of the previous work in this domain, which has tended to employ samples who were college-age or younger (cf. Krcmar & Greene, 1999; Potts et al., 1996; Schierman & Rowland, 1985). Consequently, future research in this area should attempt to add to our understanding of preferences for televised sport and whether such penchants (and the factors that affect them) vary over time as viewers mature (Sargent et al., 1998).

McDaniel (2002) was intentionally constrained to some of the most popular forms of combative and stylistic sports to avoid potential confounds presented by other types of events. Consequently, no mechanized sports were included in the

study because sports such as golf and racing have very different dynamics and arousal potential (McDaniel, 2002). However, it is possible that sports such as auto racing could be attractive to sensation seekers, given the potential for accidents and even fatalities (Litle & Zuckerman, 1986). Moreover, boxing was not examined in the study as part of the violent-combative sports category nor were baseball and soccer listed among the other aggressive-combative sports. Therefore, replications of McDaniel's study should include a broader variety of sports programming content (or focus on individual sports that were not represented). In addition, the potential influence of culture or geographic location should also be a consideration in future studies in this area because tastes for media stimuli, such as sport (or music), might differ as a result of ethnic or regional influences (cf. Hirschman, 1982). Because the arousal potential of media content might differ as a function of personal relevance, a broader array of sports programming (e.g., soccer or rugby) should be included in studies outside the United States to examine this phenomenon in other settings.

In conclusion, the results of McDaniel (2002) support the notion that accounting for differences in certain types of media content, such as televised sports, is important to sensation-seeking research on media preferences (cf. Litle & Zuckerman, 1986; Zuckerman, 1988). Broad media genres do not adequately capture differences in stimulus intensity/arousal potential, such as violence and aggression. Therefore, future studies in this area need to better account for such differences in programming within certain television genres, like those examined here. Moreover, consumer behavior research should also endeavor to examine the influence of sensation seeking in the context of live sporting events because stadium viewing exposes spectators to potentially arousing environmental stimuli that are quite different from watching television at home (Bernhardt et al., 1998; Wann et al., 2001; Zuckerman, 1994). This line of inquiry would not only add to the research literature on the consumption of sporting events but also increase the understanding, which could ultimately prove beneficial in promoting mediated spectator sports and their sponsors.

REFERENCES

Bernhardt, P., Dabbs, J. M., Fielden, J. A., & Lutter, C. D. (1998). Testosterone changes during vicarious experiences of winning and losing among fans at sporting events. *Physiology and Behavior, 65*(1), 59–62.

Bryant, J., Comisky, P., & Zillmann, D. (1981). The appeal of rough-and-tumble play in televised football. *Communication Quarterly, 29*, 256–262.

Bryant, J., & Raney, A. A. (2000). Sports on the screen. In D. Zillmann & P. Vorderer (Eds.), *Media entertainment: The psychology of its appeal* (pp. 153–174). Mahwah, NJ: Lawrence Erlbaum Associates.

Cialdini, R. B., Borden, R. J., Thorne, A., Walker, M. R., Freeman, S., & Sloan, L. R. (1976). Basking in reflected glory: Three (football) field studies. *Journal of Personality and Social Psychology, 34*(3), 366–375.

Conway, J. C., & Rubin, A. M. (1991). Psychological predictors of television viewing motivation. *Communication Research, 18*(4), 443–463.

Eastman, S. T., & Otteson, J. L. (1994). Promotion increases rating, doesn't it? The impact of program promotion in the 1992 Olympics. *Journal of Broadcasting and Electronic Media, 38*(3), 307–322.

Gan, S., Tuggle, C. A., Mitrook, M. A., Coussement, S. A., & Zillmann, D. (1997). The thrill of close game: Who enjoys it and who doesn't ? *Journal of Sport and Social Issues, 21*, 53–64.

Glasgow, M. R., & Cartier, A. M. (1985). Conservatism, sensation seeking and music preferences. *Personality & Individual Differences, 6*(3), 393–395.

Goma'-I-Feixanet, M. (2001). Prosocial and antisocial aspects of personality in women: A replication study. *Personality and Individual Differences, 30*, 1401–1411.

Guttman, A. (1996). The appeal of violent sports. In J. Goldstein (Ed.), *Why we watch: The attractions of violent entertainment* (pp. 7–26). New York: Oxford University Press.

Haugvedt, C. P., Petty, R. E., & Cacioppo, J. T. (1992). Need for cognition and advertising: Understanding the role of personality variables in consumer behavior. *Journal of Consumer Psychology, 1*(3), 239–260.

Hillman, C. H., Cuthbert, B. N., Cauraugh, J., Schupp, H. T., Bradley, M., & Lang, P. J. (2000). Psychophysiological responses of sport fans. *Motivation and Emotion, 24*(1), 13–28.

Hirschman, E. C. (1982). Ethnic variation in hedonic consumption. *Journal of Social Psychology, 118*(2), 225–234.

Hirschman, E. C. (1987). Consumer preferences in literature, motion pictures and television programs. *Empirical Studies of the Arts, 5*(1), 31–46.

Jack, S. J., & Ronan, K. R. (1998). Sensation seeking among high- and low-risk sports participants. *Personality and Individual Differences, 25*, 1063–1083.

Kassarjian, H., & Sheffet, M. J. (1991). Personality and consumer behavior: An update. In H. Kassarjian & T. Robertson (Eds.), *Perspectives in consumer behavior* (pp. 281–303). Englewood Cliffs, NJ: Prentice Hall.

Krcmar, M., & Greene, K. (1999). Predicting exposure to and uses of television violence. *Journal of Communication, 49*(3), 24–45.

Laverie, D. A., & Arnett, D. B. (2000). Factors affecting fan attendance: The influence of identity salience and satisfaction. *Journal of Leisure Research, 32*(2), 225–246.

Leone, C., & D'Arienzo, J. D. (2000). Sensation seeking and differentially arousing television commercials. *Journal of Social Psychology, 140*(60), 710–720.

Litle, P., & Zuckerman, M. (1986). Sensation seeking and music preferences. *Personality and Individual Differences, 4*, 575–578.

Madrigal, R. A. (1995). Cognitive and affective determinants of fan satisfaction with sporting event attendance. *Journal of Leisure Research, 27*(3), 205–227.

McDaniel, S. R. (2001). An examination of demographic, lifestyle and personality influences on consumer preferences for participating in promotional games. *Advances in Consumer Research, 28*, 19.

McDaniel, S. R. (2002). *Reconsidering the relationship between sensation seeking and preferences for viewing televised sports.* Paper presented to the 21st Annual Advertising and Consumer Psychology Conference, New York.

Mustonen, A., Arms, L., & Russell, G. W. (1996). Predictors of sports spectators' proclivity for riotous behaviour in Finland and Canada. *Personality and Individual Differences, 21*(4), 519–525.

Palmgreen, P., Donohew, L., Lorch, E. P., Hoyle, R. H., & Stephenson, M. T. (2001). Television campaigns and adolescent marijuana use: Tests of sensation seeking targeting. *American Journal of Public Health, 91*(2), 292–296.

Perse, E. M. (1996). Sensation seeking and the use of television for arousal. *Communication Reports, 9*, 37–48.

Potts, R., Dedmon, A., & Halford, J. (1996). Sensation seeking, television viewing motives, and home television viewing patterns. *Personality and Individual Differences, 21*, 1081–1084.

Ridgeway, D., & Russell, J. A. (1980). Reliability and validity of the sensation-seeking scale: Psychometric problems in Form V. *Journal of Consulting and Clinical Psychology, 48*(5), 662–664.

Rowland, G. L., Fouts, G., & Heatherton, T. (1989). Television viewing and sensation seeking: Uses, preferences and attitudes. *Personality and Individual Differences, 9,* 1003–1006.

Rubin, R. B., & McHugh, M. P. (1987). Development of parasocial interaction relationships. *Journal of Broadcasting and Electronic Media, 31,* 279–292.

Sargent, S. L., Zillmann, D., & Weaver, J. B. (1998). The gender gap in the enjoyment of televised sports. *Journal of Sport and Social Issues, 22,* 46–64.

Schierman, M. J., & Rowland, G. L. (1985). Sensation seeking and selection of entertainment. *Personality and Individual Differences, 6*(5), 599–603.

Schroth, M. L. (1994). A comparison of sensation seeking among different groups of athletes and nonathletes. *Personality and Individual Differences, 18*(2), 219–222.

Shapiro, L. (2001, May 13). Playing the ratings game. *The Washington Post*, pp. D7.

Shoham, A., Rose, G. M., & Kahle, L. R. (1998). Marketing of risky sports: From intention to action. *Journal of the Academy of Marketing Science, 26*(4), 307–321.

Shrum, L. J. (1999). Television and persuasion: Effects of the programs between the ads. *Psychology and Marketing, 16*(2), 119–140.

Stotlar, D. K. (2000). Vertical integration in sport. *Journal of Sport Management, 14*(1), 1–7.

Wakefield, K. L. (1995). The pervasive effects of social influence on sporting event attendance. *Journal of Sport and Social Issues, 19*(4), 335–351.

Wann, D. L., Melnick, M. J., Russell, G. W., & Pease, D. G. (2001). *Sport fans: The psychology and social impact of spectators.* New York: Routledge.

Weaver, J. B. (2000). Personality and entertainment preferences. In D. Zillmann & P. Vorderer (Eds.), *Media entertainment: The psychology of its appeal* (pp. 235–248). Mahwah, NJ: Lawrence Erlbaum Associates.

Zaichkowsky, J. L. (1994). The personal involvement inventory: Reduction, revision, and application to advertising. *Journal of Advertising, 23*(4), 59–70.

Zillmann, D. (1991). Television viewing and physiological arousal. In J. Bryant & D. Zillmann (Eds.), *Responding to the screen: Reception and reaction processes* (pp. 102–133). Hillsdale, NJ: Lawrence Erlbaum Associates.

Zuckerman, M. (1988). Behavior and biology: Research on sensation seeking and reactions to the media. In L. Donohew, H. Sypher, & E.T. Higgins (Eds.), *Communication, social cognition and affect* (pp. 173–194). Hillsdale, NJ: Lawrence Erlbaum Associates.

Zuckerman, M. (1994). *Behavioral expressions and biosocial bases of sensation seeking.* Cambridge, UK: Cambridge University Press.

Author Index

A

Aaker, D. A., 107, *114*
Abelson, R. P., 173, *176*
Abrahams, M., 117, *131*
Abrams, R. L., 35, *41*
Adaval, R., 149, 151, 152, 154, 155, *157*, 162, *174, 176*
Adler, S. A., 125, *131*
Agrawal, J., 318, *319*
Ahlm, K., 153, *159*
Ahrens, M. B., 79, 81, 83, *98*, 118, *132*
Aiken, D., 312, *320*
Ajay, K., 40, *41*
Aksoy, L., 105, 106, 109, *114*
Aldridge, A., 28, *41*
Alexander, J. K., 194, 207, *210*
Allan, K., 244, *249*
Allen, M.,197, 204, *209*
Allport, G. W., 235, *249*
Amis, J., 316, 319, *319*
Anderson, C. A., 180, *189*, 197, 198, 202, 208, *209*
Anderson, C. L., 225, *232*
Anderson, D. R., 203, *209*
Anderson, J. R., 315, *319*
Anderson, N. H., 145, 149, *157*
Andison, F. S., 196, 198, *209*
Andrews, N., 117, *130*
Antil, J. H., 276, *289*
Arms, L., 326, *334*
Arms, R. L., 314, *320*
Armstrong, G. M, 102, *115*, 128, *130*
Arnett, D. B., 324, *334*
Arnett, J. J., 286, *288*
Aron, A., 296, *305*
Aron, E., 296, *305*
Aronson, E., 317, *319*

Arpan-Ralstin, L. A., 96, *98*
Ashforth, B. E., 316, *321*
Askew, C., 119, 120, 129, *132*
Atkin, C. K., 200, 203, *210, 211*, 235, 239, *249*
Ault, J., 247, *251*
Auty, S., 118, *130*
Avery, R. J., 54, *60*, 64, *76*, 79, 80, 81, *96*
Aylesworth, A., 40, *41*

B

Babin, L. A., 46, 55, 56, *60*, 64, 65, *76*, 79, 80, 81, 82, *96*, 105, *114*, 262, *273*
Bachman, J. G., 204, *211*
Bailis, D. S., 164, 172, 173, *176*, 256, *274*
Baker, B., 245, *249*
Baker, M. J., 105, *114*
Baker, W. E., 52, 53, *60*, 126, *130*
Balasubramanian, S. K., 45, 47, 48, *60*, 100, 103, 104, 106, 110, *114*, 221, *230*
Balbach, E. D., 83, *98*
Ballard, P. B., 22, *41*
Bandura, A., 106, *114*, 194, 199, 200, 206, 208, *209, 210*, 216, 221, 291, *305*
Bannan, K. J., 64, *76*
Bargh, J. A., 17, *41*, 71, *76*, 90, 97, 142, 143, 144, 148, *157, 158*, 178, *189*, 208, *210*, 233, *249*
Barney, J., 316, *319*
Bartholomew, K., 294, 303, *305*
Barwise, T. P., 276, *288*
Basil, M. D., 83, *96*
Baumal, E., 235, *251*
Baumeister, R. F., 314, *319*
Baxter, L. A., 280, *290*
Beach, M. L., 79, *98*, 118, *132*, 280, *290*
Bearden, W. O., 281, *288*

337

Beatty, S. E., 234, *249*
Becker, M. H., 194, *209*
Belk, R. W., 59, *60*
Belson, W. A., 198, 199, 201, 204, 205, 206, 207, 208, 209, *209*
Bennett, M., 57, 58, *60*
Bennett, R., 244, *249*
Berkowitz, L., 197, 200, 206, *209*
Berlyne, D. E., 282, 283, *288*
Berman, L., 153, *159*
Bernhardt, P., 327, 333, *333*
Berscheid, E., 280, *289*
Berscheid, W. E., 317, *320*
Bettman, J. R., 284, *288*
Beville, H. M., 275, *288*
Bharadwaj, S. G., 316, *319*
Bhatnagar, N., 105, 109, *114*
Biocca, F., 86, *96*, 169, *174*
Birdsall, T. G.,19, *42*
Bischak, V. D., 180, *191*, 222, *232*
Blades, M., 127, *132*
Blaxton, T. A., 74, *77*
Bleich, D., 281, *288*
Bloom, P., 106, *114*
Bodenhausen, G. V., 140, 141, 142, *159*
Borden, R. J., 312, *319*, 327, *333*
Borges, R., 318, *319*
Boring, E. G., 21, *41*
Bornstein, R. F., 17, 40, *41*, 70, *76*
Botta, R., 302, *305*
Boush, D. M., 106, *114*
Bower, G. H., 86, *97*, 152, *159*, 315, *319*
Bowlby, J., 294, *305*
Bradley, M., 327, *334*
Braman, S., 229, *230*
Brand, M. J., 318, *321*
Brannstrom, I., 227, *230*
Branscombe, N. R., 312, *319, 322*
Braun, K. A., 56, *60*, 65, 69, 72, 73, 74, 75, *77*, 82, *97*
Breitrose, H., 194, 207, *210*
Brennan, I., 46, 56, *60*, 81, 82, *96*
Brennan, K. A., 297, 298, 303, *305*
Brewer, M. B., 240, *249*, 303, *306*
Brezgel, K., 197, 204, *209*
Bristor, J. M., 244, *249*
Brock, G. J., 258, *273*
Brock, T. C., 1, 2, *8*, 161, 163, 164, 166, 167, 168, 171, 172, 173, 174, *175, 176*, 255, 256, 258, 262, 271, 272, *273, 274*, 300, 304, *306*
Brook, J. S., 200, *210*
Brown, B. W., 194, 207, *210*

Brown, D., 179, *189*
Brown, J., 138, *158*
Brown, J. D., 226, 227, 229, *230*, 303, *306*
Brown, J. J., 286, *289*
Brown, R., 143, *158*
Bruck, M., 162, *174*
Brucks, M., 128, *130*, 145, *157*
Bruner, J., 162, *174*
Bruner, J. S., 164, 165, *174*
Bryant, J., 142, *159*, 179, 182, *189*, 257, *273, 274*, 323, 324, 325, 328, 329, 331, *333*
Bryson, S. W., 297, *308*
Buck, E. B., 279, *289*
Buckley, K. W., 244, *249*
Budesheim, T. L., 146, 147, 148, *159*
Burnett, J., 315, *319*
Burns, A. C., 262, *273*
Burroughs, J. E., 178, 187, 188, *189*
Burrows, L., 71, *76*, 143, 144, *157*
Bushman, B. J., 180, *189*, 197, 198, 202, 208, *209*, 292, *306*, 314, *319*
Buss, D. D., 58, *60*
Busselle, R. W., 170, *174*, 186, *189*
Butters, J., 303, 304, *306*

C

Cachere, J., 197, *211*
Cacioppo, J. T., 81, *97*, 111, *115*, 166, 167, 171, 173, *174, 175, 176*, 187, *189*, 194, *209, 211*, 243, *250*, 255, 262, 270, *273*, 327, *334*
Cairns, E., 197, *209*
Calder, B. J., 202, *210*
Calfee, J. E., 106, *114*
Cameron, G., 316, *321*
Campbell, D. T., 198, 202, *210*
Canary, D. J., 203, *209*
Cantor, J., 226, 227, 229, *230*, 293, *307*
Carder, S. T., 64, 65, *76*, 79, 80, 81, 82, *96*, 105, *114*
Carlston, D. E., 153, *157*, 186, *189*
Carnes, M. C., 165, *174*
Carol, J., 83, *98*
Carpenter, K. M., 162, *175*, 184, *190*
Carpentier, F., 82, 86, *98*
Carstensen, L. L., 272, *273*
Cartier 328, *334*
Carveth, R. A., 179, *189*
Cash, D. W., 303, 304, *306*
Cash, T. F., 303, 304, *306*
Cassidy, J., 294, *307*

Cattarin, J. A., 303, *306*
Cauraugh, J., 327, *334*
Ceci, S. J., 162, *174*
Celozzi, M. J., 204, *210*
Celsi, R. L., 315, *319*
Cermak, L. S., 124, *130*
Chaffee, S. H., 200, 201, 203, *210, 211*
Chaiken, S., 109, *115*, 162, 170, 173, *174*, 208, *210*
Chakravarti, D., 125, *131*
Chandler, K., 124, *130*
Chapman, J. P., 241, *249*
Chapman, L. J., 241, *249*
Chapman, S., 83, *96*
Charles, S. T., 272, *273*
Charlton, T., 117, *131*
Chartier, F., 65, *76*, 80, 81, 82, *96*, 127, *131*
Chartrand, T. L., 17, *41*
Chattopadhyay, A., 71, *77*
Chen, M., 71, *76*, 143, 144, *157*
Cheng, H., 244, *249*
Choi, J., 88, 89, 94, *98*
Choi, W. S., 84, 88, *96*
Chomsky, N., 245, *249, 250*
Choo, T., 110, *114*
Christensen, A., 280, *289*
Christenson, P. G., 83, 85, *96, 98*
Chung, S. W., 121, *131*
Cialdini, R. B., 162, *175*, 184, *190, 191*, 312, *319*, 327, *333*
Clancey, M., 276, *288*
Clark, C. L., 298, 303, *305*
Cohen, D., 104, *114*
Cohen, E. E., 201, 202, 203, 205, *210*
Cohen, J., 296, *306*
Cohen, P., 200, *210*
Colcombe, S. J., 144, *157*, 162, *176*
Cole, C. A., 227, *230*
Cole, T., 296, *306*
Collins, N., 294, *306*
Collins, P. A., 203, *209*
Collins, R. L., 303, *306*
Coltrane, S., 244, *249*
Combs, B., 184, 185, *189, 190*
Comisky, P., 325, 328, 329, 331, *333*
Comstock, G., 193, 194, 195, 196, 197, 198, 199, 201, 202, 203, 204, 205, 207, *210, 211*, 292, *307*
Conner, K. R., 316, *320*
Conway, J. C., 282, *288*, 328, 332, *334*
Conway, M., 271, *273*
Cook, F. L., 222, *232*

Cook, T. D., 198, 200, 201, 202, *210*
Cooper, C. P., 216, *230*
Coover, G., 244, *250*
Costa, P. T., Jr., 291, *307*
Costley, C. L., 145, *157*
Coussement, S. A., 325, 327, 328, 329, *334*
Craik, F. I. M., 71, *77*
Crawford, H. A., 105, *114*
Crawford, Z., 88, 89, 94, *98*
Creelman, C. D., 19, *42*
Csikszentmihalyi, M., 168, *174*, 203, *211*, 256, *273*
Culley, J. D., 244, *249*
Cuthbert, B. N., 327, *334*

D

Dabbs, J. M., 327, 333, *333*
Dacin, P. A., 217, 229, *231*
Dalakas, V., 312, *320*
D'Alessio, D., 197, 204, *209*
Dalton, M. A., 79, 80, 81, *98*, 118, *132*
Dammler, A., 127
D'Arienzo, J. D., 324, *334*
d'Astous, A., 65, *76*, 80, 81, *96*, 127, *131*
Davie, R., 117, *131*
Davis, H. L.., 278, *288*
Davis, K. E., 295, *306*
Davis, M. S., 280, 286, *288*
Davis, R. M., 83, *96*
Dawson, S., 187, *191*
Dean, D. H., 317, *320*
Dedmon, A., 324, 328, 330, 331, 332, *334*
DeFleur, M. L., 179, *189*
Deighton, J., 50, *60*, 162, *174*, 284, *288*, 310, *320*
DeJong, W., 223, *230*
DelFattore, J., 163, *174*
DeLorme, D. E., 54, *60*, 80, 82, *96*, 100, 103, 105, 110, *114, 116*
Del Rosario, M. L., 202, *210*
Denman, D. W., 244, *250*
Dennis, E., 215, 228, *230*
Devine, P. G., 143, *157*
Dholakia, R. R., 110, *115*
Diener, B. J., 83, *96*
Dijksterhuis, A., 208, *210*
Dion, K. K., 317, *320*
Distefan, J. M., 83, 84, *96*, 224, *230*
Dixon, T., 179, *189*
Dodd, C. A., 122, *131*

Dolan, R. J., 46, 49, 51, 53, *60*
Donnerstein, E., 204, *210*
Donohew, L., 324, 332, *334*
Donohue, G. A., 257, *274*
Doppler, M., 216, 223, 229, *232*
Downs, A. C., 244, *249*
Drabman, R. S., 139, *157*
Draine, S. C., 34, *41*
Drummey, A. B., 125, 126, *131*
Dubas, K. M., 46, 56, *60*, 81, 82, *96*
Dubé, L., 271, *273*
Duncan, M., 312, *320*
Dywan, J., 121, 122, *131*

E

Eagly, A. H., 109, 110, *115*, 170, 173, *174*, 208, *210*
Eastman, S. T., 324, *334*
Eaton, J., 316, *320*
Ebbinghaus, H., 20, 21, 22, *41*, 126, *131*
Eccles, J., 241, *250*
Edell, J. A., 145, *157*
Ehrenberg, A. S. C., 276, 280, *288*
Eleey, M. F., 88, *97*
Elliot, M. T., 244, *249*
Elliot, R., 127, *132*
Ellis, D. M., 125, *131*
Ellis, H. D., 125, *131*
Elton, M. P., 311, *320*
Englis, B. G., 6, *9*, 45, 53, *61*, 99, 103, *115*, 146, *158*, 220, 221, 225, 228, 229, *230*
Erdelyi, M. H., 3, *8*, 17, 19, 20, 21, 22, 23, 25, 26, 36, 38, 40, *41*
Erickson, G. A., 312, *320*
Erikson, E. H., 236, *249*, 313, *320*
Eron, L. D., 200, 206, 207, *210, 211*
Escalas, J. E., 283, 284, *288*
Esses, V. M., 255, *273*
Estes, L. S., 297, *308*
Evans, L., 297, *306*
Evans, R. I., 223, *230*
Everett, S. A., 83, *96*

F

Faber, R. J., 219, *232*
Fahy, J., 316, *319*
Farkas, A. J., 84, *97*

Farquar, J. W., 194, 207, *210*
Fazio, R. H., 82, 96, *96, 98*, 169, *174*
Feldman Barrett, L., 295, 303, *307*
Ferraro, R., 54, *60*, 64, *76*, 79, 80, 81, *96*
Festinger, L., 240, *249*, 302, *306*
Fielden, J. A., 327, 333, *333*
Finnegan, J. R., Jr., 223, 226, 227, *231*
Fischhoff, G., 184, *190*
Fishbein, M., 145, 149, *158*
Fisher, A. H., 286, *288*
Fisher, C., 14, 15, 16, 17, 19, 24, 38, *41, 42*
Fisher, R. J., 312, *320*
Fiske, J., 279, *288*
Fitzsimons, G., 145, *159*
Flavell, J. H., 161, *174*
Fletcher, C., 4, *9*, 89, 90, 91, 92, 94, *98*
Flora, J. A., 194, *210*
Ford, J. B., 244, *249*
Foster, B. L., 286, *289*
Fortmann, S. P., 194, *210*
Fournier, S., 46, 49, 51, 53, *60*, 104, *115*, 283, *288*
Fouts, G., 328, 331, 332, *335*
Fox, S., 216, 219, *231*
Fraley, R. C., 295, *309*
Freeman, S., 312, *319*, 327, *333*
Frenzen, J., 278, 286, *288*
Freud, S., 14, 25, 29, *42*, 244, *249*
Friedberg, N. L., 297, *306*
Friestad, M., 48, 57, *60*, 75, *77*, 106, 109, 110, *114, 115*, 281, *288*
Fryburger, V., ix, *x*
Furnham, A., 235, *249*

G

Gabrial, S., 303, *306*
Galley, D. J., 70, *76*
Gan, S., 325, 328, 329, *334*
Garcia, L., 302, *306*
Garcia, S., 235, *250*
Gardner, B., 314, *320*
Gardner, M., 236, *250*
Gardner, W., 303, *306*
Garnham, A., 86, *96*
Garst, J., 166, 167, 172, 173, *175*
Gentner, D., 86, *97*
Gentner, D. R., 86, *97*

Gerbner, G., 5, *8*, 88, *97*, 164, *175*, 178, 179, 180, 181, 185, *190*, 216, 219, 222, *231*, 257, *273*, 291, 292, *306*
Gerhardstein, P., 125, *131*
Gerrig, R. J., 164, 166, 167, 171, 172, 173, *175, 176*, 256, *274*
Gibbons, J. A., 75, *77*
Gibson, B., 84, *97*
Gilbert, D. T., 39, *42*, 164, 168, *175*
Gilens, M., 244, *250*
Gilpin, E. A., 83, 84, *97*, 224, *230*
Gitlin, T., 236, 243, 246, 247, *250*
Glantz, S. A., 83, *97, 98*
Glasgow, M. R., 328, *334*
Glass, G. V., 196, 197, *210*
Glenberg, A. M., 87, *97*
Goldberg, B., 245, *250*
Goldberg, M. E., 71, *77*, 128, *130*, 217, *231*
Goldstein, D., 138, *158*
Goldstein, J. H., 314, *319*
Goma'-I-Feixanet, M., 324, 326, *334*
Goodstein, R. C., 40, *41*
Gorman, T. F., 140, 141, 142, *159*
Gorn, G. J., 71, *77*, 105, *115*, 217, 221, *231*
Gould, S. J., 46, 54, 55, *60*, 100, 103, 105, *115*
Grabner-Krauter, S., 103, *115*
Graesser, A. C., 86, 87, *97*
Graf, P., 3, *8*, 67, *77*, 318, *322*
Gray, N., 297, *308*
Grayson, J., 247, *251*
Green, M. C., 1, 2, *8*, 161, 163, 164, 166, 167, 168, 171, 172, 173, *175, 176*, 255, 256, 262, 271, 272, *273, 274*, 300, *306*
Greenberg, B. S., 170, *174*
Greene, D., 241, *250*
Greene, K., 324, 327, 329, 330, 331, 332, *334*
Greeno, J. G., 86, *97*
Greenspan, S. L., 86, *97*
Greenwald, A., 34, *41, 42*
Gregory, L. G., 184, *190*
Gregory, W. L., 162, *175*
Gross, L., 5, *8*, 88, *97*, 164, *175*, 178, 179, 180, 181, 185, *190*, 216, 219, 222, *231*, 257, *273*, 292, *306*
Grossberg, J., 63, *77*
Grove, J. R., 314, *320*
Guidano, V. F., 297, *306*
Gunter, B., 127, *132*
Gupta, P. B., 46, 54, 55, *60*, 65, 66, 74, *77*, 79, 82, 87, *97*, 100, 103, 105, *115*
Gustafson, M., 91, *98*

Gutsch, K. U., 204, *210*
Guttman, A., 327, *334*
Gwinner, K. P., 316, *320*

H

Halford, G. S., 85, 86, *97*
Halford, J., 324, 328, 330, 331, 332, *334*
Hamilton, K., 293, *306*
Hanrahan, S. J., 314, *320*
Hansen, F. J., 244, *250*
Hargrove, K., 247, *251*
Harris, R. J., 291, *306*
Harrison, K., 293, 298, *306*
Harrison, S. D., 244, *249*
Harvey, J. H., 280, *289*
Harwood, J., 285, *288*
Hasher, L., 138, *138*
Hashtroudi, S., 138, *158*, 169, *175*
Haskell, W. L., 194, *210*
Hass, R. G., 170, *175*
Hastie, R., 149, *158*, 162, *175*, 186, 187, *190*
Haugtvedt, C. P., 173, *176*, 327, *334*
Hawkins, R. P., 181, 183, *190*, 223, *231*
Hawkins, S. A., 71, *77*
Hayes, B. K., 124, *131*
Hayman, C. A., 122, 124, *131, 132*
Hazan, A. R., 83, *97*
Hazan, C., 294, *307, 308*
Head, S. W., 179, *190*
Healey, E., 244, *251*
Hearold, S., 196, 197, 198, 204, 205, *210*
Heath, L., 202, *210*
Heatherton, T., 324, 328, 331, 332, *335*
Heatherton, T. F., 79, 81, 83, *95*, 118, *132*
Hebb, D. O., 283, *288*
Heckler, S. E., 74, *78*, 120, *132*, 277, 278, *290*
Heider, F., 317, *320*
Heinberg, L. J., 293, *307*
Hennessy, R., 124, *131*
Hennigan, K. M., 202, *210*
Henriksen, L., 83, 85, *96, 98*
Herbart, J. F., 21, *42*
Herman, E. S., 245, *250*
Herman-Cohen, V., 228, *231*
Hernandez, M., 216, 223, 229, *232*
Herring, L., 197, *209*
Hertog, J., 223, 226, 227, *231*
Hewstone, M., 240, *250*
Higgins, E. T., 90, *97*, 142, 148, 153, *158*

Higgins, R. L., 312, *322*
Hilgard, E. R., 155, *158*
Hillman, C. H., 327, *334*
Hines, D., 84, *97*
Hirsch, P., 179, 180, *190*
Hirschman, E. C., 187, *190*, 214, 217, 218, 224, 225, 226, 227, 230, *231*, 284, *288*, 310, 314, *320*, 324, 328, 330, 332, 333, *334*
Hirt, E. R., 312, *320*
Hoeke, S. A., 318, *321*
Hogan, M., 215, 229, *231*
Hogben, M., 197, *210*
Hogg, M. A., 208, *211*
Holbrook, M. B., 310, 314, *320*
Holden, C., 272, *273*
Holden, S. J. S., 71, *77*
Holender, D., 19, 22, *42*
Holland, B., 39, *42*
Hollingsworth, L., 247, *251*
Holmes, J. G., 139, *158*
Homer, P. M., 313, 318, *320*
Horowitz, L. M., 294, 303, *305*
Hosie, J. A., 125, *131*
Hothschild, L., 303, *306*
House, P., 241, *250*
Houston, M. J., 227, *230*
Hoyle, R. H., 324, 332, *334*
Huber, J., 316, *320*
Huesmann, L. R., 200, 201, 206, 207, *210, 211*
Hughes, M., 179, 180, *190*
Hunt, M., 195, *210*
Hunt, M. R., 244, *249*
Hunt, S. D., 316, *320*
Hunter, D., 197, *209*
Hunter, R., 145, 149, *158*
Huston, A. C., 227, *231*
Huston, T. L., 280, *288*
Hyde, J. S., 298, *307*

I

Ickes, W., 235, *250*
Isbell, L. M., 138, 149, 151, 152, *157, 158*
Iyer, P., 137, *158*

J

Jack, S. J., 326, *334*
Jackson-Beeck, M., 88, *97*
Jacobvitz, R. S., 203, *209*

Jacoby, J., 315, *321*
Jacoby, L. L., 67, 77, 121, 122, *131*, 138, *158*
Jaffe, E. D., 48, *61*
Jakobs, E., 286, *288*
James, C., 300, *307*
James, W., 22, *42*, 121, *131*
Janiszewski, C., 53, *60*, 71, 72, *77*, 119, *131*
Jasechko, J., 138, *158*
Jaworski, B. J., 315, *321*
Jeffries-Fox, S., 88, *97*
Jellison, J. M., 109, *115*, 221, *231*
Jenkins, H., III., 281, *288*
Jensen, T. D., 318, *322*
Johar, G. V., 318, *320*
John, D. R., 117, *132*, 214, 230, *231*
Johnson, J. G., 200, 201, *210*
Johnson, M. K., 1, *8*, 138, *158*, 162, 165, 169, *175*
Johnson-Laird, P. N., 86, *97*
Johnstone, E., 122, *131*
Joiner, C., 316, *321*
Josephson, W. L., 204, *210*
Judd, C. M., 241, *250*
Jussim, L., 241, *250*

K

Kahle, L. R., 311, 312, 313, 315, 317, 318, *320, 321*, 324, 326, *335*
Kahneman, D., 184, *190, 191*, 220, *232*
Kail, R. V., 125, 126, *131*
Kamakura, W. A., 318, *319*
Kambara, K. M., 311, 313, 317, *320, 321*
Kamins, M. A., 318, *321*
Kang, N., 199, 200, *210*
Kao, C. F., 167, *174*
Kaplan, N., 294, *307*
Karabenick, S. A., 235, *251*
Karrh, J. A., 46, 54, *60*, 64, 65, *77*, 79, 81, 82, *97*, 100, 105, *115*
Kasen, S., 200, *210*
Kassarjian, H., 327, *334*
Kazelskis, R., 204, *210*
Kefauver, E., 215, *231*
Keller, K. L., 107, *114*, 307, *321*
Kelley, C., 138, *158*
Kelley, C. M., 121, 122, *131*
Kelley, H. H., 109, *115*, 280, *288*
Kelman, H. C., 311, 312, 313, *321*
Kendzierski, D. A., 200, 201, *210*

Kennedy, C., 312, *320*
Kerkman, D., 227, *231*
Kernan, J. B., 314, *321*
Kessler, R., 199, 200, 201, *211*
Kielwasser, A. P., 277, *290*
Kihlstrom, J. F., 120, *131*
Kilbourne, J., 304, *307*
Killen, J. D., 297, *308*
Kim, E., 101, *115*
Kinney, L., 54, *61*
Kintsch, W., 86, *98*
Kleinbard, J., 21, 22, *41*
Kleine, R. E., III., 314, *321*
Kleine, S. S., 314, *321*
Klinger, M., 34, *42*
Klinger, M. R., 82, *98*
Kolin, E. A., 282, *290*
Komatsu, S., 125, *132*
Koomen, W., 303, *308*
Kotler, P., 102, *115*
Kozinets, R. V., 277, 286, *289*
Krcmar, M., 324, 327, 329, 331, 332, *334*
Krishnan, H. S., 72, 75, *78*, 125, *131*
Kropp, F., 312, *321*
Krugman, H. E., 126, *131*, 284, *289*
Krull, D. S., 164, 168, *175*
Kubey, R. W., 203, *211*, 256, *273*
Kuklinsky, J. H., 146, 147, 148, 151, *159*
Kunda, Z., 284, *289*, 304, *307*
Kunst-Wilson, W. R., 39, *42*, 120, *131*

L

Laird, J., 303, 304, *308*
Lang, P. J., 327, *334*
Langlieb, A. M., 216, *230*
Langston, W. E., 87, *97*
Lastovicka, J. L., 217, *231*
LaTour, M. S., 244, *249*
Laverie, D. A., 324, *334*
Law, J., 124, *132*
Law, S., 56, *60*, 65, 71, 72, 73, 74, 75, 76, 77, 82, *97*
Layman, M., 184, *190*
Leavitt, C., 110, *115*
Lee, B., 276, 277, 279, *289*
Lee, J., 288, *289*
Lee, J. Y., 244, *251*
Lee, R. G., 244, *249*
Lee, R. S., 277, 279, *289*

Leets, L., 296, *306*
Lefkowitz, M. M., 200, *211*
Lehmann, D. R., 214, 228, *231*
Leigh, T. W., 315, *319*
Leone, C., 324, *334*
Leone, D. R., 70, *76*
Lepore, L., 143, *158*
Lerner, M. J., 139, *158*
Leuba, C., 282, 283, *289*
Leung, C. C., 161, 164, 173, *176*
Levin, A. M., 316, *321*
Levinger, G., 280, *289*
Levy, M. R., 276, 277, *289*
Levy, S. J., 314, *320*
Lewis, C., 118, *130*
Liberman, A., 173, *174*
Lichtenstein, M., 186, *190*
Lichtenstein, S., 184, *190*
Lichter, L. S, 179, 187, *190*
Lichter, S. R., 179, 187, *190*
Lindblad, I., 227, *230*
Linderholm, T., 89, 90, 91, *98*
Lindsay, D. S., 138, *158*, 169, *175*
Lingle, J. H., 153, *158*, 186, *190*
Linz, D., 179, *189*, 204, *210*
Lipton, H. L., 83, *97*
Litle, P., 267, *273*, 324, 328, 331, 332, 333, *334*
Litvack, D., 71, *77*
Livingstone, S. M., 85, *97*, 277, *289*
Lockwood, P., 304, *307*
Loftus, E. F., 162, *175*
Lombardi, W., 90, *97*, 142, 148, *158*
Lorch, E. P., 324, *334*
Lord, K. A., 303, *305*
Lord, K. R., 55, *60*, 65, 66, 74, *77*, 79, 82, 87, *97*, 100, 105, *115*
Lowrey, T. M., 6, *9*
Lull, J., 286, *289*
Lumpkin, J. R., 244, *250*
Lurie, L., 153, *158*
Lutter, C. D., 327, 333, *333*
Lutz, R. J., 127, *131*, 317, *321*
Lyddon, W. J., 297, *306*
Lynch, J. G., Jr., 233, *250*
Lynn, S., 153, *159*

M

Maccoby, E. E., 203, *211*
Maccoby, N., 194, 207, *210*

MacGregor, B., 246, 247, *250*
MacInnis, D. J., 74, *77*, 120, *132*, 314, *321*
Mackie, D. M., 173, *176*
Macklin, M. C., 127, *131*
Macmillan, N. A., 19, *42*
Madon, S., 241, *250*
Madrigal, R. A., 310, 316, 318, *320, 321*, 324, *334*
Mael, F. A., 316, *321*
Magiera, M., 100, 103, 108, *115*
Main, M., 294, *307*
Maio, G. R., 255, *273*
Malkoc, S., 105, 109, *114*
Malone, P. S., 164, 168, *175*
Mandler, J. M., 126, *131*
Mann, D., 301, *307*
Manstead, A. S., 286, *288*
Markus, H., 284, *289*, 296, 303, *307*
Maslow, A. H., 236, *250*
Mast, F., 69, *77*
Maurer, J., 84, *97*
Maxwell, S. E., 223, *230*
Mazis, M. B., 244, *250*
Mazzocco, P. J., 258, *273*
McAlexander, J. H., 286, *290*
McCann, J., 316, *320*
McCarthy, M., 46, 49, 51, *60*
McClung, G. W., 58, *61*
McCombs, M. W., 257, *273*
McCracken, G., 284, *289*
McCrae, R. R., 291, *307*
McDaniel, S. R., 319, *321*
McDaniel, S. R., 324, 329, 330, 331, 332, 333, *334*
McDermott, K. B., 67, *77*
McGee, S., 83, *98*
McGriff, J. A., 214, 224, *231*
McGuire, W. J., 219, *231*
McHugh, M. P., 330, *335*
McIlwraith, R., 282, *289, 290*
McInman, A., 314, *320*
McKinley, N. M., 298, *307*
McLeod, J. M., 200, 203, *210, 211*, 244, *251*
McLuhan, M., 215, 226, *231*
McQueen, J., 50, *60*, 162, *174*, 284, *288*
Meenaghan, T., 315, *322*
Meeske, C., 318, *321*
Mehrabian, A., 283, *289*
Melnick, M. J., 326, *335*
Melone, N. P., 318, *321*
Melton, R. J., 146, 147, 148, 151, *159*

Menon, A., 315, *319*
Meri, D., 54, 55, *61*, 79, 81, 82, 90, *97*, 105, *115*
Merritt, R. K., 84, *97*
Mertin, R. K., 241, *250*
Middelman-Motz, A. V., 127, *131*
Milavsky, J. R., 199, 200, 201, *210*
Milgram, S., 291, *307*
Miller, D. T., 139, *158*
Miller, M. C., 218, *231*
Miller, N., 240, *249*
Mills, J., 109, *115*, 221, *231*
Milner, B., 66, *77*
Mischel, W., 235, *250*, 291, *307*
Mitrook, M. A., 325, 327, 328, 329, *334*
Mizerski, R., 53, 55, *61*, 64, 65, *78*, 105, *116*
Moe, J. C., 318, *321*
Moore, E. S., 127, *131*
Moore, T. E., 17, *42*, 69, *77*
Morgan, M., 178, 179, 180, 181, 185, *190, 191*, 216, 219, 222, *231*, 257, *273*, 291, 292, *306, 308*
Morgan, R. M., 316, *320*
Morley, D., 277, *289*
Morris, M., 245, *250*
Morrow, D. G., 86, *97*
Munch, J. M., 276, *289*
Murphy, S. T., 164, *175*
Murry, J. P., 217, 229, *231*
Mustonen, A., 326, *334*

N

Nabi, R. L., 87, *98*
Naito, M., 125, *132*
Nass, C., 164, *176*, 296, *307*
Neaderhiser, B. J., 75, *77*
Nebenzahl, I. D., 48, 54, 55, *61*, 81, *97*, 110, *115*
Nell, V., 167, *175*
Nelson, M. R., 128, *132*
Netemeyer, R. G., 281, *288*
Newcomb, H., 179, *191*
Newcomb, T., 234, *250*
Newcombe, N., 125, 126, *131*
Newton, B. J., 279, *289*
Nisbett, R. E., 152, *158*
Norman, A. T., 277, *290*
Novick, N. J., 303, *306*
Nuland, S., 169, *175*
Nurius, P., 296, 303, *307*

O

Oates, C., 127, *132*
Oatley, K., 170, *175*
Ogles, R. M., 180, *191*
O'Guinn, T. C., 137, 139, *158*, 164, *176*, 179, 186, 187, 181, 188, *191*, 217, 219, 220, 228, *231, 232*
Ohta, N., 124, *132*
O'Kearney, R., 296, 297, *307*
Olien, C. N., 257, *274*
Oliver, M. B., 179, *191*
Oliver, M. B., 257, *274*
Olofsson, A., 225, *230*
Olson, J., 315, *321*
Ong, B. S., 54, 55, *61*, 79, 81, 82, 90, *97*, 105, *115*
Osborne, D., 244, *250*
O'Sullivan, P., 315, *322*
Ostrom, T. M., 153, *158*, 168, *176*, 186, *190*
Ottati, V. C., 138, *158*
Otteson, J. L., 324, *334*

P

Paik, H., 196, 197, 198, 199, 201, 202, 203, 204, 205, *211*, 292, *307*
Paivio, A., 74, *77*
Palmgreen, P., 220, *232*, 324, 332, *334*
Pant, N., 316, 319, *319*
Panting, C., 117, *131*
Park, B., 186, 187, *190*, 241, *250*
Park, C. W., 58, *61*, 314, *321*
Parkin, A. J., 120, 123, 125, *132*
Paulhus, D., 235, *251*
Pavelchak, M. A., 276, *289*
Pavlov, I. P., 22, *42*
Payne, D. G., 21, *42*
Pease, D. G., 326, *335*
Pechmann, C., 128, *132*
Pecotich, A., 57, 58, *60*
Pelham, B. W., 303, *307*
Pennington, N., 149, *158*, 162, *175*
Penrod, S., 204, *210*
Peplau, L. A., 171, *176*
Peracchio, L. A., 126, *132*, 227, *232*
Perez, A. M., 74, *78*
Perfect, T. J., 119, 120, 129, *132*
Perloff, R. M., 168, *175*
Perry, E. S., 244, *250*

Perse, E. M., 276, 277, 279, 284, *289, 290*, 296, 298, *308*, 324, 327, 328, 330, 331, 332, *334*
Peters, S. M., 227, *231*
Petrich, C., 215, *232*
Petty, R. E., 73, *78*, 81, *97*, 111, *115*, 138, *159*, 166, 167, 168, 171, 173, *174, 175, 176*, 187, *189*, 194, *209, 211*, 243, *250*, 255, 262, 270, *273*, 314, *321*, 327, *334*
Pettygrew, T. F., 241, *250*
Pham, M. T., 58, *61*
Philliber, W., 216, 219, *231*
Pierce, J. P., 83, 84, *96, 97*, 224, *230*
Pietromonaco, P. R., 295, 303, *307*
Pingree, S., 181, 183, *190*, 223, *231*
Pittman, T. S., 17, *41*
Polkinghorne, D. E., 284, *289*
Posovac, E. J., 293, 304, *307*
Posovac, H. D., 293, 304, *307*
Posovac, S. S., 293, 304, *307*
Postman, N., 255, 256, 272, *274*
Potts, R., 203, *334*, 216, 223, 229, *232*, 324, 328, 330, 331, 332, *334*
Pötzl, O., 14, 31, 38, *42*
Powell, M. C., 82, *96*
Powell, R. A., 296, 298, *308*
Power, J. G., 244, *250*
Prentice, D. A., 164, 166, 171, 172, 173, *175, 176*, 256, *274*
Price, J. R., 120, *133*
Price, L., 282, *290*
Prinz, W., 143, *159*
Puchinelli, N., 69, *77*
Punj, G., 234, *250*
Putnam, R. D., 272, *274*
Puto, C. P., 53, *61*, 276, 277, 279, 285, *290*
Putrevu, S., 57, 58, *60*

R

Radvansky, G. A., 4, *9*, 80, 85, 86, 87, 88, *97*, 98, 145, 154, *159*
Raines, E. E., 223, *230*
Raju, P. S., 282, 283, *289*
Ramsay, R., 296, 297, *308*
Raney, A. A., 323, 324, 325, *333*
Rauch, A., 296, *307*
Rawlings, E., 195, 200, *209*
Read, S., 294, *306*
Read, S. J., 235, *250*
Reece, D., 220, *232*

Reeves, B., 164, *176*, 296, *307*
Reid, L. N., 54, *60*, 80, 82, *96*, 100, 103, 110, *114*
Reingen, P. H., 286, *289*
Rescorla, R., 23, *42*
Reyes, R. M., 152, *159*
Reynolds, K. D., 184, *191*
Rholes, W. S., 153, *158*
Richards, J. M., 303, *306*
Richards, J. W., 310, *322*
Richins, M. L., 187, *191*, 284, *289*
Ridgeway, D., 329, *335*
Riggle, E. J., 146, 147, 148, 151, *159*
Rindfleisch, A., 178, 187, 188, *189*
Ringold, D. J., 106, *114*, 244, *250*
Risden, K., 4, *9*, 89, 90, 91, 92, 94, *98*
Ritson, M., 127, *132*
Roberts, D. F., 83, 85, *96, 97*, 227, *232*
Roberts, K. P., 127, *132*
Robinson, J. P., 204, *132*
Rodin, J., 292, *307*
Roe, K., 227, *232*
Roediger, H. L., 67, 74, *77*
Rogers, C. R., 313, *321*
Rogers, E. M., 257, 272, *274*
Rokeach, M., 187, *191*
Romer, D., 50, *60*, 162, *174*, 284, *288*
Ronan, K. R., 326, *334*
Rose, G. M., 106, *114*, 312, 313, 315, 324, 326, *335*
Rose, R. L., 315, *319*
Rosenblatt, L., 281, *290*
Rosengren, K. E., 291, *308*
Rosenthal, R., 195, 197, 201, *211*
Roskos-Ewoldsen, B., 82, 88, *98*
Roskos-Ewoldsen, D. R., 82, 86, 88, 89, 94, 96, *96, 98*
Rosnow, R. L., 201, *211*
Ross, D., 194, 199, 200, *209*
Ross, L., 152, *158*, 241, *250, 251*
Ross, S. A., 194, 199, 200, *209*
Rosselli, F., 173, *176*
Rossi, D., 287, *290*
Roter, D. L., 216, *230*
Rothenberg, R., 100, *115*
Rothman, C., 301, *308*
Rothman, S., 179, 187, *190*
Rotzoll, K., ix, *x*
Rovee-Collier, C., 125, *131, 132*
Rowland, G. L., 267, *274*
Rowland, G. L., 324, 328, 331, 332, *335*

Rozelle, R. M., 223, *230*
Rubens, W. S., 199, 200, 201, *211*
Rubin, A. M., 257, *274*, 276, 279, 282, 284, *288, 289, 290*, 291, 296, 298, *308*, 328, 332, *334*
Rubin, D. B., 197, 201, *211*
Rubin, M., 240, *250*
Rubin, R. B., 330, *335*
Rubin, Z., 171, *176*
Ruelle, R., 247, *251*
Ruskin, G., 101, *115*
Russell, C. A., 52, 53, 56, 57, *61*, 65, 73, 74, *77*, 276, 277, 278, 279, 281, 285, 287, *289, 290*
Russell, G. W., 326, *334, 335*
Russell, J., 283, *289*
Russell, J. A., 329, *335*

S

St. Pierre, J., 96, *98*
Sanchez, D., 203, *211*
Sand, R., 21, *42*
Sandage, C. H., ix, *x*
Sandler, D. M., 103, *115*
Sanyal, A., 121, *132*
Sapolsky, B. S., 54, *61*
Sargent, J. D., 79, 81, 83, 84, *98, 118*, 132, 224, *230*
Sargent, S. L., 323, 325, 328, 329, 330, 331, 332, *335*
Saris, R. N., 84, *97*
Schaaf, D., 309, *321*
Schacter, D. L., 3, *8*, 67, 70, *77*, 122, *132*
Schallow, J., 282, *289, 290*
Schank, R. C., 173, *176*
Scharrer, E., 193, 194, 195, 198, 201, 203, 207, *210*, 292, *308*
Schierman, M. J., 267, *274*, 324, 328, 331, 332, *335*
Schiller, H. I., 218, *232*
Schimmack, U., 73, 75, *77*
Schmitt, K. L., 203, *209*
Schnuth, R. L., 83, *96*
Schouten, J. W., 286, *290*
Schroth, M. L., 324, 326, *335*
Schudson, M., 103, *115*
Schuh, E., 35, *42*
Schumann, D. W., 111, *115*, 234, 236, 237, 239, 240, 247, *250, 251*
Schupak-Neuberg, E., 293, *308*
Schupp, H. T., 327, *334*

Schwartzman, D. F., 184, *191*
Schwarz, J., 179, *191*
Scott, L., 225, 226, *231*
Secunda, E., 54, 55, *61*, 81, *97*, 103, 110, *115*
Seger, C. A., 69, *78*
Segrin, C., 87, *98*
Seguin, S., 247, *251*
Seidman, S. B., 286, *289*
Semenik, R. J., 219, *232*
Sengupta, J., 145, *159*
Shanahan, J., 178, 179, 180, 185, *190, 191*, 216, 219, 222, *231*
Shanahan, N., 257, *273*, 292, *306*
Shank, M. D., 310, *321*
Shapiro, L., 324, *335*
Shapiro, S., 72, 74, 75, *78*, 120, *132*
Sharpe, T. M., 297, *308*
Shaver, P. R., 292, 294, 295, 297, 298, 303, *305, 306, 307*
Shavitt, S., 6, *9*, 146, 147, 148, 151, *159*
Shaw, D. L., 257, *273*
Shaw, H. E., 293, *308*
Sheffet, M. J., 327, *334*
Sheppard, A., 117, 130, *132*
Sherman, S. J., 153, *159*, 184, *191*
Sherman, S. M., 280, *290*
Sherry, J., Jr., 225, 226, *232*
Shields, D. L. L., 83, *98*
Shiffrin, R. M., 233, d*251*
Shih, C. F., 128, *132*
Shisslak, C. M., 297, *308*
Shoda, Y., 291, *307*
Shoham, A., 312, 315, *321*, 324, 326, *335*
Shrum, L. J., 138, 139, *158*, 164, *176*, 178, 179, 180, 181, 183, 185, 186, 187, 188, *189, 191*, 215, 217, 219, 220, 222, 228, 229, 230, *231, 232*, 324, *335*
Sicoly, F., 241, *251*
Signorielli, N., 88, *97*, 178, 179, 180, 181, 185, *190*, 216, 219, 222, *231*, 244, *251*, 257, *273*, 291, 292, *306, 308*
Silberstein, L. R., 292, *307*
Simmons, C. H., 139, *158*
Singer, M., 86, 87, *97*
Singh, S. N., 217, *231*
Singhal, A., 272, *274*
Skelly, J. J., 173, *176*
Skinner, B. F., 313, *321*
Slack, T., 316, 319, *319*
Slamecka, N. J., 318, *322*
Slater, M. D., 163, 164, 172, 173, *176*

Sloan, L. R., 310, 312, *319, 322*, 327, *333*
Sloman, S. A., 124, *132*
Slovic, P., 184, 185, *189, 190*
Smailes, E. M., 200, *210*
Smith, S. M., 173, *176*, 234, *249*
Smollan, D., 296, *305*
Smythe, D. W., 179, *191*
Snyder, C. R., 312, *322*
Snyder, M., 235, *250*, 255, *274*
Solomon, M. R., 6, *9*, 45, 53, *61*, 99, 103, *115*, 220, 221, 225, 228, 229, *230*, 314, *322*
Spence, D. P., 32, *42*
Spieler, R. T., 86, *97*
Spitzberg, B. H., 186, *209*
Sroufe, L. A., 294, *308*
Srull, T. K., 186, *190*, 233, 235, *250, 251*
Stack, A. D., 314, *319*
Staelin, R., 145, *157*, 234, *250*
Stapel, D. A., 303, *308*
Stein, R. I., 293, *308*
Steortz, E. M., 105, *116*
Stephan, C. W., 235, *251*
Stephan, W. C., 235, *251*
Stephenson, M. T., 324, 332, *334*
Stern, B. B., 244, *251*, 281, *290*
Sternthal, B., 110, *115*
Stice, E., 293, *308*
Stipp, H. H., 199, 200, 201, *211*
Stockwell, T. F., 83, *98*
Stotlar, D. K., 324, *335*
Strange, J. J., 1, 2, *8*, 161, 163, 164, 165, 173, 174, *175, 176*, 271, *273*
Strathman, A. J., 314, *321*
Streete, S., 120, 125, *132*
Striegel-Moore, R. H., 292, *307*
Strutton, D., 244, *251*
Stucky, R. J., 312, *322*
Sunstein, C., 235, *251*
Swann, W., 235, *251*
Swayne, L. E., 245, *251*
Swets, J. A., 19, *42*
Szymanski, K., 121, *131*, 318, *321*

T

Tafarodi, R. W., 164, *175*
Talbot, N., 124, *130*
Tanner, W. P., 19, *42*
Taylor, C. B., 194, *210*
Taylor, C. R., 244, *251*

Teel, J. E., 281, *288*
Tellegen, A., 262, *274*
Terry, D. J., 208, *211*
Tesser, A., 235, *251*
Thomas, C., 303, *306*
Thomas, M. A., 139, *157*
Thomas, S. A., 200, 201, *210*
Thompson, C. J., 217, 218, 225, 227, *231*, 284, *288*
Thompson, J. K., 293, 303, *306, 307*
Thompson, W. C., 152, *159*
Thorne, A., 312, *319*, 327, *333*
Thornton, W., 203, *211*
Throckmorton-Belzer, L., 84, *97*
Thurlow, R., 4, *9*, 89, 90, 91, 92, 94, *98*
Tichenour, P. J., 257, *274*
Tickle, J. J., 79, 81, 83, *98*, 118, *132*
Tonn, B. E., 215, *232*
Toppin, T., 138, *159*
Toth, J. P., 122, *132*
Trabasso, T., 86, *97*
Treasure, J., 296, 297, *308*
Tribble, J. L., 83, *96*
Tripp, C., 318, *322*
Troup, M. L., 54, *61*
Tuggle, C. A., 325, 327, 328, 329, *334*
Tulving, E., 122, 124, *131, 132*
Turow, J., 6, *9*, 235, 240, 248, *251*
Tutko, T., 310, *322*
Tversky, A., 184, *190, 191*, 220, *232*
Tyler, T. R., 222, *232*
Tzeng, Y., 89, 90, 91, *98*

U

Unnava, R. H., 314, *321*

V

van den Broek, P., 4, 8, 89, 90, 91, 92, 94, *98*
Van den Bulck, J. 179, *191*
van der Voort, T. H. A., 127, *132*
van Dijk, T. A., 86, *98*
Vanhuele, M., 71, *77*
van Raaij, W. F., 128, *133*
Varadarajan, P. R., 316, *319*
Varey, R. J., 214, *232*
Vargas, P. T., 73, *78*
Viswanath, K., 223, 226, 227, *231*

Voigt, L., 203, *211*
Volgy, T., 179, *191*
Vollmers, S., 53, 55, *61*, 64, 65, *78*, 105, *116*
von Hippel, W., 73, *78*
Von Restorff, H., 105, *116*
Vorderer, P., 2, *9*, 257, *274*

W

Wachsmuth, J. O., 303, *307*
Wagstaff, G. F., 139, *159*
Wakefield, K., 312, *320*
Wakefield, K. L., 324, *335*
Wakshlag, J., 280, *288*
Walder, L. O., 200, *211*
Walker, M. R., 312, *319*, 327, *333*
Walker, W. R., 75, *77*
Waller, G., 293, *306*
Walls, S., 236, 239, *250*
Wallwork, L. W., 228, *232*
Walma van der Molen, J. H., 127, *132*
Walsh, D. A., 226, 229, 227, *232*
Wann, D. L., 312, 315, *319, 322*, 326, 333, *335*
Ward, A., 296, 297, *308*
Waters, E., 297, *308*
Watson, D., 235, 244, *251*
Watson, J., 313, *322*
Weaver, J., 204, *211*
Weaver, J. B., 323, 324, 325, 326, 327, 328, 329, 330, 331, 332, *335*
Weber, J. G., 303, *306*
Wegener, D. T., 138, *159*, 166, *176*
Weinberger, J., 40, *43*
Wells, W. D., 50, 53, *61*, 225, 226, *231, 232*
Werner, C. M., 280, *290*
Wertheim, E. M., 297, *306*
Whannel, G., 312, *322*
Wharton, J. D., 202, *210*
Wheeler, S. C., 164, 172, 173, *176*, 256, *274*
Whetmore, E. J., 277, *290*
Whittlesea, B. W. A., 120, *133*
Wiggins, J. S., 235, *251*
Wilcox, K., 303, 304, *308*
Williams, C. J., 213, *232*
Williams, P. T., 194, *210*
Williamson, J., 25, *43*
Willis, H., 240, *250*
Windhal, S., 276, 277, *289*
Winkeilman, P., 303, *308*
Winski, J. M., 103, *116*

Winsten, J. A., 223, *230*
Wojnicki, A., 104, *115*
Wolbarst, L. R., 124, *130*
Wolf, M. J., 257, 272, *274*
Wolf, N., 302, *308*
Wolfe, R., 315, *322*
Wong, F., 197, *211*
Wood, P. D., 104, 207, *210*
Wood, W., 109, *115*, 197, *211*
Wright, M. C., 227, *231*
Wright, P., 48, 57, *60*, 75, *77*, 106, 109, 110, *115*, 281, *288*
Wright, R. W., 316, *322*
Wyer, R. S., 4, *9*, 80, 85, 86, 87, 88, *98*, 138, 140, 141, 142, 144, 145, 146, 147, 148, 149, 151, 152, 154, 155, *157, 158, 159*, 162, 164, *174, 176*, 179, 181, 186, 188, *191*, 217, 219, 220, 228, *232*

Y

Yang, M., 88, 89, 94, *98*
Ye, G., 128, *133*

Yon, L., 117, *131*
Yonelinas, A. P., 121, 122, *133*
Young, M., 89, 90, 91, *98*

Z

Zacks, R. T., 86, 87, *97*
Zaichowsky, J. L., 330, 334, *335*
Zajonc, R. B., 39, 40, *42, 43*, 71, *78*, 120, 122, *131, 133*
Zanna, M. P., 169, *174*
Zeifman, D., 294, *308*
Zillmann, D., 2, *9*, 142, *159*, 180, 182, *189, 191*, 257, *273, 274*, 312, *320*, 323, 325, 326, 327, 328, 329, 330, 331, 332, *333, 334, 335*
Zimbardo, P. G., 291, *308*
Zimmer, M. R., 105, *116*
Zoob, I., 282, *290*
Zuckerman, M., 267, 268, *273, 274*, 282, *290*, 292, *308*, 324, 325, 326, 327, 328, 330, 331, 333, *334, 335*
Zwaan, R. A., 86, 87, *98*, 166, *176*

Subject Index

A

Accent, displacement of, 26, 27*f*
Adult attachment theory, 294–297
Adultery, television and perceptions of, 179
Advertising, *See also* Product placement
  cost of, versus product placement, 103–104
  hybrid, 221
  lifestyle, 53
  product placement as, 47
  transformational, definition of, 53
Advertising literacy, in children, 127–128
Ad-work, 25
Affective classical conditioning
  definition of, 52
  and product placement, 52–53
Affluence, television and perceptions of, 139,
  179, 219
Age
  and response to television messages, 227–228
  and violent programming–aggression links,
  199–200
Aggression
  interpersonal, definition of, 201
  risk factors for, 203
  and susceptibility to violent programming,
  292
  television and perceptions of, 219
  television violence and, pathways between,
  193–211
Alternative processing approach, 67–68
American Academy of Pediatrics, 215
Amnesia, 21
Antisocial attitudes, 206
Apparent processing, 233
Approval of violence, 206
Assimilation, and body dissatisfaction, 302–305
Associative network memory model, 315–316

Attachment orientation, and body
  dissatisfaction, 291–308
Attachment theory, adult, 294–297
Attention, management of, 236, 247
Attitudes
  change in, fiction and, 172–173
  consumer, on product placement, research on,
  54–55
  fit of product and context and, 107–108
  as link between programming and behavior,
  critique of, 193–194, 205–209
  toward placed brands, 105–106
Attribution theory, on hybrid advertising, 221
Audience heterogeneity
  need for research on, 227
  for sports entertainment, 327–328
Availability heuristic, 184, 219–220
Awareness
  learning without
    expressions of, 66–69
    influence of, 69–72
  of persuasive intent, and product placement
    efficacy, 109–110
  response without, 120
Ayers, Dean, 51

B

Backlash, consumer, 100–101, 110–111
Balance theory, 317
Basking in Reflected Glory (BIRGing), 312
Behavior
  consumption, nonadvertising television
    messages and, 213–232
  image-activated stereotypes and, 143–144
  implicit memory and, 125–126
Behavioral scripts, product placement and, 126

Belief change
    fictional involvement and, 168–169
    fiction and, 172–173
BIRGing, 312
Blurred communications
    advantages of, 100
    product placement as, 99
BMW, 49, 73, 104, 107
Body dissatisfaction, attachment orientation and,
    291–308
Bond, James, 49, 73, 104, 107
Bosch, Hieronymous, 29–31, 37*f*
Brainwashing, subliminal advertising as, 69
Brand placement, *see* Product placement

                        C

Celebrities
    connectedness with, and body dissatisfaction,
        300–302
    endorsements by, in sports, 317–318
    product association with, 80
    and smoking initiation, 84, 224
Censorship
    of fiction, 163
    Freudian, definition of, 25
    and restriction of exposure to diversity, 245
Centrality, of product placement, and
    effectiveness, 72, 74, 82, 90–91, 95
Characters, identifying with
    and body dissatisfaction, 293–294, 296–297,
        300–305
    and persuasion, 170
Children
    advertising literacy in, 127–128
    behavioral scripts of, product placement and,
        126
    implicit memory in, 124–128
    product placement and, 117–133
        research directions for, 129–130
    vulnerability of, 127
Chocolate, alleged properties of, 164, 171
Choice, product placement and, 123–124, 123*f*
Cigarette advertisements, as product placement,
    83–85
Classical conditioning
    affective
        definition of, 52
        and product placement, 52–53
    on hybrid advertising, 221

Classroom, need for entertainment in, 256–257
Coca-Cola, 81, 88, 90–91
Communication objectives, timing of induction
    of, effects of, 154–156, 155*t*
Community building, television connectedness
    and, 286–287
Compliance
    definition of, 311
    and sports affiliation, 311
Compromise formations, 39
Conceptual priming, 71
Condensation, 26–28, 28*f*
Conditioned response (CR), 23
Congruence, *see* Fit
Connectedness, to television shows/characters,
    275–290
    and body dissatisfaction, 293–294, 296–297,
        300–305
    consequences of, 283–287
    correlates of, 281–283
    definition of, 277–279
    time and, 280–281
Consumer behavior, need for entertainment
    scale and, 256
Consumer characteristics, and product
    placement efficacy, 109–111
Consumer cultivation, process model of,
    177–191, 182*f*
Consumer decision making, implicit memory
    and, 71–72
Consumer involvement, with placed claims, and
    product placement efficacy, 111
Consumption
    good versus bad, 216
    ideology of, in nonadvertising programming,
        225
    perceptions of, television and, 219
    symbolic, sport fan affiliation and, 314–315
Consumption associative viewing, research on,
    218–219
Consumption behavior, nonadvertising
    television messages and, 213–232
    theory on, 216–221
Consumption nonassociative viewing, research
    on, 217–218
Context, fit of product placement and, 107–108
Contrast, and body dissatisfaction, 302–305
CORFing, 312
Corporations, and sports properties, 315–316
Course-of-event model, 87
Cowboy Bebop, concept activation in, 91–94, 93*t*

CR, *see* Conditioned response
Cultivation effect
  process model of, 177–191, 182*f*
  psychological processes and, 180–181
  research on, 179–180
Cultivation judgments
  first-order, process model of, 184–185
  as psychological judgments, 183
  second-order, 185–188
Cultivation theory, 5, 64, 178–180, 219, 222, 257, 291–292
  criticism of, 219–220
Cultural texts, research on, 225–226
Cutting Off Reflected Failure (CORFing), 312

D

Data collection, order of, importance of, 228
Declarative memory, *see* Explicit memory
Defenses against persuasive communications, 24, 75–76
  blurred communications and, 100
  commercial type and, 50
  consumer awareness and, 109–110
  evasion of, 29, 38–40, 106
  fiction and, 164, 166, 168–169
  news media and, 247
Delay, and responses to verbal information with image, 146–148, 147*t*
Delicious paradox, 117–133
  definition of, 120
Democracy
  need for entertainment and, 272
  restriction of exposure to diversity and, 235
Demographic measures, 181–183
Desensitization, 247–248
Die Hard, 84
Direct experience, definition of, 216
Dismissing-avoidant attachment pattern, 294–295
Displacement, of accent, 26, 27*f*
Dissociation
  between awareness and response, 120
  double, in explicit-implicit memory model, 72–74
Diversity, restriction of exposure to, 233–251
Douglas, Michael, 88
Drama, and sports affiliation, 313
Drama advertisement, definition of, 50
Dramatization, 29

Dream-work, 25
  techniques in, 25*t*
Dual process models, 173, 194, *see also* Elaboration likelihood model; Explicit-implicit memory model

E

Eating disorders
  attachment style and, 297
  idealized media images and, 292
Ebbinghausian subliminality, 20–22, 20*f*–21*f*
  definition of, 13
Effect size, calculation of, 195
Efficacy, definition of, 207
Elaboration likelihood model (ELM), 111, 171–172, 194
Elderly, television and perceptions of, 219
Embedded advertising, *see* Product placement
Emotional context effects, and consumer decision making, 71, 75
Emotional priming, 71
Endorsements, in sports entertainment, 317–318
Entertainment
  as birth control, 271
  definitions of, 267–269
  gratifications of, 193, 276
Entertainment drive, 263–264, 263*t*
Entertainmentization, 257–258
Entertainment media
  power of, 161–176
  psychology of, 1–9
  uniqueness of, 8
Entertainment passivity, 265, 266*t*
  in definitions, 268
  priming, 269–270
Entertainment utility, 264–265, 264*t*
Episodic memory, in mental models, 86
E.T. The Extraterrestrial, 46, 49, 51, 63–64, 79, 81, 95
Ethics
  of product placement, 83–85
  of product placement for children, 128
Explicit-implicit memory model
  double dissociation in, 72–74
  and product placement, 63, 66–69, 120–124, 123*f*
Explicit memory, 120–123
  versus implicit, 67–68, 121–122
  measurement of, 68–69

F

Falling Down, 81–83, 88–91
False familiarity effect, and consumer decision
    making, 71
Falsehood, versus fiction, 165
False notes, identification of, 169
Familiarity, and acceptance of persuasion, 172
Fan clubs, as community, 286
Fans
    fair weather, 312
    and sporting events, 310
Fanzines, 282
Fearful-avoidant attachment pattern, 294–295
Felt security, 294
Fiction
    definition of, 165
    versus falsehood, 165
    impact of, 162–163
    power of, 161–176
        boundaries of, 170–172
    and processing style, 165–170
    response to, judgment criteria and, 170
File drawer problem, 195
First-order judgments, process model of,
    184–185
First-order measures, 181–183
Fisher, Charles, 14
Fit, of product placement and context, and
    efficacy, 107–108
Fluency, implicit memory and, 121
Focal consciousness, 38–39
Forgetting, Ebbinghaus curve of, 20, 20f
Freudian subliminality, 24–31, 26f–28f,
    30f–37f
    definition of, 13

G

GAM, *see* General aggression model
Gender
    and character identification, 298
    and connectedness, 281
    and effects of pornography, 142–143
    and need for entertainment, 271
    and response to television messages, 227–228
    and sports fan affiliation, 315, 331
        research on, 325, 330
    and violent programming–aggression links,
        199, 201

General aggression model (GAM), 208
Genre expectations, 166
Gizmo subliminality, 13–19
    beyond, 13–43
    contribution of, 31–40
    and psychological subliminality, 38
Glass, Eugene, 196–197

H

Halo effect, 317
Health belief model, 194
Hedonic consumption, sporting event as, 310
Herbart, Johann, 21
Hershey Foods Corporation, Reese's Pieces, 46,
    49, 51, 63–64, 79, 81, 95
Hippocampus, 67, 68f
Horizontal connections, in television
    consumption, 279
    and community, 286–287
Hospitality, in sports entertainment, 317
Hostile personality traits, 206
Hostility, sport fan affiliation and, 314
Hybrid messages
    definition of, 47
    future of, 221
Hypermasculinity, and susceptibility to violent
    programming, 292
Hypermnesia, 21, 21f

I

Identification
    and body dissatisfaction, 304
    definition of, 311
    and sports affiliation, 311–312
    television connectedness and, 284–285
Images
    effects of, on responses to actual people and
        events, 139–140
    Freudian subliminality and, 24–31
    and information processing, 145–153, 147t,
        151t–152t
    versus words
        and memory, 87, 137–159
        retention functions for, 21–22, 22f
Imaginal ability, and connectedness,
    281–282
Impersonal impact hypothesis, 222–223

Implicit memory, 120–123
  and behavior, 125–126
  in children, 124–128
  and consumer decision making, 71–72
    need for research on, 72–74
  duration of effect of, 124
  versus explicit, 67–68, 121–122
  measurement of, 68–69
  and product placement, 82
Impulsive sensation seeking (ImpSS),
  325
Indirect experience, definition of, 216
Information processing
  apparent versus subliminal, 233
  biased, sport fan affiliation and, 314
  fiction and, 165–170
  images and, 145–153, 147*t*, 151*t*–152*t*
  product placement and, 119–120
Infotainment, 163
Insight, 25
  as truth, 170
Interactive television, 287–288
Internalization
  definition of, 311
  and sports affiliation, 313
Internet, and sports entertainment, 318
Interpersonal utility, 276
Interpretation, 25
  versus meta-analysis, 196
  of violent programming–aggression links,
    198–205
Involvement, *see also* Connectedness
  with fiction, and elaborative scrutiny, 166–170
  with product placement claims, and efficacy,
    111
  and sports fan affiliation, 332

J

Joe Camel character, 29, 32*f*–35*f*
Joke-work, 25
Judgment
  criteria for, 170
  online, 187
  type of, 181–183
    and role of television, 177–191
  verbal and nonverbal information and,
    137–159
Just world mindset, 139–140
  challenges to, 171

K

KWZ effect, 39

L

Landscape model
  and product placement, 94–96
  of text comprehension, 89–91
  with video stimuli, 91–94
Latent content, 24
Learning
  formed associations and, 106
  without awareness
    expressions of, 66–69
    influence of, 69–72
Lectures, definition of, 50
Lifestyle advertising, 53
Lifestyle-related product choices, research on,
  220–221
Limen, 19

M

Manifest content, 24
Marketing
  connection and, 287–288
  product placement as, 47–51
  through sports entertainment
    functional approach to, 309–335
    limitations of, 318–319
    tactics for, 316–318
Market segmentation
  connection and, 287
  definition of, 245
  and restriction of exposure to diversity, 235,
    240, 245–246, 248
Masking, types of, 14
Materialism, television viewing and, 139,
  187–188, 219
Mean world mindset, 179
  mental models and, 88
Media
  characteristics of, and restriction of exposure
    to diversity, 233–251
  consumption of, and cultivation judgments,
    184–185
  credibility of
    and acceptance of message, 247
    and consumer backlash, 110–111

entertainment
  power of, 161–176
  psychology of, 1–9
  uniqueness of, 8
  exposure to, and real-world response,
    139–142, 141*t*, 219–220
  idealized body images in, and body
    dissatisfaction, 291–308
  mental models of, 85–94
  and product placement efficacy, 109–111,
    113–114
  as torrent, 247
  trust in, 106–107
  types of, characteristics of, 102
Media affinity, 332
Media effects, 177–178
Media Matters, 215
Media stimulation curve, 241–243, 242*f*
Memory
  and product placement, 66–69, 81–83, 105
  types of, brain areas and, 67, 68*f*
  verbal and nonverbal information and,
    137–159
Mental models
  definition of, 86
  of media, 85–94
  presentation modality and, 153–154
  for product placement, 79–98
Mere-exposure effect, 39
  accounting for, 122–123
  and consumer decision making, 71
  and media effects, 291
  and product placement, 53
Message
  characteristics of, and product placement
    efficacy, 107–109
  simplicity of, and restriction of exposure to
    diversity, 243–244
Meta-analysis, 195–198
Mezzatesta, Gary, 51
Modality, of product placement, and
  effectiveness, 72, 74–75
Modeling paradigm, on hybrid advertising,
  221
Motivational states, and restriction of exposure
  to diversity, 236–239, 237*f*
Music preferences, sensation seeking and,
  328
Music television, consumption imagery in,
  225–226

N

Narrative, *see* Fiction
Need for entertainment (NEnt)
  differences in, social implications of, 271–272
  scale for, 255–274, 260*t*–261*t*
  situational, 256–257
  strength and ubiquity of, 258–261, 258*f*
Network models, versus mental models, 86
News, as biased entertainment, 246–247
Nielsen ratings, 275
Nonadvertising television programming
  and consumption behavior, 213–232
    theory on, 216–221
  definition of, 213
  immediate effects of, 223–224
  long-term effects of, 223
Nonverbal information, *see* Images
Normativeness, definition of, 207

O

OLA, *See* Optimum level of arousal
OLS, *See* Optimum level of stimulation
Omission, 25, 26*f*
One-sidedness, 247–248
Online judgment, 187
Optimum level of arousal (OLA), and sports
  consumption, 325–326
Optimum level of stimulation (OLS), and sports
  consumption, 325–326
Optimum stimulation level (OSL), and
  connectedness, 282–283

P

Parasocial interaction, 275–290
  and body dissatisfaction, 293–294, 296–297,
    300–305
  definition of, 330
  gender and, 281
Pavlovian subliminality, 22–24
  definition of, 13
People meters, 275
Perception, versus reality, 163–164, 219–220
Perceptual priming, 70
Perceptual representation system (PRS), 70
Personal Involvement Inventory (PII), 332

Persuasive communications, *see also* Defenses
    against persuasive communications
    acceptance of, relevance and, 171–172
    in fiction, need for research on, 162
    significance of, 101–102
    social cognition theory on, 194
Persuasive intent, awareness of, and product
    placement efficacy, 109–110
Pertinence, definition of, 207
PII, *see* Personal Involvement Inventory
Pinocchio Circling, 169
Plastic-word representation, 29
Plausibility, of fiction, 170
Politician, image of, and responses to issue
    stands, 145–149, 147*t*
Pornography
    and aggression, 197, 204
    and real-world responses, 142–143
Pötzl-Fisher effects, 14–17, 15*f*–16*f*, 18*f*
Preoccupied attachment pattern, 294–295
    and parasocial interaction, 296
Primary-process thinking, 39
Priming
    definition of, 69
    research on, 69–71
Print media, associations of, 102
Procedural memory, *see* Implicit memory
Process model
    of consumer cultivation, 177–191, 182*f*
        limitations of, 188–189
        first-order judgments in, 184–185
        second-order judgments in, 185–188
Product category, and placement effectiveness,
    75
Product claims, trust in, 106–107
Product evaluations, product placement and,
    81–83
Product placement, 45–61
    advantages of, 103–104
    and behavioral scripts, 126
    and children, 117–133
        ethics of, 128
        research directions for, 129–130
    and choice, 123–124, 123*f*
    definition of, 45, 102–103
    effectiveness of
        factors affecting, 74–75, 99–116
        measurement of, 63–78, 104–107, 112–113
        research on, 55–56
        television connectedness and, 285
    effects of, 80–85

ethics of, 83–85, 128
landscape model and, 94–96
long-term effects of, need for research on,
    59
as marketing communication, 47–51
mental models for, 79–98
multidimensional nature of, 51–52
negative effects of, 52–53, 95
as Pavlovian subliminality, 24
prevalence of, research on, 54
prices for, 46
    calculation of, 66
    strength and, 108
    processing, 119–120
product characteristics and, need for research
    on, 58–59
psychological processes and, 52–54
research on, 54–56, 65*t*
    future directions for, 57–59
shelf-life of, 81
in sports entertainment, 318
strength of
    and efficacy, 108–109, 108*f*
    need for research on, 57–58
Professions, television and perceptions of, 179
PRS, *see* Perceptual representation system
Psychological processes
    and cultivation effect, 180–181
    and product placement, 52–54
Psychological subliminality, 13, 19–31
    definition of, 14
    and gizmo subliminality, 38
Psychological well-being, and aggression, 203
Publicity
    disadvantages of, versus product placement,
        104
    product placement as, 47
Public policy recommendations, on
        nonadvertising television messages,
        226–230

R

Rape
    perceptions of, media influence and, 139–143
    pornography and, 142–143
Real world
    versus fiction, 163–164
    perceptions of, television and, 219–220
    versus portrayal, 179

responses to, fiction exposure and, 139–140,
    161–176
Recall, and product placement, 64–66
Receiver operating characteristic (ROC) curve,
    19
Recognition, and product placement, 64–66
Reese's Pieces, 46, 49, 51, 63–64, 79, 81, 95
Regulation, of commercials, versus product
    placement, 81, 113
Relevance, and acceptance of persuasion,
    171–172
Research, future directions for
    on audience heterogeneity, 227
    on implicit memory and consumer decision
        making, 72–74
    on long-term effects of product placement, 59
    on persuasive communications in fiction, 162
    on product characteristics and product
        placement, 58–59
    on strength of product placement, 57–58
Restriction of exposure to diversity, 233–251
    consequences of, 238f, 240–241
    definition of, 234
    model of, 236–241, 237f–238f
Retention functions, 21, 21f
    for images versus words, 21–22, 22f
Reverse hypothesis, on violent programming
    and aggression, 198–199, 201
Risk taking, nonadvertising television
    programming and, 223–224
ROC curve, 19
Romantic programming, and expectations,
    87–88
Rub-off effect, 315

                            S

Seamlessness, of product placement, 51
    and attitudes, 105–106
    need for research on, 57–58
    strength and, 109
Secondary-process thinking, 39
Second-order measures, 183
Secure attachment pattern, 294
Seinfeld, 72–73
Selective exposure, 255
    and media effects, 291
Self-concept, development of, television
    connectedness and, 283–284
Self-identity, definition of, 234

Semantic memory, in mental models, 86
Sensation seeking
    and connectedness, 282–283
    and consumption of televised sports, 323–335
        research on, 325–326, 329–330
    and susceptibility to violent programming,
        292
Sensation-seeking personality, research on,
    326–329
SES, *see* Socioeconomic status
Sexuality, and Freudian subliminality, 24–31
Signal detection theory, 19
Simulation heuristic, 184
Situation, definition of, 86
Smoking initiation, 224
    product placement and, 83–85
Soap Operas for Social Change, 213
Social cognitive theory, 194
Social comparison
    processes of, 302–305
    television connectedness and, 284–285
Social contagion, 206
Socioeconomic status (SES), and violent
    programming–aggression links, 201
Sponsorships, in sports entertainment, 316–317
Sporting event, definition of, 310
Sports entertainment
    affiliation with, 311–314
        consequences of, 314–315
    marketing through
        functional approach to, 309–335
        limitations of, 318–319
        tactics for, 316–318
    research on, 313–314
    televised, consumption of
        decline in, 324
        research on, 325–330
        sensation seeking and, 323–335
    uniqueness of, 309–311
State-of-affairs model, 87
Stereotypes
    image-activated, and behavior, 143–144
    reinforcement of, and restriction of exposure
        to diversity, 244–245
Stimulus, and forgetting, 21
Subliminal effects
    conceptions of, changes in, 40
    current status of, 17–19
    Pötzl-Fisher, 14–17, 15f–16f, 18f
    power of, 38–40, 69–72
    processing of, 118

Subliminal processing, 233
Surveillance, 276
Susceptibility
    definition of, 207
    to interpersonal influence, and connectedness, 281
Symbolic consumption, sport fan affiliation and, 314–315
Symbolization, 28–29, 30*f*–31*f*

T

Tachistoscope, 14
Telethnography, 225–226
Television, *see also* Nonadvertising television programming
    as addictive, 256
    attachment to, measurement of, 258–261, 258*f*
    as birth control, 271
    consumption of, 276–277
        connections within, 278–279, 278*f*
    content of
        classification of, issues in, 328
        research on, 225–226
    critiques of, 214–215
    heavy viewers of
        beliefs of, 179, 219
    definition of, controversies in, 226
    interactive, 287–288
    and larceny theft, 202
    research on, critique of, 215–216
    role of, judgment and, 177–191
    uses of, 327–328
    watching
        definitions of, 275–276
        motives for, 193, 276
    and worldview, 137–139, 179, 219–220
Text comprehension, landscape model of, 89–91
Threshold of consciousness, 21
Tie-ins, 49
Time
    and connectedness, 280–281
    and violent programming–aggression links, 200–201
Transformational advertising, definition of, 53
Transportation by narrative, 300
    and elaborative scrutiny, 166–170

Trust, in brand claims/media, 106–107
Truth status, of fiction, 165

U

Ultra-thin body type, 298, 302, *see also* Body dissatisfaction
Unconditioned response (UR), 23
Unconditioned stimulus (US), 23
Unconscious, simplicity of, 35
Understanding, of media, 85
    landscape model and, 89–91
    mental models and, 85–94
UR, *see* Unconditioned response
US, *see* Unconditioned stimulus

V

Values
    and communication bias, 153–154
    reinforcement of, and restriction of exposure to diversity, 245–246
    and sports fans, 313
Value-system measures, 183
Verbal information, *see* Words
Vertical connections, in television consumption, 278–279
Vertizontal connections, in television consumption, 279
Viewing, goal of, 85
Violent programming
    and aggression, pathways of, 193–211
    history of criticism of, 215
    and mental models, 88
    and real-world responses, 139–142, 141*t*, 219–220

W

Weldon, Fay, 101
Willis, Bruce, 84
Winning, 310–311
Withdrawal, from television, 256
Women, *see also* Gender
    idealized media images of, and body dissatisfaction, 291–308
    vulnerability to media effects, factors affecting, 293–294

Words
  versus images
    and memory, 87, 137–159
    retention functions for, 21–22, 22*f*
  processing of, images and, 149–152,
    151*t*–152*t*
Worldview
  fiction and, 161–176
  television and, 137–138, 179, 219–220

Y

You've Got Mail, 47, 51

Z

Zapping, 257
  product placement and, 80